PETTICOAT PILOTS

MICHAEL TRAYNOR

PETTICOAT PILOTS

BIOGRAPHIES AND ACHIEVEMENTS
OF
IRISH FEMALE AVIATORS

1909–1939

VOLUME ONE

Text © Michael Traynor

First published 2019 by Michael Traynor

traynormichael0@gmail.com

00-353-87-6440572

Editing, design and layout and cover design by Alicia McAuley Publishing Services

www.aliciamcauley.com

Maps by Martin Gaffney

www.martingaffney.ie

Printing by Best Value Printing, Guinness Enterprise Centre, Taylor's Lane, Dublin 8

www.bestvalueprinting.ie

A CIP record for this book is available from the British Library.

ISBN Volume One 978-0-9549194-1-2

ISBN Volume Two 978-0-9549194-2-9

This book is set in Baskerville 10/13.

CONTENTS

PREFACE

IT WAS POINTED out to me in June 2011 that the achievements of early Irish female pilots had gone unrecognised for the best part of a century. In pondering this idea, I considered my own collection of some 260 books on all aspects of Irish aviation. References to these women were scarce and, despite the fame several of them enjoyed while they were alive, history had largely forgotten them. With this in mind, I set about the task of compiling a list of such women. As an initial source, I consulted records of those issued with an Aviator's Certificate by the Royal Aero Club of the United Kingdom. As I delved into the lives of these aviators, other names emerged. Research into newspapers in the National Library of Ireland in Dublin and issues of *Flight* magazine from 1909 onward revealed further information. And so the journey began.

I selected 12 families and decided to compile a chapter on each. The lives of three of the women in question had already been researched and information on them was available to the public. Fortunately, the authors of their respective biographies were very generous in making their work (which is referenced in the relevant chapters) available to me; consequently, these sections required minimal research. The stories of the other nine amazing women took a considerable amount of primary research and took almost seven years to complete.

All the museums, libraries and archives I contacted proved to be exceptionally helpful and provided some vital information from their records. Luckily, in most instances, family photograph albums, some dating back over a hundred years, were still in the possession of the women's descendants. There are several hundred photographs in these two volumes that have not hitherto appeared in the public domain.

I have included the ancestral lineage of each family in order to provide some background to the lives of these women. The lives they led after their aviation careers and details of their descendants are also included. This satisfying task has taken me on an eight-year odyssey. A conservative estimate of 12,000 hours of research has resulted in this publication, which comprises approximately 205,000 words of text and 773 images spread over two volumes comprising approximately 600 pages. Any opinions expressed in this publication are my own, except where expressly attributed to a particular individual.

The research brought me to all the counties associated with these women. In those cases where their homes were still standing, I had the good fortune to see where they spent their early childhood years. Sadly, some of their houses have been demolished to make way for developments or have suffered the ravages of time. It was very gratifying for me to discover that, although not all of these women married and had children, those who did have descendants still living across several continents. In making contact with these relatives, I found fantastic support for the research I was undertaking. In some cases they were not fully aware of the aeronautical achievements of the ancestor in question. Many went to great lengths to locate and share with me their old family photograph albums, some of which were in the family for over a century. It has been a genuine pleasure to have family members share in my efforts to have their loved ones remembered.

As well as acknowledging their achievements I also discovered that in several cases there was grief in many of these women's lives. These chapters contain instances of tragedy. Whether it was the death of their parents or the loss of their children in war or other fateful circumstances, these women bore the same losses as many other families. I opted for the start of the Second World War as a cut-off point, mainly because civil aviation in Ireland was curtailed at that time.

The achievements of Irishwomen of the early decades of the twentieth century are finally being recognised and it is anticipated that this publication will help bring these women the attention they deserve. It is hoped that pilots of the twenty-first century will admire these women and acknowledge what they achieved at a time when aviation was in its infancy. The women in these chapters were trailblazers and mixed with pioneers of aviation and achievers in that field. They hailed from each of the four provinces of Ireland and flew pioneering routes for women.

The efforts of these valiant and adventurous Irishwomen were chronicled by the international media of the time and, luckily for me, many newspaper reports of their successes are available in libraries and museums throughout the world. I was fortunate that many archivists and curators assisted me by offering their cooperation, for which I am grateful. When the research was completed I was grateful that descendants gave the final seal of approval to the text and photograph captions.

These women made exploratory flights over long distances. They competed in air races and persevered in the face of ridicule and hostility from their male counterparts. Their determination and valour inspired me to bring their memories to life.

Michael Traynor
October 2019

FOREWORD

IRELAND'S FASCINATION – INDEED, obsession – with flying and aviation has been documented for at least 900 years. It is recorded in *Buile Shuibhne*, the dramatic saga of the bird-man King of Dál nAraide, which was later the inspiration of several of T.S. Eliot's most wonderful lyrics and brilliantly recreated in Seamus Heaney's *Sweeney Astray*. W.B. Yeats immortally described in 1918 the fascination with flight in his poem 'An Irish Airman Foresees His Death', the tragic protagonist from Kiltartan being his friend Robert Gregory.

The island of Ireland and its people were positioned, both by geography and by human history, to make a completely unique contribution to the earliest days of world aviation. Our experience as islanders defines us, not just in our physical geography, but also in the geography of our minds, of our communities, our societies, our political outlooks, of how we see and relate to the world beyond our coastal horizons. Island nations are so often outward-looking, perhaps by necessity – interested in the world beyond, in its promises and its dangers. It is, therefore, hardly surprising that Ireland became, over the course of the twentieth century, a major world player in aviation. From aircraft leasing to commercial airline operations, Ireland has been pioneering and innovative and has spearheaded the aviation sector's growth.

The legacy of those early beginnings continues to thrive today. Irish people now travel by aeroplane more often than any other national group worldwide, and more than 40 per cent of large commercial jets crossing the skies of the world are financed or leased by Irish-based companies, which employ approximately 5,000 people directly and indirectly on these shores. Ireland is now recognised globally as a centre of excellence

for the industry and the top four global lessors are located here. More broadly, Irish airlines, managers, flight crews, engineers and financiers swarm across the aviation industry everywhere.

As Uachtarán na hÉireann, I am proud of this remarkable Irish phenomenon.

Commercial aviation, perhaps more than any other invention of human ingenuity, has contributed to the cause of bringing people together in peace. By making the world smaller through increased accessibility, it has enabled island states like Ireland to grow and prosper economically, socially and culturally, and has opened up the far-flung corners of our planet to enable a reciprocal sharing of cultures and ideas as well as forging multiple symbioses. This cultural diversity brings innovation, opportunity, dynamism and a creative energy that enriches our society.

Like so many aspects of history, the role that women played in critical movements and pivotal events is often unrecorded, unacknowledged or, at the very least, frequently given less space than it deserves. This can be said of Irish aviation history. Women were among the first so-called 'Éire-nauts' and, like so many areas of history, their role seems to have been forgotten in some form of collective amnesia. This book attempts to address this notable deficit in the historical accounts of this country in the early twentieth century.

Containing detailed biographies of Irish female aviators who earned their Aviators' Certificates prior to the outbreak of the Second World War, this book forensically charts the achievements of these trailblazing women, only about a dozen of whom fall into the aforementioned category. The book provides details regarding their ancestry, their aeronautical achievements and their subsequent lives in biographical format, with a full chapter devoted to each of the 12 selected so-called 'aviatrices', to use the language of the time.

This book fittingly addresses the knowledge gap on the role of women in early Irish aviation, honouring them in their rightful place in Irish history. From the earliest pioneers, including Violet Dunville, Ireland's first female balloonist, to Lilian Bland, who became the first female in the world to design, build and fly her own aircraft in August 1910, the book contains fascinating accounts of these sometimes-larger-than-life individuals who demonstrated passion, bravery and skill, not to mention fortitude, given the sexism that was evident at the time.

Challenges clearly still remain. While research indicates that women on every continent had begun to fly within the first two decades of powered flight, the global number of women airline pilots in contemporary times is just 3 per cent. This indicates that, regrettably, we have still a long way to travel if we are to achieve gender equality in the aviation sector.

Furthermore, we must be cognisant that aviation is responsible for contributing about 2.5 per cent of global greenhouse-gas emissions, with the sector consuming five million barrels of oil every day. While modern aircraft are 70 per cent more fuel-efficient than 40 years ago, carbon emissions from international aviation could grow sevenfold over the next 30 years, according to the International Civil Aviation Organisation (ICAO). The best solution here is for the sector to become part of a global scheme to limit emissions, such as the Carbon Offsetting and Reduction Scheme for International Aviation (CORSIA), which is being developed currently by ICAO.

This book, *Petticoat Pilots*, is a unique collector's treasure-trove, not just for historians or scholars of Irish aviation, but for all those Irishwomen and Irish men at home and around the world who wish to learn and celebrate the undeniably world-class, but too-often unsung, achievements of the women whose stories are told within it.

The volume of research underpinning this book, conducted over a seven-year period, and the level of detail that has been provided, including some 773 beautifully reprinted historical images, is truly remarkable. I congratulate Michael Traynor for this *tour de force*. It is undoubtedly the ultimate reference source on the topic of women's aviation history in Ireland, and it will surely become internationally recognised as a foremost title on the subject.

Michael D. Higgins
President of Ireland

ACKNOWLEDGEMENTS

A PUBLICATION OF this magnitude requires the input, assistance and cooperation of a considerable number of people – too many to individually thank in a single page. It would conceivably require another chapter. There are librarians, archivists, curators and custodians in establishments across many countries that have delved into their records to produce information and data to support the stories of Ireland's early female aviators. Aviation historians have offered great assistance in providing primary accounts of the events of the period.

As regards the 773 images contained in these two volumes, I am extremely grateful to the many people who made extraordinary efforts to obtain high-resolution digital copies of the images that I wished to include. They have been individually acknowledged as the source in the attributions that accompany each photograph. To anyone I have inadvertently omitted, I sincerely apologise. Be assured that your assistance was very much appreciated.

I am very grateful to the family members of each of the women who appear in this book, many of whom retain family albums that have survived in some instances for over a century. They willingly made those images available to be included here for readers' enjoyment. The majority of photographs have come from family albums not hitherto seen in the public arena and for that I am particularly grateful.

Family members of the women also greatly assisted in providing ancestral information regarding their family pedigree and lineage. I wish also to extend my sincere thanks to my own family for their support during this lengthy process.

I could well be labelled as something of a disaster when it comes to grammar, punctuation and the like. This was where I have relied on the services of Helen Walsh and aviation historian Guy Warner. On International Women's Day, 8 March 2018, I met Alicia McAuley in the Public Record Office of Northern Ireland (PRONI), Belfast. She agreed to undertake the mammoth assignment of editing, designing and laying out my efforts of the previous seven years. I gasped when she said it could take a full year; but she was right.

In the intervening 12 months I had the considerable challenge of locating high-quality versions of each of the images identified during the research stage. Many photographs were located in a variety of museums, libraries and with commercial photographic companies. In addition to sourcing the photographs I had to ensure copyright laws were adhered to in all instances and that meant acquiring permissions and licences for use in this book. For any omissions in the credits of photographs I apologise.

Creating easy-to-understand maps was entrusted to the professional custody of the meticulous and patient Martin Gaffney. The onerous task of creating 18 family trees fell also to Alicia McAuley.

After a year spent putting a wonderful shape on my seven years of research, Alicia handed the entire document to Dr Conor Reidy, who proofread the 205,000-word book meticulously in an effort to make sure no errors had escaped us. The final stage in the lengthy process was the printing.

This project would not have made it to the finish line without the generosity of my sponsors. For their support and confidence in the project I am truly grateful. They are individually listed opposite.

Thanks to all of those mentioned here, this work will go some way towards honouring the lives and achievements of the first Irish female aviators.

I am grateful to the following corporate and private sponsors, who have contributed financially to this publication. Without their vital financial input, the completion of this project would not have been possible. I thank them all sincerely.

CORPORATE SPONSORS

PRIVATE SPONSORS

Mark Appleby, Dublin

Howard Fee, Belfast

Ronny Vogt, Zurich

PROLOGUE

AT A TIME when we are honouring the achievements of other Irishwomen, many of our early female aviators have been forgotten. These are the brave and pioneering women who ventured aloft in machines sometimes comprised of little more than wood and canvas. Engines of the time were somewhat experimental, navigation aids were non-existent and aeronautical charts were not yet developed. Aeronautical meteorology had not been perfected by weather forecasters.

At the time of the first all-female transcontinental air race in the United States of America, in 1929, headline writers dubbed the race the 'Powder Puff Derby'. The pilots participating were jestfully called 'Petticoat Pilots'. Ruth Nichols was one prominent female pilot of that period. In her autobiography, *Wings for Life* (1957), she refers to her fellow pilots as 'Petticoat Pilots'. Similarly, Judy Lomax uses the same term of endearment in her autobiography, *Women of the Air* (1987). As this publication covers that era, I have adopted the phrase as its title.

The introduction to this book outlines the aspirations of males as the exponents of early aviation in Ireland. A relatively small number of women are referred to in historical sources dealing with aeronautical attempts. It was the sport of balloon racing that tempted Violet Dunville, the first Irish female aeronaut, a native of County Meath, to venture into the atmosphere. She was followed by Lilian Bland, a woman from County Antrim who travelled to England to examine some early aircraft. She returned home and drew up her own plans for a glider. Following its success, she added an engine; thus, in 1910, she became the first woman in the world to design, construct and fly her own aeroplane.

There were no formal flight-training facilities in the new Irish state of the early 1920s and pilots with ambitions to fly were required to go to established flying schools in England or France. The first woman to do this was Sophie Eliott-Lynn from County Limerick. She travelled to London in 1925 to earn her Aviator's Certificate. She achieved international acclaim and accolades when she became the first woman to fly solo from Cape Town, South Africa, to London, before almost losing her life in a dreadful plane crash in Cleveland, Ohio. In 1926, two women from Counties Cork and Monaghan were successful in obtaining their Aviators' Certificates. Sadly, one of these women, Sicele O'Brien, had the tragic distinction of becoming the first Irish female to die in an aviation crash. The other, Lady Bailey, went on to achieve worldwide recognition for her pioneering flights over Africa and was awarded a royal DBE for her contribution to aviation.

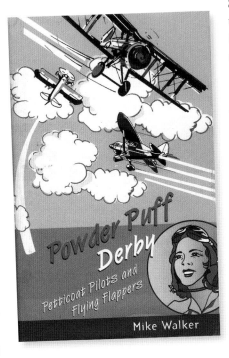

The book by Mike Walker about the 1929 Women's Air Race from California to Cleveland, entitled Powder Puff Derby: Petticoat Pilots and Flying Flappers *(2004).*

It was 1930 when Adelaide Cleaver, a Belfast-born woman, then living near London, earned her Aviator's Certificate and travelled in an open-cockpit aircraft on a return flight from London to India. She then shipped her aircraft across the Atlantic and flew from New York to California.

The Irish Aero Club was rejuvenated following the *Bremen* flight from Ireland to America in 1928. The club began formal tuition for female pilots during the summer of 1931. The first woman in Ireland who earned her licence to fly here was Jean 'Shamrock' Trench, a native of County Galway. Others were still travelling to the United Kingdom for flying lessons. On returning to Dublin in 1933, a County Wexford-born woman, Lady Nelson, acquired a flying field north of Dublin city and ran a commercial aviation operation as well as offering flying lessons and giving joy-rides to many hundreds, introducing them to the pleasures of flight.

History was made when Margaret, Helen and Mairi Stewart, three sisters from County Down, earned their Aviators' Certificates and departed regularly from a flying field near their home that had been created by their air-minded father, Lord Londonderry. Around the same time, sisters Mabel and Sheila Glass from Belfast travelled to London and achieved similar aeronautical status in 1934. These latter sisters flew their aeroplane to Cairo to compete successfully in an aerial race over the Egyptian desert. Mabel Glass flew approximately 900 military aircraft from factories to Royal Air Force bases in the United Kingdom while serving as a pilot with the Air Transport Auxiliary during the Second World War.

Ruth Hallinan, a County Cork-born woman, despite contracting polio at an early age, was the first woman in Munster to earn her flying certificate. She was instrumental in the development of the Cork Aero Club during the 1930s. Nancy Corrigan was a County Mayo woman who tragically lost her father at an early age. She was brought to America in 1929, at the age of 16, leaving the poverty-stricken island of Achill behind. Secretly she took flying lessons in Cleveland and, from her earnings with a top model agency in New York, further enhanced her flying credentials. During the Second World War she was a Chief Flying Instructor at a college in Oklahoma and taught United States Air Force cadets to fly. She finished in a creditable position in one of the most prestigious air races in America in 1948.

Other women learned to fly in the years under review and they are listed in an appendix to this publication. Their stories are perhaps something another researcher will take up.

A group of women welcoming 'Petticoat Pilots' to the airport at Greenville, North Carolina, in August 1965.
Courtesy J.Y. Joyner Library, East Carolina University, North Carolina

THE FIRST ÉIRE-NAUTS
EARLY ATTEMPTS AT FLIGHT IN IRELAND

For centuries flight has fascinated men and women. Throughout history, attempts to emulate our feathered friends failed, often with fatal consequences. Until relatively recently, winged flight seemed impossible and the first successful aerial ascents were by balloon. These early ascents were followed by attempts at gliding and, eventually, by the achievement of powered flight. Internationally, members of the female sex undertook aerial voyages from their earliest days. The same was the case in Ireland.

The aviator Hilda Hewlett.

COURTESY GAIL HEWLETT, *OLD BIRD: THE IRREPRESSIBLE MRS HEWLETT* (2010)

IRELAND'S FIRST AERONAUT was Richard Crosbie. He was born around 1755 in Crosbie Park, Baltinglass, County Wicklow, with family origins traced to Counties Kerry and Laois. He was the second son of Sir Paul Crosbie and his eldest brother, Sir Edward Crosbie, was executed in June 1798 for an alleged role in the rebellion of that year. Sir Edward's wife was Lady Castiliana, a daughter of Warner and Hester Westenra of Rossmore Park, County Monaghan.

On 16 August 1784, Richard Crosbie unveiled his *Grand Aeronautic Chariot*, a hydrogen balloon, in Ranelagh Gardens, Dublin. Over the next few months, Dublin witnessed considerable interest in balloon flights, which had already been taking place in England. Crosbie released numerous small balloons over the city almost daily to publicise the forthcoming launch of his 'chariot'. A cat was sent up in a balloon launched in early September 1784 and, on 2 October, Crosbie launched a balloon measuring 36 feet in circumference. Further launches planned before the end of 1784 were postponed because of poor weather and the fact that Crosbie was suffering from fatigue.

A launch was scheduled for 4 January 1785, with the Duke of Rutland ordering a number of vessels to be spread across the Irish Sea. This was to be Crosbie's first manned flight. This launch was unsuccessful, however, because of unsuitable weather. The next date set for Crosbie's attempt at manned flight was 19 January 1785. Estimates put the number of spectators at Ranelagh Gardens at between 20,000 and 35,000. The launch, scheduled for 11am, was delayed and it was 1pm when Crosbie boarded his 'chariot'. More hydrogen was added and, at 2.40pm, Richard Crosbie lifted off to become the first man to ascend in a balloon in Ireland. Contemporary estimates suggested he reached a height of 18,000 feet before he opened a valve to allow him to descend and alight at the North Strand in north Dublin. This figure is probably an exaggeration, given the rarefied air at that altitude.

A further attempt, which took off on 10 May 1785 from the Palatine Square, Royal Barracks (later Collins Barracks), Dublin, was unsuccessful and Crosbie began to draw the wrath of the public for his many failures. His next attempt was two days later but, owing to the 12 stone of ballast on board, as well as other items, the basket became overladen. It was too heavy to bear the weight of Richard Crosbie, a 16-stone man. So as not to disappoint the crowd, which was getting angrier, he selected a young Trinity College student, Richard McGwire, to take his place. The balloon was released and it carried

An artist's impression of the scene at Ranelagh Gardens, Dublin, when Richard Crosbie ascended on 19 January 1785 to become Ireland's first aeronaut.

McGwire across Dublin and out over the Irish Sea, descending into the water about nine miles from Howth. McGwire was rescued in an exhausted condition and brought to Howth by boat.

Crosbie made one last ascent in Dublin when he rose from Leinster Lawn on the Merrion Square side of Leinster House on 19 July 1785 in the presence of a reported 60,000 spectators. He estimated that he was about 35 miles offshore from Howth when he was rescued by boat and brought back to Dunleary (now Dún Laoghaire) at 4am. He was celebrated for the perceived success of that adventure. There are no further reports of attempts by Crosbie or any other aeronaut to cross the Irish Sea until 27 years later. Crosbie did make one final ascent but this time he relocated his efforts to Limerick, to the House of Industry on the North Strand (later Clancy Strand) beside the River Shannon. This launch went ahead at 4.30pm on Thursday, 27 April 1786 and he was carried westbound over the River Shannon. Having crossed parts of County Kerry, he eventually descended near Newmarket-on-Fergus, County Clare, after almost two hours in the air. The life and aeronautical experiences of Richard Crosbie are documented in the publication *Ascend or Die: Richard Crosbie, Pioneer of Balloon Flight* (2010) by Bryan MacMahon.

While Richard Crosbie was achieving great things in aeronautics on the western side of the Irish Sea, another aeronaut was making equally good progress with his achievements in England. James Sadler was baptised on 27 February 1753 in St Peter-in-the-East Church in Oxford. His father, also named James, was a cook, and the younger James followed his father's career path and became a pastry cook. On 5 November 1775, James married Mary Harper and they lived in Abingdon, Oxfordshire. By the middle of January 1784 Sadler was developing his own designs for an 'aerostatic globe of a large size'. James Sadler's first experiment with an unmanned hydrogen-filled balloon, 36 feet in circumference, took place on 9 February 1784 from Cowley House, St Clements, Oxford. It travelled 79 miles. Sadler experimented with several other ascents over the coming months and achieved his first manned ascent on 4 October 1784. This flight carried him six miles at a maximum altitude of 3,600 feet and made him the first Englishman to ascend in a balloon.

James Sadler made six ascents throughout 1785 at various locations in England. After his ascent from Stroud, Gloucestershire, on 19 October 1785, he turned his attention to the development of steam engines. In 1795 he obtained employment with the Royal Navy at Portsmouth as Barrack Master on a good annual salary of £300. Sadler's engineering skills produced the first steam engine erected in Portsmouth Dockyard and possibly at any naval establishment. He also designed furnaces for naval ships and ships' guns and cannons. James Sadler's naval gun designs were brought to the attention of Admiral Horatio Nelson, who professed he 'could wish my upper-deck completely to be mounted with them'. Before sailing for the Battle of Trafalgar on 14 September 1805 in HMS *Victory*, Nelson had hoped to be equipped with Sadler's guns, but Sadler was too ill to comply with the Admiral's wishes. Sadler's naval career ended in 1809.

James Sadler was 57 years of age when he resumed his interest in aeronautics after a break of 25 years and ascended near Christ Church College, Oxford, on 7 July 1810, watched by an estimated crowd of 50,000. Seven ascents later, he decided to make an attempt to cross the Irish Sea, which Richard Crosbie had failed to do 27 years previously. For this attempt he used a balloon 55 feet in circumference and launched it from Belvedere House, Drumcondra, Dublin, on 1 October 1812. The sea crossing to Anglesey in Wales is 60 miles long. Sadler travelled approximately 237 miles, carried in different directions because of changes in wind direction, but failed to make landfall. He ditched south-east of the Isle of Man and was rescued and brought to Liverpool.

James Sadler's youngest son, Windham, who was born on 17 October 1796, showed an interest in ballooning and made his first

Engraved for the Dublin Magazine.

James Sadler was the first successful aeronaut in England. He turned his attention to balloon ascents from Ireland in 1812.
COURTESY RONNY VOGT

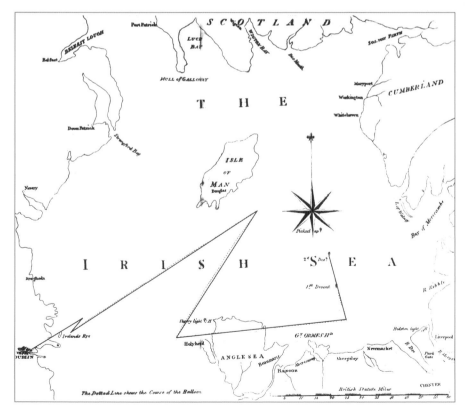

The approximate track James Sadler's balloon followed during his unsuccessful attempt to cross the Irish Sea from Dublin on 1 October 1812. After being carried 237 miles, he ditched in the Irish Sea.
COURTESY RONNY VOGT

A colour print depicting Windham Sadler crossing the coastline during his attempt to become the first person successfully to cross the Irish Sea by air on 22 July 1817.
COURTESY SCIENCE AND SOCIETY PICTURE LIBRARY, SCIENCE MUSEUM, LONDON

ERIN GO BRAH

solo ascent on 7 September 1813, aged 16. When Windham ascended from Piccadilly, London, on 29 July 1814, he carried as a passenger Mary Thompson, who, 'though acquainted with Mr Sadler's family from earliest life, never ascended before. She availed herself of the opportunity with firmness and resolution not excelled in any example of female courage,' according to one contemporary source. Mary Thompson was probably the first female to fly in England since Madame Garnerin at Vauxhall in 1802. They descended successfully 45 miles away near Coggeshall, Essex. She again took to the air with Windham Sadler on 15 September 1814, ascending from Pontefract in west Yorkshire.

By mid-1816 the Sadlers had again turned their attention to Ireland. Windham made an ascent from the military barracks in Cork on 2 September 1816. His next two ascents were in Ireland, both from Dublin. The ascent of 5 November 1816, with Edmund Livingston as a passenger, left from Richmond Barracks and landed in the Bog of Allen. Next was an attempt to cross the Irish Sea on 22 July 1817. Rumours abounded as to who would be on board – James and Windham Sadler, Edmund Livingston or Mary Thompson. On the day, Windham ascended solo. The launch was from the Cavalry Barracks at Portobello, Dublin, at 1.20pm. At about 4pm he approached the Welsh coast. He stated: 'At five minutes after seven o'clock I trod on the shores of Wales.' His landing was about 1.5 miles from Holyhead. The Irish Sea had successfully been crossed by an aeronaut for the first time. Twenty-year-old Windham Sadler returned to Dublin on board the *Chichester* steam packet ship, which departed Holyhead at 1am and arrived in Dublin at 6am. He was honoured by the Lord Lieutenant in the Phoenix Park later that day.

To assuage the disappointment of both Edmund Livingston and Mary Thompson for not being part of the historic crossing of the Irish Sea, Windham Sadler helped them to make a joint ascent from Dublin on 20 August 1817. The balloon was displayed at the Dublin Society House and the flight from the military barracks at Portobello was of relatively short duration. The pair descended on the edge of the estate of David La Touche at Marley Park, Rathfarnham, having covered a distance of about five miles. Mary Thompson received the honour of becoming the first woman ever to ascend

in Ireland. The life and aeronautical experiences of James Sadler are documented in the publication *King of All Balloons: The Adventurous Life of James Sadler, the First English Aeronaut* (2015) by Mark Davies.

There is no further evidence that Mary Thompson or any other Irish female embarked on balloon flights for approximately a further 90 years. The next mention in historical sources of an Irish female aeronaut was Violet Dunville (*née* Lambart), a member of a well-established County Meath Anglo-Irish family.

There is very little reference to aeronautical challenges in Ireland during the middle years of the nineteenth century. The first Irishman to attempt flight in earnest was Professor George Francis Fitzgerald of Trinity College, Dublin, in the latter years of that century. In the early 1890s, a German engine builder, Otto Lilienthal, had conducted experiments with 'soaring machines' in Berlin. In January 1895, Professor Fitzgerald wrote to Lilienthal requesting information on his latest apparatus. He subsequently purchased one for £25 and had it delivered to Trinity College.

The *Irish Times* of Wednesday, 3 April 1895 informed its readers:

> Shortly after one o'clock yesterday a novel exhibition was witnessed by crowds who lined the College wall in Nassau Street. Professor Fitzgerald made attempts to soar in his aerial machine which is composed of white canvas attached to a strong frame and has somewhat the appearance of the outstretched wings of a bird. The tail is formed of four small fans. After several failed runs through the College grounds the machine was raised about two feet from the ground and, aided by a brisk breeze, it and the Professor were carried for a short distance.

This is regarded as the first successful attempt by an Irishman to fly in a glider. However, Professor Fitzgerald received a considerable amount of ridicule from the public and he abandoned any further attempts to fly. On 9 August 1896, Lilienthal died in a crash outside Berlin during one of his experiments. Had this tragedy not occurred, he might have beaten the Wright brothers, who became the first to achieve sustained controlled

The bearded, bowler-hat-wearing Professor Fitzgerald commenced his first unsuccessful run in an attempt to become airborne at Trinity College, Dublin, on 2 April 1895.
COURTESY RONNY VOGT

Professor Fitzgerald launched himself into the air after gaining momentum by running down a ramp at Trinity College, Dublin, on 2 April 1895.
COURTESY DENIS WEAIRE, GEORGE FRANCIS FITZGERALD (2009) VIA PHILIP BEDFORD

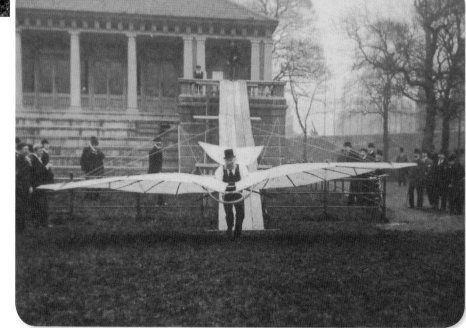

flight in a heavier-than-air machine on 17 December 1903. English aviator Percy Pilcher delivered a talk to the Military Society of Ireland on Thursday, 21 January 1897. This lecture gave detailed accounts of his and Lilienthal's experiments with gliders. But over 14 years elapsed after Professor Fitzgerald's attempts before the first successful powered flight by an Irish person took place. Harry Ferguson achieved this honour when he flew for 130 yards at Hillsborough, County Down, on 31 December 1909.

Professor Fitzgerald rose approximately two feet off the ground in his Lilienthal glider on 2 April 1895 in the grounds of Trinity College, Dublin.
COURTESY NATIONAL LIBRARY OF IRELAND, DUBLIN

Enter the female pilots.

In her book *Before Amelia: Women Pilots in the Early Days of Aviation* (2002), Eileen F. Lebow detailed the international spectrum of female pilots and how they influenced each other. The following women would have given encouragement to Irish females wishing to challenge their male counterparts.

On 22 October 1909, at Châlons, France, a fragile aeroplane manoeuvred across the field, turned and, with its motor at full throttle, rushed and lifted into the air for a distance of some 300 metres before settling down again. With roars of approval, the ground crew ran to help the pilot out and a tall, elegant woman, smiling broadly, stepped into history. Raymonde de Laroche had just driven a heavier-than-air machine into the air alone and is generally recognised as the first woman in the world to have done so. Five months later, on 8 March 1910, she was issued Aviator's Certificate number 36 by the Aéro-Club de France, becoming the first woman in the world to receive such a certificate. The Baroness, as she was nicknamed, resumed her flying career after the end of the Great War. She was killed, aged 36, in a flying accident at Le Crotoy in northern France on 18 July 1919.

Raymonde de Laroche became the first woman in the world to fly in a powered aircraft at Châlons, France, on 22 October 1909. She died, aged 36, in a flying accident on 18 July 1919.
COURTESY SMITHSONIAN NATIONAL AIR AND SPACE MUSEUM, WASHINGTON DC

In a Blériot XI aircraft of this type, Edith Maud Cook became the first Englishwoman to fly successfully. She was an aerial performer and died on 14 July 1910 when a parachute jump went tragically wrong. She was 31 years of age.
COURTESY CANADA AVIATION AND SPACE MUSEUM, OTTAWA, CANADA (REFERENCE CASM-4937)

Spencer Kavanagh, a balloonist and parachutist, took flying lessons at the Blériot School at Pau, southern France. She continued her instruction at the Claude Grahame-White School when he opened it, also at Pau. She almost certainly soloed in early 1910 to become England's first woman to fly.

Spencer Kavanagh's real name was Edith Maud Cook, but at different times she used the names Elsa Spencer, Viola Fleet, Viola Spencer-Kavanagh, Viola Spencer and Viola Kavanagh, depending on which company she was working for as an aerial performer. One writer commented that Kavanagh changed her name as often as others did their dresses. Her exhibition career was short lived. She died in hospital on 14 July 1910, five days after a failed parachute jump from a balloon at Coventry, England. She was aged 31 and, although she never earned an Aviator's Certificate in her brief career, it was not for lack of courage.

Harriet Quimpy was the first woman to earn her Pilot's Licence in America on 1 August 1911. She became the first woman to cross the English Channel on 16 April 1912. She died on 1 July 1912 aged 37, after inexplicably being thrown from her aircraft during a landing descent at a thousand feet. She landed in the water below and was killed instantly.
COURTESY INTERNATIONAL WOMEN'S AIR AND SPACE MUSEUM, CLEVELAND, OHIO

An autograph and photograph of Hilda Hewlett.
COURTESY SCIENCE AND SOCIETY PICTURE LIBRARY,
SCIENCE MUSEUM, LONDON

On 29 August 1911 Hilda Hewlett became the first British woman to earn an Aviator's Certificate issued by the Royal Aero Club. For this photograph she posed beside a Hanriot flying machine.
COURTESY GAIL HEWLETT, *OLD BIRD: THE IRREPRESSIBLE MRS HEWLETT* (2010)

In 1911, America gained its first licensed woman pilot, Harriet Quimpy, who earned Pilot's Licence number 37 on 1 August by successfully completing her tests before two representatives of the Aero Club of America. She was deemed an ideal choice to break the sex barrier in America: glamorous, clever, definitely a modern woman yielding nothing to men. Harriet Quimpy was born on 11 May 1875 in Michigan. She was killed in an aviation accident near Boston, Massachusetts, on 1 July 1912, aged 37.

Hilda Beatrice Herbert was born in England on 17 February 1864. After her marriage to Maurice Hewlett, she helped to establish the Hewlett-Blondeau Flying School. Eventually she began to take flying lessons herself and, on 18 August 1911, passed her tests to become the first Englishwoman to obtain her Aviator's Certificate (number 122, issued on 29 August 1911). Representatives from the Royal Aero Club, down from London, were curious observers when she took her tests.

Ireland's first female pilot was Lilian Bland, who flew her own machine in County Antrim in August 1910 and became credited as the first woman in the world to design, build and fly an aeroplane. She never received any formal flying tuition and consequently was not issued with an Aviator's Certificate. After her achievement she abandoned aviation and within a year she took an interest in motor cars. Following her marriage in December 1911, she moved to Canada

and, in 1935, she returned to England, eventually settling in Cornwall in 1955. She died near Land's End on 11 May 1971, aged 92.

The first Irishwoman to earn her Aviator's Certificate was Limerick-born Sophie Eliott-Lynn (*née* Peirce), later to become Lady Heath. She was the only woman presented with her Aviator's Certificate in 1925: her 'A' Certificate was issued on 4 November of that year. She was only the eighth woman in Britain to be so presented, since certificates were first issued in 1910. On 18 October 1926, two Irishwomen successfully passed their flight tests for their 'A' Certificates at Stag Lane Aerodrome, London. They were Cork-reared Sicele O'Brien and Monaghan-born Lady Bailey (*née* Mary Westenra). The fourth Irish female to be issued her 'A' Certificate was Belfast-born Adelaide Cleaver, who received it on 3 June 1930.

In August 1931, the first 'A' Certificate issued to a female in Ireland was presented to Jean 'Shamrock' Trench. Wexford-born Lady Nelson (*née* Cathleen Bryan) received her certificate in London on 16 December 1932 and became only the sixth Irish female to be issued an Aviator's Certificate in seven years.

In Ireland itself, a limited amount of private flying took place. Military aviation existed, since 23-year-old Major Sholto Douglas had helped to identify the first military aerodromes during the summer of 1917 for the Royal Flying Corps. In his autobiography, *Years of Combat: the First Volume of the Autobiography of Sholto Douglas, Marshal of the Royal Air Force, Lord Douglas of Kirtleside* (1963), he wrote:

> Most of what are to-day the principal aerodromes in Éire and Northern Ireland were selected by me on that trip during the early summer of 1917, and they included such places as Collinstown, Baldonnel and Aldergrove. I also found a site for an aerodrome near Fermoy and another one at the Curragh.

Following the successful transatlantic crossing by Alcock and Brown in June 1919, there was real interest in developing aviation on the island. It waned after a period and was not revitalised until another transatlantic achievement gripped the nation. During the decade from 1918 to 1928, there were very few private aeroplanes in the country. During that period, the Guinness brewing family were the most prolific operators of private aircraft in Ireland. Following his transatlantic crossing in the *Bremen* in April 1928, Colonel James Fitzmaurice turned his attention to revitalising the Irish Aero Club, which had been formed in November 1909.

This resurgence led to the club finding a home at Baldonnel Military Aerodrome outside Dublin and, thanks to men like Colonel Fitzmaurice, it was revived in August 1928. This time it prospered and developed and grew each year. It was eventually able to purchase three de Havilland Gipsy Moths. In April 1934, the club decided to expand its operations and supported requests for a branch in Cork.

For almost 28 years after the first heavier-than-air flight, no woman obtained an Aviator's Certificate in Ireland. There were no proper training facilities for civil pilots in Ireland until the early 1930s. Pilots were required to go to England, usually to the London Aeroplane Club at Stag Lane. Here, successful applicants were issued with their Royal Aero Club Aviator's 'A' Certificate.

In October 1931, Amy Johnson travelled to Ireland and gave a talk entitled, 'My Flight with *Jason* to the Land of the Golden Fleece' (that is, the eastern end of the Black Sea) to audiences in Belfast and Baldonnel. A talk by such a high-profile aviator would have inspired many Irishwomen to begin an interest in aviation. A full-size model of the aircraft in which Amy Johnson flew to Australia was exhibited in Clery's in Dublin's O'Connell Street.

A small number of Irishwomen were aeronautically adventurous in the three decades prior to the outbreak of the Second World War, when civil aviation was banned. Aircraft were still relatively primitive at that time, aviation navigation was in its infancy, aeronautical charts were non-existent and aviation meteorology had not yet been introduced. Pilots had to know the mechanics of their machines intimately, because they were frequently required to perform their own routine maintenance.

The following chapters deal individually with the Irishwomen who earned distinction as they progressed through achievements in aviation. Each chapter outlines in biographical form the ancestry, lives, achievements and descendants of these early Irish women aviators. The purpose of this publication is to bring to light the aeronautical accomplishments of those adventurous, brave and pioneering women. We deal firstly with one who distinguished herself as the first Irish-born woman to leave *terra firma* in a balloon.

BIBLIOGRAPHY

Mark Davies, *King of All Balloons: The Adventurous Life of James Sadler, the First English Aeronaut* (Stroud: Amberley Publishing, 2015).

Eileen F. Lebow, *Before Amelia: Women Pilots in the Early Days of Aviation* (Washington, DC: Brassey's, 2002).

Bryan MacMahon, *Ascend or Die: Richard Crosbie, Pioneer of Balloon Flight* (Dublin: History Press Ireland, 2010).

Richard O. Smith, *The Man with His Head in the Clouds: James Sadler, the First Englishman to Fly* (Oxford: Signal Books, 2014).

The trio of Irishwomen who learned to fly at Stag Lane Aerodrome, London, and in 1925 and 1926 became the first three Irish females to earn their Aviator's Certificates. Left to right: Sophie Eliott-Lynn, Lady Bailey and Sicele O'Brien.

COURTESY DE HAVILLAND MOTH CLUB ARCHIVE (PHOTO BY W. NORTH)

VIOLET DUNVILLE
RISING ON THE STRENGTH OF WHISKY

In the early years of the twentieth century, ballooning became a popular sport among the aristocratic classes. One of the early exponents of the craze was John Dunville of the successful whisky-distilling family from Belfast. In 1892 he married Violet Lambart from County Meath. Violet also became keen on aeronautics and, in 1907, she acquired her own balloon. She entered races throughout England and on the Continent. She achieved many awards and accolades for her successes. The First World War saw the demise of ballooning activities and sadly the death of Violet Dunville's son, who was posthumously awarded the Victoria Cross for his military achievements. Another son was the victim of a rebel attack during the Easter Rising of 1916. Violet Dunville died in Belfast in 1940 and was buried in her adopted town of Holywood, County Down.

A photograph of Violet Dunville dated 28 June 1922.
COURTESY GORDON THOMPSON

VIOLET LAMBART WAS descended from the ancient family of Lambart VI, Count of Louvain, Belgium, who died in the year 1015 and whose sons had estates in Flanders. Randulph de Lambart fought alongside William the Conqueror at the Battle of Hastings in 1066. The Lambertini family are also descended from him. Prospero Lambertini became Pope Benedict XIV in August 1740, serving until May 1758. By the middle of the twelfth century, the Lambarts had settled in Skipton, Yorkshire, and this became their seat for several centuries. Some Lambart descendants relocated to Preston in Yorkshire during the seventeenth century. One of these was John, who died around 1474. He had a son, Richard, whose son Walter married Margaret Gaynesford. They lived in Preston until Walter's death on 11 September 1545. Walter had a son, whom he also christened Walter. He married Rose Wallop and they lived at Southampton, Hampshire. Walter and Rose's only son was called Oliver. During the Anglo-Spanish War, Oliver took part in the storming of Cadiz in southern Spain, which took place in June 1596 under the command of Robert Devereux, the second Earl of Essex. Following this successful battle, the Earl made Oliver a knight. The Earl led the Crown forces against Irish rebels in March 1599.

Essex's military campaign, part of the Nine Years War, failed in Ireland and, on 24 September 1599, he returned to London and appointed Oliver Lambart Master of the Camp at Enniscorthy, County Wexford, and Chief Commander in Leinster. (Essex was later tried for treason and beheaded in the Tower of London on 25 February 1601.) On 19 July 1601, on the recommendation of Lord Mountjoy, Lambart was appointed Governor of Connaught, thus establishing the Lambart family in Ireland. During 1611 Oliver was granted about 2,000 acres of land in County Cavan. On account of his military successes throughout Ireland on behalf of King James I, Oliver Lambart became Member of Parliament for County Cavan between 1613 and 1615. On 16 February 1617 he was created

The second Earl of Essex, who led the Crown campaign against Irish rebels in 1599 and made Oliver Lambart a knight.
COURTESY NATIONAL PORTRAIT GALLERY, LONDON

Lord Lambart, first Baron of Cavan. Oliver married Hester, daughter of Sir William Fleetwood, Knight, of Carrington Manor, Bedfordshire. Oliver died on 9 July 1618 and was buried in Westminster Abbey, London. He was succeeded by his eldest son, Charles.

Charles Lambart was born around April 1600 and succeeded as second Lord Lambart in July 1618 upon the death of his father. Charles inherited sizeable estates in Westmeath, Roscommon, Cavan and King's County (later County Offaly). By 30 June 1625, he had married Jane Robartes and held several official titles, including Commander of the infantry forces in Ireland that quelled the 1641 Rising. He was given the title first Earl of Cavan on 14 January 1646. He died on 25 June 1660 and is buried at St Patrick's Cathedral, Dublin.

Charles and Jane had four children, two sons and two daughters. Charles was succeeded by his youngest son, Richard, born in 1628, as the second Earl of Cavan. On 12 November 1648, Richard married Rose Ware, a daughter of Sir James Ware of Macetown, County Dublin. When Richard died in May 1691 he was succeeded by Charles, his only son from his marriage to Rose. Charles was born on 7 September 1649 and subsequently became third Earl of Cavan. In 1670 Charles married Castilini Gilbert of Kilminchy, Queen's County (later County Laois). He died on 5 December 1702 and was buried at St Patrick's Cathedral in Dublin. The title of fourth Earl of Cavan went to his second son, Richard Lambart.

Richard Lambart first sat in the House of Lords on 25 November 1703. He served in the Queen's army in Spain, Portugal and the West Indies and, while in Barbados, he met and married Margaret, the daughter of Richard Trant, Governor of Barbados. They had four children. On 21 June 1729 he was appointed to the Privy Council of Ireland. Richard Lambart died on 10 March 1741 at Lambarton House, Queen's County. Richard and Margaret's second daughter was

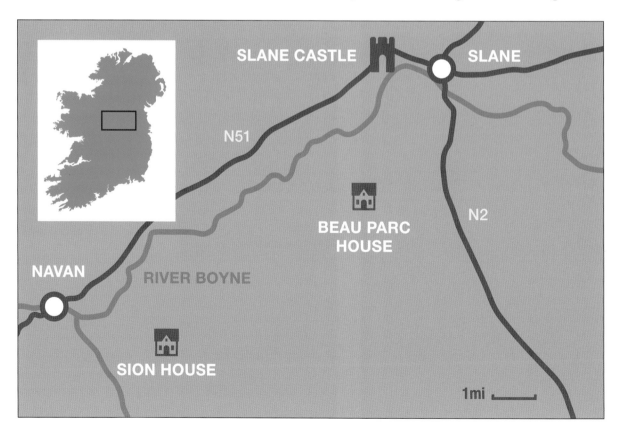

A map showing locations associated with the Lambart family.

Map © Martin Gaffney

BEAUPARC HOUSE, BOYNE VALLEY. 7794.W.L.

Lady Hester Lambart. On 13 December 1738, she married Warner Westenra. Warner and Hester had a son called Henry who married Harriet Murray. They became great-great-grandparents to Mary Westenra (Lady Bailey), the subject of another chapter in this publication. Warner and Hester's daughter, Castiliana, married Sir Edward Crosbie, an older brother of Ireland's first aeronaut, Richard Crosbie.

Charles Lambart (1600–60), the first Earl of Cavan, had another son called Oliver. Oliver married Eleanor Crane and their only son Charles married Elizabeth Hamilton, whose son Gustavus Lambart married Thomasine Rochfort. Gustavus Lambart was the Member of Parliament for Kilbeggan, County Westmeath, between 1741 and 1776. He built a three-storey mansion around 1755 at Painstown, between Slane and Navan, County Meath. Beau Parc House was to become the home of the Lambart family for the next 230 years. This Palladian building overlooks a bend on the south bank of the River Boyne and is located high above the river, two miles south-west of Slane village. The south-west-facing rectangular house is a large block, two rooms deep and three storeys high,

above a full basement. In 1837 the demesne contained about 300 acres.

On 6 February 1892, *Irish Society* described the house as follows:

> Beau Parc House, with its wood crowned heights and leafy banks, in one of the most picturesque spots in Ireland, is the exquisite and delightfully situated residence of the Lambart family. It occupies a most commanding situation on the summit of a high bank rising boldly from the Boyne and enjoys a magnificent view of the river and its richly wooded banks.

Gustavus and Thomasine had a son, Charles, who married Frances Dutton. In 1810, Charles and Frances's son, also called Gustavus (1772–1850) married Anna Butler Stevenson. In 1799 Gustavus built the Church of Ireland church at Painstown. (This building survived until the mid-twentieth century. It was deconsecrated in 1958 and demolished in 1961.) His marriage to Anna produced a son, whom they christened Gustavus

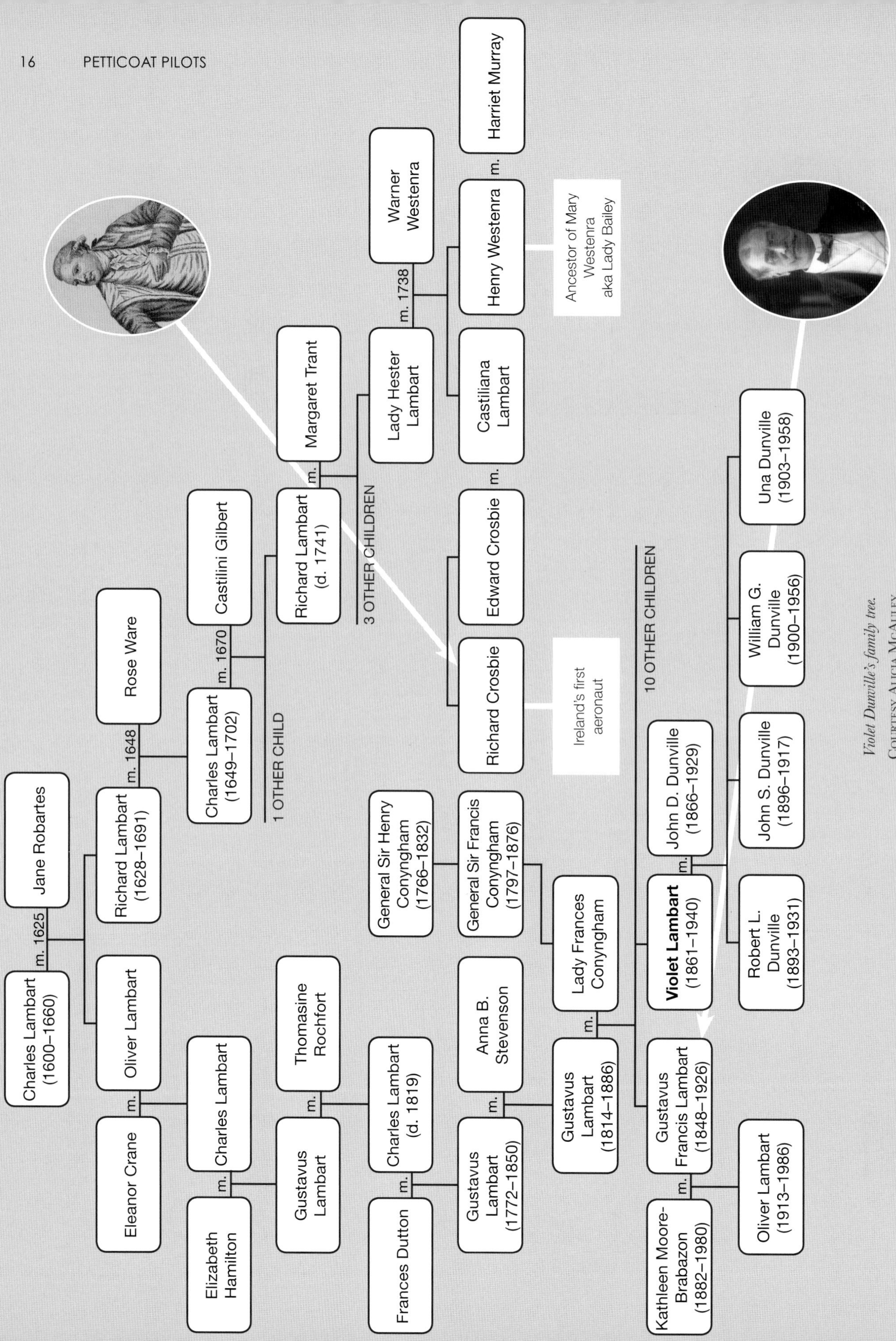

Charles Lambart (1600–1660) — m. 1625 — Jane Robartes

Richard Lambart (1628–1691) — m. 1648 — Rose Ware

Charles Lambart (1649–1702) — m. 1670 — Castilini Gilbert

Richard Lambart (d. 1741) — m. — Margaret Trant

1 OTHER CHILD

Warner Westenra

Lady Hester Lambart — m. 1738 — Henry Westenra

Castiliana Lambart

Harriet Murray — m. —

Ancestor of Mary Westenra aka Lady Bailey

3 OTHER CHILDREN

Edward Crosbie — m. —

Richard Crosbie

Ireland's first aeronaut

Oliver Lambart

Eleanor Crane — m. — Charles Lambart

Elizabeth Hamilton

Gustavus Lambart

Thomasine Rochfort — m. — Charles Lambart (d. 1819)

Frances Dutton — m. —

Gustavus Lambart (1772–1850) — m. — Anna B. Stevenson

General Sir Henry Conyngham (1766–1832)

General Sir Francis Conyngham (1797–1876)

Lady Frances Conyngham

Gustavus Lambart (1814–1886) — m. —

Gustavus Francis Lambart (1848–1926) — m. — Violet Lambart (1861–1940)

Kathleen Moore-Brabazon (1882–1980) — m. —

Oliver Lambart (1913–1986)

Violet Lambart (1861–1940) — m. — John D. Dunville (1866–1929)

10 OTHER CHILDREN

Robert L. Dunville (1893–1931)

John S. Dunville (1896–1917)

William G. Dunville (1900–1956)

Una Dunville (1903–1958)

Violet Dunville's family tree.
COURTESY ALICIA McAULEY

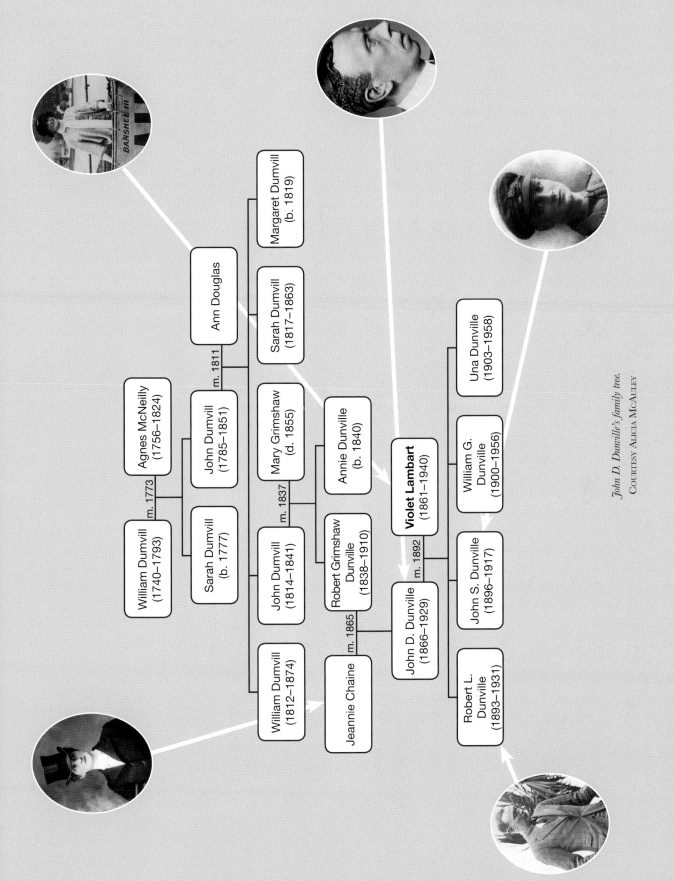

John D. Dunville's family tree.
COURTESY ALICIA MCAULEY

The overgrown and neglected entrance to the underground burial vault
of the Lambart family in Painstown Cemetery, Navan, County Meath.
For approximately 200 years members of the Lambart family were
interred beneath the foundations of the Church of Ireland church at
Painstown. The church was demolished in 1961 and only the ivy-clad
foundations remain above the Lambart vault.
AUTHOR'S PHOTOGRAPH

William Lambart (1814–86). Gustavus married Lady
Frances C.M. Conyngham in 1847. Up until the
time of his death, Gustavus W. Lambart was Deputy
Lieutenant for County Meath. He had a brother,
Charles James, who became Rector of Navan Parish in
1857. Additional details regarding the Lambart family
can be found in *The Peerage of Ireland* by John Lodge
(1789) and *The Complete Peerage*, Volume 3 (1913) by
George E. Cokayne.

Lady Frances Conyngham was known in her time
as Lady Fanny and was the third daughter of Sir
Francis Conyngham, second Marquess Conyngham
(1797–1876). He held numerous titled positions and
senior government offices and rose to the rank of
General in the armed forces. He was Lord Lieutenant
of County Meath between 1869 and his death in 1876.
His father was General Sir Henry Conyngham, first
Marquess Conyngham (1766–1832), who also held
senior positions in government and other administrative
positions in England and Ireland. On 5 July 1794,
Henry Conyngham married Elizabeth Denison, who
gained some notoriety as the last mistress of King
George IV. Four weeks after his Coronation on 19 July
1821, the King arrived at Howth, County Dublin, for
a state visit. Elizabeth spent a considerable portion of
the three weeks he was in Ireland in his company. The
King stayed at her home in Slane Castle between 23
and 27 August 1821.

Henry Conyngham was created first Earl of
Mountcharles on 15 January 1816. The eighth
Marquess Conyngham is Henry Conyngham,
predominantly known as Henry Mountcharles, who at
the time of writing resides at the former Lambart family
home of Beau Parc House, Slane, County Meath. He is
also owner of the nearby Conyngham ancestral family
home of Slane Castle.

The Lambarts had considerable influence in
Ireland and succeeded in persuading the Great
Northern Railway to locate a station near their estate.
Construction of the railway line between Drogheda
and Navan commenced during the years of the
Great Famine and the line was officially opened on
15 February 1850. The station was located in the
townland of Painstown, opposite the main entrance to
the Lambart estate, and was called Beau Parc Station.
Four steam trains each way stopped there daily. The
Lambart family could depart in first-class carriages
on the 9am train and arrive in Dublin by 10.30am.
Day trips would arrive at Beau Parc Station by special
carriage from colleges and various other organisations
to see the grounds, the big house and the river.

In his publication *Yellow Furze Memories*, Conor
Brennan described working conditions on the Lambart
estate:

The Lambarts were rated a good family to work with. In the demesne at least 30 were employed outdoors and indoors about half that number, so this place set the headline regarding wages, hours and estate house rents. Working conditions were good. In Beau Parc many of the workers had estate houses. The Lambarts were very popular with the employees and also the residents of the area. There was great respect for the Lambart family. Eventually, the cost of keeping Beau Parc became almost impossible as wages increased and year by year a number of men were let go and so the garden and grounds were not kept up as in the past.

Gustavus William and Lady Frances Lambart had 12 children, the eldest of whom was Sir Gustavus Francis William Lambart (1848–1926), known as Sir Francis, who was created first Baronet Lambart of Beau Parc on 13 July 1911. He married Kathleen Moore-Brabazon (1882–1980) on 13 September 1911. The Moore-Brabazon ancestral home was Tara Hall, in close proximity to the Hill of Tara in the townland of Cabragh, south of Navan and about ten miles from Beau Parc. They had one son, Oliver Francis Lambart, born on 6 April 1913 in Beau Parc House.

On the death of Sir Francis on 16 June 1926, 13-year-old Oliver became the second Baronet. When Painstown Church was deconsecrated in 1958, several artefacts and memorials dedicated to the Lambart family, including a stained-glass window, were relocated to St Patrick's Church of Ireland in Slane village. In the 1960s the Irish Land Commission purchased about 300 acres of the Beau Parc Demesne. Lady Kathleen Lambart died in December 1980, aged 98, by which time the estate had few employees. Sir Oliver was the last member of the Lambart family to reside at Beau Parc House. He died on 16 March 1986 in Our Lady's Hospital, Navan. He was unmarried and upon his death the baronetcy became extinct. Beau Parc House came into the possession of his relative, Lord Henry Mountcharles, the eighth Marquess Conyngham.

Kathleen Moore-Brabazon's younger brother was John T.C., who was granted Aviator's Certificate number one by the Royal Aero Club on 8 March 1910. He served with the Royal Flying Corps in the First World War and later held a number of corporate directorships and parliamentary positions. In 1919 he

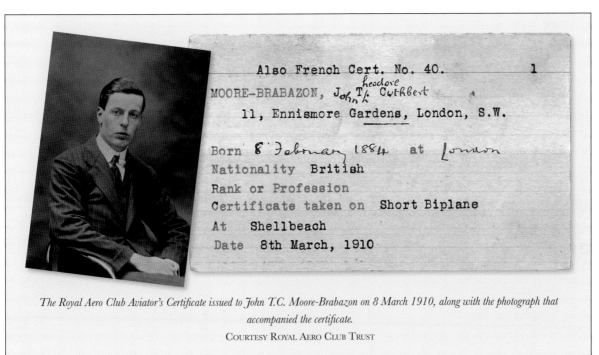

The Royal Aero Club Aviator's Certificate issued to John T.C. Moore-Brabazon on 8 March 1910, along with the photograph that accompanied the certificate.

COURTESY ROYAL AERO CLUB TRUST

Sir Gustavus Francis William Lambart,
first Baronet, with his wife, Lady Kathleen
Barbara Lambart (née Moore-Brabazon)
and their only child, Sir Oliver Francis
Lambart, second Baronet, in a portrait by
Bassano, taken on 7 May 1923.
COURTESY NATIONAL PORTRAIT GALLERY,
LONDON

was appointed Parliamentary Private Secretary to the Secretary of State for War, Winston Churchill. In 1941 and 1942, Moore-Brabazon was Minister of Aircraft Production under Prime Minister Churchill. Following this he was granted the title Lord Brabazon of Tara. As will be seen, he also featured in the aviation life of Violet Lambart.

The seventh of Gustavus William and Lady Frances's 12 children was Violet Anne Blanche Lambart, born on 14 August 1861 and destined to become the first Irish-born female aeronaut.

Like many children of Anglo-Irish aristocratic families, Violet Lambart enjoyed a privileged lifestyle. As a young woman, she engaged in hunting and other equine pastimes. Her mother, Lady Lambart, was generous to the local population around Slane and Navan and allowed her estate to host cattle, horse, sheep and dog shows, dog trials and bull sales. Cricket matches were also held on the grounds of Beau Parc House. The Lambart family integrated with the local community in a positive manner. Violet and her siblings were well regarded in the community. Violet attended shows and horse-race meetings at other locations. She went to bloodstock sales with her father. As a débutante she had a full social calendar and attended the St Valentine's Day Ball and Hunt Ball, to name but two. It is conceivable that Violet met John Dunville at one of these social occasions. The Dunvilles owned Sion House near Navan and primarily used it as a place where the Dunville family could enjoy hunting away from their home in Holywood, County Down. Sion House and Beau Parc House are about eight miles apart.

On 7 January 1892, 30-year-old Violet Lambart married 25-year-old John Dunville Dunville. Over the generations the Dunville family surname had a variety of versions, among them Dumvill, Dumville and Domville. The English line of Dumvills descended from Hugh of Avranches, from Donville-les-Bains in Normandy, northern France, who came to Cheshire, England, around the time of William the Conqueror. John Dunville's family could trace their lineage back to Edmund Dumvill, born in 1570 in Rostherne, Cheshire. The Dumvill family line of interest to this story relates to William Dumvill (1740–93), who was born in Belfast and remained there all his life.

The headstone of William Dumvill (1740–93) in Shankill
Cemetery, Belfast. He was an ancestor of the generations that
developed the successful Dunville whisky empire.
AUTHOR'S PHOTOGRAPH

William's brother, Robert, and many of his close Dumvill relatives emigrated to places in America like South Carolina, Tennessee, Arkansas, Kentucky and Missouri. Several other branches of the family resided in villages in Yorkshire and Durham. On 6 June 1773, William Dumvill married his second wife, Agnes McNeilly (1756–1824) at Carnmoney Parish Church, County Antrim. They had two children – a daughter, Sarah, born on 26 December 1777, and a son, John, born on 15 June 1785. William died on 1 November 1793, aged 53.

The website www.dumville.org has extensive details about the Dumvill family history and contains the following account of the whisky business started by John Dumvill:

> John Dumvill joined the whiskey blenders and tea importers Napier & Company of Bank Lane, Belfast in 1801 at the age of sixteen. Six years later he became a partner of the firm with William Napier, and the name of the firm was changed to Napier and Dunville. The spelling of John's surname had been changed from 'Dumvill' to 'Dunville'. William Napier's son Joseph became Lord Chancellor of Ireland.
>
> John Dunville married Ann Douglas (1788 to 1865) on 9 November 1811. They had four children: William born on 25 December 1812, John born on 14 October 1814, Sarah born on 9 July 1817 and Margaret born on 20 November 1819. In 1825 the name of the whiskey firm was changed to Dunville and Company and the business moved from Bank Lane to Callender Street near Donegall Square in Belfast. With their increasing prosperity they moved to 12 Donegall Square East which was then in a fashionable middle-class area. John Dunville became a town alderman and a manager of the Academical Institution. On 1 June 1837 John Dunville junior (1814–1841) married Mary Grimshaw, daughter of Robert Grimshaw, Deputy Lieutenant, of Longwood, County Antrim. The Grimshaw family were the cotton barons of the nineteenth century in Belfast and it was Nicholas Grimshaw that built the first water driven cotton mill in Belfast in 1781.
>
> Dunville & Co. launched their best-known brand of whiskey, V.R., in 1837 after Queen Victoria (Victoria Regina) ascended the throne.

The Dunville mausoleum in Clifton Street Cemetery, Belfast, where members of the Dunville family were interred between 1824 and 1874.
AUTHOR'S PHOTOGRAPH

The Dunville Mausoleum in Clifton Street Cemetery in north Belfast was erected in 1832 by John Dunville (1785–1851) around the grave of his mother, Agnes, who died on 25 December 1824, aged 68.

John (1814–41) and Mary had two children – Robert Grimshaw Dunville, born on 28 May 1838 in Belfast, and Annie Dunville,

A sketch of Richmond Lodge. This was the Dunville family home between 1845 and 1874.
COURTESY REVEREND CON AULD

born on 2 October 1840. Sadly their father died on 15 April 1841 aged just 26. He was buried in Clifton Street Cemetery.

The history of the Dunville whisky business continues:

In 1845 John senior and Ann Dunville moved to the stately Richmond Lodge, which had been built on the Holywood Road in County Down at the end of the eighteenth century. When John Dunville senior died aged 65 years on 21 March 1851, Dunville & Co. had been a large, thriving whiskey business for many years and his surviving son William Dunville (1812–1874) succeeded him as Chairman. On 24 November 1864 William Dunville married Anne Georgina Knox, daughter of the Venerable Edmond Dalrymple Hesketh Knox, Archdeacon

of Killaloe, and granddaughter of the Honourable Right Reverend Edmund Knox, Bishop of Limerick. They had one son who was still-born on 13 December 1865. As well as being Chairman of Dunville & Company, William Dunville was an active member of the Liberal Party and a Justice of the Peace.

In about 1860 William Dunville took in as partners his nephew, Robert Grimshaw Dunville (1838–1910), and James Bruce and James Craig. These energetic and ambitious young men spurred the development of Dunville & Co., and with William Dunville succeeded in building the Royal Irish Distilleries. Robert Grimshaw Dunville's father John Dunville Junior had died when Robert was two, and his mother had died when he was sixteen. James Craig's son, born in Belfast in 1871 and also named

The plan of the 86-acre estate surrounding Richmond Lodge when it was occupied by William Dunville between 1845 and his death in 1874. The entrance was off the Holywood to Belfast road.

Courtesy Public Record Office of Northern Ireland (PRONI), Belfast

The extensive buildings of Dunville's Distillery and the Royal Irish Distilleries in west Belfast following the opening of the Royal Irish Distilleries in 1869. The railway line into Belfast city centre, which was important to the business, is in the foreground.

COURTESY PRONI, BELFAST

Contemporary sketches of the extensive Dunville's Royal Irish Distilleries buildings in west Belfast. The steam locomotive in the foreground (top image) shows its proximity to the important Belfast railway network.

COURTESY WWW.DUMVILLE.ORG

James Craig, became the first Prime Minister of Northern Ireland …

A charity, the Sorella Trust, was founded by William Dunville on 19 November 1873, in memory of his unmarried sister, Sarah (1817–1863). Sorella is the Italian word for sister. The initial aim of the trust was to improve the houses of the working classes and this was achieved by building better houses in the Grosvenor Road area. Money from the trust was used to fund scholarships for primary and secondary education and for exhibitions in Queen's College which became Queen's University Belfast.

The major employers in Belfast in the late nineteenth century were the shipyards of Harland and Wolff and Workman, Clark and Company. The cotton and linen industries were also thriving and the whisky-distilling business was an important force in the city. The levy of duty on whisky was a real fiscal advantage to the British Government. Dunville's was one of the more successful distilleries in Belfast. It produced over 2.5 million gallons of whisky per year and employed 450 men. The granaries could hold 250,000 bushels of grain. The water came from Lough Mourne, 12 miles away, and in the distillery grounds there were two wells, 160 feet deep. In 1869, the Royal Irish Distilleries

Dunville's used the Scottish spelling of 'whisky' for their promotional material and labelling of products. The standard Irish spelling is 'whiskey'.
COURTESY WWW.DUMVILLE.ORG

were dominated by a 160-foot chimney. Bonded warehouses covered a total area of 13 acres in Adelaide Street, Alfred Street, Clarence Street and Franklin Street. The Royal Irish Distilleries are described in detail by Alfred Barnard in his book *The Whisky Distilleries of the United Kingdom* (1887).

premises were built on the Grosvenor Road in the west of the city, not far from Great Victoria Street Railway Station. Dunville and Company Limited owned and operated the Royal Irish Distilleries. Coal and grain were brought by rail to the distilleries' own siding and the railway wagons took the final product away. The distillery grounds covered about seven acres and

In promotional material displayed in hotels and bars, Dunville and Company opted to spell their brand of Irish whisky without an 'e'. Generally the Irish version is spelt 'whiskey'.

The Vienna Universal Exhibition was held in the Austrian capital between 1 May and 31 October 1873. The only British firm displaying whisky was Dunville

The distillery yard of Dunville and Company in west Belfast.
COURTESY THOMAS HOLMES MASON COLLECTION
VIA NATIONAL LIBRARY OF IRELAND

The bonded warehouse at Alfred Street, Belfast, which was one of several storage buildings around Belfast that housed the vast quantities of Dunville's distilled whisky.

COURTESY THOMAS HOLMES MASON COLLECTION VIA NATIONAL LIBRARY OF IRELAND

Robert Grimshaw Dunville married Jeannie Chaine from Larne on 14 December 1865 and they built the magnificent Redburn House near Holywood, County Down.

COURTESY CHRISTOPHER DUNVILLE

and Company. This was a major honour and achievement for the Belfast distillery and testified to their prominent place among British whisky producers.

Robert Grimshaw Dunville married Jeannie Chaine of Larne, County Antrim, on 14 December 1865. At a cost of £28,000 they built the magnificent Redburn House, two miles from Richmond Lodge on the Holywood Road, County Down. It was the most opulent of all the north-County Down mansions. It was constructed using the finest Scrabo stone obtained from the nearby estate of Lord Londonderry at Newtownards. It had 70 rooms, the grandest of which were the entrance hall and the ballroom, illuminated by a magnificent Waterford Crystal chandelier. It was set in 170 acres with views of Belfast Lough and the distant Glens of Antrim. Domestic and sanitary arrangements at Redburn House were decades ahead of the mid-nineteenth-century norm, as were the comforts of the servants' accommodation. Around the grounds were many cottages for those servants who did not live in the big house. Robert and Jeannie's only child, John Dunville Dunville (his surname was also one of his forenames), was born in Redburn House on 20 October 1866.

When William Dunville died on 18 May 1874 at 54 Princes Gate, London, he became the last of the Dunville family to be laid to rest in the

Palace Barracks. Holywood. 620.

family vault at grave number 109 in Clifton Street Cemetery. Richmond Lodge had been the Dunville family home since it was acquired by John Dunville in 1845. Shortly after William's death, however, Robert sold Richmond Lodge and around 1879 he purchased Sion House near Navan, County Meath. It had 26 rooms and 11 outbuildings. Redburn House then became the principal Dunville residence, while the family primarily used Sion House as a base for hunting and shooting. Robert G. Dunville became High Sheriff of County Meath in 1882. By 1886 he owned 5,360 acres in County Down. In 1911, Robert's son John became Master of the Meath Hounds, a position he retained until 1915.

The story according to www.dumville.org continues:

> When William Dunville died in 1874 his nephew Robert Grimshaw Dunville succeeded him as the third Chairman. Robert Grimshaw Dunville was a Justice of the Peace, a Deputy Lieutenant of County Down and a High Sheriff of County Meath. Dunville & Company was incorporated in 1879, becoming Dunville & Company Limited.
>
> The V.R. Distillery Cricket Club was formed in 1879 and to enable the members of the cricket club to remain active during the winter months, the Distillery Football Club was formed in 1880. The Directors of Dunville gave the Football Club their support and filled in a waste pond at the back of the distillery to create the club's first football ground.

Sion House near Navan, County Meath, was acquired by Robert Grimshaw Dunville as a location for the family's leisure activities from the 1850s.
COURTESY SAM CHRISTIE

Under the chairmanship of Robert Grimshaw Dunville, the annual output of whiskey from the distillery increased from one and a half million gallons in 1887 to two and a half million gallons in 1890. The four acres of Dunville Park were opened to the citizens of the City of Belfast in 1891 as its first public park.

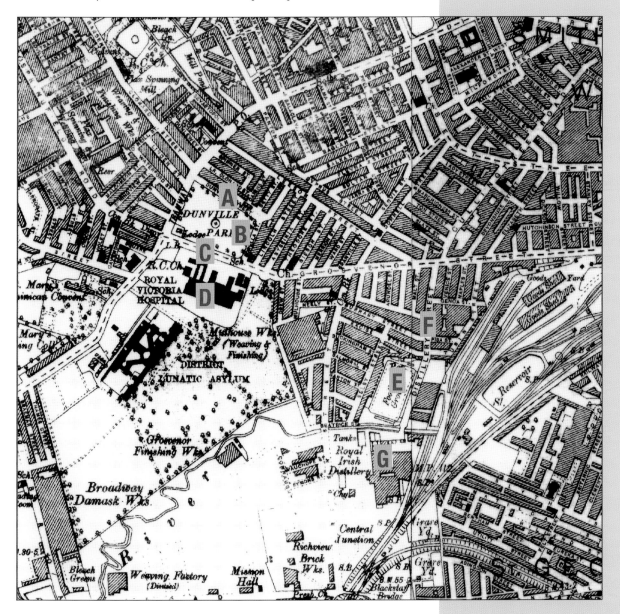

West Belfast in the 1890s, reflecting the influence of the Dunville family and their whisky empire.

A: *Dunville Street*   **D:** *Royal Victoria Hospital*   **F:** *Distillery Street*

B: *Dunville Park*   **E:** *Distillery Football Ground*   **G:** *Royal Irish Distilleries*

C: *Grosvenor Road*

COURTESY ORDNANCE SURVEY OF NORTHERN IRELAND

Beaufort Buildings in Westminster, London, was the location for the head office of Dunville and Company in London.

From the early 1880s, Dunville and Company had offices at 4 Beaufort Buildings in the St Clement Danes area of Westminster in the heart of London. They also had agencies located at: 112 Bath Street, Glasgow; 25 Westgate Road, Newcastle; 2 Coates Crescent, Edinburgh; Cavendish House, 9 Cavendish Row, Parnell Square, Dublin; and Queen Insurance Building, Dale Street, Liverpool.

At the time of the census of England on 3 April 1881, Robert's only child, 14-year-old John Dunville Dunville, was a second-year boarder at Eton College, Berkshire. He left Eton in 1883 aged 16 and went to Trinity College, Cambridge, where he gained a Master of Arts degree. While he was at Cambridge he was Master of the Cambridge Staghounds for two seasons, 1886 and 1887. On completion of his education he joined the 5th Battalion, Prince of Wales Leinster Regiment, and was commissioned as Second Lieutenant on 11 April 1887. In 1890 he was appointed Private Secretary to the Duke of Devonshire.

John Dunville spent a considerable amount of his leisure time as a young man at Sion House, hunting and pursuing other sporting activities. It may well have been on one of these visits that he became acquainted with Violet Lambart, who lived eight miles away. On 7 January 1892, John Dunville married Violet Anne Blanche Lambart by special licence in the Church of Ireland church at Painstown, County Meath. Violet was the fifth daughter of Gustavus William Lambart, Deputy Lieutenant, of Beau Parc House, County Meath. The *Irish Times* of Friday, 8 January 1892 detailed the wedding ceremony under the heading, 'Fashionable Marriage at Beau Parc, Co.

Meath'. Two columns outlined the notable guests and wedding presents and described in detail the attire of the bride and her bridesmaids. Diamonds and other precious stones featured among the gifts. The report also synopsised the groom's speech. The choir of St Bartholomew's Church, Dublin, conducted the choral part of the service. The guests were entertained at Beau Parc House. That evening the couple left by special train for Dublin, from where they proceeded to the Continent.

The popular weekly one-penny publication *Irish Society* detailed the lives of the aristocratic class in Ireland during its years of circulation. The issue of 16 January 1892 devoted a full page to Violet Lambart's wedding under the heading, 'Fashionable Irish Marriage'. It listed those in attendance and the lavish gifts that were bestowed on the couple.

Irish Society serialised articles over five weeks entitled 'The Lambarts and the Dunvilles', commencing on 16 January 1892. Their opening lines read:

> The greatest, most interesting and attractive
> event of late in the Irish fashionable world

John Dunville (right), aged 20, was Master of the Cambridge Staghounds in 1886 and 1887.
COURTESY SAM CHRISTIE

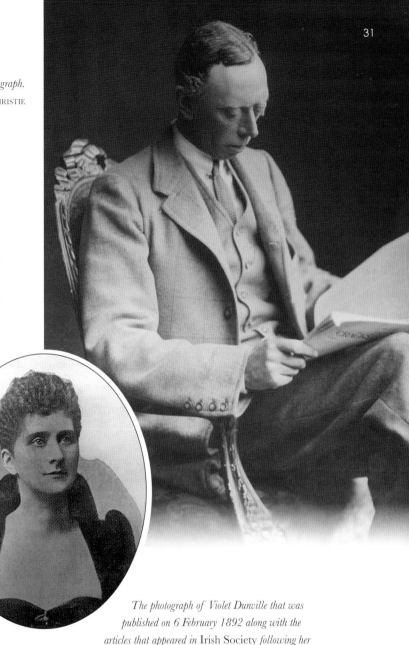

John D. Dunville in a relaxed pose in an undated photograph.

took place last Thursday in the suitable and prettily situated Church of Painstown, when Miss Violet Anne Blanche Lambart of Beau Parc House, Slane, Co. Meath, one of the lovely, beautiful and charming daughters of Lady Fanny Lambart and the late lamented Major Gustavus William Lambart, D.L., J.P., was married to John Dunville of Redburn, Holywood, Co. Down, a most popular, amiable and courteous gentleman, who for some time has been a frequent and welcome visitor amongst all classes in Royal Meath.

The articles gave considerable detail regarding the family connections and relationships between the Lambarts and the Dunvilles and many of the lords, ladies and other titled families throughout Ireland and England. Several pages were devoted to these connections. During the years when Violet was growing up, the house hosted royalty and nobility from different parts of Ireland, England and Scotland. The articles lavished considerable praise on both families. In relation to Violet, they added:

The photograph of Violet Dunville that was published on 6 February 1892 along with the articles that appeared in Irish Society *following her marriage on 7 January.*

The marriage of Miss Violet Lambart must most undoubtedly be looked upon with a very special degree of interest and delight above the ordinary events of the kind which are frequently taking place in our country, in consequence of not only her own personal charms of beauty, her amiability and winsome manners, her tenderness of heart and disposition, but also the high, honoured and dignified place the noble and illustrious house of Lambart has occupied – up to the present – for years, both in the Court of Victoria and the Irish Viceregal Court.

Prior to her marriage, Violet was Lady-in-Waiting to 33-year-old Princess Beatrice, fifth daughter and youngest child of Queen Victoria. She performed a similar role for Queen Alexandra, wife of King Edward VII, Queen Victoria's eldest son. Violet's older sister, Constance Una, was Lady-in-Waiting to the Duchess of Albany. The Lady-in-Waiting attended all state ceremonies and presided at the household table.

Bertha, Violet's younger sister, when aged 20, was Maid-of-Honour to Queen Victoria between January 1890 and the Queen's death on 22 January 1901. The Maids-of-Honour to Queen Victoria were all young ladies of good family, who were personally selected by Her Majesty. They enjoyed for life the courtesy title 'Honourable' and were in constant attendance on the Queen.

The *Irish Society* article further referred to Violet in the following context:

> She has left the exquisite abode of her ancestors and the fond and loved ones there, likewise the happy and delightful and picturesque spots and scenes of her gay childhood and youth, but more especially the poor to whom she was a kind and sympathetic friend at all times, brightening and gladdening many of their homes by her cheerful, sweet, and lively presence. Through her personal worth, sympathy, tenderness and kindliness both of heart and manner, she is so justly entitled.

The infant son Billy seated on his mother's lap, while Bobby stands alongside them with his arm around his mother. It was customary in the Edwardian era to dress a male child in a frock or dress.
COURTESY CHRISTOPHER DUNVILLE

John and Violet Dunville established their home in London and started a family there. They had four children: Robert Lambart Dunville, born on 18 February 1893; John Spencer Dunville, born on 7 May 1896; William Gustavus Dunville, born on 13 June 1900; and their only daughter, Una Dunville, born on 22 February 1903.

The census for England of 31 March 1901 recorded John and Violet Dunville and their sons, Robert, William and John as living at 46 Portland Place, Marylebone, in the Borough of Westminster, an affluent area of London. In 1873 the property was the residence of James Sinclair, the fourteenth Earl of Caithness, the most northerly land mass in Scotland. After Sinclair's widow's death in 1895, John Dunville acquired 46 Portland Place. In addition to the members of the Dunville family, the census also listed 12 servants: a butler, two footmen, a lady's maid, a cook, two nurses, two housemaids, two kitchenmaids and a hall boy. Redburn House, Holywood, and 46 Portland Place became centres of lavish entertainment, expertly organised by Violet as the fashionable hostess. The James Adam-designed block of fashionable houses containing numbers 34 to 60 Portland

Place was constructed in 1774. Numbers 46 and 48 formed the centrepiece of the building. It was located between Regent's Park and Hyde Park in central London.

The family's summer vacations and Christmas holidays were spent at Redburn House, Holywood, the head of the family there being John's father, Robert Grimshaw Dunville. The house was looked after by 16 house staff and 10 ground staff. The stables housed 60 horses for hunting and 4 horses for drawing carriages, all tended by 16 grooms. On the night of the census of Ireland of 31 March 1901, Sion House, Navan, was occupied by Robert and Jeannie Dunville, aided by ten domestic servants. On the same night, eight miles to the east, Beau Parc House near Slane was occupied by Violet's unmarried brother, Sir Gustavus Francis (53), and her unmarried sisters, Cecil (46), Lilian (36), Bertha (31) and Adeline Lambart (29), along with ten servants.

In 1906, Dunville and Company extended its Belfast offices from 16 to 18 Callender Street through to Arthur Street. (The only major building once used by Dunville and Company that remained 80 years after the closure of the company was

46 Portland Place, Marylebone, London, was the residence of Violet and John Dunville and their family between 1895 and 1930, photographed on 21 May 1903.
<small>COURTESY HISTORIC ENGLAND ARCHIVE</small>

25 to 39 Arthur Street.) Their equally impressive offices in London were in Shaftesbury Avenue.

Robert Grimshaw Dunville died on 17 August 1910 aged 72 years, after an illness lasting a few weeks, at his residence, Redburn House. He had been Chairman for 36 years. He was the first of the Dunville family to be interred in the new family grave in the Priory Cemetery, Holywood, County Down. The *Irish Times* published his obituary the following day. It included comments such as:

> He was head of the firm Messrs Dunville & Co. Ltd., Royal Irish Distilleries and much of the prosperity of this extensive firm was due to his indefatigable labours. He presented Dunville Park to the City of Belfast on 29 July 1899. Mr Dunville also defrayed the entire cost (£5,000) of enclosing and laying out the park, erecting a beautiful terracotta fountain and building an ornamental park-keepers house. He was a Deputy Lieutenant for Belfast and a Justice of the Peace for County Down. The late Mr Dunville was highly respected by all who had the pleasure of his acquaintance.

Robert Grimshaw Dunville (1838–1910) was Chairman of the Dunville whisky empire for 36 years.
COURTESY CHRISTOPHER DUNVILLE

The magnificent four-acre Dunville Park with its terracotta fountain was presented to the citizens of Belfast in 1899 by Robert Grimshaw Dunville. The buildings of the Royal Victoria Hospital form a backdrop to the park. The chimney in the background belongs to the Dunville distillery.
COURTESY WILLIAM LAWRENCE COLLECTION, NATIONAL LIBRARY OF IRELAND

The principal feature of Dunville Park was the magnificent terracotta fountain built by the Royal Doulton Company. As a tribute to the generosity of Robert G. Dunville, two Belfast streets surrounding Dunville Park were named in honour of the family, namely Sorella Street and Dunville Street. Nearby is Distillery Street, also named in memory of the Dunville distillery. Robert was succeeded as fourth Chairman of Dunville and Company Limited by his only child, John Dunville Dunville. In 1911, Royal Irish Distilleries took over the defunct Bladnoch Distillery near Wigtown, about 26 miles to the east of Stranraer in south-west Scotland. This family-run distillery had been operating since 1817 but was closed in 1905 during a period of over-supply and low sales of Scotch whisky. By the time the *Titanic* was launched in April 1912, Belfast was producing almost half of Ireland's whisky. The largest distillery was Dunville's.

According to the National Archives of Ireland in their exhibition of the 1901 and 1911 censuses:

> Belfast in 1911 was enjoying the greatest boom in its history. The chimneys of its linen mills and the cranes which stretched above its shipyards framed the commercial success of the city. This success ensured that Belfast was a place unlike any other in Ireland. Wealth in Belfast was the product of industry. By 1911 Belfast rolled out into the counties of Down and Antrim. The transformation of a century of industrialisation had entirely redrawn its scale and style. In 1808 [when the distillery firm of Napier and Dunville was established] only around 25,000 people lived in Belfast; by 1841, this number had increased to 70,000; and by 1911, it had reached 386,947. That was an increase of 10% from the previous census in 1901. It was, by 1911, the largest city in Ireland. Dublin had 304,802 inhabitants and Cork had 76,673.

On the night of the census of 2 April 1911, John D. Dunville was in Redburn House, Holywood, County Down, with his widowed mother, Jeannie. This would be explained by the fact that he had recently taken over the chairmanship of the Dunville whisky empire following the death of his father the previous year. Also present that night was Violet's nephew John Claude Brownrigg, Managing Director of Dunville and Company Limited. Eleven servants were also in residence. Violet was spending the night at Sion House, Navan, County Meath, attended by a further 11 servants, while her brother Gustavus Lambart was in nearby Beau Parc House, Slane, along with his unmarried sister, Lilian, and 12 servants.

John Dunville served for 18 years as Private Secretary to Spencer Cavendish, the eighth Duke of Devonshire, until the latter's death on 24 March 1908. While fulfilling this role he developed an interest in aeronautical pursuits that had become popular with the Edwardian aristocratic class in the early years of the twentieth century – flying gas balloons.

The photograph of John D. Dunville submitted to the Aero Club of the United Kingdom when he applied for his Aviator's Certificate in 1907.
Courtesy Royal Aero Club Trust

John Dunville (left) and Charles Rolls (right). In the centre is Henry Edmunds, often known as the 'Godfather of Rolls-Royce', as he introduced Charles Rolls to Henry Royce in 1904.

The Aero Club of the United Kingdom was founded during a balloon ascent from Crystal Palace, London, on 24 September 1901 by three wealthy motorists: Frank Hedges-Butler, his daughter Vera and Charles Stewart Rolls, and modelled on the Royal Automobile Club. (The Aero Club was granted the prefix 'Royal' on 15 February 1910 for its achievements and status.)

The initial ballooning years of John Dunville Dunville were documented on 10 October 1978 by Gordon Bruce, Company Secretary of Short Brothers Limited, Belfast. The following is a summary of his unpublished work.

John Dunville was brought up as a sportsman and it is surprising he did not take up the Edwardian sport of ballooning, which by then had become respectable for both aeronauts and spectators alike, until 1906. Charlie Rolls recognised that the first Gordon Bennett Cup race would require the services of the country's best balloon builders. In the same way he selected Henry Royce as the premier car builder, he sought out Eustace and Oswald Short to build the 80,000-cubic-foot balloon *Britannia* to enter the inaugural race on 30 September 1906 in Paris, France.

Dunville's introduction to ballooning happened when he flew with Charlie Rolls in *Venus* on 13 June 1906. The flight was from Shorts' new balloon factory at Battersea on the south bank of the River Thames in London to Liphook in Hampshire, a distance of 45 miles. Dunville had found his *métier*.

He had three further flights with Rolls before he took delivery of his first balloon from Shorts at Battersea on 1 August 1907, with Rolls as pilot. It measured 50,000 cubic feet and he called it *La Mascotte*, which was the pet name of his wife, Violet Anne. The usual price for a balloon of that size was about £200 and each ascent cost about £10. Dunville trained about three times a week to obtain Aero Club Aeronaut's Certificate number nine, issued on 3 December 1907. Violet's brother-in-law, John T.C. Moore-Brabazon, Lord Brabazon of Tara, had already been flying balloons with distinction since 1903.

Shorts were appointed Official Aeronauts to the Aero Club and the careers of Dunville and Shorts were inextricably linked over the following years, with Shorts building and launching most of Dunville's balloons. John Dunville trained in long-distance flying and learned the skills of searching for favourable air streams at various heights – rising by jettisoning ballast and descending by valving coal-gas. On 30 May 1908, Dunville competed in the International Balloon Race at the Hurlingham Club, London, and on 24 June he won the C.S. Rolls Cup for the Hare and Hounds Race. The race involved a 'quarry' balloon, usually flown by Rolls, which was given a head start and pursued by the other balloons. The winner was the balloon that landed nearest the 'Hare'. On 11 August 1908, John Dunville flew *La Mascotte* on his first crossing of the English Channel from Battersea to St Omer, a distance of 125 miles, covered at a speed faster than Louis Blériot's first powered crossing on 25 July 1909. (Dunville's average speed was 57 miles per hour, while Blériot's was 51 miles per hour).

John Dunville was elected to the Aero Club's Executive Committee in 1908 and was nominated as one of the three aeronauts to represent the United Kingdom in the third annual Gordon Bennett Cup. *La Mascotte* was replaced by the larger Shorts-built 77,000-cubic-foot balloon *Banshee*. Dunville funded his entry from his own resources. The 23 entrants, representing 8 countries, left Berlin on 11 October 1908. *Banshee* flew over Hamburg and the Kiel Canal and was heading towards the North Sea when prudence dictated that Dunville should land. He alighted one mile from the coast on the German-Danish border. He had been in the air for 36 hours and 54 minutes, the longest duration by a British-built balloon thus far, and had covered a distance of 272 miles. His wickerwork basket measured 5 feet and 3 inches long, 4 feet and 8 inches wide and 3 feet and 6 inches high. While it was generally accepted that *Banshee* was the winner, a Swiss entrant, aided by a tow from a boat, was controversially awarded the prize.

John Dunville (left) and Charles Pollock (second from left), photographed at the start of the Gordon Bennett Cup in Berlin on 11 October 1908. While it was generally accepted that they won the race, the award was controversially awarded to a Swiss entrant.

Flight by powered aircraft was becoming more popular. Nonetheless, the Dunville name continued to be associated with the Aero Club's diminishing band of balloon enthusiasts in the years before the First World War. Dunville's new Shorts-built 80,000-cubic-foot balloon *Banshee II* flourished between 1911 and 1914, especially in long-distance competitions.

The first time Violet Dunville ascended in a balloon was on Monday, 27 May 1907, almost one year after her husband entered the sport. It was a night-balloon flight in the *Nebula*, owned by Mrs Assheton-Harbord, along with Charles Pollock. The flight was from the Shorts factory at Battersea in London to Sevenoaks in Kent. Shorts' premises were located under the arches of the railway bridge adjacent to the Battersea Gasworks. Their balloons were inflated using coal-gas from the gasworks.

It was over a year later that Violet's name appeared again in historical sources as a balloon passenger. The occasion was the International Balloon Race of Saturday, 30 May 1908 from the Hurlingham Club, Fulham, London. *La Mascotte* was one of the 31 entrants. The pilot was her husband and the other passengers were Captain

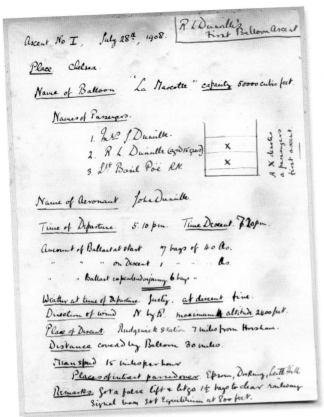

*Robert L. Dunville's record of his first
balloon flight, which he took aged 15,
on 28 July 1908.*
COURTESY ROYAL AERO CLUB TRUST

B. Corbet and Mr Vere Ker-Seymer. The field of entrants established a world record for the number of balloons in a race. Unfortunately *La Mascotte* landed 7.5 miles away from the winning post. John T.C. Moore-Brabazon also took part, in *Venus*.

Two months later, Violet's 15-year-old son, Robert Lambart Dunville, made his first ascent. It was in the 50,000-cubic-foot *La Mascotte*. The ascent began at Chelsea at 5.10pm on 28 July 1908. His mother and Lieutenant Basil Poe, Royal Navy, who was also embarking on his first balloon ascent, were also on board. They travelled south for about 30 miles and landed near Horsham, West Sussex, having spent 2 hours and 20 minutes aloft.

On Saturday, 21 November 1908, John and Violet Dunville, Charles Pollock and Phillip Gardner attempted to win the Northcliffe Cup for the longest-distance balloon flight. They departed Battersea, south of London, in *Banshee* at 2.15pm and crossed the coast at Dover to Calais, France, and then onward over Brussels, but the winds changed and carried them north over the Zuiderzee towards the North Sea in a snowstorm. With the weather deteriorating, they descended in a gale at 1.20am on Sunday morning in Baelen, Belgium, near the Dutch border. After narrowly avoiding the roof of a cottage, the balloon was safely landed in a potato patch. The aeronauts spent the night in the cottage. This was the first time a balloon with four persons on board had crossed the English Channel.

*The scene at the Hurlingham Club, Fulham, London, as the 31 balloons prepared to
ascend for the International Balloon Race on 30 May 1908. This was the first time
Violet Dunville participated in such an event.*
COURTESY ROYAL AERO CLUB TRUST

A further attempt was made on 11 December 1908 when, accompanied by Charles Pollock and Phillip Gardner, they started from Chelsea Gas Works and descended at Crailsheim, north-east of Stuttgart in Germany, a distance of 485 miles. The channel crossing of 35 miles took only 37 minutes. This was John Dunville's fifty-fifth balloon flight and he was awarded the Northcliffe Cup for the longest balloon journey during 1908.

The International Aeronautic Federation Conference on 11 January 1909 discussed the decision to award the Swiss balloon, *Helvetia*, first position in the Gordon Bennett Cup on 11 October 1908. The conference accepted there was nothing it could do but accept the outcome of the decision of the Berlin Aero Club. It would not go instead to John Dunville.

At the Annual General Meeting of the Aero Club of the United Kingdom on 10 March 1909, John Dunville was re-elected by ballot to the committee for 1909. He was also appointed Chairman of the Balloon Sub-Committee of the Aero Club.

He presented to the Aero Club a challenge cup to be awarded to any member that performed the longest journey by balloon, airship or aeroplane during 1909. On 18 May 1909, Violet Dunville was elected a member of the Aero Club of the United Kingdom.

The International Balloon Race commenced from the Hurlingham Club on Saturday, 22 May 1909. *Banshee* was piloted by John Dunville. Fourteen balloons entered the race and, when Dunville

The Northcliffe Cup was won by John Dunville for the longest balloon flight during 1907 and 1908. As the winner for two consecutive years, he retained the cup perpetually. It was presented to the Officer's Mess, RAF Aldergrove, by Violet Dunville.

descended at Buckhold near Pangbourne, Berkshire, he was declared the winner. Violet was one of the four passengers and she sent a telegram to her sons Robert and John at Eton College announcing her husband's victory.

Violet was given ownership of *La Mascotte* and, on 12 June 1909, she entered this balloon in the International Point-to-Point Race, starting from the Hurlingham Club in Fulham under the auspices of the Aero Club of the United Kingdom. The race was postponed because of the weather. Later the balloon ascended with Charles Pollock as pilot and Mrs Assheton-Habord as the other passenger and landed at Angmering, West Sussex. Between 13 June and 21 June 1909 John Dunville piloted four ascents in four different balloons to gain further experience.

On Saturday, 17 July 1909, the closing balloon event of the season took place in the form of the Hare and Hounds Race from the Hurlingham Club. Charles Rolls acted as the Hare in his midget balloon *Imp* and he led away from six entrants. Three of the balloons were owned by women. Violet entered *La Mascotte* with John as the pilot. They travelled southward over London, often just a few hundred feet above the rooftops. After two hours and ten minutes the *Imp* landed at Rayleigh, Essex. *La Mascotte* landed two miles away in a disappointing fifth position.

Violet attended a banquet at the Hotel Ritz, London, on 27 July 1909, to honour the crossing of the English Channel by Louis Blériot two days previously. One hundred guests attended the hastily organised event.

John Dunville later suggested a prize fund be established for the encouragement of flying in Ireland. Around the same time he was elected a member of the Aeronautical Society of Great Britain.

Gordon Bruce's account of John Dunville's aeronautical achievements continued:

In an attempt to cross the Irish Sea from Dublin on 24 January 1910 the envelope on *Banshee* was badly torn in a gust of wind. Dunville was successful on 15 February 1910 in *St Louis* when he flew from the Dublin Gas Works, Barrow Street, Ringsend to Macclesfield, 15 miles south of Manchester. The flight time of under five hours reached an estimated altitude of 10,000 feet where the temperature in the open car was 27 degrees of frost. Their average speed was 34 mph for the 160 miles they covered. This was the first successful crossing of the Irish Sea since Windham Sadler on 22 July 1817,

Mrs John Dunville.

Violet Dunville in a 1909 portrait by Bassano. In September 1909 Violet became a founder member of the Ladies' Committee of the Aero Club of the United Kingdom.
Courtesy National Portrait Gallery, London

> Father crossed Irish Channel
> february 1910.
>
> Ascended at Dublin gas works.
>
> Descended at:
> Macclesfield. (Cheshire).
> —
> Passenger :- C. F. Pollock.
> Mother was going but had to get out at the last minute as the gas was bad & would not lift suff-icient amount of Ballast with her.
> —
> First complete crossing ever been done.
> ——— " ———
> —
> RLD.

93 years previously. Robert later recorded: 'Mother was going but had to get out at the last minute as the gas was bad and would not lift sufficient amount of ballast with her.' Understandably it would have been a major disappointment for Violet not to have been part of such an historic flight.

On 2 July 1910, Violet won the Point-to-Point Race in *St Louis* from Hurlingham to Maldon, Essex, landing five miles from the spot selected for the descent. Six balloons took part.

Tragically Charlie Rolls, the Dunvilles' mentor in ballooning, was killed on 12 July 1910, aged 32. His close friends, John Dunville, John T.C. Moore-Brabazon, Claude Grahame-White, Samuel F. Cody and others were present when his French-built Wright Brothers aeroplane crashed at the Bournemouth Flying Meeting. Charlie Rolls received Aviator's Certificate number two on 8 March 1910, the same day as John

T.C. Moore-Brabazon received his certificate. Rolls was the first Briton to die in a powered aviation accident. John Dunville headed up a sub-committee of the Royal Aero Club to consider a memorial for Rolls.

The Point-to-Point Race, scheduled for Saturday, 23 July 1910 at Hurlingham, was abandoned because of

The mangled wreckage of Charles Rolls's Wright biplane, in which he lost his life at Bournemouth on 12 July 1910. He was the first British pilot to be killed in a flying accident.
COURTESY *ILLUSTRATED LONDON NEWS*

the unsuitable weather. However, the wind later decreased and John found conditions suitable for a cross-channel flight. He departed at 4.13pm. Along with Violet, Lady Milbanke and Charles Pollock, they alighted at Boulogne on the French coast around 8.20pm in the *St Louis*. The 100-mile trip was completed in 4 hours and 7 minutes.

When the Aero Club of Ireland was formed at 34 Dawson Street, Dublin, on 5 November 1909, John Dunville was not on the inaugural committee. Shortly thereafter, however, he was elected Chairman. He occasionally held the position of Acting Chairman of the Royal Aero Club of the United Kingdom. He used his influence within the latter organisation to secure Messrs Drexel, Grace and Dickson for the very successful inaugural Aviation Meeting at Leopardstown Racecourse, Dublin, on 29 and 30 August 1910. In the programme for the event, the Honorary Secretary acknowledged the role of John Dunville:

> My committee is under a lasting debt of gratitude to Mr John Dunville for his deep and abiding interest in the Club's welfare ever since its inception. I would also like to acknowledge his practical help in connection with our inaugural meeting. Without his influence it would have been impossible for us to submit such an attractive programme.

The Motor News of 3 September 1910, in an article about the Leopardstown meeting, praised Dunville:

> The Aero Club has in Mr John Dunville one of the greatest technical experts in aeronautics and who has contributed not less to the success of the meeting because a family bereavement prevented him from appearing on the grounds to witness the consummation of all the many voluntary labours in which he had engaged to ensure success.

The family bereavement referred to was that of his father, Robert Grimshaw Dunville, who died on 17 August 1910.

On 11 February 1911, a statue commemorating the eighth Duke of Devonshire was unveiled at the entrance to Horse Guards Avenue, Whitehall, London. John Dunville and sculptor Herbert Hampton had previously presented the design to King Edward VII at Buckingham Palace for his approval. The statue measured 13 feet in height and rested on a 16-foot plinth. As previously mentioned, John Dunville had been Private Secretary to the Duke from 1890 to 1908.

The Royal Aero Club Annual General Meeting was held on 30 March 1911 at 166 Piccadilly, London. Robert Loraine was awarded the silver medal for his aeroplane flight from Wales to Ireland and a silver medal was also awarded to John Dunville for his Irish Sea balloon journey from Ireland to England. At the same meeting John Dunville was re-elected as one of the 18-member committee for 1911.

The next balloon to be owned by Violet was called *Banshee II* and measured 80,000 cubic feet. The first race she entered it for was the Point-to-Point Race organised by the Royal Aero Club of the

Banshee II ascends from the Hurlingham Club, watched by several thousand spectators who enjoyed the aristocratic Edwardian sport of balloon racing.
COURTESY ROYAL AERO CLUB TRUST

United Kingdom. Eight balloons started the 1911 season's first balloon race from the Hurlingham Club on Saturday, 27 May 1911. Violet's husband piloted and they finished in fourth position, having landed 35.5 miles from the official destination of Challow Railway Station near Wantage, Berkshire (now in Oxfordshire).

Violet focused her attention on long-distance races using her latest balloon acquisition. The Royal Aero Club hosted the Challenge Cup for the race from Battersea Park, south London, to Roye in the Somme area of northern France, which *Banshee II* completed on 16 July 1911. They covered about 174 miles in 6 hours and 40 minutes. This was the second-longest balloon flight in a British balloon during 1911. The balloon was piloted by Charles Pollock and the passengers included Violet and her son Robert.

The Car magazine on 20 September 1911 carried a photograph of Violet's sister-in-law, Lady Lambart, with the added comment:

> Our portrait this week is one of Lady Lambart. Before her marriage last week on 13 September 1911 to Sir Francis Lambart, she was Miss Kathleen Moore-Brabazon. Like her brother, Mr J.T.C. Moore-Brabazon, who won the *Daily Mail*'s prize of £1,000 for the first flight of a circular mile on an all-British aeroplane on 2 November 1909, Lady Lambart is fond of travelling in the air, and has made balloon ascents with Mr Frank Butler. On the 13 July 1911, the bridegroom was made a baronet on the occasion of King George V's visit to Ireland. Sir Francis's title then became 1st Baronet Lambart of Beau Parc.

For the fourth consecutive year, John Dunville presented the Challenge Cup for the longest balloon flight in 1912. He was also Chairman of the Aero Club of Ireland and continued to represent them at the Royal Aero Club meetings.

The long-distance balloon race for the Hedges-Butler Challenge Trophy started from the Hurlingham Club at 5.16pm on Saturday, 22 June 1912. *Banshee II* landed at 3.10am the following morning across the Moors at Grosmont near Whitby, on the east coast of Yorkshire, a distance of 220 miles, to win the trophy. The pilot was Charles Pollock and Violet Dunville and Phillip Gardner were the passengers.

At the twelfth Annual General Meeting of the Royal Aero Club, held on 19 March 1913, John D. Dunville was re-elected to the committee for 1913. He continued to be the representative of the Aero Club of Ireland. On Saturday, 28 June 1913, four balloons ascended from Hurlingham as part of the Mortimer Singer Cross-Channel Race to France. *Banshee II* landed near Hastings, Kent, on the south-east coast, and did not finish. On Saturday, 19 July 1913, *Flight* magazine reported on Violet's good fortune:

> The last British balloon race for the present season started from Hurlingham on Saturday, 12 July 1913. It was a long distance race for the Hedges-Butler Challenge Cup and was won by Violet Dunville for the second year in succession. She used the *Banshee II* and the pilot was Charles Pollock. In addition to the Challenge Trophy, Violet received a souvenir from Mr Frank Hedges-Butler. The following are the approximate distances accomplished by the competitors:–

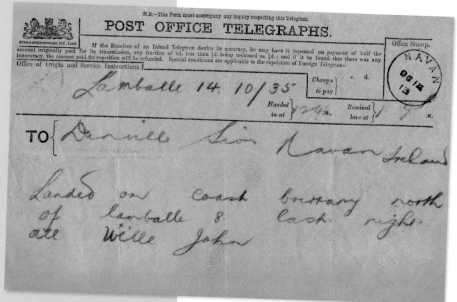

POST OFFICE TELEGRAPHS.

N.B.—This Form must accompany any inquiry respecting this Telegram.

Lamballe 14. 10/35

TO { *Dunville Sion Navan Ireland*

Landed on coast brittany north of lamballe 8. Cash. night.
all wille John

1st. *Banshee*. Mrs John Dunville. Distance 120 miles.

3rd. *Polo*. Pilot John Dunville. Distance 98 miles.

The Gordon Bennett Cup for 1913 was held on 12 October, starting from central Paris. As in 1912, the representatives for the United Kingdom were John D. Dunville and Jean de Francia. There were 18 entrants and Dunville's *Banshee II* finished in fourteenth position, having landed at Pléneuf on the Brittany coast, north of Lamballe.

The long-distance balloon race for the Mortimer Singer Cup started from the Hurlingham Club on Saturday, 27 June 1914 and was won in Violet's balloon *Banshee II*, piloted by her husband. The descent was made at Hythe near Folkestone, Kent. (This was the day before Archduke Franz Ferdinand was assassinated in Sarajevo, Bosnia.) Two weeks later, on 11 July 1914, Violet was again triumphant in the Hedges-Butler Long-Distance Challenge Race from the Hurlingham Club. She descended at Nesscliffe near Shrewsbury, Shropshire, in the early hours of the following morning. This being Violet's third consecutive victory in this race, the cup now became her absolute property. This was the final balloon event before the declaration of war on 4 August 1914. The onset of war caused the curtailment of general aviation, including civilian balloon flights.

The Great War was to have a devastating effect on Violet's family. Her eldest son, Robert Lambart Dunville, had been born on 18 February 1893 at 6 Green Street, Park Lane, London. This area was a popular residential suburb for the aristocrats of Westminster. Robert's preparatory school was Ludgrove School, Wokingham, Berkshire, which he attended between 1902 and 1906. He went to Eton College between 1907 and 1911. He joined the Cavalry and was appointed Second Lieutenant (on probation) with the 1st Life Guards on 20 November 1912, aged 19. He resigned his commission on 25 October 1913.

Following the outbreak of the First World War, he joined the Territorial Force with the Yeomanry and was appointed Second Lieutenant with the Royal Buckinghamshire Hussars on 6 October 1914. This regiment suffered heavy casualties during the Gallipoli Campaign in Turkey between April 1915 and January 1916. Robert, however, had been sent home to Holywood, County Down, in April 1915 by a medical board in Malta, suffering from acute appendicitis. When he recovered from his appendectomy in November 1915, he returned to service with the Grenadier Guards. In 1916, he was accepted as a member of the prestigious White's gentlemen's club on St James's Street in London. He was back in Holywood when the Easter Rebellion broke out in Dublin.

On Easter Monday, 24 April 1916, Second Lieutenant Robert L. Dunville was travelling by chauffeur-driven motor car from Holywood to Kingstown (later Dún Laoghaire) to board a boat to return to service in England. At Castlebellingham, County Louth, at ten minutes to seven that evening, the car was stopped by a large party of armed insurgents. Robert and his chauffeur were placed against a railing along with three members of the Royal Irish Constabulary. One of the rebels opened fire on the group of five at the railing and Constable McGee was mortally wounded. Lieutenant Dunville was shot in the chest and through a lung. Although left for dead by the rebels, he survived. Both of these men were 23 years of age. Four rebels were tried by courts martial for killing a policeman and attempting to kill a military officer. Three received the death penalty, which was later commuted to a prison sentence.

John and Violet's second son also saw military service during the First World War. John Spencer Dunville, who was born on 7 May 1896, was the first of the children to be born at 46 Portland Place, London. John arrived at Ludgrove School in September 1905 and left in April 1909. He attended Eton between 1909 and 1914. On 16 September 1914, 7 weeks after the outbreak of war, 18-year-old John was appointed Temporary Second Lieutenant as a Cavalry officer with the 1st Royal Dragoons and very swiftly confirmed in that rank.

The website www.dumville.org records the following about Second Lieutenant John S. Dunville:

> He was educated at Ludgrove School and Eton, where he was a member of the Officers' Training Corps from May 1912 to July 1914. He passed matriculation for Trinity College, Cambridge, but joined the army instead, serving as a Second Lieutenant in the 5th Reserve Regiment of Cavalry. In April 1915 he applied to join the Royal Flying Corps and was accepted but his course of instruction in aviation was cancelled a few days before he was due to start. He transferred to the 6th (Inniskilling) Dragoons and went to France in June 1915. There he took part in the Battle of Loos in September 1915, and transferred to the 1st (Royal) Dragoons in January 1916. In April he contracted trench fever and was invalided out to England. He returned to the 1st (Royal) Dragoons in France in December 1916.
>
> Second Lieutenant John Spencer Dunville was fatally wounded during a raid on the German lines near Épehy in France, part of the Hindenburg Line, on 25th June 1917.

Épehy is a village in the Somme area of northern France, about 40 miles south-west of the border with Belgium. Despite his arm being surgically amputated, John died the following day in a hospital in Villers-Faucon and was buried in the Communal Cemetery on the north-west of the village, in Row A, Grave 21.

The War Office issued the following notice on 2 August 1917:

Robert L. Dunville, aged 19, in the dress uniform of the 1st Life Guards in 1912.
COURTESY CHRISTOPHER DUNVILLE

His Majesty the King has been graciously pleased to approve of the award of the Victoria Cross to 2nd Lieutenant John Spencer Dunville, late Dragoons.

For most conspicuous bravery.

When in charge of a party consisting of scouts and Royal Engineers engaged in the demolition of the enemy's wire, this officer displayed great gallantry and disregard of all personal danger.

In order to ensure the absolute success of the work entrusted to him, 2nd Lt. Dunville placed himself between an NCO of the Royal Engineers and the enemy's fire, and, thus protected this NCO was enabled to complete a work of great importance.

2nd Lt. Dunville, although severely wounded, continued to direct his men in the wire-cutting and general operations until the raid was successfully completed, thereby setting a magnificent example of courage, determination and devotion to duty, to all ranks under his command.

This gallant officer has since succumbed to his wounds.

The painting of Second Lieutenant John Spencer Dunville that hangs in the Warrant Officers' and NCOs' Mess of the Household Cavalry Regiment, Combermere Barracks, Windsor, Berkshire.
COURTESY PETER STOREY, CURATOR, HOUSEHOLD CAVALRY ARCHIVE

Twenty-one-year-old John Spencer Dunville, Victoria Cross (VC), the Royal Dragoons, was buried in the Communal Cemetery in Villers-Faucon, Somme, France.
COURTESY COMMONWEALTH WAR GRAVES COMMISSION

The Victoria Cross awarded to Second Lieutenant John Spencer Dunville was accepted by his father, Squadron Commander John D. Dunville, on 29 August 1917.
COURTESY MINISTRY OF DEFENCE, CROWN COPYRIGHT, VIA HOUSEHOLD CAVALRY, LONDON

The Victoria Cross that John Spencer Dunville was posthumously awarded was received by his father, Squadron Commander John Dunville Dunville, from King George V at Buckingham Palace on 29 August 1917. It is on display at the Household Cavalry Museum in Horse Guards, Whitehall, London. He was also awarded the 1914–15 Star, the British War Medal 1914–20 and the Victory Medal 1914–19.

Violet bequeathed sufficient funds to ensure that a wreath could be laid in memory of her son Jonkins at the War Memorial, Holywood, each Remembrance Day. This practice was still continued in November 2018, over a century after Jonkins's death.

The life of Violet's beloved son, nicknamed Jonkins, is commemorated in many ways: two memorial plaques in St Philip's and St James's Church, Holywood, County Down; the pulpit in the Garrison Church in Palace Barracks, Holywood; the War Memorial, Holywood; the War Memorial, Eton College, Berkshire; the Victoria Cross Memorial, Eton College; and the War Memorial, Trinity College, Cambridge.

The War Memorial in Redburn Square, Holywood, commemorates the only Holywood native to receive the Victoria Cross in the First World War.
AUTHOR'S PHOTOGRAPHS

IN GRATEFUL MEMORY
OF THE MEN OF
HOLYWOOD
AND DISTRICT
WHO GAVE THEIR LIVES
IN THE GREAT WAR
1914 — 1918

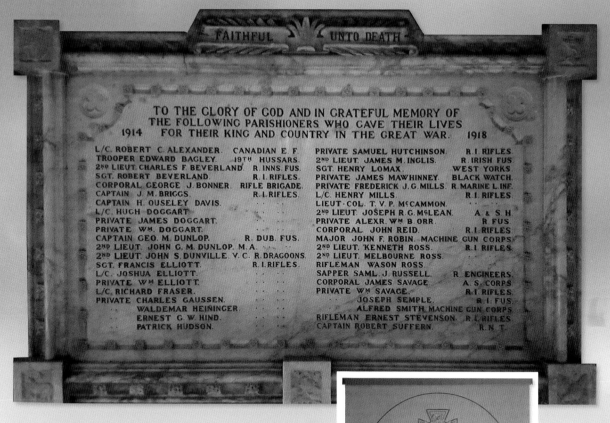

FAITHFUL · **UNTO DEATH**

TO THE GLORY OF GOD AND IN GRATEFUL MEMORY OF
THE FOLLOWING PARISHIONERS WHO GAVE THEIR LIVES
1914   FOR THEIR KING AND COUNTRY IN THE GREAT WAR.   1918

L/C ROBERT C. ALEXANDER.   CANADIAN E.F.   PRIVATE SAMUEL HUTCHINSON.   R.I. RIFLES.
TROOPER EDWARD BAGLEY.   19TH HUSSARS.   2ND LIEUT. JAMES M. INGLIS.   R. IRISH FUS.
2ND LIEUT. CHARLES F. BEVERLAND. R. INNS. FUS. SGT. HENRY LOMAX.   WEST YORKS.
SGT. ROBERT BEVERLAND.   R.I. RIFLES.   PRIVATE JAMES MAWHINNEY.   BLACK WATCH.
CORPORAL GEORGE J. BONNER. RIFLE BRIGADE.   PRIVATE FREDERICK J.G. MILLS.   R. MARINE L. INF.
CAPTAIN J.M. BRIGGS.   R.I. RIFLES.   L/C HENRY MILLS.   R.I. RIFLES.
CAPTAIN H. OUSELEY DAVIS.   LIEUT-COL. T.V.P. McCAMMON.
L/C HUGH DOGGART.   2ND LIEUT. JOSEPH R.G. McLEAN.   A. & S.H.
PRIVATE JAMES DOGGART.   PRIVATE ALEXR. WM B. ORR.   R FUS.
PRIVATE WM. DOGGART.   CORPORAL JOHN REID.   R.I. RIFLES
CAPTAIN GEO. M. DUNLOP.   R. DUB. FUS.   MAJOR JOHN F. ROBIN. MACHINE GUN CORPS
2ND LIEUT. JOHN G.M. DUNLOP. M.A.   2ND LIEUT. KENNETH ROSS.   R.I. RIFLES.
2ND LIEUT. JOHN S. DUNVILLE. V.C. R. DRAGOONS. 2ND LIEUT. MELBOURNE ROSS.
SGT. FRANCIS ELLIOTT.   R.I. RIFLES.   RIFLEMAN WASON ROSS.
L/C JOSHUA ELLIOTT.   SAPPER SAML. J. RUSSELL.   R. ENGINEERS.
PRIVATE WM ELLIOTT.   CORPORAL JAMES SAVAGE.   A.S. CORPS
L/C RICHARD FRASER.   PRIVATE WM SAVAGE.   R.I. RIFLES.
PRIVATE CHARLES GAUSSEN.   JOSEPH SEMPLE.   R.I. FUS.
     WALDEMAR HEININGER.   ALFRED SMITH. MACHINE GUN CORPS
     ERNEST G.W. HIND.   RIFLEMAN ERNEST STEVENSON. R.I. RIFLES.
     PATRICK HUDSON.   CAPTAIN ROBERT SUFFERN.   R.N.T.

Above & right: *Two wall-mounted plaques in the Church of St Philip and St James in Holywood commemorate John Spencer Dunville, VC.*

Below: *John Spencer Dunville, VC, is commemorated on the family gravestone in Priory Cemetery, Holywood (left) and by a memorial plaque in Holywood Parish Church (right).*

AUTHOR'S PHOTOGRAPHS

Although civilian ballooning events did not take place during the war years, the administrative functions of the Royal Aero Club continued and at their Annual General Meeting on 23 March 1915 John Dunville was re-elected to the committee. He was re-elected for each of the war years until 1919.

With both his eldest two sons serving with the armed forces from the beginning of the First World War, John Dunville Senior recommenced his military service. Eight months after the outbreak of the war, the Admiralty granted him a temporary commission as Flight Lieutenant with the Royal Naval Air Service (RNAS) on 30 March 1915. On 10 December 1915, *Flight* detailed a descent by parachute made by Lieutenant Colonel E.M. Maitland from a balloon piloted by Flight Lieutenant John Dunville and Flight Commander Corbett Wilson. Lieutenant Colonel Maitland jumped from the basket at an altitude of 10,500 feet and landed safely. On 1 January 1916, Dunville was promoted to Flight Commander, with further promotion on 30 June 1917 to Squadron Commander within the RNAS. On 31 December 1917, he was further promoted to Acting Wing Commander, with 450 officers and 2,000 men under his command at the No 1 Balloon Training Wing at RNAS Roehampton in south-west London.

When the Royal Flying Corps and the RNAS became the Royal Air Force (RAF) on 1 April 1918, John Dunville assumed the rank of Lieutenant Colonel, RAF.

The *London Gazette* in its New Year edition dated 1 January 1919, announced the following on behalf of King George V, St James's Palace:

In 1916, Wormwood Scrubs, London, was the main base for balloon and airship crew instruction before the opening of RAF Cranwell College as a dedicated airship-training station. The three officers seated in the front row are: Squadron Commanders John Dunville (Balloon Instructor) (third from right), A. Corbett Wilson (Commanding Officer) (second from right) and Charles F. Pollock (Balloon Instructor) (right).

COURTESY BRIAN TURPIN, *COASTAL PATROL: ROYAL NAVY AIRSHIP OPERATIONS DURING THE GREAT WAR, 1914–1918* (2016)

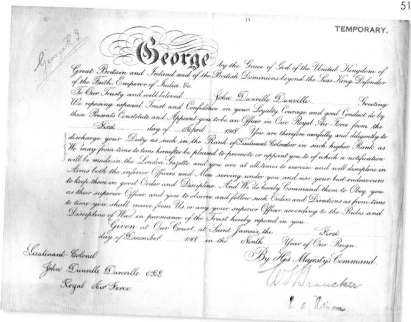

The certificate of appointment of John Dunville Dunville to the rank of Temporary Lieutenant Colonel in the newly formed RAF on 1 April 1918.
COURTESY ROYAL AERO CLUB TRUST

The King has been graciously pleased to give orders for the following promotions in, and appointment to, the Most Excellent Order of the British Empire, in recognition of valuable services rendered in connection with the war:–

Royal Air Force, Lieutenant Colonel John Dunville.

To be Officer of the Military Division of the Most Excellent Order (OBE).

Lieutenant Colonel John Dunville was listed on 3 June 1919 on His Majesty's Birthday Honours list 'in recognition of distinguished services rendered during the war'. He was further elevated and granted the title Commander of the Military Division of the Most Excellent Order of the British Empire (CBE). He resigned his service with the RAF on 5 September 1919, aged 52.

On 9 April 1918, Robert (Bobby) Dunville married his cousin Winifred Phyllis Combe of 45 Belgrave Square, London, in the Royal Military Chapel, Wellington Barracks, London. A guard of honour was furnished by a detachment of the Grenadier Guards, who provided an archway formed from Lewis guns as the bride and bridegroom left the chapel. Phyllis's mother was Lady Jane Seymour Combe, who was a daughter of Lieutenant General George Conyngham, the third Marquess Conyngham (1825–82). Robert's grandmother (Violet Dunville's mother) was Lady Frances Conyngham, who was a sister of Lieutenant General George Conyngham. Robert and Phyllis had one daughter, Maureen Eileen Anne, born on 18 September 1919. Following the birth of his daughter, Robert moved out of their family home in Chapel Street, Belgrave Square, London, and returned to live with his parents at 46 Portland Place. On 21 May 1920, Phyllis Dunville obtained 'a decree of restitution of conjugal rights to be obeyed within 21 days'. On 5 September 1920, Robert was acquitted at Marylebone Police Court on a charge of being drunk in charge of a motor car and assaulting a police sergeant. The marriage did not survive and, on 21 January 1921, a decree nisi was granted. Phyllis married the Honourable Francis N. Curzon on 27 April 1922 and, on 10 June 1927, Robert married Kathleen Kirkpatrick Shaw, daughter of Mr Justice Morice and Mrs Isabel Morice, late of the High Court in Pretoria, South Africa.

The edition of *Flight* magazine dated 11 November 1920 announced the appointment of Lieutenant Colonel John Dunville to command the newly formed Ulster Special Constabulary in Belfast. The War of Independence (1919–21) and the Irish Civil War (1922–3) made for a dark period in Belfast's history. From summer 1920 until the autumn of 1922, political violence in Belfast cost 465 lives, with over 1,000 injured. It started on 21 July 1920, with a loyalist march to the city's shipyards to expel 7,000 Catholic workers. (At that time Henry Glass was General Manager of the Workman, Clark and Company shipyard. See the chapter on the Glass sisters.) Dunville's had 650,000 gallons of whisky destroyed in bonded warehouses at the port of Dublin on the night of 6–7 April 1922. They lodged a compensation claim for £450,000 to cover the loss.

The final balloon Violet Dunville owned was Banshee III, *which was registered G-FAAH with the UK Department of Civil Aviation in August 1921.*
COURTESY GORDON THOMPSON
VIA CHRISTOPHER DUNVILLE

Despite the pressures of that position, John Dunville retained his role on the committee of the Royal Aero Club for 1920, 1921 and 1922. He also maintained his involvement in balloon racing. The Air Navigation Act 1920 required all lighter-than-air balloons and airships to be registered with the United Kingdom Department of Civil Aviation. The register for these types commenced with G-FAAA and they were classified as 'Spherical Free Balloons'. Consequently, when Violet acquired her balloon *Banshee III* in August 1921, it was given the registration mark G-FAAH. On 18 September 1921, *Banshee III*, entered by Violet, was one of the two British representatives in the Gordon Bennett Cup in Brussels. Violet was joined by her husband, who was the pilot, and Squadron Leader F.A. Baldwin. Their balloon was nominated as first of the eighteen balloons (representing five nations) to depart. They were unsuccessful. The winner was the Swiss entrant, Captain Armbruster, who travelled 756 kilometres as the crow flies in *Zurich* and stayed aloft for 27 hours and 23 minutes, finally landing on Lambay Island off Howth, County Dublin.

The next year's Gordon Bennett Cup took place in Geneva, Switzerland, on 6 August 1922. Violet's *Banshee III* was one of the three British entries, but unfortunately it failed to start.

At a committee meeting of the Royal Aero Club held on 18 April 1923, Lieutenant Colonel John D. Dunville was unanimously elected Vice-Chairman of the club for that year. Lieutenant Colonel John T.C. Moore-Brabazon was retiring Chairman. Dunville was re-elected to the same position on 9 April 1924.

On 4 August 1923, aged 56, John Dunville sailed from Liverpool, accompanied by a nurse, Margaret Ellerington, bound for a 25-day stay in New York. Dr Clive Pitt of Knightsbridge, London, was recorded as the person who authorised his sea journey. The ship's manifest included the comments: 'Med Cert, blind in left eye. Landing justified.'

The Gordon Bennett Cup race took place from Brussels on 23 September 1923. Violet entered *Banshee III* and, as was customary, her husband was the pilot. There were 15 starters and they soon encountered a severe lightning storm. Three balloons burst into flames, which resulted in the deaths of five aeronauts. At Herpen in the Netherlands, *Banshee III*'s grappling hook caught on some roofs, tearing off chimneys, and the aeronauts were thrown under the balloon car and suffered injuries to their faces and legs. They were able to return to Brussels on 24 September and were placed sixth, having covered 130 kilometres.

On 29 February 1924, Lieutenant Colonel Dunville, his wife, Violet, and her lady's maid, E. Williams, departed Southampton on board the

This photograph of Violet, dated 28 June 1922, carries the inscription, 'Better luck next time, best love, Mother'.
Courtesy Gordon Thompson

Banshee III *entered the Gordon Bennett Cup race, departing from Solbosch, Brussels, Belgium, on 23 September 1923. It was placed sixth. Tragically, five aeronauts lost their lives during the race. In the car prior to the race are Violet Dunville and, on the right, Robert L. Dunville (Bobby).*
Courtesy Gordon Thompson

RMS *Arundel Castle*, bound for Cape Town, South Africa. Their departure from South Africa was from the port of Durban and they arrived back in Southampton on 5 May 1924. The Royal Aero Club nominated Violet as one of its two representatives for the Gordon Bennett Cup in Brussels on Sunday, 15 June 1924, in *Banshee III*. On this occasion, the pilot was Squadron Leader F.A. Baldwin and the assistant was Lord Edward Grosvenor. They finished in a disappointing tenth place, having covered just 210 kilometres.

Three months later, on 13 September 1924, along with their Head Nurse, Margaret Ellerington, John and Violet sailed from London on board the RMS *Ormonde*, bound for Sydney, Australia. In early 1925, they both crossed the Atlantic and returned on board the RMS *Scythia* from New York, arriving in Liverpool on 28

March 1925. John Dunville was again re-elected to the committee of the Royal Aero Club *in absentia* at their Annual General Meeting on 25 March 1925.

The Gordon Bennett Cup race on Saturday, 7 June 1925 again had Violet as one of the three representatives for Britain in *Banshee III*. She had on board her husband and Squadron Leader Baldwin. They landed at Cap de la Hague and finished eighth out of 18 starters. *Flight* magazine reported that two weeks later:

On 21 June 1925 Violet, accompanied by her son Captain Robert Dunville and Commander Baldwin, made an ascent in *Banshee III* from the Welsh Harp, Hendon at 1am and landed near the Belgian frontier later that morning.

Banshee III, registration G-FAAH, prior to departure in the Gordon Bennett Cup race in Brussels, Belgium, on 15 June 1924. Left to right: Squadron Leader Baldwin (pilot), Violet Dunville (owner) and Lord Edward Grosvenor (aide).

COURTESY ROYAL AERO CLUB TRUST

At a committee meeting of the Royal Aero Club on 22 July 1925, Robert Lambart Dunville was elected a club member.

Wing Commander and Violet Dunville, accompanied by their valet and maid, began a maritime journey that averaged 29 days at sea each way on 14 November 1925. The departure was from the port of London on board the SS *Orama*, destined for Sydney, Australia. They continued to New Zealand and returned from Wellington to Southampton, where they disembarked from the SS *Athenic* on 18 May 1926. For that journey they brought their valet and maid with them again.

Violet entered *Banshee III* for the Gordon Bennett Cup race at Antwerp, Belgium, on 30 May 1926. She had on board her son Bobby and Squadron Leader F.A. Baldwin. Another disappointing result followed, when they travelled north-east of Eindhoven and only reached Veghel in the Netherlands, having covered 50 miles. John and Violet did not enter for any further competitive balloon races. They had enjoyed participation in balloon racing for 20 years, since Charlie Rolls had first introduced them to the sport on 13 June 1906.

While still fulfilling the position of Chairman of Dunville and Company, John returned to the RAF as Wing Commander on 17 August 1926. The same four persons sailed from London on board the SS *Orama* on 13 November 1926, again bound for Sydney, Australia. Such journeys were always undertaken first class. They then travelled to New Zealand with a party of British anglers and spent several weeks big-game fishing. They returned to Australia and sailed from Brisbane on board the SS *Hesperides* and arrived in Liverpool on 20 May 1927. John Dunville's final sea voyage was a sailing from Durban, South Africa. He arrived on board the RMS *Arundel Castle* at Southampton on 28 January 1929. At the Annual General Meeting of the Royal Aero Club held on 27 March 1929, Wing Commander John D. Dunville was re-elected to the committee.

John Dunville was a committee member of the Royal Aero Club when Aviator's Certificates were

A commemorative medallion presented by Aéro Club de Belgique to Violet Dunville for her participation in the Gordon Bennett Cup race on 7 June 1925.
COURTESY SAM CHRISTIE

Below: *While big-game fishing in New Zealand in 1926, Violet was photographed beside a 288-pound swordfish.*
COURTESY GORDON THOMPSON VIA SAM CHRISTIE

granted to several of the Irish female pilots that feature in this publication. They included Sophie Eliott-Lynn, Sicele O'Brien and Lady Bailey. In 1927 there were 145 Aviator's Certificates granted in Britain. That figure almost doubled for 1928, when 283 were issued.

Gordon Bruce continued the life of John D. Dunville:

> He flew in the 11th Gordon-Bennett balloon race in Geneva, Switzerland on 6 August 1922 and Brussels on 23 September 1923 using *Banshee III*. The end of John Dunville's competitive career was marked by the entry of his son Robert L. Dunville to balloon racing in the 1926 Gordon-Bennett Race at Antwerp, Belgium.

On 17 August 1926 John Dunville CBE, was appointed Wing Commander of No 502 (Ulster) Special Reserve Squadron of the Royal Air Force based 15 miles west of Belfast at RAF Aldergrove on the east shores of Lough Neagh. It was supplied with twin-engined Vickers Vimy heavy bombers on its formation on 15 May 1925. He retained this position until a few months before his death. No 502 (Ulster) Squadron became part of Coastal Command during the Second World War and was heavily involved in the war at sea as successors to Dunville's airships of the First World War. In 1936 Short Brothers Limited merged with Belfast shipbuilders Harland and Wolff to form Short and Harland to construct aircraft at Belfast Harbour – ironically about three miles from the Dunville family home at Redburn House, Holywood, County Down.

Following a brief illness, John Dunville Dunville died in his residence at 46 Portland Place, London, on 10 June 1929, aged 62. The *Belfast Telegraph* paid tribute to Dunville the following day and referred to his position as Chairman of Dunville and Company Limited. It added:

> Always very keen on sport, Colonel Dunville when a young man was an enthusiastic cross-country rider and skilful polo player. For two seasons

Violet in a relaxed pose in an undated photograph.
COURTESY CHRISTOPHER DUNVILLE

(1886–1887) he was Master of the Cambridge Staghounds and Master of the Meath Hounds 1911–1915.

The newspaper summarised his national and international achievements in balloon competitions and events and later his career with the RNAS and the RAF. He served for a number of years in the Meath Militia, 5th Battalion Leinster Regiment, where he got his army rank. He became one of the few servicemen to have held commissioned ranks in all three services – army, navy and air force.

Flight magazine paid tribute to Lieutenant Colonel John Dunville Dunville on 13 June 1929:

> He was one of our pioneer balloonists. He began his ascents with the late Hon. C.S. Rolls and in 1907 he had a balloon built for himself by Short Bros. Subsequently, he owned many balloons and at one time held the record for the longest time in the air by a British spherical balloon made during a race from Berlin in 1908. At the Gordon-Bennett balloon race he took financial responsibility for assisting Great Britain to be represented. With the advent of the aeroplane he helped to organise flying meetings in England and Ireland. He joined the RNAS in 1915 and served until after the Armistice, receiving a CBE for his services in 1919. In 1926 he was made Hon. Wing Commander RAF. For many years he was an active member of the Royal Aero Club committee.

He was buried in the Priory Cemetery, Holywood. His will was proved in March 1930 at £33,812.

The Dunvilles had made 46 Portland Place their family home for approximately 35 years. The *Times* of 8 April 1930 contained a notice stating that Violet moved to number 76 Portland Place, where she lived accompanied by up to nine servants and house staff. (Her former home at 46 Portland Place became a Grade II listed building on 10 September 1954.)

Following the death of his father, Robert became the fifth Chairman of Dunville and Company. The *Times* of London carried the following death announcement on 12 January 1931:

> On the 10th January 1931, at Johannesburg suddenly of heart failure Robert Lambart son of the late Wing Commander John Dunville, CBE and Mrs Dunville, of Redburn, Holywood, Co. Down, Northern Ireland and 46 Portland Place, W. London.

The *Belfast Telegraph* of 10 January 1931 informed its readers:

> His passing removes one of the best known figures in Ulster sporting and social life and brings to a close a career which was remarkable in many respects. The deceased gentleman was a fine business chief under his capable direction this noted company extended in many respects.

Robert was aged 37 at the time of his death. He was on a visit to South Africa to meet his wife's family and had planned to travel to Australia to visit his only surviving brother, William. The possibility exists that Robert never fully recovered from the gunshot wounds he had received on Easter Monday 1916 in Castlebellingham. Robert Dunville kept an extensive private zoological garden at his home, Redburn House, Holywood, County Down, for which animals had been gathered from a variety of locations around the world. After his death, the animals from Robert's private zoo formed the nucleus of the collection that inaugurated the Belfast Zoological Gardens, which opened to the public on 28 March 1934. He had been the fifth Chairman of Dunville and Company for only 19 months.

Following the death of Robert L. Dunville, Sion House, in the townland of Alexander Reid near Navan, County Meath, was offered for sale. It was acquired in July 1936 by the Sisters of Charity of St Vincent de Paul for use as a college of agriculture and domestic science. In later years it became St Stephen's National School. The house and entrance gates were classified as protected properties. Robert left an estate valued at £43,026 8s 7d.

Portland Place, in recent years, has been occupied by several foreign embassies and been home to the British Broadcasting Corporation since 1932. On 23 December 1932, accompanied by her nursing sister, Mai Rafferty, Violet sailed first class from Southampton on board the MS *Baloeran* to Port Said, Egypt.

The third son of John and Violet Dunville was William Gustavus, who was born on 13 June 1900 at 46 Portland Place, London. In the 1911 census, he was ten years old and boarding at Stubbington House, a preparatory school in Hampshire. Like his two older brothers, he went to Eton College in 1912, aged 12. He remained there until 1917. On 2 April 1921, 20-year-old William sailed from Southampton to New York. He was described on the manifest of the RMS *Aquitania* as a 'marine engineer'. In less than a year he was back in England.

The website www.dumville.org contains the following additional information about William:

> On 23 March 1922 William married Ruth Glover from the Newtownards Road, Belfast in the Trinity Church, Marylebone, London. Her father Samuel Glover was an iron turner. William and Ruth were both twenty-one years old when they married. Shortly afterwards the couple relocated to Australia to run a 21,000 acre sheep farm at Barry Station, Nundle, New South Wales.

Robert Lambart Dunville with a zebra in his private zoo at Redburn House. After his death, his animals formed the nucleus of Belfast Zoological Gardens, which opened in March 1934.

COURTESY CHRISTOPHER DUNVILLE VIA SAM CHRISTIE

William's wife was listed living on her own in the 1925 Electoral Roll for the Division of Robertson, Subdivision of Gloucester, New South Wales. In October 1926 Ruth Dunville petitioned for a divorce in Australia on the grounds of desertion and a decree absolute was announced in the *Sydney Morning Herald* on 11 May 1927. There were no children from the marriage of William and Ruth.

Shortly after Robert's death, William returned to Northern Ireland. Thirty-one-year-old William was then the only surviving male descendant of the Dunville family; his father and two older brothers were dead. Nonetheless, he did not head up the Dunville whisky empire. William met 25-year-old Ivy Evelyn Coombs in Portsmouth, England, and together they travelled to Canada. Ivy became William's second wife. Their first daughter, Shirley June Dunville, was born on 17 June 1933 in Canada. Over the next few years they lived in several rented properties close to the city centre of Sault Ste Marie in Ontario, close to the border with the United States. Their second daughter, Avis Zoe Pamela Dunville, was born on 14 April 1935. It seems that William drank heavily and this affected his life. He was receiving regular payments from his family in Northern Ireland on the understanding that he would remain in Canada and thus avoid any embarrassment to his family. Shirley married Garth Harmond Thorkilson and they had four children. Avis married firstly Murray Daynard and secondly Leonard McLeod. Avis had one son, Michael Daynard. William died on 22 August 1956 in Sault Ste Marie, Ontario. His widow, Ivy, lived for a further 11 years. Avis died on 2 July 1977 and Shirley died on 11 November 1994.

The National Prohibition Act, known also as the Volstead Act, banned the sale and distribution of alcohol in the United States of America. It came into effect in 1920 and lasted until 1933. The Prohibition period reduced the demand for legal whisky and had a detrimental effect on sales of Dunville's whisky. Robert Dunville was the last heir and Chairman and the company, without a suitable person at its head, foundered. By the end of 1935, Royal Irish Distilleries had ceased whisky production – it had vast quantities of spirit in bond but no market. Dunville and Company went into receivership and was liquidated in 1936, with the loss of 400 jobs. Its distillery assets were disposed of and all legal matters were finalised over the next 12 years. The Dunville-owned Bladnoch Distillery in Scotland went into liquidation in 1937.

Violet was 41 years of age when her only daughter, Una, was born on 22 February 1903. When Una was four, it was decided that she required professional residential medical care.

William Dunville in 1944 with daughters Shirley (left) and Avis.
COURTESY KIRSTEN YOUNG

Normansfield Hospital was established in 1868 by Dr John Langdon Haydon Down (1828–96) as a private home for the 'care, education and treatment of those of good social position who present any degree of mental deficiency'. An extra chromosome was identified as the cause of the particular syndrome he treated there, which was subsequently named after him.

In 2007 Andy Merriman documented Down's legacy in his publication *Tales of Normansfield: The Langdon Down Legacy*. One of the chapters is entitled 'A Distillery, Several Balloonists and a Red Head' and documents the period when Una Dunville was resident at Normansfield Hospital. The following paragraphs are a synopsis of that chapter.

On 4 October 1907 John Dunville contacted Normansfield Hospital, Teddington, London, concerning Una's admission. He wrote:

> Dear Sir,
> I am anxious to place my little girl aged four years in some establishment where she could be taken care of and Dr Savage has mentioned your name to me saying that you undertake the charge of children whose

brain has not developed. I shall be glad to know whether you could consider a proposal to take charge of my little child.
> John Dunville.

He received a positive response from the hospital and plans were made for Una's admission. The fees were 250 guineas *per annum*. Having cared for their daughter at home for four years, it was a heartrending decision for Violet. Nonetheless, it was requested that she should be admitted at the earliest opportunity. John wrote on 16 October 1907:

> I think that my wife, having at last reluctantly made up her mind that she must be parted from the child, is anxious that it should not be delayed.

By the end of October 1907 Una became a resident of the girls' south wing of Normansfield. Her admission documents included the following comments:

> Is like a child of two, walks does not speak, can indicate wants, incontinent, difficulty in swallowing, stuffy in nose and throat, rather spiteful, used to hang her tongue out, does not play well with toys, throws them, does tear clothes, very determined, good natured, never been ill, won't take medicine, frightened of having her hair cut, when she screams she is sick, never could be left alone.

After a few months Violet wrote to Percival Langdon Down, John Langdon Down's son:

> I am so happy that she is so happy now and I do hope you will allow me to go down to see her. I always am wondering if she knows any more things than she did.

William and Ivy Dunville at the wedding of their daughter Shirley on 19 March 1955. At the time of printing there are 34 descendants (excluding spouses) of William and Ivy residing in Canada.
COURTESY KIRSTEN YOUNG

Further correspondence from Violet during 1908 included these remarks:

> I want her to look as nice as if she was at home. I should like blue ribbon for her. Please let her wear the little diamond crescent brooch which she has and her brothers wore. I thought her so much improved when I saw her.

Violet often sent Una toys and gifts, including an old chair that she liked. Letters from Violet always ended with her expressing her gratitude for the care that Una was receiving at Normansfield. She wrote: 'Her surroundings are all so nice I think and I feel confident and happier about Una being away from home.'

In early February 1912 Violet's letter to the hospital included the following:

> I am sending a little pram for Una which you will please keep for her birthday on 22nd of this month. I saw her the other day and I was so pleased with her in every way she looked so nice and beautifully turned out, but I was utterly sorry I could not take her away with me, but I know she is in the best keeping.

The birthday was Una's ninth.

A series of letters from Percival Langdon Down between 1913 and 1916 to the Dunvilles exhibits the level of care, attention and education that Una received at Normansfield.

On 22 February 1924 Una came of age. Under the Mental Deficiency Act of 1913 there were formalities to be dealt with if she was to remain at Normansfield. It was decided that she should indeed remain there.

Meanwhile, Violet had been ill and her husband had taken her on a voyage to South Africa. On Violet's return from South Africa she visited Una. She wrote:

> I went down there today to see her. I was delighted at the improvement in her every way. She dressed up in her birthday clothes and she looked so nice I thought. Miss Cheek [Matron] gave me a graphic description of the whole entertainment. I wished I could have seen it.

Following the death of her son Bobby on 10 January 1931, Violet received a letter of condolence from Reginald Langdon Down, John Langdon Down's other son. She responded from her home in Redburn, Holywood on 19 February 1931:

> My grateful and true thanks for your kind thoughts of me in my misery. Blessed Bobby was the light of my life and his love for me quite incomparable. So with his dear father's loss you can believe how stricken I am. I hope Billy will come home and you have Una.

Una lived at Normansfield until her death on 28 September 1958, aged 55. She died from the effects of influenza and a duodenal ulcer. The informant on her death certificate was Norman Langdon Down, John Langdon Down's grandson. Una outlived her parents and her three brothers.

Despite the fact that John and Violet Dunville had four children, there was no male heir to continue the Dunville family name. Their eldest son, Robert Lambart, had one daughter, Maureen Eileen, who married Canadian Herbert Robertson, Wing Commander RAF, on 17 March 1941 in Saskatchewan, Canada. They had four daughters. William Gustavus had two daughters from his second marriage to Ivy Coombs in Canada. Shirley June married Garth Thorkilson on 19 March 1955 and they had three daughters and one son. Avis Zoe married Clifford Murray Daynard on 2 June 1953 and they had one son.

Violet standing on the running board of her yellow and black Rolls Royce. The car was a 1913 Silver Ghost model with Barker Torpedo engine. It was exhibited at the 1913 Olympia Show and then supplied to Violet. Looking on is her chauffeur, Paddy Kelly.

COURTESY SAM CHRISTIE

Violet Dunville is interred on the left side of the Dunville grave in Priory Cemetery, Holywood, County Down. Violet planted part of a privet bush from her son Jonkins's grave in France in front of his memorial stone on the right-hand side of the grave.

With war looming, Violet left 76 Portland Place in London. (In 1957 the building was demolished to make way for a new building, which was occupied by the City and Guilds Institute. In 1996 it became the offices of the Institute of Physics. It underwent further refurbishment and in 2015 became the headquarters of the Royal Institute of British Architects.)

Violet returned to Redburn House, Holywood, County Down. She died on Thursday, 7 March 1940 at 14 Lower Crescent, Belfast, aged 78. The house is an end-of-terrace red-brick building located near Queen's University, Belfast. Her death certificate states: 'Acute Appendicitis operation. Cardiac Failure. Certified.' This indicates she suffered a heart attack during or shortly after an appendix operation. In attendance at her death was her mother-in-law's nephew John Claude Brownrigg, who was former Managing Director of Dunville and Company Limited.

Two days later, the *Belfast Newsletter* informed readers of Violet's death in the list of death notices on page one with the remark, 'Funeral strictly private. No flowers.' There was no obituary. The *Belfast Telegraph* made no reference to her passing. Brownrigg was an executor to her will. Violet left an estate in England and Northern Ireland of £196,569. In her will she remembered her native County Meath and bequeathed money to Painstown Church, Beau Parc and Meath County Infirmary, Navan. The Dunville family had resided in Holywood for 95 years and Violet was the last remaining member of the family to occupy Redburn House. To quote the Reverend Con Auld:

The family's capacity to employ local labour and the magnanimous generosity made the Dunvilles the toast of the town. The family's quixotic and sumptuous lifestyle gave them fame throughout Ireland and beyond. Hunting, shooting, fishing, yachting and ballooning all found sporting favourites among the versatile Dunville family. The Dunvilles owned Ireland's largest distillery and one of the biggest in the world by the early 20th century. Family wealth, social position and a diary full of sporting events set the Dunvilles well above the daily chores of running the Royal Irish Distilleries. This task was carried out by a Board of Directors. Family guests were met in Redburn Square at Holywood railway station and brought to Redburn House in the elegant Dunville

The catalogue for the six-day public auction of the contents of Redburn House that took place ten weeks after the death of Violet Dunville.
COURTESY PRONI, BELFAST

carriage drawn by four of the finest horses. Evening dinner was a formal occasion. John and Violet Dunville were generous employers and mindful of those in retirement who had served the family well. They repaid business success with generous gifts to the local community. Violet adored her yellow and black Rolls Royce and frequently drove at speed along the untarred roads and dust tracks around Holywood.

Ten weeks following Violet's death, the contents of Redburn House were sold by public auction. The auction was conducted by J.D. Nicholl and Company Limited, 43–7 Chichester Street, Belfast. It took place at Redburn House over six days from 20 to 27 May 1940 and contained 2,500 lots.

During the Second World War, Redburn House was commandeered by the Air Ministry and occupied by the

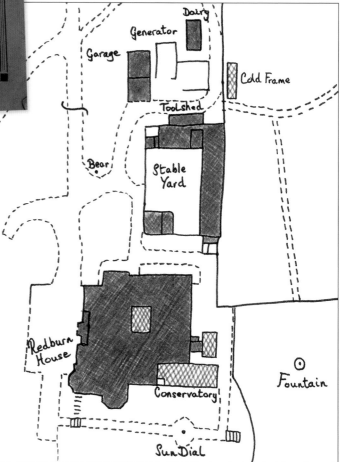

A sketch of Redburn House and its surrounding buildings.
COURTESY ROSEMARY MASEFIELD

Women's Auxiliary Air Force. In 1950 the once-majestic mansion and its 170-acre estate was acquired by Holywood Urban District Council for £14,700. A new cemetery was consecrated in the grounds in 1953. Ownership of the house over the years passed through several occupiers until the building was left derelict, damaged by arson and demolished around 1972.

Some of Redburn Estate was used for public housing; the remainder was developed by the Department of the Environment (Northern Ireland) as Redburn Country Park. It contains five miles of walkways and an escarpment, from the top of which are spectacular views of Belfast City, Belfast Harbour and the south-Antrim hills.

To accommodate construction of the A12 Westlink road linking Belfast city centre with the M1 motorway in the 1970s, most of the distillery buildings belonging to Dunville's were demolished. In addition to Redburn Country Park in Holywood, however, the legacy of the Dunville dynasty survives and is perpetuated in Belfast. Dunville Park was opened by Robert G. Dunville in 1891 and was the first public park in Belfast. Belfast Zoological Gardens benefitted from Robert Dunville's private zoo. The former head office of Dunville and Company Limited is now a B1 listed building and street names synonymous with the family and business survive. The whisky brand name has been revived. Violet's family home near Slane, County Meath, has been restored and is now open to the public. Testimony to Ireland's first female aeronaut and her family survives.

The former Dunville estate surrounding Redburn House was developed by the Department of the Environment (Northern Ireland) as Redburn Country Park for use as a public amenity area for the citizens of Belfast and surrounding areas.
COURTESY ROSEMARY MASEFIELD

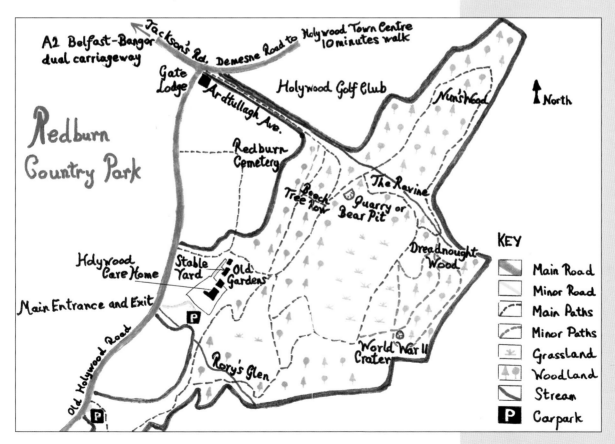

EPILOGUE

After the liquidation of the company in 1936, the former head office of Dunville and Company Limited at 25–39 Arthur Street, Belfast, was converted for use as a branch of the Belfast Savings Bank in 1938. In January 1986, Belfast City Council categorised it as a B1 listed building 'of special architectural or historic interest'. During the 1990s it was occupied by the First Trust Bank. In recent years it has been used as a licensed premises.

The Echlinville Distillery, Kircubbin, County Down, became the first new distillery in Northern Ireland in 125 years when it commenced distilling in June 2013. It revived the Dunville VR and other Dunville's Irish whisky brands among its leading products after a 77-year absence.

On Tuesday, 13 August 2013, Dunville Park in Belfast was reopened and rededicated after a £2 million restoration project by Belfast City Council. This followed several decades of neglect and vandalism. The park boasts many modern facilities for the citizens of Belfast and is a testament to the generosity of the Dunville family.

The Lambart ancestral home at Beau Parc House, Slane, County Meath, has been restored, with some original paintings

The Echlinville Distillery, Kircubbin, County Down, commenced distilling in 2013 and revived the Dunville's brand.
COURTESY ECHLINVILLE DISTILLERY

Dunville Park was reopened free of charge to the citizens of Belfast on 13 August 2013. It is located at the junction of Grosvenor Road and Falls Road in west Belfast. On the far side of the park is Dunville Street and on the right-hand side of the image is Sorella Street. The buildings in the foreground are part of the Royal Victoria Hospital.
COURTESY BELFAST CITY COUNCIL

The Echlinville Distillery produces several Dunville's-branded products.
COURTESY ECHLINVILLE DISTILLERY

and artefacts returned to the house. It is now open to the public. This is the house in which Violet Lambart was born on 14 August 1861. Beau Parc House featured in the 1955 Universal Pictures film *Captain Lightfoot*, starring American actor Rock Hudson.

On 27 April 2017, a ceremony was held in Westminster, London, to mark the centenary of the award of the Victoria Cross to John Spencer Dunville. Before the ceremony, music was played by the Band of the

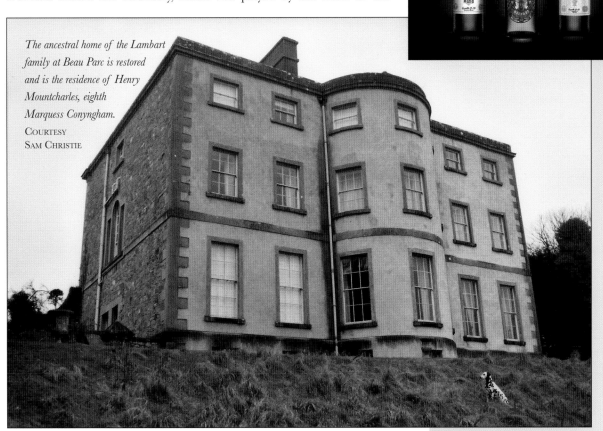

The ancestral home of the Lambart family at Beau Parc is restored and is the residence of Henry Mountcharles, eighth Marquess Conyngham.
COURTESY
SAM CHRISTIE

Robin Masefield's guide to Redburn Country Park.
COURTESY ROBIN MASEFIELD

Household Cavalry. The address was read by the Lord Mayor of Westminster, Councillor Steve Summers, and the response was read by Colonel Crispin Lockhart MBE, Chief of Staff, London District of the Household Division. The Lord Mayor of Westminster read the Victoria Cross citation and unveiled the commemorative stone, which was then blessed by the Reverend G. Scott, Chaplain to the Household Cavalry.

Holywood Library, County Down marked the centenary of Lieutenant John Spencer Dunville's death on Wednesday, 7 June 2017 by hosting a talk given by Sam Christie and the launch of a booklet compiled by Robin Masefield: *Redburn Country Park: A Community Guide.*

The Dunville family memory survives in Violet's native County Meath. Sion House was the Dunville hunting residence, located in Athlumney, south of Navan. It was sold to the Sisters of Charity of St Vincent de Paul in 1936 for use as St Martha's College of

Agriculture and Domestic Science. It ceased to function in that role in 1982 and lay idle for about 21 years until redeveloped as St Stephen's National School, founded on 1 September 2003. Sion House and the main entrance gates are protected structures. Close to Sion House are Dunville Road and Dunville Park. The Dunville name was not forgotten when a residential development containing 298 units was constructed in the locality. The development is called Dunville.

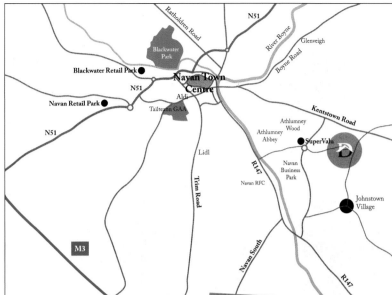

BIBLIOGRAPHY

Con Auld, *Forgotten Houses of Holywood* (Holywood: Con Auld, 2003).

Con Auld, *Holywood Then and Now: Essays by an Old Resident at the Beginning of a New Millennium* (Holywood: Con Auld, 2002).

Conor Brennan, *Bits and Pieces of Yellow Furze Parish* (privately published, 2000).

Conor Brennan, *Yellow Furze Memories* (privately published, n.d.).

Frank Hedges-Butler albums, c/o The Royal Aero Club Trust, RAF Museum, Hendon, London (unpublished, n.d.).

Jill and Miles Holroyd, www.dumville.org.

Andy Merriman, *Tales of Normansfield: The Langdon Down Legacy* (Middlesex: Down's Syndrome Association, 2007).

Flight magazine (1909–30).

Note: The website www.dumville.org includes further bibliographies.

ACKNOWLEDGEMENTS

Sam Christie, Holywood, historian.

Andrew Dawrant, The Royal Aero Club Trust, RAF Museum, Hendon, London.

Christopher Dunville, great-great-grandson of Violet Dunville and Dunville family genealogist.

Jill and Miles Holroyd, creators of www.dumville.org. Additional acknowledgements for contributors to that website are listed thereon.

John N.W. Scott, genealogical researcher.

COURTESY McPEAKE AUCTIONEERS, TYRRELSTOWN, DUBLIN

LILIAN BLAND

A WORLD'S FIRST ACHIEVER

Ireland was being introduced to aviation by the success of Harry Ferguson and his first flight in Ireland on 31 December 1909 and by the Aviation Meeting at Leopardstown, County Dublin, in August 1910. Meanwhile, in County Antrim, 31-year-old Lilian Bland designed, constructed and flew her own aircraft to become the first woman in the world to attain such an achievement. Afterwards, she turned her back on aeronautical experiments. She married her first cousin and they established a home in a remote part of Vancouver Island, Canada. They cultivated the land like many pioneers but when the marriage experienced difficulties she came back across the Atlantic. She spent the twilight years of her life near Land's End in England and died there in 1971, aged 92.

Lilian Bland in 1898, aged 19.
COURTESY WWW.LILIANBLAND.IE

FOR SEVERAL GENERATIONS it was customary to reward English military leaders with large estates in Ireland or England. This was particularly true during the reign of King Charles I, when he waged war against his own parliament during the 1640s. In return for military service to the King, large tracts of lands were either given gratis or sold to military leaders at affordable prices. Thomas Bland is typical of the soldiers of that time. On 30 August 1642, King Charles I bestowed on Bland the title of Baronet of Kippax Park (near Leeds, Yorkshire) for 'Active zeal and devotion to the Royal cause'. The Bland family name appears a century earlier in Blands Gill, Sedbergh, which is now in Cumbria but was once part of west Yorkshire. Some members of the Bland family moved to Ireland from Yorkshire around 1670.

The Bland family lineage of interest to this story appeared in Blandsfort, four miles east of Abbeyleix, Queen's County (later County Laois) in the early eighteenth century. John Bland purchased land in Queen's County and built Blandsfort House in 1715. When he died in 1728 he left the Blandsfort Estate to his brother General Sir Humphrey Bland (1685–1763), who was Governor of Gibraltar from 1749 to 1754. Humphrey Bland commanded the cavalry at the Battle of Culloden, Scotland, on 16 April 1746 as Major General. He died on 8 May 1763, aged 77, without leaving any children. Humphrey's younger brother was William, who served as Captain with the 8th Dragoons. On 14 September 1720, William married Elizabeth Jones Cock from Liverpool. William Bland died in 1746, leaving three sons, the eldest of whom was John (1723–90).

In 1763 John Bland married Sarah, a daughter of Charles Birch of Birch Grove, County Wexford. He died in 1790 and was succeeded at Blandsfort by his eldest son, also called John, who married Elizabeth Birch from Turvey, Donabate, County Dublin, on 27 November 1790. This marriage produced four sons and three daughters. The eldest son was John Thomas Bland, who was successor to the estate. He married Margaret Bond of Bath, England, and when he died childless in 1849 he bequeathed Blandsfort Estate to his youngest brother, Loftus Henry.

Loftus Henry, the fourth and youngest son (1805–72), married Charlotte Elizabeth Annesley on 20 August 1840, second daughter of Lieutenant General Arthur Grove Annesley of Annesgrove, County Cork. They had one son, John Loftus Bland, born on 6 June 1841. Loftus Henry was elected Member of Parliament for King's County (later County Offaly) on 26 July 1852 and Chairman of the Quarter Sessions for Cavan in 1862. He succeeded to the estates of his eldest brother, John Thomas, at Blandsfort, skipping the entitlement in succession of the second son, Robert Wintringham Bland (1794–1880). The third son was Charles Humphrey Bland (1795–1811). At the age of 16, Charles was one of 838 sailors and soldiers who lost their lives when the HMS *St George* sank in a storm off Jutland, Denmark, on 24 December 1811 in one of the worst maritime disasters at that time.

Robert Wintringham Bland was born on 21 February 1794 at Blandsfort in Queen's County. He became a clergyman and was the Perpetual Curate at St George's Parish in Upper Falls, Belfast, the oldest place of Anglican worship in Belfast. He married Alicia Evans on 14 July 1826. Alicia was the daughter of the Reverend Edward Evans, Justice of the Peace, of Gortmerron, Dungannon, County Tyrone. Robert and Alicia's marriage produced six children: Marianne Sinclair, born on 6 April 1827; John Humphrey, born on 20 May 1828; Edward Loftus, born on 10 December 1829; Sarah Maria, born on 21 May 1832; Robert Henry, born on 4 October 1834; and Alice Louisa, born on 2 October 1841. Between 1845 and 1849, the Reverend Robert was District Curate of St John's Parish at Whitehouse, a few miles north-east of Belfast City, on the northern shore of Belfast Lough. The children were raised at Abbeyville and then Woodbank, Whiteabbey, a mile or so along the coast from Whitehouse. (On 1 April 1958 the Urban District of Newtownabbey was formed by the merging of seven ancient villages including Carnmoney, Whiteabbey and Whitehouse.)

Robert Wintringham Bland was born in Blandsfort House, near Abbeyleix, County Laois, in 1794. He became a clergyman and moved to Whitehouse, north-east of Belfast.
COURTESY WWW.LILIANBLAND.IE

The Bland family home at Abbeyville, Whiteabbey, County Antrim, from a painting by John Humphrey Bland dated August 1871.
COURTESY WWW.LILIANBLAND.IE

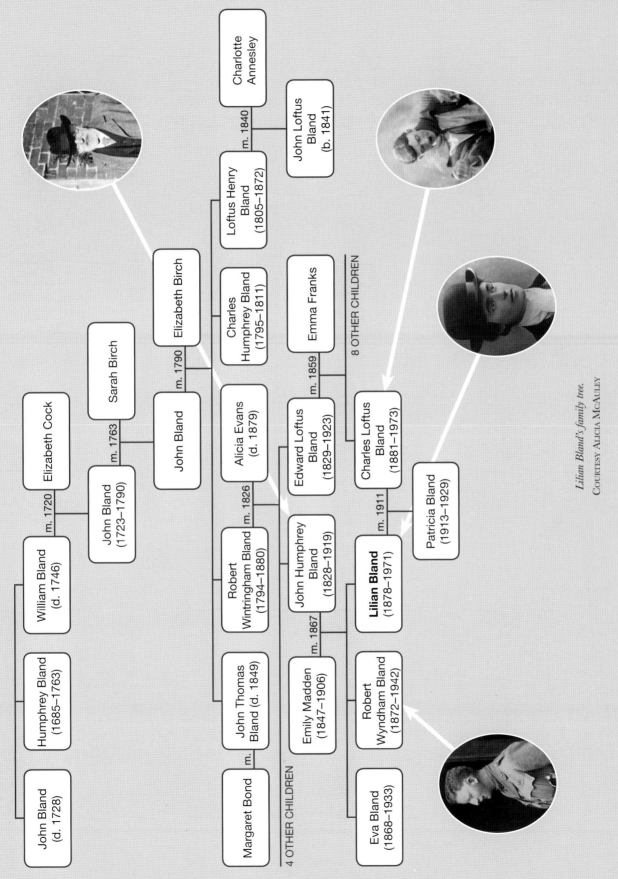

Lilian Bland's family tree.
COURTESY ALICIA MCAULEY

The Reverend Robert and Alicia's eldest son, John Humphrey Bland, became an artist and owned Fernagh House, Whiteabbey, County Antrim, not far from the family home. Between 1848 and 1861, having gained a Bachelor of Arts degree at Trinity College, Dublin, he studied art in Paris at the École des Beaux-Arts and in the studios of François-Édouard Picot and Thomas Couture, exhibiting his work at the Royal Academy in London and the Belfast Art Society.

On 30 October 1867, 39-year-old John Humphrey Bland married 20-year-old Emily Charlotte (born on 16 January 1847), daughter of the Reverend Wyndham Carlyon Madden (1793–1864) and Charlotte Leeke of Bergh Apton, near Norwich, Norfolk. John and Emily lived in Fernagh House. Three children were born of this marriage. The eldest was Eva Charlotte, born on 10 November 1868 in Fareham near Portsmouth, Hampshire. She was followed by Robert Wyndham Humphrey on 27 January 1872 in south Kensington, London, and finally Lilian Emily, who was born on 28 September 1878 in Maidstone, Kent. Their grandmother Alicia died on 10 October the following year and the Reverend Robert Wintringham Bland died a year later, on 21 December 1880, aged 86, at Abbeyville, Whiteabbey, County Antrim. At the time of the census for 1881, two-year-old Lilian and her parents and siblings were living at 33 Willington Street, Maidstone, Kent. They employed a cook, a nurse, a governess and a housemaid. Her father described his occupation as artist and painter.

From the time of John and Emily's marriage in 1867 over the following 33-year period, the family lived at several locations in Ireland, England and Europe. These included London, Arcachon near Bordeaux in south-west France, Maidstone in Kent, Paris, Rome, Geneva in Switzerland and St Ives in Cornwall, along with several other places. A cousin of Lilian's father died near Lake Geneva and left him a number of duties to perform. Lilian and her mother accompanied their father to Geneva for that period.

The three Bland children were mostly educated by a governess and Lilian spent a short period in 1891 at a private boarding school on the north-west Kent coast, when she was 12 years of age. She boarded at 4 the Grove, Thanet, Westgate-on-Sea.

When his wife became ill in 1900, John Humphrey brought his family back to Ireland, where he moved in with his sister at Tobarcooran House, Glebe Road West, Carnmoney, County Antrim. His sister was Sarah Smythe, the widow of General W.J. Smythe, RA, FRS, who had died in 1887. Shortly after moving to Carnmoney, Emily became so ill that she had to live in a warmer climate. By the time of the census of 31 March 1901 she had moved to Cannes in south-east France on the Mediterranean with her daughter Eva, while Lilian and her father remained at Tobarcooran House.

By 1902 Lilian had already made a name for herself as a journalist for local and national Irish newspapers and London magazines, and she was an acclaimed press photographer. She took numerous photographs at equestrian events including hunts and polo matches. On 10 February 1902, 23-year-old Lilian, on a trip to see to her ailing mother, visited Monte Carlo, Monaco, where she photographed the airship flight by Alberto Santos-Dumont. This would have been her first experience of an aeronautical event. Back in Ireland, on 2 July 1903, Lilian was among the press photographers to record the first Gordon Bennett Cup road race in Ireland. This was a significant event for Ireland, as there were only about 300 motor vehicles on the island at that time and a statutory exemption permitted the 12 entrants to breach the national speed limit of 14 miles per hour. She described her coverage of the race thus:

> I started off on a bicycle taking photographs of all the dangerous corners the cars would have to round and aiming at getting original views so as to avoid the type of pictures professionals were taking. We sometimes rode 50 miles a day and this with a 7 pound penalty in the shape of my Reflex camera.

Her report and photographs of the race were published in *The Golden Penny* magazine. Her appetite for things mechanical would have been whetted at this international motoring event.

Throughout the period 1905–8, Lilian penned numerous articles relating to equine interests. She imparted her knowledge and understanding of horses to readers of many popular international publications. These publications included *The Badminton Magazine of Sports and Pastimes* and *Fores's Sporting Notes and Sketches*.

Lilian's mother, Emily, died in Cannes on 27 December 1906. Lilian further astonished her contemporaries in Carnmoney, and scandalised her

In 1899 20-year-old Lilian travelled to Tuscany, northern Italy, to study music for two years.
COURTESY WWW.LILIANBLAND.IE

Twenty-five-year-old Lilian in her riding attire in 1904.
COURTESY WWW.LILIANBLAND.IE

To photograph the Gordon Bennett Cup road race on 2 July 1903, Lilian cycled the course, carrying her camera on her back.
COURTESY GUY WARNER

The standard practice in Edwardian England was for ladies to ride a horse side-saddle (top). Lilian Bland broke with protocol and rode astride in the same manner as gentlemen (bottom). This caused a degree of scandal at the time.
COURTESY WWW. LILIANBLAND.IE

aunt Sarah, by wearing riding breeches, smoking cigarettes in public, tinkering with motor-car engines and riding astride rather than side-saddle. She was also one of the first ladies in Ireland to apply for a jockey's licence. She rode for a training stables, performing riding exercises and trial gallops, schooling and breaking in hunters and qualifying thoroughbreds for point-to-point races. She hunted in Counties Antrim, Down, Kilkenny, Tipperary, King's County and Queen's County in Ireland and with the Pytchley, Atherstone, North Warwick and Warwickshire Hunts in England. Lilian spent considerable time during the hunting season of 1906–7 living in Rugby, Warwickshire, where she became a member of the Pytchley Hunt. Moreover, she was a crack shot and was not averse to lying in wait for poachers before sending them and their lurchers packing with a well-aimed burst of shotgun pellets. All of these characteristics were sufficient to make her stand out anywhere in the British Isles during

Tobarcooran House, Carnmoney, County Antrim, home to Lilian Bland from 1900 to 1912 (painting by Carl Schwab).
COURTESY NORA SCHWAB VIA GUY WARNER

A portrait photograph of Lilian in 1907, aged 28.
COURTESY WWW.LILIANBLAND.IE

the Edwardian period – and rather more so in Presbyterian Ulster.

Lilian became interested in aviation through her hobby of photographing birdlife. In particular, she was fascinated by the seagulls wheeling in the skies over the west coast of Scotland. She was staying with internationally renowned artist Jemima Blackburn on her estate at Roshven beside Kinlochmoidart near Fort William, Inverness, in the summer of 1908.

Lilian subsequently wrote about this visit:

> I was off to the Highlands to photograph sea birds, with a large trunkful of negatives and Lumiere colour plates. At Glenfinnan Miss Blackburn would row me out to a small island and there she would leave me plenty of food for the day. I would lie for hours studying the great black backed gulls soaring, using their tails as balancing rudders to the shifting breeze – how lovely it would be to fly. Each variety of gull had its own location, intruders would be chased away, a tweak at the tail feathers upsetting the enemy's balance so that they looped the loop and honour was satisfied. I think they were the first colour plates of live birds and I showed them at the Royal Photographic Society in London.

Between 17 September 1908 and 24 October 1908, the Royal Photographic Society's Annual Exhibition was held in London. A selection of 12 of the colour photographs that Lilian had produced were exhibited, which may have been the first colour plates of live birds ever taken.

The following year, when Louis Blériot flew across the English Channel on 25 July 1909, Lilian's uncle Robert sent her a postcard of the Blériot XI monoplane. He included a note of the machine's dimensions. Thus, her aviation ambitions were further kindled. She read all the books and magazine articles she could find about aeroplanes – including the weekly *Flight* magazine, which was first published on 2 January 1909. Later that year, she had the opportunity to visit the Blackpool Aviation Meet, which took place from 19 to 23 October 1909 and was the first officially recognised air display to be held in the United Kingdom.

She wrote a letter home to her father on 20 October:

> I have seen them fly, and looked over all the flying machines; they are all made very much the same way and they looked smaller than I expected. After hours of waiting Latham brought his machine out and it

Lilian attended the Blackpool Aviation Meet in October 1909. There she studied aeroplanes and spoke with early aviators and aircraft builders.
COURTESY BLACKPOOL INTERNATIONAL AIRPORT VIA GUY WARNER

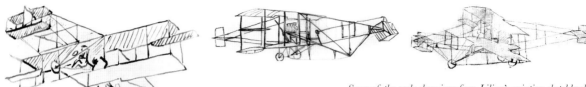

Some of the early drawings from Lilian's aviation sketchbook.

started running along the field and then gradually rose and flew half a circuit, when its wings or skid caught in a ditch, and broke the skid and bent the propeller. Paulhan flew in a Farman machine, several rounds of the course and alighted quite gracefully … in flying they keep their heads to the wind and turn a corner by drifting round tail-first … the Gnome motor is the best. The few English machines are, I imagine, no good – much too small and fitted with motor-bike engines … most of them are covered with tyre fabric, lashed on like lace boots sewn or tacked … the wheels are on castors with small springs.

Hubert Latham and Louis Paulhan were French pioneering aviators and contemporaries of Louis Blériot.

As can be judged from the above, Lilian was highly observant and by no means uncritical. She was not overawed by either the magnificent men or their flying machines. She made careful inspections of the aircraft, measuring and recording their dimensions, examining their structures, their methods of construction and their engines. Many years later the Department of Aeronautical Engineering at Queen's University, Belfast, examined her notebooks and technical drawings and commented very favourably on her technical skills and grasp of the subject.

Back at Tobarcooran House, Lilian made full use of the late General Smythe's well-equipped workshop at the back of the house and constructed a model biplane glider with a wingspan of six feet, which successfully flew under tow. During the winter of 1909–10, satisfied with this proof of concept, she designed and manufactured her glider. It was constructed of spruce, ash, elm and bamboo, then covered with unbleached calico, which she soaked in a home-mixed concoction of gelatine and formalin to make it rainproof. Lilian obtained the metal parts from Samuel Girvan of Ballyclare, County Antrim, and the A.V. Roe Company in Manchester.

After the individual sections were made in the workshop, she carried them across to the coach-house, where the full-scale biplane glider was assembled. When finished, it had a wingspan of 27 feet and 7 inches. Lilian then wrote her first letter to *Flight* magazine, which was published on 11 December 1909, in which she discussed the possibility of taking off in her glider using the skids in the manner of a toboggan on snow. She also discussed the use of metal parts, the recipe for a good varnish to proof calico and the advantages of ash over spruce. She finished her letter, 'Hoping this information may be of use.' The founder and editor of *Flight*, Stanley Spooner, commented as follows:

Lilian working on designs for her glider in the workshop at Tobarcooran House.

It is at all times a pleasure to us to receive such a thoroughly helpful letter as the above, and the fact that it comes from a lady not only enhances the interest which attaches to it, but shows how far-reaching is the fascination of flight. We expect much from Ireland in aviation, as in every other phase of daring sport, and we cordially wish success to our correspondent.

The first successful aeroplane flight in Ireland took place on 31 December 1909. Harry Ferguson, in a machine he designed himself, flew for approximately 130 yards at a maximum height of 15 feet at Lord Downshire's Park at Hillsborough, County Down. He achieved his goal of making the first flight in Ireland by an Irishman in an Irish aeroplane before the end of 1909.

Lilian decided to name her aircraft the *Mayfly*. We can speculate on the reasons why she chose that name. She perhaps thought that it may fly – or, indeed, that it may not; alternatively, like the insect, she perhaps did not expect it to last more than one day. Following the first tethered trial flight, Lilian wrote to *Flight* magazine again and her letter appeared in the issue of 19 February 1910:

Lilian holding the wing of her glider outside the workshop at Tobarcooran House, Carnmoney.
COURTESY WWW.LILIANBLAND.IE

I enclose two photos of my biplane, the '*Mayfly*'. I made her entirely myself, with the exception of the metal clips, and, of course the sockets, strainers, etc., were bought from English firms. I think she is the first biplane made in Ireland.

I had her out again to-day, wind of 18 mph. My only difficulty is at present to prevent her flying when I do not want her to. To-day I had three men to assist me, two of them knew nothing about it, and she ran the rope through their hands and soared up 20 feet before anyone was prepared. Fortunately the third man and myself had hold of a long rope, which saved the situation, in fact we got the machine soaring beautifully for some time until a down-wind caught the elevators which I had fastened, when she dived down and broke both skids, but did no other damage. It is quite a new sensation being charged by an aeroplane.

We then had quite a lively time sailing her downhill to the shed; a 4 foot bank was cleared in fine style, and indeed the only drawback was the pace, for she wants to go about 30 mph. I have now altered the steering arrangement so that the elevators can be controlled from the ground, which I naturally ought to have done from the first. I am also fitting two side panels, as I cannot very well work the balancing wings from the ground.

I have not yet had a chance of ascertaining the gliding angle exactly, but she soars with vertical ropes, and I imagine her angle is about 7 degrees. As I told you, she rises straight off the ground when faced to the wind. If we bring her gliding down in a steady wind she lands as softly as a feather. A few hours' work has made the skids stronger than they were before; they both broke where the wood was cross-grained, but I have the greatest difficulty here to get hold of good wood. The skids are American elm, which is very springy, and I must say they were severely tried.

Lilian E. Bland

Joe Blain, who assisted Lilian Bland with her experiments with a glider and then with an engine-driven aeroplane. Joe is photographed with a cup he won for shooting.

COURTESY BOMBARDIER, BELFAST, VIA GUY WARNER

The editor of *Flight* added:

> [Other aviators in embryo will not fail to have read with pleasure Miss Bland's breezy letter of her preliminary experiments nor to wish her success in all future trials, particularly when she becomes the pilot of her machine – Ed]

Throughout the spring of 1910 the *Mayfly* was flown as a glider on the slopes of Carnmoney Hill, a volcanic neck that rises to a height of 785 feet above sea level. Lilian's chief assistant was her aunt's gardener's 'boy', Joe Blain. Joe was 32 years old at that time and loved the outdoors, shooting and other sports. He was also an early exponent of the new-fangled bicycling craze.

Convinced by the demonstration that she was on the right path, Lilian Bland then wrote to the aviation pioneer and emerging aircraft manufacturer Alliott Verdon Roe, asking if he could supply her with a two-stroke, air-cooled engine. Roe had become the first Englishman to build and fly his own aeroplane on 12 July 1909. He agreed to make or source a suitable engine at a cost of £100. In the meantime, Lilian carried out further research in the observation of the flow of air over lifting surfaces, simply by passing the aerofoil shapes through her steam-filled bathroom.

Over the early months of 1910, Lilian contributed several weekly articles and engaged in correspondence with readers of *Flight* about a variety of technical issues involving aircraft construction and flight. On 5 March 1910 she wrote to *Flight*:

> The last time she [the *Mayfly*] was out she soared very well. She was up about 20 minutes in a wind of 10 mph and we then started her down the hill and she did a slow glide of 190 yards' distance and she soared up to 50 feet. She holds the height and distance record for Ireland.

Subsequently, four stalwart members of the Royal Irish Constabulary from nearby Glengormley Barracks also gave a hand. Their job was to hold onto the glider during the initial series of tethered flights by Lilian and Joe. The lifting qualities of the *Mayfly* were so good that on one occasion the four constables were in danger of becoming airborne, so they released their hold suddenly, leaving Joe Blain to cling on, turn the glider out of wind and bring it back to earth. Before and after the flight trials the glider was stored in a nearby shed beside a quarry belonging to Tom Smith.

Lilian's main problem was getting enough male assistants available when the winds were right to assist with holding the ropes and controlling the glider. If only three or four men were present, they were likely to go soaring with the machine because of its lifting efficiency. She remarked how the Wright brothers had given up soaring as the men could not hold their machine. She stated that her glider was very well balanced. The *Mayfly* was built in three sections and, when dismantled, could be stored in a space of 15 feet by 10 feet.

By 21 May 1910, Lilian was corresponding with *Flight* about various features on her glider and her ongoing experiments and trials. These included a combination of wood and steel skids that would not break each time the craft made a heavy landing caused by a sudden drop in wind speed. These experiments also brought about improvements in rudder and elevator controls. She was also considering attaching floats for operation on water.

On 11 June 1910, she updated the readers of *Flight* with some additional technical details of her glider:

In a wind of 20 mph the machine has lifted 698 pounds which includes my own weight. On a recent occasion two men were sitting on the main plane and I was standing on a wing tip taking off a panel when the machine rose and started to glide down the hill at an angle of 7 degrees and with a wind of 15 mph. We naturally hastily dropped off. The men weighed about 12 stone each and I weigh 8 stone 5 pounds. She can rise from a standing position with a wind against her of 14 mph and can rise with a gentle pull of the ropes. I have not flown her since Easter due to no suitable wind. My engine was due to have been ready early in May but I now expect it in a week. My machine was built from the first to take an engine. All my clips and many bolts are homemade at very little

An original painting by Norman Whitla, commissioned by Guy Warner, of an early flight by Lilian Bland in her glider Mayfly *on Carnmoney Hill.*
COURTESY NORMAN WHITLA VIA GUY WARNER

cost and in flying order will weigh 526 pounds. She is now fitted with two 24 inch motor bicycle wheels, one each side of a Farman type skid.

By 2 July 1910, Lilian had tested the strength of construction of the *Mayfly* and found the main spars could bear a load of 400 pounds without any appreciable bending. Her 20-horsepower Avro engine and Avro propeller measuring 6 foot and 6 inches in diameter were ready. Two weeks later she went to England herself to collect the items, which fitted into the railway carriage.

The engine was test run with the aid of a whisky bottle filled with petrol and her aunt's ear trumpet as a filler tube. An engine mounting was added to the trailing edge of the lower wing. A seat made from a remnant of carpet was furnished for the leading edge; a proper petrol tank arrived; a T-bar control yoke was fitted; and a tricycle undercarriage was constructed. The *Mayfly* was configured as a pusher with the engine behind the pilot. Joe Blain started the engine by standing between the tail booms and swinging the propeller – not a task for the faint-hearted, as Lilian noted: 'It was not a good engine, a beast to start and it got too hot. But once it was coaxed into action it ran satisfactorily enough.'

The small field on Carnmoney Hill was judged to be inadequate for flight trials. Instead, Lord O'Neill's 800-acre park at Shane's Castle, Randalstown, County Antrim, was made available and a hut was erected. Small wheels were fitted to the skids, while the front and rear booms were removed, which enabled the *Mayfly* to be towed to its new location and then reconstructed. Apparently the field was also home to a bull, of whom Lilian wrote to *Flight*: 'If it gets annoyed and charges I shall have every inducement to fly!' When the weather was suitable (that is, calm with little or no wind), Joe and Lilian would cycle the 12 miles from Carnmoney to Randalstown.

The first tentative hops were made in August 1910. At first Lilian could scarcely believe that she had left the ground until viewing the evidence – the cessation and resumption of the wheel tracks marking her flight path. The flights increased in length to nearly a quarter of a mile and the *Belfast Evening Telegraph* declared on 7 September 1910:

FIRST IRISH BIPLANE TO FLY
Co. Antrim Lady's Successes in Aviation

Miss Bland of Carnmoney, Co Antrim, who is the first lady to design and construct an aeroplane, has been making short flights with her machine near Randalstown. The biplane was first tested as a glider, and proved so successful that Miss Bland decided to fit it with a motor. Since the aeroplane has been on its flying ground the weather has been most unfavourable but the machine at its first trial rose from the ground after a run of thirty feet and flew for some distance a few feet above the ground. The machine is built somewhat on the lines of a Curtiss biplane but has two elevators working separately or together in connection with the horizontal tailplanes. The machine carries over 2 pounds per square foot, and weighs, with the pilot, under 600 pounds. The motor is a 20 hp Avro, two-cylinder opposed type and has so far proved most satisfactory and reliable.

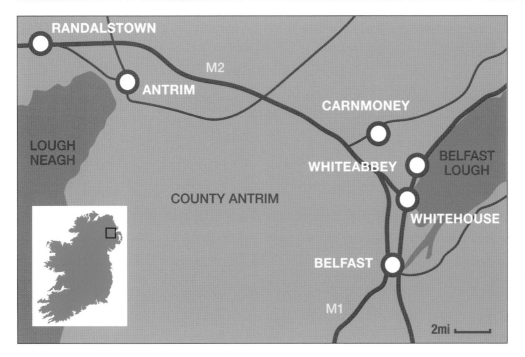

Map showing areas associated with Lilian Bland.
MAP © MARTIN GAFFNEY

The 10 September 1910 issue of *Flight* included a letter from Lilian under the heading, 'Miss Lilian Bland Flies'. It opened with the joyous exclamation:

I have flown! All this time I have been learning my engine and getting shipshape. Then for five weeks we had foul weather. At last on Wednesday [31 August 1910] she rose 30 feet which I carefully measured. As the grass was wet it was easy to see where the wheels left the ground. It was dead calm and the quaintest thing was I did not know I was off the ground! The Avro engine is splendid, although I frequently have fights with it to get it to start, it has never stopped unless I stop it on purpose.

World aviation history had been made. Lilian was now the first woman to design, construct and fly her own powered aircraft. In the same letter she added:

I always start her on one cylinder and let her pick up slowly as I think it less strain on the engine, but, I have it now in perfect control and can go as slow or fast as I want to. The propeller is also excellent. I am naturally awfully pleased having made and designed her myself. It is a very small but promising start anyway.

The previous week, *Flight* had given an account of the first Irish Aviation Meeting, which had taken place at Leopardstown Racecourse, Dublin, on Tuesday, 30 August 1910. Another first in Irish aviation was recorded in August 1910. Miss Rita Marr was born in Liverpool, but her father was from County Kildare and her mother from County Mayo. Harry Ferguson, who had made the first flight in Ireland on 31 December 1909, brought his monoplane to Magilligan Point, County Derry, in August 1910. He invited Miss Marr to join him there and she pluckily undertook to accompany him in flight. The 35-horsepower, 8-cylinder engine sped them along the strand and rose into the air, travelling a considerable distance. Rita Marr thus became the first female aircraft passenger in Ireland. (Lord Carberry was another aviator who carried female passengers,

Lilian at the controls of the Mayfly *after her first successful and historic flight on 31 August 1910.*
<small>COURTESY *FLIGHT* VIA
GUY WARNER</small>

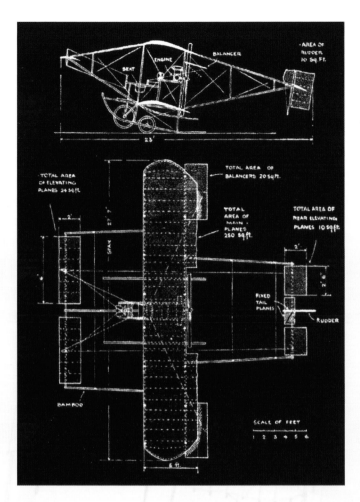

The side elevation and plan view of the Mayfly *that was published in* Flight *magazine on 17 December 1910.*

among them Miss Townsend in Clonakilty, County Cork, on 9 July 1914, and his wife, José Metcalfe, during exhibition flights.)

Further letters and photographs relating to Lilian Bland appeared at regular intervals in *Flight*, culminating in a three-page article, written by Lilian herself, in the 17 December 1910 issue. This also included a scale drawing of the aeroplane and precise sketches of technical details:

> When the engine starts, the draught from the propeller lifts the tail and the tip of the skids off the ground, and the machine balances on the two wheels; the third wheel in front only comes into action over rough ground, and to prevent the machine from going on her nose; it answers the purpose admirably, as my practice ground is rough grass with ridge and furrow.

She outlined the costs of her machine as follows:

> I may say that I got all my wire, bolts etc from Messrs A.V. Roe and

Co., and was very well satisfied. The actual cost of a biplane is not very serious, as sufficient good wood costs about £3 or £4. With regard to the fabric, I now use unbleached calico which is 6 feet wide and costs 9d a yard. The running gear is the most serious item. My own machine has a 20 h.p. engine and the expenses have not yet amounted to £200 although the machine has been practically rebuilt and has had two propellers, several pairs of skids and three different tails.

Lilian concluded her article with the following practical observations:

> I should not advise any amateurs to commence building aeroplanes unless they have plenty of spare time and money, but there are nevertheless many people who like myself have the time, but lack the necessary £.s.d. As a result of my experience I am certain that the only way to build an aeroplane cheaply is to put the best of everything into it. One can learn a great deal by watching good pilots. Unfortunately we have none in Ireland at present, but I have been fortunate in seeing Farman, Paulhan and Latham, all masters of the art.

Left: *Two photographs of the Mayfly that accompanied Lilian's article to* Flight *magazine on 17 December 1910.*
COURTESY *FLIGHT* VIA GUY WARNER

Below: *From her home in Carnmoney Lilian improved the design of the Mayfly. These illustrations show the improvements in design between February 1910 and February 1911.*
COURTESY PETER LEWIS, 'AN EDWARDIAN ECHO' IN *AIRCRAFT ANNUAL* 1973, VIA GUY WARNER

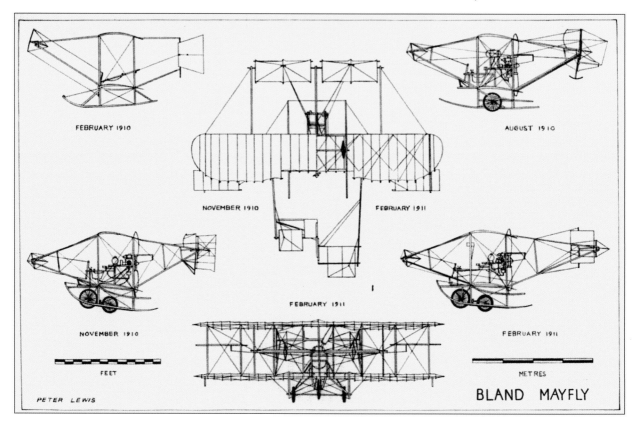

FEBRUARY 1910

AUGUST 1910

NOVEMBER 1910

FEBRUARY 1911

FEBRUARY 1911

NOVEMBER 1910

FEBRUARY 1911

FEET

METRES

PETER LEWIS

BLAND MAYFLY

To sum up the various points one has to settle before starting the construction of a machine:–

Firstly – A place to fly it in. Bad ground is a waste of time and takes much longer to learn on.

Secondly – The engine, if of low hp, the aeroplane must be light and have a large area to weight.

Thirdly – The placing of engine and pilot and whether main planes will carry all the weight.

Fourthly – To draw out every detail to scale, and if trying an original design, to make a good-sized model, and see if any new point in controls or design is going to work as intended.

Fifthly – Design the machine so that it can be easily taken to pieces for transport (by turning the skids round, my machine will wheel along any road when the outriggers are taken off).

In conclusion … the engine and propeller must be reasonably efficient, otherwise it is only a waste of time.

Lilian then built a quarter-scale model of the *Mayfly* and inserted the adjoining advert in *Flight* early in 1911. The issue of 18 March 1911 carried an article and photographs of the model built by Lilian, which had a span of seven feet and seven inches and weighed five and a half pounds. It behaved like a full-size machine.

Lilian advertised in Flight *magazine for the gliders she planned to manufacture and sell.*
COURTESY *FLIGHT* VIA GUY WARNER

Both Lilian Bland and Harry Ferguson turned their back on aviation after their respective achievements and neither attempted to gain Aviator's Certificates from the Royal Aero Club. Harry Ferguson became famous in the field of automotive invention, particularly tractors, and in 1911 Lilian was bribed by the offer of a motor car from her father to pursue less hazardous activities. She collected the car, a 20-horsepower Model T Ford, in Dublin and the drive back to Belfast was her first and only driving lesson. She then set up a sub-agency in Belfast selling Fords. This was announced in *Flight* on 29 April 1911 and brought ire from her aunt Sarah as being most unladylike. Aviation played no further part in Lilian's life.

Lilian's father, John Humphrey, had a younger brother, Edward Loftus Bland, who rose to the rank of Major General in the service of the Royal Engineers. Edward married Emma Franks from Jerpoint, Kilkenny, on 4 January 1859 and they lived at Woodbank, Whiteabbey, County Antrim. They had nine children, the second-youngest of whom was Charles Loftus Bland, born on 21 October 1881 in St Helier, Jersey. He boarded at Wellington College, Crowthorne, Berkshire, and then at Woolwich Army School. In 1901 Charles attended the Royal Garrison Artillery training school at Aldershot where, on 3 April 1901, he was promoted to Lieutenant. Four of his elder brothers already had successful military careers. Two later became generals, and they and two other brothers eventually merited an entry in *Who's Who*.

The 1911 Model T Ford given to Lilian by her father on the promise, by her, that she would give up the dangerous activity of flying.
COURTESY WWW.LILIANBLAND.IE

Woodbank House, the home of Major General Edward Loftus Bland, at Whiteabbey, County Antrim, in 1896.

<small>COURTESY WWW.LILIANBLAND.IE</small>

Charles was despatched to China, where he took part in the Boxer Rebellion, which ended on 7 September 1901. He was offered a position in the British Intelligence Department, having made a report on German railway building in China, but instead he chose to seek work in America. He resigned from the army on 9 November 1904 and his resignation was amended to: 'placed on retired pay with effect 13 December 1904'. Some of his family formed the opinion that sunstroke in China had affected his mental stability and this had contributed to his departure from the army. They committed him to an asylum, but his brother John bought his passage to New York and, on 20 November 1905, 24-year-old Charles sailed from Queenstown, Cork, on board the RMS *Oceanic*. He claimed residence in Blarney, County Cork. He spent a short time in New York as a labourer, working on skyscrapers. He then moved further west to work in a gold mine in California, and he was there when the great earthquake devastated San Francisco on 18 April 1906.

The Bland brothers (left to right): Edward Loftus, Robert Henry and John Humphrey. Edward's son Charles married John's daughter Lilian on 3 October 1911. It was Robert who sent Lilian the details of Louis Blériot's aircraft in July 1909, which generated her interest in designing her own machine.

<small>COURTESY WWW.LILIANBLAND.IE</small>

Two years later, Charles moved to Victoria, Vancouver Island, British Columbia, just inside the Canadian border on the west coast. He found employment with Gus Lindeman as a trapper and prospector 300 miles further north in Quatsino on the north-western shores of Vancouver Island. Here he settled and, with the aid of a £100 loan from his brother John, he purchased 160 acres at Quiet Cove on the mouth of the Johnson River at Quatsino Sound. He returned across the Atlantic in Autumn 1911 in the hopes he could persuade his cousin Lilian to marry him.

On 3 October 1911, Lilian again surprised her family and friends when she married, by licence, her first cousin Charles Loftus Bland in Tonbridge Registry Office, Kent. Their address was quoted as Broadford House, Horsmonden, Hastings, Kent. This was just 12 miles from Maidstone, where she was born 33 years previously. Charles was nearing his thirtieth birthday at this time. Eight days after their wedding, Lilian bid Charles *bon voyage* at Southampton Pier when he boarded the SS *Saint Paul* for New York. Charles returned to Quatsino to set up their homestead and Lilian returned to County Antrim to tell her father about the wedding and her plans to go to Canada. On 14 October 1911, Lilian wrote a letter to Charles from Tobarcooran House and included her father's reaction to the news of their marriage: 'He was vexed and was most awfully surprised but took it better than I had expected.'

Lilian was getting excited about the move and, in a letter to her husband dated 21 November 1911, she expressed her keen desire to join him as soon as possible:

> Not counting luggage it will cost me at least thirty two pounds to get to Victoria. The boat is twelve pounds. I can let you have another fifty pounds by selling rubber shares at their present dumpy state. I haven't tackled freight rates yet but they tell me ten pounds per ton right through to Vancouver. Your last letter took seventeen days to get here.

She sailed to Fleetwood, Lancashire, and then travelled by train to Broadford House, Horsmonden, Kent, on 24 November. Less than two months after her own marriage, on 30 November 1911 her older sister, Eva Charlotte, married Geirge Kycas Blackey Borton. There were no children born to Eva.

In its 23 December 1911 issue, *Flight* wished Lilian and Charles well and noted that Charles had read of his cousin's exploits in copies of the same magazine while he was still in Vancouver. From these articles he had come to the conclusion that Lilian would be a suitable bride for the pioneer life. She offered for sale her aeroplane, glider, engine, propeller, plant and machines to cover the cost of her carriage to Canada. The issue of 6 January 1912 confirmed that she passed her biplane glider to the newly formed 'Dublin Flying Club' (a possible reference to the Irish Aero Club, formed in Dublin on 5 November 1909). The engine and two wheels were purchased for £25 by 19-year-old Sydney Camm of 10 Alma Road, Bristol, who used Lilian's engine to study the workings of aeronautical

Lilian's father, John Humphrey Bland, who was 'vexed' with Lilian for secretly marrying her first cousin Charles Loftus Bland. He is photographed here on 30 September 1914, aged 86.
COURTESY WWW. LILIANBLAND.IE

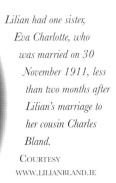

Lilian had one sister, Eva Charlotte, who was married on 30 November 1911, less than two months after Lilian's marriage to her cousin Charles Bland.
COURTESY WWW.LILIANBLAND.IE

The land that Charles and Lilian had cleared to make space for their homestead and garden by 1914. The line of the forest had previously come as far as the stump in centre foreground.
COURTESY WWW.LILIANBLAND.IE

power plants. In 1924 Camm joined the Hawker Aircraft Company and in 1934 he was appointed Chief Project Engineer. He was responsible for the design of such Hawker aircraft as the Hurricane, Typhoon, Tempest and Sea Fury. Lilian's engine sowed the seed of aeronautical engineering with Sydney Camm.

By now aviation in Ireland was developing and great interest was aroused by the first successful crossing of St George's Channel, which Denys Corbett Wilson achieved when he landed in a field at Crane, near Enniscorthy, County Wexford, on 22 April 1912. He departed Goodwick in south Wales just before 6am and covered the 65 miles in 1 hour and 40 minutes. However, this historic aviation event was overshadowed in the media by the tragic sinking of the RMS *Titanic* on 15 April 1912.

Six days after the *Titanic* tragedy, on 21 April 1912, Lilian sailed from Belfast on board the SS *Lake Manitoba*, bound for Montreal. She was one of 308 passengers on board, of whom 294 were Irish emigrants. The ship's manifest listed her as a 'tourist', though she stated her intended permanent residence was Canada. The sea crossing took about eight days. From Montreal she boarded the daily Canadian Pacific Railway to Vancouver, a journey of approximately 3,000 miles. A departure at 21.40 on a Monday from Montreal would arrive in Vancouver at 11.50 on the following Saturday – a journey time of over four and a half days. From Vancouver it then took several hours in a steamship to cross the 50 miles to Nanaimo on Vancouver Island in British Columbia. The journey to Quatsino was a further 250 miles to the north-west of the island. In 1912 the railroad only went as far north as Courtenay, 60 miles north of Nanaimo. From there Lilian had the option of horse-drawn transport by land (where there were dirt tracks rather than roads) or 200 miles by motor boat, which would have taken two or three days. The journey from Belfast must have proved exhausting and it probably took most of three weeks before she was reunited with her husband.

Charles had become a lumberjack in Canada and Lilian joined him to establish a farm on 160 acres of land at Quiet Cove on the south side of Quatsino Sound, Vancouver Island. The nearest town was Quatsino, seven miles across the sound by boat. To replace the shack he had originally constructed for himself, Charles built a house of hand-hewn

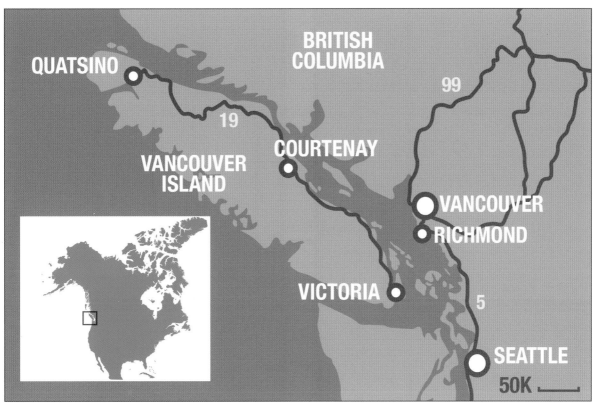

Locations on Vancouver Island associated with Lilian Bland after her move to Canada in 1912.
Map © Martin Gaffney

The shack on Vancouver Island that Charles Bland erected was home for Lilian during her first year in the Canadian outback.
Courtesy www.lilianbland.ie

Charles Bland emigrated to Vancouver Island to work as a trapper and prospector. After his marriage to Lilian he returned to the Canadian province to establish a home for them both.
Courtesy www.lilianbland.ie

Above: *The land around their homestead was tilled and cultivated.*
COURTESY WWW.LILIANBLAND.IE

Above: *Patricia Lilian Bland was born on 13 April 1913, when Lilian had been on Vancouver Island for one year.*
COURTESY WWW.LILIANBLAND.IE

Left: *A two-man saw was used to fell the large spruce trees in Quiet Cove.*
COURTESY WWW.LILIANBLAND.IE

logs with pieces of lumber found on the beach. The house did not contain a single nail. There was no road to the homestead and the construction of the house was completed by the time their only daughter, Patricia, was born on 13 April 1913. Lilian's pioneering traits were revealed when she threw herself into the physical work at hand. She worked through all the available hours of daylight, uprooting stumps, clearing the land, tending the cattle and other animals they had obtained and carrying out the innumerable chores common to the chosen life of pioneers.

Meanwhile, back in Ireland, Lilian's father John was recuperating from an illness at St Anne's Hill Hydro, Blarney, County Cork. From there he wrote to Lilian on 1 July 1913, congratulating her on the birth of

Lilian in front of her snow-covered homestead at Quatsino during the winter of 1916.
COURTESY WWW.LILIANBLAND.IE

The west view of the Bland homestead at Quiet Cove, Quatsino, British Columbia, in 1920, eight years after Lilian's move to that part of Canada.
COURTESY WWW.LILIANBLAND.IE

her baby and expressing his delight at the news of the progress she was making on their lands. Her brother, Robert Wyndham Bland, had joined the 18th Royal Irish Rifles and on 15 March 1915 he was promoted from Captain to Temporary Lieutenant. On 9 June 1915 he married Mildred Dorothea Mordaunt at St Mary's Church, Bryanston Square, London. Mildred was born in Dinapore (now Danapur), West Bengal. There were no children of this marriage. Lilian's father, John Humphrey Bland, died on 1 February 1919, aged 90, and left Lilian a legacy.

In 1917, to assist with domestic chores, the Blands sent for a cousin of Lilian's, Mary Madden, from Victoria, who came and acted as a housekeeper. Mary had been in

poor health and Lilian suggested to her parents that a change of air in Quiet Cove might be of benefit. Mary Evelyn Madden was born on 15 July 1902 to the Reverend Wyndham Madden and his wife, Evelyn (née Bather). The Reverend Wyndham was a younger brother of Lilian's mother, Emily Charlotte. Mary Madden was a first cousin of Lilian's. In 1911, the 62-year-old Reverend Wyndham Madden and 46-year-old Evelyn decided to make a new life for themselves in Canada. The Maddens, with their four daughters and two sons, moved from Longford Hall Rectory, Newport, Shropshire, to Waldo, British Columbia. Waldo was about 600 miles east of Vancouver and was a prospectors', miners' and pioneers' hamlet. The Maddens later moved to Victoria on the southern shores of Vancouver Island. The census return for the Bland homestead in Quatsino, Vancouver Island, taken on 1 June 1921, listed Charles Loftus Bland (aged 39), his wife Lilian Emily (aged 41), their daughter, 8-year-

Below: *The clearing that Charles and Lilian had created by 1917, after five years at Quatsino.*
Courtesy www.lilianbland.ie

Left: *Lilian's only brother was Captain Robert Wyndham Bland, who served with the Royal Irish Rifles during the First World War.*
Courtesy www.lilianbland.ie

Lilian carrying her infant daughter, Patricia.
Courtesy www.lilianbland.ie

old Patricia, and 18-year-old Mary Evelyn Madden. They all listed their nationality as Canadian.

Later in 1921, Charles and Lilian, along with Patricia, moved 1,580 miles south to Napa Valley, north of San Francisco, California, to develop a prune orchard. Mary Madden joined them when she sailed from Seattle, Washington, to San Francisco on 9 March 1922. On 18 July 1922, while in Calistoga, Napa County, California, Mary Madden gave birth to Charles's son, John Robin (Jackie), three days after Mary's twentieth birthday. They stayed there for four years and then Charles, Lilian, Patricia and Jackie returned to Quatsino in 1925. At that time, Mary

Patricia and Jackie playing at Quiet Cove,
Quatsino, in the 1920s.
Courtesy www.lilianbland.ie

Charles Bland enjoying some time with his daughter, Patricia.
Courtesy www.lilianbland.ie

Lilian's only child was Patricia. Patricia got a sliver of wood in her foot and developed tetanus. Nothing could be done for her and, tragically, she died in September 1929 at the age of 16.
Courtesy www.lilianbland.ie

Madden returned to Victoria, in the south of Vancouver Island, to care for her father, who had contracted tuberculosis and died in 1926. Charles and Lilian raised both Patricia and Jackie at Quiet Cove. Charles's father, Major General Edward Loftus Bland, died on 26 February 1923, aged 93 years.

In her memoirs, written in 1930, Lilian gave an insight into the family's existence, and also what pioneers in western Canada were experiencing in those days:

> We have literally cut a home out of the forest, cleared land and turned it into fertile soil. We grow enough of our own food supply with a surplus to sell, mostly in small fruits and vegetables. Partly it is market garden work and is very familiar to work of the same kind at home, except there are no roads, except the inland Sound and all traffic is by motor boats, all settlers being located at the waterfront. We cut our own wood supply and clear a little more land each year. This means the use of big saws and axes.
>
> We have poultry and cows which means cutting hay with a scythe. We have the carpenters, plumbers and mechanics to keep things in repair and we provide our own meat and fish supply with troll and gun, never killing for 'sport' but only for necessary food supply which is canned for winter use. Fishing, logging and mining are the main industries here and there is a pulp mill 16 miles away. The woods are full of deer, black bear, elk, some cougars and small animals – coon, mink and marten.

Lilian wrote of her husband:

> My husband is one of many sons of an old Irish family. His father was a General in the Royal Engineers so Charles had no choice and was trained for the army. He was posted to China but he didn't care for the profession of legal slaughter so he resigned the first opportunity he got and came home to catch hell from his family. When he further told them that he wished to become a workman and follow out his own line of thought there was one howl of 'Disgrace', so he was shipped out west as the disgrace of the family and after working in a gold mine and on a ranch as a carpenter's help he finally came with some other men who were looking for cheap land to Quatsino. This location had a future as the finest inland harbour.
>
> Having got a piece of land and built a bachelor's shack, his thoughts turned to a companion for help. I for my part was studying life. My mother was a society woman, my father was an artist and with these two opposite interests I saw both sides of life, the Bohemian and the fashionable.

She wrote also of her own life:

I had a thirst for knowledge and a strong dislike for society, their empty lives, empty talk, fashions, gambling etc. Before I was twenty I had been to many cities of Europe, studied art in Paris, studied music in Rome, life everywhere. Finally I came back to Ireland where my father had settled down with his sister. Here I started to ride and became a good rough rider, training horses, often riding in a man's saddle as I found it easier, having ricked my back in a side-saddle when a horse bolted with me. Riding cross-legged was then considered a terrible thing for a lady to do. A fanatical priest in Tipperary told the people to stone me, but they cheered me on. Other work I took up was photography and my photos and copy were in many well-known London papers, dealing chiefly with sport and natural history.

She described how she became involved in aviation:

Louis Blériot flew the Channel and I studied aeroplanes – the few that had been made – and I lay for hours on the cliffs watching the gulls soaring. Then I said I would make a machine that would fly. Hoots and derision – which did not worry me at all. I made a glider and turned the RIC [Royal Irish Constabulary] out to help me to control and test it. I then got a twenty horse power engine from A.V. Roe. Finally I was ready to fly and flew only short distances it is true but it was the first machine in Ireland to fly and I had made it all myself.

My dad was horrified with my success when the machine flew and as I was loyal and respectful to him I agreed to quit. My dad had also bribed me with a motor car so my next step was to become an agent for the Ford motor car, the first in the North of Ireland. As an agent I was another family disgrace, 'black sheep', 'crazy' etc.

Following the death from tetanus of Patricia Bland in September 1929 Lilian and Charles experienced marital difficulties. In September 1932, Charles and ten-year-old Jackie left the homestead in Quatsino and went to Vancouver, where they both got a bad dose of influenza. Mary Madden went to Vancouver from Victoria to care for them. Lilian returned to England alone, in 1935, to live with her brother, Captain Robert Bland, at Penshurst in Kent. In May 1935, Charles, Mary and Jackie returned to the homestead in Quatsino.

The Japanese attack on Pearl Harbor took place on 7 December 1941. Nine days later, Jackie joined the United States Navy at Seattle, Washington. In the years after the war he became a fisherman. On 4 January 1962 he married Margaret Thornton at Upper Agbrigg, Yorkshire. On 6 September 1962, Jackie was skippering his boat, the *Loretta B*, when it capsized and sank on the Fraser River near Richmond, south of Vancouver. Jackie Bland (aged 40) and three others were drowned and their bodies were never recovered.

Charles remained in Quatsino for the remainder of his life. He died there on 6 January 1973, aged 91. He was survived by Mary, who bore him other children: a daughter, Dora (born in 1933), a son, Robert (born in 1935) and twins, Charles and Mary (born in 1937). All the children were educated by correspondence, using the kitchen as a schoolroom and the table as a desk. Most of them finished sixth grade. Mary Madden died in December 1991, aged 89, and is buried in Quatsino Cemetery.

On 5 May 1964, Hugh Graham Conway, Managing Director at Short Brothers and Harland Limited, Belfast, wrote to Lilian by way of recognition of her achievement of 54 years earlier.

SHORT BROTHERS & HARLAND LIMITED
P.O. BOX 241
QUEEN'S ISLAND BELFAST 3

LONDON OFFICE:
BERKELEY SQUARE HOUSE   Telegrams: AIRCRAFT BELFAST
BERKELEY SQUARE W1   Telephone: BELFAST 58444
Telephone: MAYfair 954f   Telex: 74-539

HGC/NGC/10519   5th May, 1964

Mrs. Lilian Bland,
Sennen,
Lands End,
CORNWALL

Dear Mrs. Bland,

    I can at last send you photocopies of the local paper dealing
with Harry Ferguson's first flight and then yours. You will see that
you were the first biplane but that he was the first aeroplane proper.
At any rate you must have been the first woman in the world to build
and fly an aeroplane, which isn't so bad.

                                    Yours sincerely,

                                    H.G. Conway

Encl:

In 1964, Hugh Graham Conway, Managing Director at Short Brothers and Harland Limited, Belfast, wrote to Lilian, acknowledging her achievement in the field of aviation.
COURTESY GUY WARNER

Lilian Bland enjoyed her retirement at Sennen Cove, Cornwall.
COURTESY WWW.LILIANBLAND.IE

In 1965 she told the *New York Times*:

> When I came back from Canada I became a gardener. I gambled my wages on the stock market and was very lucky. I made enough to come here [Sennen in Cornwall] ten years ago. I now spend my time painting, gardening and gambling a little.

Lilian retired to Briggeruwell, Maria's Lane, Sennen Cove, Penzance, Cornwall. She had visited that part of the United Kingdom with her father on a painting trip in 1893, as a 13-year-old. In an interview for *The Western Morning News*, Cornwall, on 8 February 1966, when asked about her self-imposed exile near Land's End, she replied:

> I love it. I keep busy, I have my plants, I paint and I gamble. Very occasionally I watch television at a neighbour's house, but only the horse racing – I back five horses a day, with success, I may add and, great fun!

Lilian Bland died on 11 May 1971 at the age of 92. Her death certificate reported her cause of death as cardiac failure, severe arteriosclerosis and myocarditis. She was buried in the churchyard of the village of Sennen on 17 May 1971. Lilian Bland had been involved in the world of aeronautics for approximately 18 months. It was a brief but significant period. In that relatively short time, she blazed a trail for aviators and, in particular, made aviation a subject that other women followed.

EPILOGUE

The Ulster History Circle raised a blue plaque in memory of Lilian Bland in 1997 and placed it near her former homestead of Tobarcooran House. The house has since been demolished.

On 29 July 2003, as part of its celebration of the Centenary of Flight, An Post issued a set of four postage stamps in the Republic of Ireland, one of which featured Lilian and the *Mayfly*.

The centenary of Lilian Bland's first flight occurred on 31 August 2010. To commemorate the occasion, Guy Warner published a booklet celebrating her life.

Meanwhile, Randalstown Historical Society raised a plaque to Lilian at Station House, Shane's Castle, Randalstown, County Antrim, on 31 August 2010. It was unveiled in the presence of Imogen Holmes, Lilian's great-niece.

Also on Tuesday, 31 August 2010, a memorial gathering was held beside Lilian's resting place at Sennen Cemetery, Cornwall. The event was organised by Guy Warner, and as part of it the Reverend Edward Pratt spoke in tribute to his great-aunt. In attendance on behalf of the Ulster Aviation Society was Kate Welsh. As part of the ceremony, two light aircraft from MSH Flight Training at Land's End Airport performed a fly-past in salute of Lilian.

In 2009 Ernie Cromie and Guy Warner of the Ulster Aviation Society proposed to Newtownabbey Borough Council that a park in Glengormley, County Antrim, be renamed and a replica model of Lilian's aircraft be placed on permanent display there. On 24 August 2011, the Mayor of Newtownabbey, accompanied by the Reverend Edward Pratt and Imogen Holmes, unveiled a full-scale model of the *Mayfly* in Glengormley Park, which was renamed Lilian Bland Memorial Park.

The University of British Columbia in Vancouver holds a special collection containing 1,391 glass-plate negatives, glass lantern slides, celluloid prints and celluloid negatives, the majority of which were taken by Lilian Bland between 1900 and 1935. They are retained under the title 'Lilian Bland Fonds'.

The blue plaque in memory of Lilian Bland.
AUTHOR'S PHOTOGRAPH

The postage stamp commemorating Lilian Bland, issued in 2003 by An Post.
COURTESY AN POST

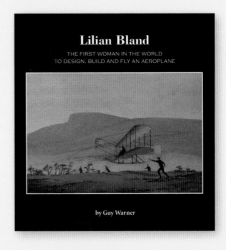

Guy Warner's booklet celebrating the life of Lilian Bland.
COURTESY GUY WARNER

Icon Films, Bristol, produced a short film that was broadcast on the BBC's The One Show *in January 2016. Guy Warner was one of the people interviewed for the programme.*
COURTESY ICON FILMS

The plaque commemorating Lilian Bland at Station House, Shane's Castle, Randalstown.
COURTESY RANDALSTOWN HISTORICAL SOCIETY

The Reverend Edward Pratt and the Ulster Aviation Society's Kate Welsh at a memorial gathering at Sennen Cemetery, Cornwall, in 2010.
Courtesy Ulster Aviation Society

BIBLIOGRAPHY

Bob Montgomery, *Early Aviation in Ireland* (Garristown, County Meath: Dreoilín Specialist Publications Limited, 2013).
Colm O'Rourke, www.lilianbland.ie.
Guy Warner, *Lilian Bland: The First Woman in the World to Design, Build and Fly an Aeroplane* (Belfast: Ulster Aviation Society, 2010).

Aircraft Annual (1973).
Flight magazine (1909–12).

ACKNOWLEDGEMENTS

Dora and Mary Bland, compilers of the Bland family tree (1993).
Professor James Farrell, historian, University of New Hampshire.
Colm O'Rourke, from whose website, www.lilianbland.ie, much of the text for this chapter was extracted.
Brian Russell, Bland family historian.
Guy Warner, from whose publication *Lilian Bland: The First Woman in the World to Design, Build and Fly an Aeroplane* much of the text of this chapter has been extracted.

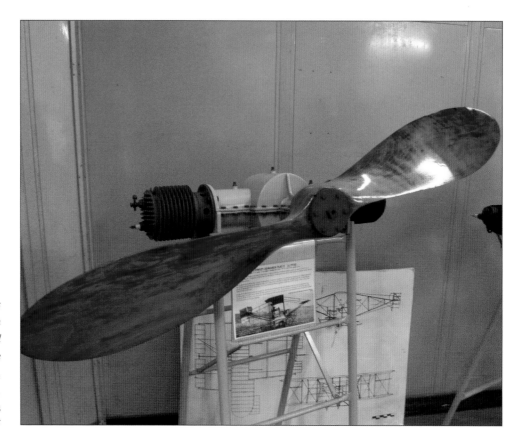

The engine and two wheels from Lilian's aeroplane are on loan from the Windsor and Royal Borough Museum to the Brooklands Museum Trust, Weybridge, Surrey.
Courtesy Brooklands Museum Trust

A model of the Mayfly *was unveiled in Glengormley Park, which was renamed Lilian Bland Memorial Park, in 2011.*
COURTESY ULSTER AVIATION SOCIETY

LADY HEATH

LADY ICARUS: LIMERICK'S LADY PILOT

Limerick-born Sophie Peirce was a renowned athlete who achieved world records. In 1925 she became the first Irishwoman to be granted an Aviator's Certificate. She challenged the British aviation establishment to allow women to earn an Aviator's B (Commercial) Certificate and was successful in becoming the first female in Britain to attain one. This allowed her to spend a short period as a KLM co-pilot. She married Sir James Heath and became Lady Heath. Her adventurous solo flight from South Africa to London earned her world acclaim and was followed by a successful tour of America, where she became the first woman to earn an aviation engineer's licence. However, a near-fatal crash in Cleveland, Ohio brought an end to her aviation career; later, a tragic fall on a tramcar in London ended her life.

A photograph of Lady Heath presented to Chris Bruton at the time she was operating Dublin Air Ferries at Kildonan, County Dublin, in 1935.

COURTESY CHRIS BRUTON VIA BRENDAN BRUTON

IN RURAL IRELAND in the mid-nineteenth century the local doctor was a highly respected member of the community. He was held in even greater esteem when he was related to the local aristocratic families. Such was the case in the Newcastle West area of County Limerick, where the Peirces and the D'Arcys were among the most prominent families. Through marriage, the Peirces were related to the owners of many of the big houses in the locality. Heathfield belonged to Edward Locke Lloyd and Castleview to Thomas Locke, and later to Robert Peirce. Perhaps the best known of the big houses was Cahirmoyle, where the artist Dermod O'Brien, a grandson of the Irish rebel William Smith O'Brien, lived until 1920; he was an acquaintance of the Peirce family.

The D'Arcy Evans family were gentlemen farmers who had come to Munster as planters following the Desmond Rebellion in 1582. Knockaderry House was a substantial residence, built about 1780, on the outskirts of Knockaderry village, and this was where they settled. The village is a small one, situated on a crossroads four miles north-east of Newcastle West on the road to Ballingarry. Knockaderry House was 'pleasantly situated beneath the shelter of a hill and surrounded by thriving plantations', said the historian Samuel Lewis in his 1837 history of Limerick City and County.

Early in the 1820s, a Dr McCarthy had been the only medical man in Newcastle West but he abandoned his practice after buying a brewery in the town. An advertisement was placed in the Dublin newspapers looking for a replacement doctor, and so it was that John Peirce came to the County Limerick town. John Peirce was originally from King's County (now County Offaly), where his family, originally from England, had settled in Cromwellian times. He took over a house in the Square. The building adjoined the demesne of the Earl of Devon, a typical absentee landlord, who spent most of his time at the family's main property in Exeter.

Across the Square lived Thomas Locke, who was a distant cousin of the earl and agent of his vast interests in County Limerick. Locke's daughter Frances caught the young doctor's eye and they married soon afterwards. Three of their sons were to follow in the family tradition by becoming doctors. One of them, George, born in 1833, studied at the University of Glasgow in Scotland and was destined to take over the family medical practice in Newcastle West.

George Peirce married twice. His first wife was Catherine D'Arcy Evans of Knockaderry House. The couple had five children. The eldest child and only boy was John (usually known as Jackie), born on 16 March 1864. From the start, Jackie was wild and difficult and became more so after the death of his mother in 1889. This behaviour did not improve after his father's subsequent

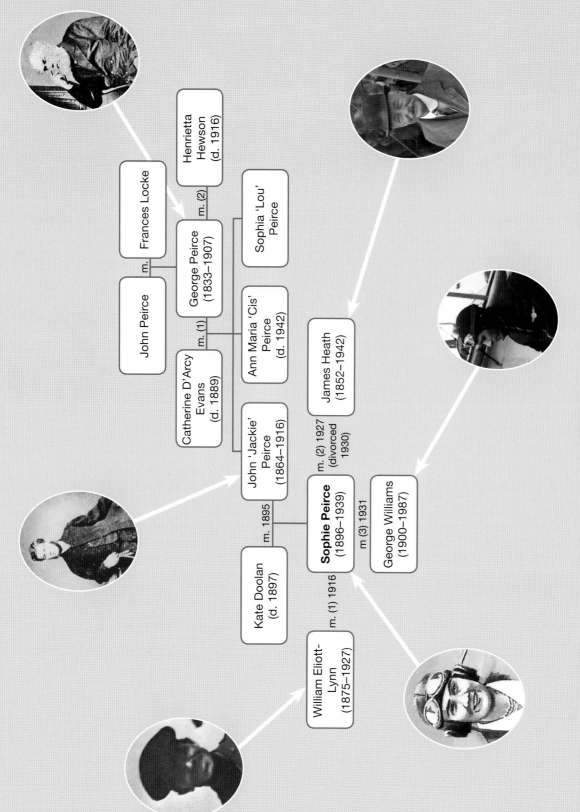

Lady Heath's family tree.
COURTESY ALICIA McAULEY

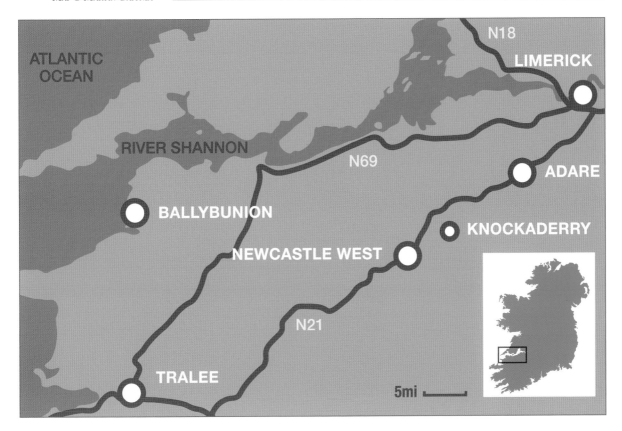

marriage to Henrietta Georgina Hewson from Ballybunion, County Kerry, a woman in her forties. Hewson was completely incapable of coping with his large family. While he was a good doctor and a respected medical officer, George was a hopeless father.

At home Jackie's exuberance was uncontrollable but in his maternal uncle, Thomas D'Arcy Evans (or Old Tom Evans, as he was called) he found a kindred spirit. The elderly man was an irredeemable drunk and George Peirce, none too pleased by his son's association with him, attempted to separate the pair by finding Jackie a job with the Provincial Bank in Kilrush, across the River Shannon in County Clare. The dull routine of life as a banker did nothing to calm Jackie down. He soon lost his job with the bank and returned to Knockaderry where, to the despair of his father, he continued to spend most of his time with Old Tom Evans. On the death of his uncle Tom, on 18 September 1886, Jackie inherited Knockaderry House.

The slide into disaster began. Soon the Peirce house was a refuge for 'the lowest blackguards' from Newcastle West, who were in and out of the workhouse and the jail. According to the judge during one of Jackie's many appearances in court, all respectable persons avoided its owner. Since none of his sisters was willing to help him manage the large house, Peirce was forced to advertise for a housekeeper. The first woman to take on this role was Catherine Keane, a labourer's wife. She was terrified of her new boss, with whom she was soon forced into a sexual relationship, and she frequently attempted to run away. Peirce would then scour the countryside until he found her. His long list of appearances before the magistrates began when he was found guilty of assaulting Mrs Keane's husband; he

was later convicted of assaulting Mrs Keane herself, for which he was sentenced to a month in jail. This horrified his Church of Ireland father, who consulted the local Catholic bishop, Dr O'Dwyer, about his son's dealings with Mrs Keane. Denounced from the pulpit by the local Catholic priest for adultery, Mrs Keane fled the parish.

The next housekeeper to arrive at Knockaderry House was Kate Doolan, who around 1888 had left her mother's home in Castlemaine, County Kerry, to work for a farmer near Ballybunion. After two years, she had found a job in Mrs McCarthy's Hotel in Limerick. She made the fateful move to Knockaderry around 1893. By then she was close to 40 years old, about 10 years older than Peirce. From the start the relationship was abusive and, true to form, her new boss regularly assaulted the housekeeper and expected her to share his bed. She suffered at least one miscarriage, known to Dr George Peirce, who treated her at the time. She found herself pregnant more than once, and was to spend at least one period in hospital after Jackie gave her a preparation of agricultural chemicals in an attempt to bring on an abortion. In June 1894, near the docks area of the city, a Limerick policeman came across an angry crowd surrounding Jackie Peirce, who had badly beaten his pregnant housekeeper.

A sensational trial a few months later heard allegations by Peirce and Doolan of rape against a neighbour, William Power. By then Doolan was again pregnant, which may have triggered the events that followed. All began late one night in February 1895, when Jackie Peirce banged on William Power's door and accused him of raping Doolan. Power, who had suffered the half-crazed Peirce's antics for years, contacted his solicitor and sued Peirce for slander. In April the case was heard in Dublin's High Court, with the outraged Power seeking the considerable sum of £1,000 in damages. By then, Peirce had withdrawn the accusation of rape but still insisted that Power had 'immoral intercourse' with his housekeeper.

Power was a wealthy Catholic bachelor farmer in his fifties, whilst Peirce was on his uppers and desperate for cash. It is likely that Peirce invented the rape story as a means of extracting money from Power. In the confusion of evidence given to the court, the true story gradually became clear. Earlier that day in February, Peirce had given Doolan a severe beating, perhaps because she had told him she was again pregnant. John Bouchier-Hayes, a medical doctor from Rathkeale, confirmed the assault in his evidence. Although he made no mention of rape, he said she had:

> marks of vile usage about the generative organs and finger marks and nail scrapes on the buttocks, the result of considerable violence committed on her by some person.

In presenting the case, one counsel described Peirce and Doolan as half-mad and the case was thrown out of court when the jury failed to reach a unanimous decision.

On 29 May 1895, a month after the court case, Jackie Peirce married Kate Teresa Doolan in the Dublin Registry Office. They were still in Dublin attempting to sort out the aftermath of the rape case, since Peirce not only had to pay Power but also had to underwrite all the costs of an expensive week in court. By now, Peirce was entirely destitute. The fine building of Knockaderry House was stripped of all but the most basic furniture and the family lived in the kitchen. He was declared bankrupt following the disastrous case and the bank sold his possessions in an effort to pay off his debts,

while his property was placed into receivership. Since they had only a small allowance and no money to pay for help, Peirce and his wife were the sole occupants of the large house. Their families ostracised them.

Back home, Peirce continued to abuse his wife and was convicted several times of assaulting her. Eventually, after one court appearance, both were sent to jail. In August 1896, Kate Doolan was charged with drunkenness and 'grossly obscene' conduct in Limerick. She did not appear to be 'right in the head', the court heard before she was sentenced to two months in jail.

On 10 November 1896, Sophia Theresa Catherine Mary Peirce Evans was born in Knockaderry House. Her arrival had no effect on her parents' troubled life. How much Sophie knew of her origins, at least in her early years, is open to question. Whatever stories she had been told, her background was tragic. In Newcastle West, Jackie's father, his stepmother and his sisters looked on in despair. Sophie Peirce's grandfather registered a new will in January 1897 mentioning neither his eldest child (and only son) nor his newborn granddaughter.

On 8 December 1897, a small paragraph appeared in the Dublin *Evening Herald* about a horrific crime that had taken place in County Limerick. The paper reported that on 6 December 1897, Sophie's father, Jackie Peirce, had brutally battered her mother, Catherine Teresa Doolan, to death at their home.

The case became known as the 'Knockaderry murder' and it packed the courtroom, where onlookers gaped at the perpetrator with awe and horror. In the

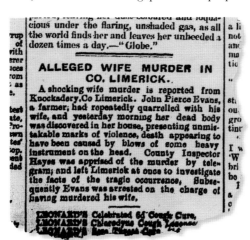

cious under the flaring, unshaded gas, as all the world finds her and leaves her unheeded a dozen times a day.—"Globe."

ALLEGED WIFE MURDER IN CO. LIMERICK.

A shocking wife murder is reported from Knockaderry, Co Limerick. John Pierce Evans, a farmer, had repeatedly quarrelled with his wife, and yesterday morning her dead body was discovered in her house, presenting unmistakable marks of violence, death appearing to have been caused by blows of some heavy instrument on the head. County Inspector Hayes was apprised of the murder by telegram, and left Limerick at once to investigate the facts of the tragic occurrence. Subsequently Evans was arrested on the charge of having murdered his wife.

A report on the murder of Kate Peirce (née Doolan) appeared in the Evening Herald *newspaper on 8 December 1897.*

COURTESY LANGFORD FAMILY VIA ASHFIELD PRESS, DUBLIN

Knockaderry House, where Sophie Peirce was born on 10 November 1896 and where she lived for one year until her father murdered her mother in their home on 6 December 1897.

COURTESY LANGFORD FAMILY

Limerick Chronicle, the death of Sophie's mother was described as a story 'so startling and revolting that the townspeople were slow to believe the news, although fully aware that the two parties concerned in the tragedy have led an unhappy life'.

The woman was so badly battered that the shinbone on one of her legs was visible through the blood and skin. Since Peirce was well known to be eccentric at the very least, few had any difficulty believing that the murder happened as the result of a bout of temporary insanity. The initial hearing before the resident magistrate took five hours. The local police sergeant, Thomas Mongey, told how he had arrived at Knockaderry House early the morning after the murder to find the cold, stiff body of Mrs Peirce lying on the floor, covered with old clothes. 'Near her was the little girl, who was wrapped in peaceful sleep,' said the sergeant. The woman was dead: 'I put my hand on her face and found it cold and rigid.' There were marks over each eye and on the nose and jaw, with no blood evident, although the wounds were clearly fresh. The room 'was all in confusion'. 'Near the body was a bent pair of tongs, fragments of a broken hazel stick and a basin containing dirty, reddish water.'

When the case was finally heard in March 1898 at the Limerick Spring Assizes, the jury returned the verdict that 'Peirce was guilty of the murder but was insane at the time'. The judge then ordered the prisoner to be detained as a criminal lunatic in Limerick Prison 'until the pleasure of the Lord Lieutenant was made known'. He was to spend the rest of his life at the Central Lunatic Asylum, Dundrum, County Dublin.

After the tragic death of her mother, one-year-old Sophie was brought to the house of her grandfather, Dr George Peirce, in Newcastle West, and she was educated at home. While his 69-year-old wife did her best, she was neither young nor capable and the day-to-day job of looking after the infant girl soon fell to her spinster aunts, in particular Ann Maria (aged 32), usually called Cis, and Sophia Louisa (aged 27), usually called Lou. The arrival of a baby in the house must have been cheering for the aunts but, as the years went by and especially after the murder trial, money was increasingly a problem, with a broken-hearted Dr Peirce unable to maintain his medical practice.

From an early age, Sophie was clearly her father's daughter – fearless and difficult to control. Whether or not she would also inherit his mental instability was unknown at the time. For a vivacious child like Sophie, the atmosphere in the house on the Square was suffocating, especially while her grandfather was still alive.

By the time Knockaderry House was sold off to the Hannon family in April 1907, Dr Peirce's health was failing. Despite this, he is said to have instructed Cis and Lou, his two daughters in Newcastle West, to look after the young Sophie, then ten years old. He died on 20 October 1907 aged 73 years. He left £4,712 in his will, with all of it going to his wife and four daughters. Life opened up for Sophie after the death of her grandfather and she was at last permitted to leave the stifling confines of the house in Newcastle West for boarding school.

Despite the best efforts of her aunts – or maybe because of them – Sophie was a wild youngster and did not change much as she progressed into early adulthood. Even in her young days she must have cut a striking figure. From her mother she took her mass of dark hair and her height, reaching almost six feet, at a time when the average height for a woman was at least six inches less. With her stature and her intelligent, mobile face, she was hard to ignore. She was quick witted, loved playing pranks and, like her father, craved attention. 'My childhood has made me love freedom of every kind today,' she was later to say. She claimed that her aunts disapproved of sport for girls and moved her from one school to another when hockey or athletics figured too prominently on the timetable.

After stints at schools in Cork and perhaps Belfast she arrived at St Margaret's Hall in Dublin, then a small day and boarding school for Protestant girls on Mespil Road. At St Margaret's Hall Sophie received the same Classics-based education as any boy of her background would. She was a keen hockey and tennis player. For Sophie, coming from an oppressive small-town existence in a house ruled by penny-pinching and the baggage of the family's history, it must have been like heaven. Wealthier uncles and cousins probably helped to pay for Sophie's education. St Margaret's provided the intellectual stimulation she craved as a gifted young woman. From the start she was a brilliant student and, before she left, her name was engraved on the school's board of honour, prominently displayed in the entrance hall.

Her father's crimes had ruined her immediate family financially and Dr Peirce had not left enough to keep his family of non-earning daughters comfortably. For the rest of her life, Sophie would be preoccupied by money. Despite the norms of the time, she was absolutely adamant that she had to earn her own living. She had no intention of turning into one of her aunts. After the sale of the Peirce family home in 1915, Lou finally found the courage to leave Newcastle West, a move Sophie approved of. Cis moved to Ballybunion, County Kerry.

In September 1914, her secondary-school days over, the 17-year-old Sophie enrolled in the Royal College of Science for Ireland in Dublin as an associate student on a variety of scientific courses. (In recent years the Department of the Taoiseach has occupied the same building.) Dublin was then the second city of the British Empire, a bustling and lively metropolis with a population of 370,000 and growing. The family's financial problems had cast a shadow over Sophie's ambitions and she had abandoned plans to enter the medical profession, which would have proved costly. Still, Sophie, never one to pay much attention to what others expected, was all set to enjoy her college years. In her first year, Sophie achieved consistently high marks in all subjects and in her second year she did even better, earning herself two pounds when she took a first prize for Geology and also finishing second in Zoology. By now, she was well settled in the college and, as part of a

The building on the left of this photograph was the Peirce family home in the Square, Newcastle West, County Limerick. Sophie Peirce was raised there after the murder of her mother on 6 December 1897. The entrance to Desmond Castle is on the left.
COURTESY LANGFORD FAMILY

small group of students, decided to publish a students' magazine called *The Torch*.

Sophie's wild streak was never too far from the surface. Once, when dared by fellow students, she stepped out of a college window several storeys off the ground and walked around the entire building, leaping from one precarious foothold to the next and from windowsill to windowsill when necessary.

On 22 June 1916, when Sophie was 19 years of age, her father Jackie died of general paralysis in the Dundrum Lunatic Asylum, aged 52. An inquest was held two days later. Nothing untoward was found. Almost no one was present at his funeral. It seems unlikely that Sophie, although protected from her family history during her childhood, could have remained entirely ignorant of this, or of how her father's illness had affected the family circumstances. She must surely have been aware that, although he died intestate, he had left a tidy sum of £1,138, probably from the sale of Knockaderry House, to which administration had been granted to her aunt Cis.

Money was probably on Sophie's mind, too, when she met someone that summer who would alter the course of her life. Captain William Davies Eliott-Lynn was born in Liverpool on 12 June 1875 and was 21 years her senior. He was an officer with the Royal Engineers, based temporarily in Beresford Barracks at the Curragh, County Kildare, not much more than an hour's drive from Dublin. Despite living in South Africa, he had volunteered in August 1915, taking a few years off his true age, and is listed under 'Temporary and Acting Captains' for the duration of the First World War. Hardly an ideal candidate for the horrors of trench warfare, Eliott-Lynn had fortuitously lost part of a finger in a

A portrait of Sophie taken by the Werner Company in Dublin at the time of her marriage to Captain William Eliott-Lynn.
COURTESY LANGFORD FAMILY

motorcycling accident at Poperinghe (now Poperinge) just a month after arriving at the Belgian Front. When he recovered, he was sent to Ireland in the aftermath of the 1916 Easter Rising. Sophie, by now very aware of her family's impoverished status and the impending sale of their house in Newcastle West, probably saw marriage as her only salvation from a life of poverty. Therefore, she was unlikely to dismiss a reliable earner with a healthy bank balance, even one who had escaped matrimony until this stage in his life.

In the autumn of 1916 Sophie embarked on the third year of her studies. On 26 November 1916, five months after the death of her father and two weeks after her twentieth birthday, she stunned her fellow students by marrying Captain Eliott-Lynn, by now Officer Commanding, No 1 Works Company, Royal Irish Rifles:

Considerable interest was manifested in college when it became known that Miss S.C. Peirce, one of our most popular lady students, had been married to Captain W.D.E. Lynn, R.E., on November 26 in Rathmines Parish Church. During the past few years, Mrs Lynn has occupied a prominent position in the social, athletic and literary life of the College. From its inception, she has taken a deep interest in *The Torch* both in her capacity as a member of the committee and as a constant contributor. On the hockey field, she is a leading figure, her fine defensive play contributing materially to the success of the club last year, while she also earned the thanks of that club by her able management of their teas. The students of the College will be pleased to

hear that she proposes finishing her course here and we are sure all will unite in wishing Captain and Mrs Lynn every success and happiness.

Sophie's decision to marry was sudden even by her impulsive standards and, for such an outgoing character, remarkably low key. Since she had just turned 20, it is difficult to believe that her aunts approved of her marrying, although they perhaps hoped that she would now be financially secure, at least. Owing to the fact that she was raised as an orphan by maiden aunts, Sophie had little idea of what marriage meant and the entire experience came as something of a shock to her. Initially, at least, her life appears to have continued as normal. After the wedding she remained in her 'digs' in Dublin and continued to pursue her studies and her literary endeavours with *The Torch*. Her new husband was based in the Curragh Military Camp.

But it was to be a year full of personal drama for Sophie. A month later, on 12 December, her step-grandmother, Henrietta Peirce, died, leaving less than £300 to be divided among her stepdaughters and Sophie. In January 1917, her father's estate was finally settled, presumably bringing her a small income and, when Cis moved to Doon Cottage in Ballybunion, where she was to live for the rest of her life, the family's links with Newcastle West ended. Soon after, the house on the Square was sold to the Munster and Leinster Bank (later Allied Irish Bank) and it opened for business on 7 May 1924.

Sophie with her husband Captain William Davies Eliott-Lynn at Miltown Malbay, County Clare, following their marriage on 26 November 1916. Note the missing little finger on Captain Eliott-Lynn's left hand, a loss sustained during the First World War.
COURTESY LANGFORD FAMILY

Sophie wearing the uniform of the Women's British Transport Unit in France during the First World War.

Less than six months after her wedding, the new Mrs Eliott-Lynn offered her services to the War Office as a motorbike despatch rider, abandoning her studies, at least temporarily. Her husband had already fled the marriage, returning to his family duties. Sophie may have been attempting to escape both her husband and the mundane reality of domestic life. There was also the perennial question of money. Her work as a despatch rider meant that Sophie would be earning her own income for the first time. More crucially, she would be embarking on her first great adventure, unchaperoned and free to come and go as she wished, with no aunts or husband holding her back. According to *The Torch*, no sooner had Sophie been accepted by the War Office than she took the ferry to Wales and rode her new motorbike from Holyhead to London.

She was based with the Women's Army Auxiliary Corps, probably at Boscombe Down, Salisbury. With the rest of the women, Sophie was billeted in a hut at the camp's married quarters, about a mile from the aerodrome:

> The quarters themselves are rather jolly, two in a room, and there's a priceless sort of rivalry between us as to who should have the most 'outré' Kirchner pictures up and the largest amount of 'frillies' negligently laid in conspicuous places the day the Colonel inspects the billets!

This was not a huge leap from the boarding-school existence she had relished just a few years earlier. Boscombe Down had opened in October 1917 as a training depot station for the Royal Flying Corps (RFC), to train pilots for operational roles in France. Several squadrons of the RFC were based there and this is where Sophie would have encountered early aviation at first hand. Driving the Crossley Tenders to pick up the pieces and clean up after air crashes provided the most interesting work at the station.

Soon after, Sophie was sent to France. Since the first detachment of the Women's Army Auxiliary Corps had arrived in France towards the end of March 1917, the numbers of women in service had risen to 6,023 within a year. They fulfilled all sorts of non-military functions, freeing up men for the trenches. While close to the front, Sophie possibly worked with an ambulance unit, since she claimed later in life to be an experienced nurse. She would certainly have witnessed the horrors of war at first hand, because women operated first-aid stations close to the action – although, officially, they were not allowed within three miles of the trenches. Sophie's knowledge of motorbikes and cars would certainly have come in useful, given the woeful lack of skilled drivers for the heavy Napier ambulances and the assortment of other vehicles. The experience undoubtedly formed the basis of her enduring skill with engines.

Life was tough for the nurses and their drivers and while, according to later friends such as Elinor Smith, Sophie never spoke of her experiences, many others did, giving a graphic picture of those dreadful times. Although Sophie had learned early on to block out anything unpleasant in her life, what she witnessed in France can hardly have left her unmoved.

When Eliott-Lynn was pronounced fit for action, he was spared a return to the dreaded trenches of Europe and, by April 1917, was on his way to British East Africa. In August, he was appointed Works Officer at the coastal town of Lindi in Tanganyika Territory and was later given other jobs in the area. He was finally promoted to the rank of Temporary Major in October 1918. The war ended just weeks later, on 11 November 1918. In the New Year's Honours list of 1919, Eliott-Lynn was made an Officer of the Most Excellent Order of the British Empire (OBE). All was going well until early 1919, when he contracted a life-threatening case of malaria in Tanganyika. He was sent to hospital in Alexandria in Egypt, where he lingered between life and death, losing three stone in weight and becoming very depressed. By April of that year he was claiming that he had quite recovered his strength and energy

Part of Sophie's role in France during the First World War was to drive a British Transport Unit vehicle like the one pictured here. In addition, she drove an ambulance and performed nursing duties close to the front line.
Courtesy Langford family

In this portrait by Sir John Lavery, Sophie is dressed in the uniform of the Women's Army Auxiliary Corps. It was painted in 1919, while she was still serving in France.

COURTESY SOPHIE C. ELIOTT-LYNN, *EAST AFRICAN NIGHTS* (1925)

and was ordered back to London, but he suffered relapses in June and August. Since his condition was considered to be 'fair only', it was recommended that he be demobbed. In January 1920, Eliott-Lynn left the army while still in London.

Even though her husband was struggling with a serious and recurring illness, Sophie remained in France until at least July 1919, where, dressed in the uniform of the Women's Army Auxiliary Corps, she had her portrait painted by Sir John Lavery. At the time Lavery, like his fellow Irish painter William Orpen, was an official war artist; both men were later knighted for their work. Commissioned to produce a series of paintings for the collection entitled 'Women's Work' at the newly established Imperial War Museum, Lavery had travelled to France. There he had recorded the work of women in hospitals, canteens, graveyards and improvised offices. The Lavery portrait of Sophie is now in a private collection.

By autumn of that year, Sophie was seriously considering her future and applied to the Department of Agriculture and Technical Instruction in Dublin for a training grant so that she could resume her studies in Dublin. Although such grants were available only to men, the department took up her case and applied for a grant on her behalf to the Treasury Office in London:

> Mrs Eliott-Lynn was a student of the Royal College of Science for Ireland before joining the Women's Army Auxiliary Corps. Her grading in the Army was that of Driver-Mechanic, and the Department understand that she acted as Motor-Cyclist Dispatch Rider in France for a considerable period.

Her first battle with the authorities for equal treatment of men and women ended in failure. Sophie's request was turned down because she was a married woman, presumably supported by a husband.

Sophie emerged from the war a mature and self-sufficient woman and, like many others, found readjusting to civilian life difficult. The war had changed the role of women beyond recognition. For her, the cage door had been unlocked and there was no going back.

After she was demobbed, 22-year-old Sophie returned to Dublin where, in July 1919, she was reunited with her husband. After eight uneasy months, Eliott-Lynn set sail for Africa to find work as an engineer. Under the Soldier Settlement Scheme, he was awarded a large farm in east Africa on easy terms to be paid back over 30 years. In autumn 1920 his young wife returned to the Royal College of Science to complete her studies in Agriculture, which her husband felt would prove useful in Africa. When compared to the stifling dullness of life in rural Ireland, this seemed like a good plan. However, the rifts already apparent in the marriage were steadily growing wider. Sophie's inability – or perhaps unwillingness – to manage money, or repay the £60 Eliott-Lynn had lent her for her trousseau, were a source of frequent disagreements between them.

Sophie was clearly anxious to make her own way in the world. Previous generations of divorced or widowed women mostly relied on the outcome of court cases and settlements for their financial survival. Despite her war experiences – or perhaps because of them – Sophie was quite unready for the humdrum life of the typical wife. 'She is just at the age when she thinks herself very much wiser than half-a-dozen aunts or husbands,' said her exasperated husband at the time.

Taking on such a young wife had proved to be an expensive indulgence for Eliott-Lynn. Between the time Sophie had arrived back from France at the beginning of July 1919 and the following April, when he sailed for Africa, she had cost him £528. This included paying off debts, which she passed on to him, although she had been drawing her usual allowance from the bank. 'I am

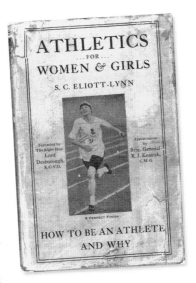

Sophie wrote the above book in 1925. It was one of the first books published about women's athletics.
Courtesy John Cussen

being rather forced to the conclusion that Sophie's idea of marriage is to extract just as much money as possible from one's husband and have as good a time as possible,' said Eliott-Lynn. He could not understand how she was failing to manage on an income of over £300 a year. On the evidence, it is hard to disagree. Sophie's aunt Cis had clearly told Eliott-Lynn something of Sophie's background and he commented:

> From what you have told me of her parents, I should think most of her faults in this particular line are hereditary, and she is more to be pitied than blamed.

With a mark of 80 per cent, 24-year-old Sophie graduated first in her class on 7 July 1921 with an Associateship in Agriculture. Throughout her life, Sophie would proudly append the letters ARCScI to her name. Eliott-Lynn had never refused Sophie money but, once she graduated, he insisted that she must find herself a job. So, in the autumn of 1921, his profligate young wife ended up at the University of Aberdeen in Scotland, apparently studying for a postgraduate degree and earning some money as a zoology demonstrator. During her period in Scotland, she made quite an impression on the hockey field, where she excelled in her usual defensive position. More crucially, Sophie had discovered the emerging sport of women's athletics: 'I once entered for the sports at a famous college when I was attending a postgraduate course,' she wrote in her book *Athletics for Women and Girls*, published in 1925. On the programme were four events for women. Sophie, an increasingly grudging wife, had found herself a new passion, one that would bring her the attention she craved and distract her from the querulous admonishments of her faraway husband.

Already an enthusiastic hockey, tennis, golf and lacrosse player, Sophie was inspired to take up athletics, beginning her competitive career in the autumn of 1921. Before a large crowd at the Dublin Tramway Sports in Lansdowne Road, she beat 12 others to win the high jump with a modest jump of 4 feet. A considerably better jump of 4 feet 6 inches at the Clonliffe Harriers Sports in Lansdowne Road was enough to rank her second in Britain and Ireland for the year 1921. Even better was a leap of 4 feet 9 inches in Ballygar, County Galway, which equalled the best known performance in the world at that time. Sophie, with clear pretensions to the grand life, was now calling herself Sophie Eliott-Lynn rather than plain Mrs Lynn and, although just a few months in the sport, had somehow emerged as an outstanding athletics talent. Meanwhile, women's athletics continued to progress at a heady rate.

For reasons that are unclear, she lasted only a few months in Aberdeen and moved over to London in

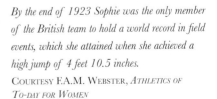

March 1922. In May 1922 she competed at a sports day organised by the King's College, at Mitcham, London, winning the high jump and 220 yards and finishing third in the long jump. In early August 1922, at a meet in Paddington, she made her first appearance in a two-handed javelin competition, where the best of three throws with either arm were added together for the total. She finished a commendable second. Highlight of the 1922 season for Sophie was the first Women's World Games, which began at the Pershing Stadium in Paris on 20 August. The competition was eagerly awaited and attracted 20,000 spectators. In the two-handed shot, Sophie finished ninth. At the first annual meeting of the British Women's Amateur Athletic Association (WAAA), held in the autumn of 1922, Sophie was invited to join as Secretary and Treasurer. The WAAA was an affiliate organisation of the Fédération Sportive Féminine Internationale (FSFI), which had been formed shortly after the 1921 Women's Olympiad in Monte Carlo.

In October 1922, Sophie finally set sail for east Africa to join her husband at their farm at Pangani, in the Tanganyika Territory. This small provincial settlement, on the coast near the Kenyan border, was about 400 miles south-east of Nairobi. Her relationship with her husband continued to be fraught. By the spring of 1923, Sophie was back in England, immersing herself in athletics. At the third Monte Carlo meet in early April, again dominated by the British women, the training she had put in while in east Africa paid off. She finished third in both the high jump and the javelin. These were her first international medals. On 6 August 1923, at Brentwood, Sophie claimed that she had jumped 4 feet 10 inches and this mark was listed by the FSFI as the best jump of the year and a world record.

By the end of 1923 Sophie was the only member of the British team to hold a world record in field events, which she attained when she achieved a high jump of 4 feet 10.5 inches.
COURTESY F.A.M. WEBSTER, *ATHLETICS OF TO-DAY FOR WOMEN*

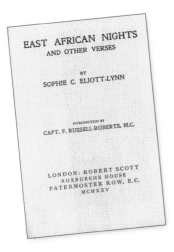

East African Nights *was a book of verse published by Sophie in 1925 about her visits to her husband's farm in east Africa.*
COURTESY JOHN CUSSEN

Sophie in safari attire. She enjoyed hunting and other similar activities while on visits to her husband in east Africa.
COURTESY SOPHIE C. ELIOTT-LYNN, *EAST AFRICAN NIGHTS* (1925)

On 18 August 1923, the inaugural English Women's Athletics Championships took place at the Oxo Sports Ground, Bromley, London, and Sophie became the country's first women's javelin champion, while also finishing second in the 120-yard hurdles and third in the shot.

By the end of 1923, her 4 feet 10.5 inches for the high jump had her sharing the women's world record on the FSFI lists with Elizabeth Seine of the USA. Officially, Sophie was then the only remaining British-based female athlete credited with a world record.

Despite her marital difficulties, Sophie departed for east Africa as soon as the athletics season was over. It was to be her last prolonged visit. Although there were many aspects of colonial African life that she loved, she was not happy there. She and Eliott-Lynn had been a mismatched pair from the start and whatever love ever existed between them was gone. Later, Sophie would claim her husband 'beat her up in the bush'. From her poems recorded in her collection *East African Nights*, published in 1925, it can be sensed that she put on a brave face. Compounding their marital problems was the failure of their farming efforts: their coffee crop failed and their animals died. This, however, was typical of the time.

With the experiment in farming a failure, Sophie returned to England in early 1924 determined to seek a divorce. Eliott-Lynn's battle with malaria continued, meanwhile, leaving him listless and depressed for months and incapable of the physical effort vital for farming. His wife's return to London meant that their marriage was effectively over.

All her life, Sophie came across as a woman torn between the need for adventure and a longing for acceptance in society. There is little doubt that, like many women of her time, she married for money. Even at this point, she was still regarded by some in athletics as a 'gold digger'. Unlike other women, accepting that their part of the deal was to stay at home and look after their husbands and children, Sophie married precisely so she would not have to do so. Little wonder, then, that her husband failed to understand her. She may also have become prone to bouts of depression, which, when contrasted with her usual outgoing and positive attitude, leads to suspicions that she may have inherited a mild form of her father's mental illness.

Sophie's finest moment as an athlete came at the second annual English Women's Championships in the Woolwich Stadium, London, on 28 June 1924,

Sophie, sitting second from left in the front row, at the inaugural English Women's Athletics Championships at the Oxo Grounds, Bromley, London, on 18 August 1923.
COURTESY WWW.RUNNINGPAST.COM VIA PAUL BROWNING

where she was dominant in both the high jump and the javelin. In the two-handed javelin there was no disputing her magnificent aggregate total of 173 feet and 2 inches, the best athletics performance of her life. The book she had just written, called *Athletics for Women and Girls*, was broadcast by the BBC on 9 April 1925, with Sophie reading its preface. It was one of the first of its kind, written by a woman for her sister athletes.

From 29 May to 4 June 1925, her life was to take another huge turn. She attended the eighth Olympic Congress in Prague as part of the FSFI delegation, travelling for the first time in her life by aeroplane. On her flight home an enthralled Sophie fell into conversation with a pilot, Captain Reid, who told her about a national air-club scheme promoted by Sir Sefton Brancker, the director of the Civil Aviation Advisory Board, which had been founded three years earlier in London. Coming up soon would be the launch of the London Aeroplane Club at the Stag Lane Aerodrome off Edgware Road, north London. Since Sophie had taken to the air with such enthusiasm, Captain Reid suggested that she go along.

She needed little prompting and, on 19 August 1925, was part of a large crowd of attentive listeners when Sir Philip Sassoon, Under-Secretary for Air, officially opened the London Aeroplane Club at Stag Lane. Sophie, 'a well-known and forceful sportswoman', was one of the first 15 members to sign up. Although David Kettel won the ballot for the club's first half-hour flight, he gallantly gave his place to Sophie. Consequently she became the club's first passenger, taking to the air in the club's dual-control de Havilland Moth. News reporters, by now obsessed with all things aerial, swarmed around her after she returned to earth. After her well-publicised

Using the two-handed throwing method, Sophie achieved her best javelin performance of her athletic career on 28 June 1924 at the Woolwich Stadium, London, with a throw of 173 feet and 2 inches.
Courtesy F.A.M. Webster, *Athletics of To-day for Women*

Sophie waiting to be taken aloft on 19 August 1925 to become the first female passenger in the newly inaugurated London Aeroplane Club at Stag Lane, London.
Courtesy British Pathé

A selection of the trophies and medals won by Sophie during her four-year involvement with athletics.
COURTESY DE HAVILLAND MOTH CLUB ARCHIVE

first flight at the opening of the London Aeroplane Club, she decided to take flying lessons. As her skill as a pilot increased, her involvement in athletics inevitably lessened. It had been a short but glorious career and her influence was permanent.

Sophie continued to take flying lessons at Stag Lane during August 1925 and worked there as the Club Secretary. Among her instructors were Sir Alan Cobham, one of the best-known aviators in England, and James Milo St John Kearney, later the first instructor with the Shannon Aero Club in Limerick. It is easy to see what attracted Sophie to the new and thrilling world of aviation. Not only was it glamorous, attracting only those wealthy enough to support an

expensive hobby, but it also had an enticing whiff of the daring and the dangerous. Always on the lookout for activities that would bring her notice, Sophie was astute enough to see that a woman pilot could attract enough publicity to generate a steady income.

Sophie proved a naturally gifted pilot. On 18 October 1925 she flew solo for the first time and made some excellent landings. She later described it as 'the most thrilling adventure of my life'. Twelve days later, she took the first test for her Aviator's 'A' Certificate, flying a de Havilland Moth with a Cirrus engine. A few days later she took her final test, flying to 6,000 feet and then, with the engine cut off, descending and landing at the aerodrome. On 4 November 1925, less than a week

before her twenty-ninth birthday, Sophie received her 'A' Certificate (number 7975). It was handed over to her personally on 30 November by Colonel F.C. Shelmerdine of the Air Ministry, who was to feature again in her story, though in less happy circumstances, eight years later.

Having obtained her 'A' Certificate, she set herself the challenge of obtaining an Aviator's 'B' (Commercial) Certificate in order to achieve a self-sustaining career in commercial aviation. In April 1924, however, the International Commission for Air Navigation had passed a resolution that 'women shall be excluded from any employment in the operating crew of an aircraft engaged in public transport'. Sophie was already struggling to be accepted as a private pilot by her male peers and, by challenging the aviation authorities to be granted a commercial licence, she

exacerbated this struggle. Sophie's battle on behalf of women pilots was described at length in her book *Woman and Flying*, published in 1929:

> When I first flew, I took my pilot's licence, and only afterwards did I discover that I had no right to a commercial one. I needed money very badly, as I had staked my last dollar on flying. I simply hounded the various ministries until they felt at last that if I insisted upon flying and being killed,

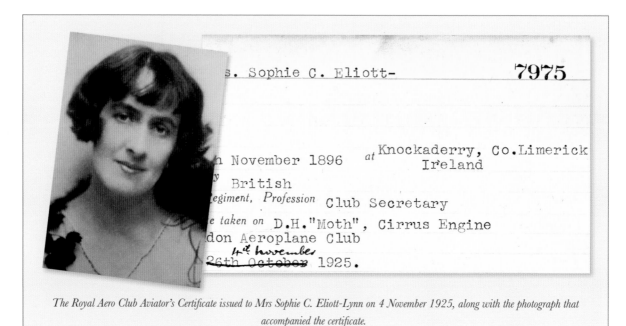

The Royal Aero Club Aviator's Certificate issued to Mrs Sophie C. Eliott-Lynn on 4 November 1925, along with the photograph that accompanied the certificate.
COURTESY ROYAL AERO CLUB TRUST

James Norman, Chief Designer of the DH.60 Moth, standing beside the prototype aircraft, G-EBKT, for its inaugural flight on 22 February 1925.
COURTESY DE HAVILLAND MOTH CLUB ARCHIVE

perhaps it would be a happy release all round. But in the end because the men saw that it was unjust and were sympathetic, I gained my point, and it was agreed between countries that women should fly freely to make a living.

This was because of the great unmentionable, only hinted at in Sophie's account: women's menstrual cycle. Menstruation was generally considered a disability that prohibited women from flying, although not all

agreed. As far as Sir Sefton Brancker, the Director of Civil Aviation, was concerned, women pilots were absolutely the equal of men.

Meanwhile, she undertook a special test on her ability to manage light machines and engines, such as the de Havilland Moth, which became standard equipment for private pilots after its launch in 1925. To earn a living, Sophie gave exhibitions and indulged in various headline-grabbing stunts. For example, on 3 April 1926, in Hereford, she became the first woman to make a parachute jump from an aeroplane in public. On 17 April 1926 she acquired a de Havilland Moth, G-EBKT; it was her first aeroplane. This aircraft had

Sophie sitting proudly and happily in the cockpit of her first aircraft, DH.60 Moth G-EBKT, at Christchurch, Dorset, on 1 June 1926.
COURTESY TIME LIFE PICTURES VIA GETTY IMAGES

851 LBS.

The only way to start a Moth aircraft, and many other aircraft types of that era, was to hand-swing the propeller.

COURTESY DE HAVILLAND MOTH CLUB ARCHIVE

the distinction of being the prototype of the famous DH.60 Moth series of aircraft. Its maiden flight was at Stag Lane on 22 February 1925, piloted by Captain Geoffrey de Havilland himself.

Sophie had found her life's passion. Her years at the Royal College of Science and as a driver during the First World War had given her a solid knowledge of mechanics, which she would call on during her career as a pilot. Flying gave focus to her considerable energies, as well as providing her with a desperately needed income.

After winning her battle to apply for a 'B' Certificate, Sophie was unexpectedly invited by the British aviation authorities to present herself for a physical examination 'during a certain period', as it was tactfully put in her book. Despite dancing until three o'clock that morning, she went at once to the Air Ministry and had no difficulty passing the 'special' examination, in front of a panel of male examiners.

She then needed to pass the written technical examination. She easily passed the tests on navigation and meteorology. By the end of April 1926, she had flown for over 20 hours and passed the cross-country test. During the first month of ownership of her Moth she flew for 52 hours.

Later on, her ability to land an aeroplane was tested and approved. She could now conclude her 'B' Certificate evaluation. On 31 May 1926, she successfully completed her night-flying test, despite a recently broken wrist. On 26 June 1926 Sophie became Britain's first officially recognised female commercial pilot. At last she was legally entitled to earn a living as a commercial pilot and carry fare-paying passengers.

Royal Aircraft Factory SE.5a, G-EBPA, was acquired by Sophie on 30 July 1926 and she entered several races with it. It was originally designed as a First World War fighter and only ten of this type had civilian ownership.

COURTESY A.J. JACKSON, *BRITISH CIVIL AIRCRAFT 1919–1972* (1988)

Portrait of Sophie.

COURTESY ASHFIELD PRESS, DUBLIN

Sophie was the only female entrant at the Concours d'Avions Économiques, Orly Airport, Paris, in her de Havilland Moth, G-EBKT, on 9–15 August 1926.
COURTESY DE HAVILLAND MOTH CLUB ARCHIVE

Sophie was well aware that she had won only the first battle and was already contemplating her future. She would have to earn a good living – or find herself a rich husband – if she were to continue with her new and expensive profession. Sophie's hard work on behalf of women pilots meant that, with backing from aviation organisations in Sweden, Norway, Czechoslovakia and France, the ban on women pilots was unanimously rescinded. The only remaining problem was the compulsory medical examination. By July 1926, it was agreed that women should be examined every three months, twice as often as men.

A month earlier, on 7 June, Sophie gave another Irishwoman, Lady Bailey, her first joy-ride and Lady Bailey was soon under instruction. (Lady Bailey's life is discussed in a separate chapter in this publication.) Also taking flying lessons at Stag Lane was Sicele O'Brien, another of this celebrated trio of Irish women pilots. O'Brien became the second woman pilot in Britain to receive a commercial licence. Sicele's life is also discussed in a separate chapter.

Sophie won three of the seven competitions she entered for during the Concours d'Avions Économiques at Orly Airport, Paris, in August 1926. She is seen here navigating her aircraft, with folded wings, through measured gates.
COURTESY FLIGHT ARCHIVES VIA ASHFIELD PRESS, DUBLIN

Sophie became the owner of an SE.5a Viper, G-EBPA, on 30 July 1926. It was previously a Royal Air Force (RAF) machine, D7016, and was put up for sale by the Aircraft Disposal Company. It had a 200-horsepower Viper engine. So began a frantic few years of flying. If there was a flying display or an air show taking place anywhere in England, Sophie was likely to be there and hogging much of the publicity. She was determined to keep her name to the fore and had a nose for a good story. A couple of weeks later, Sophie was the only woman competitor in the French Air Association's Concours d'Avions Économiques at Orly Airport, just south of Paris, which took place from 9 to 15 August 1926. After finishing with three wins from the seven tests, she was celebrated in the French

The de Havilland Moth, G-EBKT, that Sophie owned from 17 April 1926 until 4 February 1927. During this time she entered several races and competitions.
COURTESY ROYAL AERO CLUB TRUST

Lady Bailey and Sophie disembarked at Hamble Aerodrome, near Southampton, on 18 May 1927, after creating a world altitude record of 15,748 feet.
COURTESY FLIGHTGLOBAL ARCHIVES
VIA RBI LIMITED

press as 'un sport'. Her participation in the competition received extensive coverage in *Flight* on 19 August 1926.

Her hectic schedule continued after she returned home. At a two-day air festival in Bournemouth on 21 and 22 August 1926, she competed in a number of races, winning the fifth race on the programme, the Light Aeroplane Club Members' Scratch, for a prize of £20. She entered the race in de Havilland Moth, G-EBLI, borrowed from the London Aeroplane Club.

Sophie was busy flying at air shows in Lympne near Folkestone, Woodford in Lancashire and Sherburn in Yorkshire. She had started giving flying instruction at the London Aeroplane Club, where the first of her pupils was Lieutenant George H.N. Larden, Royal Artillery. He successfully passed his tests for his Aviator's Certificate on Tuesday, 28 September 1926 at Stag Lane. Later that month, at an air display to honour the visit of members of the Empire Conference at Croydon, Sophie demonstrated how easy it was to manage a small plane. She wheeled her de Havilland Moth out of a temporary building on the site, unfolded the wings, started up the engine and, after a short flight, rehoused the plane briskly and efficiently.

By now, she was the most prominent female pilot in Britain, but her forceful personality and tendency to seek the limelight had earned her the sobriquet 'Lady Hell-of-a-Din', a play on her married name. In December 1926, she travelled to Africa, where she flew a de Havilland 51 Moth belonging to her distant cousin John Evans Carberry, a man as fanatical about flying as she was herself. On 4 February 1927, following her return to England, she sold her Moth, G-EBKT, to the London Aeroplane Club.

On 1 May 1927, Sophie's estranged husband, Major William Davies Eliott-Lynn, was found drowned in the River Thames with just a single copper penny in his pocket. Aged 52, he had returned from Africa after the failure of the couple's coffee farm a few years earlier and had been living in London. Ever since his life-threatening bout of malaria in Africa during the final months of his war service, his health had been poor. He had struggled to find work, his second wife told the inquest into his death. The coroner returned an open verdict.

A couple of weeks later, on 18 May 1927, Sophie was back in the headlines when she set a new altitude record. For the ambitious pilot, anxious to prove her worth, altitude records had the great advantage of being comparatively easy to arrange. So, with Lady Bailey as front-seat passenger, Sophie took off from Hamble Aerodrome near Southampton in an Avro Avian fitted with a Cirrus Mark II engine and climbed steadily upwards to a height of 15,748 feet. Just three days later, Charles A. Lindbergh in the *Spirit of St Louis* became the first pilot to fly the Atlantic solo, a feat many had thought impossible. Thanks largely to the efforts of the publisher and publicist George Putnam, Lindbergh became a household name. Lindbergh's book, *We*, published within three months of his flight, proved a phenomenal success. With Lindbergh hysteria putting aviation on the front pages of newspapers worldwide, it was a good time to be a pilot. Sophie was well aware of this when she was interviewed by the *Daily Mail* on 'The Exhilaration of Flying'.

According to the article, she never trained for racing, not even for feats such as her recent altitude record. Nor did she diet:

> I live very simply and never diet. I eat what I like and plenty of it. Also I have a cigarette whenever I want one and I believe in the advice given by St Paul – to take a little wine for thy stomach's sake.

To keep fit, she played tennis and continued to make trips to Battersea Park to throw the javelin. In the Ladies' Air Race at the Bournemouth Meet on a weekend in early June 1927 Sophie used her superior cornering to beat Sicele O'Brien, with Lady Bailey third. 'All three handled their machines excellently, making very good turns at the aerodrome turning point, those of Mrs Eliott-Lynn being particularly good and practically vertical,' said *Flight* magazine.

An appearance in Birmingham followed in early July, but it was Sicele O'Brien's turn to capture the limelight when she won what was billed as the first Aerial Oaks, a women-only race. Then on 5 July, Lady Bailey, flying Geoffrey de Havilland's own Moth and with his wife, Louie, as passenger, broke Sophie's altitude record when she reached a world-best height of 17,283 feet. Sophie believed the Irish could fly well – Lady Bailey, Sicele O'Brien and Sophie were just three examples of successful flying Irishwomen.

Sophie, while publicly congratulating her sister pilots, was determined to regain her place as Britain's top female pilot. Although a DH.60 Moth, G-EBMV, was registered to her on 11 July 1927, Sophie had obviously struck some kind of a deal with the A.V. Roe Company, based near Manchester. A week later, on 19 July 1927, an Avro 594 Avian, G-EBRS, was also registered in her name. She was now the registered owner of three aircraft simultaneously. Sophie grabbed back the headlines that day when, 'emulating a grasshopper', she flew the Avian 1,200 miles around Britain at an average speed of 80 miles per hour, making 79 landings. She had set off from Woodford, Manchester, at 3.20am on 19 July, after dozing in the

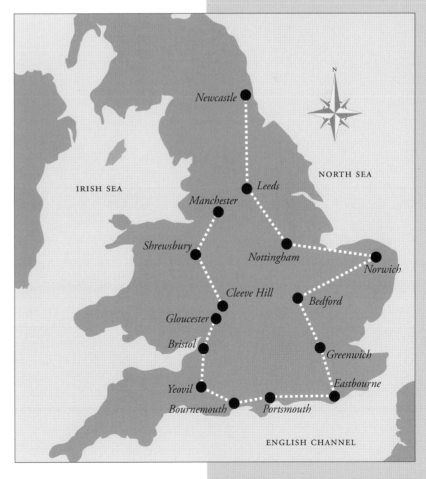

A map outlining the course taken by Sophie on 19 July 1927, when she flew to 79 airfields in 18 hours in her Avian, G-EBRS – a journey of 1,200 miles.

MAP © ASHFIELD PRESS, DUBLIN

While demonstrating the capabilities and benefits of the Avro Avian around Europe in mid-August 1927, Sophie sold her own Avian, G-EBRS, to help form a new flying club at Basle, Switzerland.
COURTESY FLIGHTGLOBAL ARCHIVES VIA RBI LIMITED

hangar overnight. Following a triangular course over England, she stayed mostly airborne for over 18 hours, completing the course at 9.27pm. In Britain at the time, many prominent buildings, usually railway stations, had their names painted on the roofs to help pilots above them find their way.

Sophie had always kept in touch with her Irish roots, making at least one annual visit to her Aunt Cis in Ballybunion, County Kerry. On 25 July 1927, she made a visit to Dublin. With mechanic Henry Hollingdrake, she had started off from Manchester at 11am for Flint in Wales and, from there, flown to Kirkcudbright in Scotland. Then she had crossed the Irish Sea at its narrowest point and gone on to Aldergrove near Belfast, where she lunched after landing in the middle of the afternoon. Just before six o'clock, she touched down in the broad spaces of the Fifteen Acres in Dublin's Phoenix Park. She had flown a total of about 500 miles. There, Commandant Fitzmaurice of the Irish Air Corps welcomed her and, flying an Irish Air Corps aeroplane, accompanied her to Baldonnel, about ten miles distant. Here, after landing officially in order to clear customs, she was the honoured guest of the Irish Air Corps. Her Avro Avian, the light aeroplane she had used in her tour of Britain the previous week, was the latest type of flying machine and was equipped with folding wings, a fact she recounted to the reporters. It could be housed in an ordinary garage and cost only £750. The flight was her first to Ireland and she had enjoyed every minute of the trip.

On the bank-holiday weekend, 30 July 1927, the annual King's Cup Race took place at Hucknall in Nottinghamshire. Sixteen of the original twenty-five aircraft listed took to the skies, with Lady Bailey the only woman, though a broken valve spring soon forced her out of the race. Strong winds hampered the competition and only six finished. Sophie boycotted the race due to a new handicapping formula but went some way towards making up for her boycott when she gave an exhibition of looping in an Avian. She created history by winning the Grosvenor Cup, the chief short race of the day, in a de Havilland Moth prototype with a 60-horsepower Cirrus Mark I engine at an average speed of 88.5 miles per hour. With 15 pilots entered and despite a handicap of 1 minute 41 seconds, she still beat Colonel the Master of Sempill in the final by a considerable margin. The victory was widely publicised as the first by a woman in an open race against men.

By the middle of August 1927, Sophie was flying the Avian in central Europe, again accompanied by Henry Hollingdrake. At Breslau in Germany (now Wrocław, Poland), she gave an exhibition of aerobatics, particularly impressing the German pilots with her vertical banks. In Switzerland, she participated at a flying-club meet in Zurich with her Avro Avian, G-EBRS. She achieved maximum marks for 'construction, workmanship, accessibility for repairs, and highest points for comfort and luggage capacity', according to later A.V. Roe advertising material. While in Switzerland, she sold G-EBRS to the Basle Air Transport Company, who immediately established a flying club using her Avian. The aircraft was removed from the UK civil-aircraft register on 26 August 1927.

By September, her Avro promotional work with Hollingdrake had taken her to Scotland. In Dundee, a crowd of 8,000 gathered to hear her speak on the history and progress of aviation, while at Aberdeen the numbers swelled to 10,000. Over the next few weeks, she was back in the north of England at the Hooton Park meet, held as part of Liverpool's Civic Week, where she won her race. On 29 September 1927, another Avro 594 Avian, G-EBQL, was registered to Sophie, but this was returned to Avro after five days.

At a meeting in Sherburn, Yorkshire, on 1 October 1927, she won the Wattle Handicap Race at an average speed of 116 miles per hour in her SE.5a, G-EBPA.

Sophie, by now, was looking for a new husband, preferably one who could pay for her flying obsession. She believed quite firmly that ambitious women needed financial security. Finding a husband required meticulous planning, she was later to tell the young American airwoman Elinor Smith, when describing her pursuit of Sir James Heath, who was to become her second husband:

> My dear, do you think that Sir James wanted to marry me? Of course not! I had to convince him how good it would be for him to have a nurse at his beck and call, and then I had to see to it that he thought the whole thing was his own idea!

She told Elinor that, to net her wealthy husband, she had put together a list of the oldest and wealthiest bachelors in the British Empire. After narrowing that down to those needing nursing care, she came up with about five possibilities. According to this account, Sir James was then spending most of his time in South Africa, home of his first wife. Sophie's choice was eminently practical.

James Heath was born on 26 January 1852 in north Staffordshire, the eldest son of a colliery and ironworks owner. He inherited the business on the death of his father in 1893. James was Member of Parliament for Staffordshire from 1892 to 1906

Sir James Heath, first Baronet, who became Sophie's second husband on 11 October 1927. From this date she acquired the title Lady Heath.

and was made Baronet in 1904. On 12 July 1881 James married Euphemia Celina Vanderbyl of Cape Town, South Africa, who died on 21 August 1921. He married Mrs Joy Smith on 6 February 1924, but this marriage was annulled in 1927. When he met Sophie, by now calling herself by her middle name, Mary, he was 75 years of age, while Sophie had just turned 30. Her future husband, an aviation fan, appeared besotted by his glamorous and high-flying wife-to-be, but the proposed alliance confirmed her reputation as a 'gold digger'.

Since Sophie had written to her aunt on 27 August 1927 saying that she intended travelling to South Africa on 1 October, it could be that the wedding was hastily arranged. The future Lady Heath refused to marry Sir James until he had agreed to settle £20,000 on her, bringing in an annual income of between £725 and £925. This meant that the wedding, originally planned for a month before her thirty-first birthday, 10 October 1927, at Christ Church in London's Mayfair, was delayed by a day to finalise the nuptial agreement. Few friends knew of her plans and fewer than a dozen people were in the church for the ceremony, having been summoned at the last minute by telephone calls from the unblushing bride. She was to be known publicly as Lady Heath for the rest of her life, clearly relishing the status conferred by a *bona fide* title. However, Sir James was evidently not a complete fool. Just minutes after the

The Royal Aero Club issued an updated Aviator's Certificate to Lady Heath following her marriage to Sir James Heath.

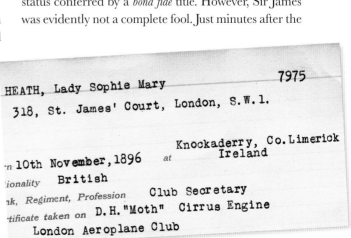

HEATH, Lady Sophie Mary   7975
318, St. James' Court, London, S.W.1.

                                    Knockaderry, Co.Limerick
                                         Ireland
...n 10th November,1896   *at*
...ionality   British
...k, Regiment, Profession   Club Secretary
...tificate taken on   D.H."Moth" Cirrus Engine
        London Aeroplane Club

Before sailing for South Africa on 18 November 1927, Lady Heath sold her de Havilland Moth, G-EBMV. She had owned this aircraft since 11 July 1927.
COURTESY RICHARD T. RIDING

wedding, he told his new bride that he would be making a will of which the daughter of his first marriage would be the principal beneficiary.

On 8 October, three days before her wedding, Sophie took off from Woodford Aerodrome near Manchester to attempt to break the altitude record of 17,283 feet set by Lady Bailey. Despite being chilled to the bone in the extreme cold, she landed without incident near Frodsham, Cheshire, in a small field only 90 yards long and lined with 40-foot-high hedges. Here she sat tight, waiting for the barograph to be collected by observing officials, since a further flight would affect the readings. When the machine was assessed and a height of 19,200 feet announced, it was greeted as a triumph for the A.V. Roe Company, which was determined to take on de Havilland and the assortment of records held by the Moth.

With her wealthy husband now roped in, the newly-minted Lady Heath was financially secure and immediately ordered the latest Avro Avian to add to the two planes still registered in her name. She had ordered the new Avro 594 Avian III for her trip to South Africa, where a tour of local aero clubs was scheduled. It was registered to her as G-EBUG on 29 October 1927. In the meantime, she continued a hectic schedule of flying and lecturing, seeing little of her new husband. The Air League of the British Empire, incorporated by the Duke of Sutherland in 1908 to encourage private and civil aviation, had a more open attitude to women pilots than other organisations. Both Lady Bailey and Elsa Mackey were on the Advisory Committee of Pilots, while Lady Heath was to chair the Ladies' Sub-Committee after her return from South Africa. Prior to departing England she put her Moth, G-EBMV, up for sale. The sale was completed while she was in South

Africa and the plane was registered to A. Fowler on 12 November 1927.

On 18 November, just over a month after their marriage, Sophie and her new husband set off on a three-week sea voyage to Cape Town, South Africa. Her violet-coloured Avro Avian biplane, G-EBUG, with its Cirrus engine, was carefully boxed and stowed in the liner's hold. The newlyweds arrived at the Cape on 5 December, after a 17-day trip. Despite much work by the Air Ministry after the First World War, flying conditions in the continent least explored by westerners were challenging. At the end of 1927, Lieutenant (later Captain) Richard Bentley, flying a de Havilland Moth, G-EBSO, took just 23 days to travel from London to Cape Town. While in South Africa he married Dorys and a few months later the couple decided to fly back to London, proving themselves useful both to Lady Heath and Lady Bailey.

Lady Heath and G-EBUG left Cape Town on a flight that would ultimately see her arriving in Johannesburg. In *Woman and Flying*, she claimed that she could find no information in Cape Town on a likely route to Cairo. The trip to Johannesburg began soon after dawn on 5 January 1928, when Lady Heath's tiny craft wobbled into the air at Cape Town. She gave lectures, joy-rides and newspaper interviews and assisted fledgling flying clubs with fundraising to the tune of £1,200 at the various towns she stopped at, including East London, Durban and Pietermaritzburg. On 8 January, she was the first woman to land an aeroplane at Port Elizabeth's

The Avro Avian G-EBUG was unpacked from its crate on arrival at Cape Town, South Africa, after Sir James and Lady Heath arrived there on 5 December 1927.
COURTESY FLIGHTGLOBAL ARCHIVES VIA RBI LIMITED

flying field. The mayor presented a new £700 Westland Widgeon monoplane to the President of the newly formed Port Elizabeth Light Aeroplane Club. Lady Heath smashed a bottle of champagne over the Widgeon's propeller hub, christening it *The Lady Heath*. She finally arrived in Johannesburg's Baragwanath Airport on 22 January, where she received a magnificent welcome. Waiting to greet her was her husband, Sir James.

While she was in Durban, news came through that Lady Bailey had been named Lady Champion Aviator of the World by the International Union of Aviators (Charles A. Lindbergh was the Gentleman Champion). The woman who had given Lady Bailey her first joy-ride, beaten her in races all over Britain and broken her altitude record responded with dignity, although she must have been disappointed that her own pioneering efforts had been ignored. A week after her arrival in Johannesburg, Lady Heath was the star attraction of a Ladies' Day, which was hosted in her honour and which attracted over 6,000 cars to Baragwanath Airport, one of the largest crowds ever seen in the city. It was the first aviation event of its kind in South Africa.

Lady Heath's Avian, G-EBUG, overtook Dick Bentley's de Havilland Moth, G-EBSO, in a 12-mile handicap race that she won on Ladies' Day in Johannesburg, 28 January 1928.

Courtesy FlightGlobal Archives via RBI Limited

Lady Heath broke a bottle of champagne as part of the christening ceremony for the Westland Widgeon named The Lady Heath *at Port Elizabeth, 8 January 1928.*

Courtesy Mary Evans Picture Library via National Aerospace Library, Farnborough, Hampshire

While travelling, she told the *Rand Daily Mail*, she favoured clothes that would roll up without creasing or showing the dirt: 'When I am flying and likely to be away from home for some days, I have to take the minimum of personal luggage with me.' She would take with her a black-beaded evening dress, an embroidered shawl and a pair of evening shoes to ensure that she was fit to be seen. For her flying kit, she brought a black leather coat, leather flying helmet and long leather boots and always flew prepared for any social occasion:

> I wear a neat, well-cut tailored navy blue coat and skirt with white silk shirt under my flying kit, so that I can go suitably clad into any hotel dining room after slipping off my jacket and gauntlet gloves.

On 7 February 1928, Lady Heath confirmed her solo flight from South Africa to London, starting on 26 February. At last, what she had been broadly hinting at was to become a reality. If she were to succeed in such a flight, she would firmly re-establish herself as the foremost woman pilot of her time. On her three previous trips to Africa, Lady Heath had visited different areas on her proposed route and gathered important local information on the terrain, the climate and the all-important availability of fuel. With no maps available, she made tracings from borrowed atlases and pieced together what information she could. Whatever her reasons for setting off on the trip, the logistics of flying over unknown, uncharted and possibly hostile territory would have deterred most pilots, male or female. Lieutenant Bentley later announced that he planned to accompany her across the swamps with his wife. Lady Heath said that she had no plans to hurry over her route. She loved all of Africa and wished to linger in some areas. Nonetheless, she must have been frustrated at Bentley's decision, which would detract from the achievement of her own

The Avro Avian G-EBUG at Pretoria, South Africa, before leaving on its flight to London.
<small>COURTESY JOHN ILLSLEY</small>

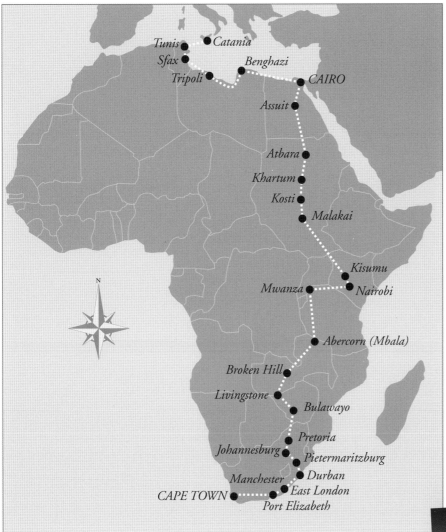

Lady Heath's flight from Cape Town to Catania, Sicily. 5 January to 6 May 1928.
MAP © ASHFIELD PRESS, DUBLIN

solo effort and possibly slow her down – she would have to keep pace with a de Havilland Moth carrying two people. For keeping the aeroplane in tune, she would carry a set of tools and plenty of spare parts. She expected to spend most of her non-flying time overhauling the engine, believing that prevention was better than cure.

She had already completed the first leg of her journey when she flew from Cape Town to Pretoria. The South African Air Force at Roberts Heights Aerodrome, Pretoria, made last-minute adjustments to her Avro Avian. Converted into a single seater, it had more room for baggage and a special petrol tank had been fitted successfully to allow her carry 60 gallons of fuel. This was enough for over ten hours' flying, the consumption of the engine being 4.5 gallons per hour and the average cruising speed 80 miles per hour.

Lindie Naughton's book *Lady Icarus: The Life of Irish Aviator Lady Mary Heath*, published in 2004 by Ashfield Press, Dublin, gives extensive coverage of Lady Heath's journey from Cape Town to Croydon. What follows is a summary in extract form of that journey, drawing also on Lady Heath's own account in *Woman and Flying*.

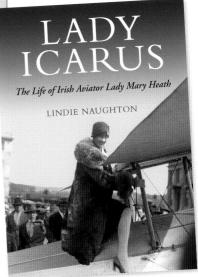

Lindie Naughton's biography of Lady Heath appeared in 2004.
COURTESY ASHFIELD PRESS, DUBLIN

On the morning of 25 February 1928, the overloaded turquoise-blue Avro Avian, G-EBUG, climbed unsteadily into the air from Roberts Heights, Pretoria, after taking 150 yards to lift off. For the 400-mile trip to Bulawayo, Lady Heath was carrying 42 gallons of fuel. She was exhilarated to be in the air and, after all the vicissitudes she had experienced, she reckoned that the first day out of Pretoria ranked second only to her first solo flight as the best adventure of her life. Six hours into her flight, she had passed the meandering Limpopo River and was soon flying over the great quartz hills of Matobo in Southern Rhodesia (now Zimbabwe).

She suddenly became aware of a pain in her head, neck and shoulders. She had suffered from sunstroke twice before and knew the symptoms. Even more ominously, in her more recent experience, she had passed out. The pain got worse and she started to see black blobs dancing in front of her eyes. Fortunately, she saw Fort Usher, Rhodesia, straight ahead. The last thing she remembered was aiming the plane north-east to some clear ground. When she recovered consciousness, she found herself under some thorn bushes, with three native girls 'in various stages of scanty undress, sitting back on their haunches and laughing at me'. She had been unconscious for about four hours and had come down just ten miles from her target of Bulawayo, where she was due at 2pm. Her disappearance had made front-page headlines in the South African press. She was taken to Bulawayo, where she rested for a few days.

On 28 February 1928, after recovering from her sunstroke, she went to Bulawayo Aerodrome. Soon she was airborne again, heading for Livingstone in Northern Rhodesia (now Zambia), the town nearest the mighty Victoria Falls. There was a dawn wake-up call on 1 March and, soon after, weighed down with 50 gallons of petrol, the Avian staggered into the air from Livingstone with the greatest of difficulty. Having it even worse were the Bentleys: 'I cannot speak too highly of Lieutenant Bentley's Moth, which with Mrs Bentley, two large suitcases, 30 gallons of petrol and spares took off in 200 yards,' wrote Lady Heath, who

was plainly exasperated with having to fly in convoy with a pair who were much slower.

The two aeroplanes flew towards Broken Hill (now Kabwe), Northern Rhodesia, in pleasant conditions. The railway proved a good navigational guide and the smoke from the zinc and lead mines guided them into the 'extraordinarily fine' aerodrome at Broken Hill. After five hours in the air, they touched down at exactly midday. Lady Heath landed safely despite the problems with her aeroplane's undercarriage, which had been damaged in her forced landing near Bulawayo. She quickly enlisted the help of an ex-Air Force mechanic at the local mine's workshops to make a new undercarriage with a bit of mild steel. The rain broke with a vengeance that afternoon, persuading both fliers to rest for two days. She continued to have mixed feelings about her decision to fly with the Bentleys, which 'took from the credit of a solo flight'. It would also slow her down considerably, since Dorys Bentley found flying in a small aeroplane with her new husband an arduous business and needed frequent rests.

From a rain-saturated boggy runway, the two small planes left Broken Hill on 4 March 1928 in light rain and headed northwards into what looked like more bad weather. After two and a half hours they reached Ndola, Northern Rhodesia. The next morning, Lady Heath was at the aerodrome early and had both machines prepared when the Bentleys arrived. Three hours of unpleasant flying in rainy weather over vicious-looking swamps followed. Fortunately, the visibility was good and they easily found their target town of Abercorn (now Mbala), on the southern tip of Lake Kampolombo. After a few days' rest, the two planes set off again and followed a straight road through the bush to Tabora, a railway-junction town in Tanganyika Territory, which she knew from her first visit to Africa. The three adventurers were airborne again by half past eight the following morning for Mwanza, where they took some time for rest and relaxation. This included a buffalo shoot on the other side of the vast Lake Victoria.

After six days' rest, the far less fit Dorys Bentley had practically recovered her strength. Lady Heath was just about managing to conceal her impatience. On 14 March, the two planes set off for Nairobi. Amongst those waving goodbye was a Signor Bonini, who insisted that Lady Heath visit Mussolini when she got to Italy, an offer she would remember later in her trip. Flying conditions were bumpy, with downdraughts a problem. Nairobi, Kenya, with its large aerodrome six miles south of the city, was a welcome sight. To their alarm, they saw a crashed aeroplane near the aerodrome. After they landed, they were told to their horror that it was the plane of Maia Carberry, 'our dear little friend who had so pluckily flown from Mombasa to Nairobi only two weeks before'.

Maia Carberry had met Sophie at Stag Lane a year earlier in August 1927, when she came to London with her husband, John, originally from Castle Freke in County Cork. Within a fortnight, Maia had passed flight, landing and altitude tests for her Aviator's Certificate and soon afterwards competed in her first international air race, attracting much media attention. After flying back to Nairobi in Kenya in January 1928, she set herself the target of becoming the first person to fly non-stop from Mombasa to Nairobi. This she did in just three and a half hours on 16 February 1928, bringing the first east-coast to highland mail with her.

On 12 March 1928, Carberry attended Kenya's first Air Fair, taking friends up for joy-rides. With a budding young aviator, Dudley Cowie, as passenger, the plane began circling to descend at 500 feet, when it appeared to lose speed. To the horror of those watching, it then spun out of control, before diving to earth with a sickening crash. The two occupants were killed instantly. Maia was just 24, her passenger 22. The Nairobi community was still in shock after the accident, Kenya's first flying tragedy. Two days later, a

Maia Carberry, aged 24 years, flew with Lady Heath in London in August 1927. Maia was killed in Nairobi on 12 March 1928, two days before Lady Heath arrived there. Maia is photographed with her daughter Juanita shortly before her fatal crash. Juanita was 2 years and 10 months old at the time of Maia's fatal crash.
Courtesy Juanita Carberry, *Child of Happy Valley* (1999)

deeply affected Lady Heath laid a wreath on Maia's grave and wrote a letter to *East Africa Standard* asking that an aerodrome be built at Mombasa and called after Maia Carberry. Instead, a hospital in Nairobi was named in her honour.

While she was in Nairobi, Lady Heath asked a local garage to remake the Avian's undercarriage and repair the petrol tank. She was annoyed to find that few of the telegrams she had sent, at considerable personal cost, to make the authorities aware of her whereabouts had been delivered and those that had got to their destination were mutilated and virtually unreadable. Lady Heath confessed that in Nairobi, she and her two travelling companions were so downhearted that they 'could have sat down and howled'. The lack of publicity for her adventure was undoubtedly one cause of her despondency, the enforced company of the Bentleys another.

On 22 March, the dispirited trio were off again. With the Avian heavily loaded, it took nearly 300 yards for the craft to become airborne, the longest run yet. Having negotiated around the 10,000-foot Kijabe escarpment she reached Kisumu, 270 miles distant on the north-east shore of Lake Victoria, ahead of Lieutenant Bentley, who had taken another route. Making the most of it, she stopped only to refuel before continuing on for another 200 miles, sticking to the northern shore of the lake until she reached Jinja. This meant that she had become the first woman pilot to fly over the equator, a feat she failed to mention in her book, but one that was widely publicised at the time by the world's press. The equator lies 90 miles north of Nairobi.

When Dick Bentley arrived at Jinja he got to work on his engine, while Lady Heath, having finished with her own engine and put in new gaskets, continued to

Lady Heath carried out daily maintenance on her Avian throughout her journey through Africa.
COURTESY FLIGHTGLOBAL ARCHIVES VIA RBI LIMITED

Entebbe, just south of the Ugandan capital, Kampala. There she spent a couple of days at Government House with Sir William Gowers, the Governor of Uganda and a renowned aviation enthusiast, whom she wished to consult about the next stage of her journey. At the time no woman was allowed to fly solo the 1,200 miles between Juba, just north of the border in the Sudan (now South Sudan), and Wadi Halfa, south of the Sudanese border with Egypt, without permission from the RAF Headquarters at Khartoum. To appease the RAF, Lady Heath proposed paying Lieutenant Bentley five pounds an hour to accompany her safely over the treacherous swamp. At last he was proving useful.

On 28 March 1928, they set off for Mongalla in the Sudan. With the River Nile as a guide, they had no navigational problems on the way to Malakal. Although it was now midday and she preferred to fly in the cool of the morning to spare her engine, Lady Heath decided to press on alone for Khartoum, continuing to follow the Nile. Clearly she had tolerated the Bentleys' company for long enough. Because of the extreme heat, she decided to land at Kosti and overnight there. Next morning she continued the 190-mile journey for two and a half hours, despite sandstorms, and reached Khartoum, where she decided to rest for a few days.

On 9 March 1928, Lady Bailey set off from Croydon in her DH.60 Moth, G-EBSF, in an attempt to fly to the Cape. This was four weeks after Lady Heath made the official announcement of her solo flight to London and predicted that a rival company would organise a flight around the same time as her own. On 1 April 1928, Lady Bailey arrived in Khartoum. That evening, a dinner was given in honour of those two Irishwomen, who could not have been more different.

The Sudanese government were unused to women doing much of anything on their own, let alone flying, and were still nervous of Lady Heath's plans. To appease them, she set off the next morning, in tandem with a Fairey service aeroplane, heading north for Wadi Halfa. She soon left the slower machine in her slipstream. Landing at Atbara a couple of hours later, she accepted an invitation to play tennis and stay the night. Airborne again the next morning, she took five hours to reach Wadi Halfa, following a railway line through the desert. On 4 April, Lady Heath made a marathon nine-hour trip all the way to Cairo, Egypt, about 700 miles away, using a page torn from an atlas as a very rough guide.

After her arrival at Cairo, she remarked that her engine was still running 'like a sewing machine' and better than when she had started out. This she attributed largely to her own diligence:

> I did the tappet clearances every day, no matter how short the flight was, and cleaned the petrol and oil filters. Only once did I fly in the heat of the day and I never flew at less than 7,000 feet to get the cool air. I ran my engine at 1,700 rpm [revolutions per minute] throughout and did one to three hours' routine work daily.

She had taken 38 days to fly from Pretoria to Cairo, a distance of 5,100 miles, flying on 16 of those days and spending just over 72 hours in the air:

> I had come safely through the heart of Africa and I felt my machine was a live entity and a very faithful one to have brought me so well and truly over mountain ranges and swamps, over forests and deserts, without ever faltering.

Like Lady Bailey before her, Lady Heath ran into difficulties in Cairo. She woke from a 15-hour sleep to find that the local authorities had impounded her aeroplane and locked it in a hangar at Heliopolis. The Egyptian authorities were concerned about allowing a lone female to cross the Mediterranean. They suggested she ask the RAF for assistance, but this request was refused as it would create a precedent. Not until Lady Heath wired Mussolini using the address, 'Mussolini, Italy', was the next stage of her flight assured. The following morning, she was delighted to receive a reply from Mussolini; he had put a seaplane at her disposal and she would meet up with the pilots in Tunisia. She was relieved to set off for the frontier port of Sollum (Sallum) on 15 April 1928, especially since, for the first time on her trip, she now had a set of decent maps, sent to her from London. Just over six hours later, she reached Sollum Aerodrome. Mussolini's assistance towards Lady Heath was not assured – two years previously, on 7 April 1926, another Irishwoman, Dublin-born Violet Gibson, suffering mental illness, had shot him in the face at point-blank range in Rome. The badly aimed shot just grazed his nose. Gibson was returned to England to spend the remainder of her life in a mental institution.

However, disaster struck the next morning as she attempted to take off from the boulder-strewn runway. Caught between two rocks, the rear part of the machine was pulled right off and trailed forlornly in the dirt. Lady Heath now needed to replace the entire rear quarter of the Avian. She obtained assistance from the Italian military fortress at Amseat. The incident delayed her by several days. Not until 23 April was she airborne again. As she headed towards the coast, what was a following wind turned into a strong headwind because of the Ghibli – a hot, dry, dust-bearing Sirocco wind

predominant in spring around Libya. Approaching Benghazi, she experienced her first north-African rain. A fever she had felt coming on at Sollum took full hold and she slept for the rest of the afternoon; the squadron's doctor found she had a temperature of 103 degrees.

As soon as she felt better she continued along the coast until she touched down in the Libyan capital of Tripoli on 25 April. There she expected to meet her seaplane escort, to which she had telegraphed from Sirte that she was on her way. However, at Tripoli she heard the disturbing news that the seaplane that had set out from Syracuse in Sicily had been less lucky than she had when it ran into the Ghibli – it had been forced down about 40 miles off the coast. Despite an extensive search, the seaplane was not found until the fifth day, fortunately with all its crew alive and well.

With Lieutenant Bentley also planning to cross the Mediterranean, Lady Heath reluctantly decided to meet up with him in Tunis and offer him the same fee she had paid him before for escort duties. She finally left Tripoli ten days later than planned. On her way past a nearby port, she saw the stricken seaplane being towed towards Tripoli by a destroyer. Using a succession of distinctive salt lakes and a road map to guide her, she

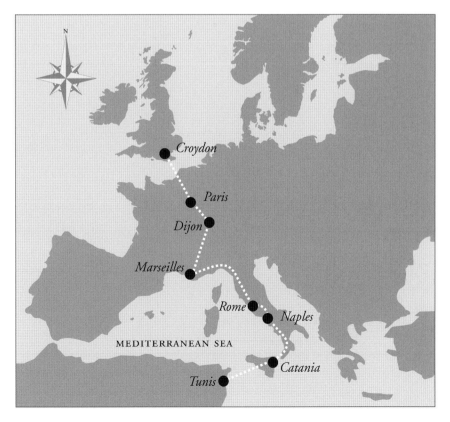

Lady Heath's flight from Catania, Sicily, to Croydon, London, from 6 to 17 May 1928.
MAP © ASHFIELD PRESS, DUBLIN

crossed over into the French territory of Tunisia on 5 May 1928. At Tunis she had to repair the undercarriage and main spar, which had been damaged on departure from Tripoli, when her left wheel had hit a pile of stones. One of the mechanics also discovered a bullet hole in one of the Avian's wings. The locals, it transpired, had a reputation for taking pot-shots at planes flying overhead, particularly if they were Italian. Lady Heath could only express relief that they had missed her petrol tank.

On Sunday, 6 May 1928, Lady Heath finally left Africa behind, flying again with the Bentleys across the Mediterranean from Cap Bon, near Tunis, to Sicily, a distance of 95 miles. As she crossed the Mediterranean she was able to see both Europe and Africa. Ahead Mount Etna pierced the clouds, making a perfect landmark on the way to the aerodrome at Catania on the east coast of Sicily. She landed in mid-morning, with the Bentleys arriving half an hour later. No sooner had they reached Sicily than Lady Heath sped on ahead, flying alone and enduring a bumpy ride as she headed over the Strait of Messina to Naples. After eight and a half hours' flying, as it grew dark, she approached Naples.

A tired and somewhat forlorn-looking Lady Heath arrived at Le Bourget Airport, Paris, on 16 May 1928.

COURTESY AGENCE DE PRESSE MEURISSE, PARIS VIA BIBLIOTHÈQUE NATIONALE DE FRANCE

On departure the next morning her overloaded machine just cleared the trees beside the runway at Naples and she followed the wind to Rome. There she stayed for a week, partly to convalesce from her rheumatic fever and partly because of the Italians' 'wonderful hospitality'. There was also the fact that General Balbo, head of the Italian Air Force, offered her a free overhaul of her engine, so that she could be certain of a 'a strong finish' to her adventure. While in Rome she was invited to meet Mussolini and she was, like many others of the time, enchanted by the dictator, describing him as 'that great man who is more of a national monument than an individual'.

London was now just a few days distant and, early on 14 May, she left Rome for Marseille. Following the coastline, she arrived there in the late afternoon. In Marseille, she met her friend and co-author of *Woman and Flying*, Stella Wolfe Murray. Next day, low clouds and driving rain hampered her progress during a four-hour flight as she flew northwards in her open-cockpit Avian along the Rhône Valley as far as Dijon. The next morning, 16 May, she departed for Paris.

Following a safe landing at Le Bourget Airport, she was an honoured guest at a party hosted by Clifford Harmon, President of the International League of Aviators. Le Bourget

THE VICTORIA FALLS
This picture of the Victoria Falls, seen from the cockpit of an aeroplane, gives an idea of the wonderful stability in the thin air of Africa.

WOMAN AND FLYING

By
LADY HEATH
AND
STELLA WOLFE MURRAY

ILLUSTRATED

London
John Long, Limited
34, 35 & 36 Paternoster Row
[All Rights Reserved]

was the Parisian airport that had welcomed Charles A. Lindbergh a year earlier, after his successful transatlantic solo flight, on 21 May 1927. After a good night's rest, Harmon drove Lady Heath from the Hôtel Claridge on the Champs-Élysées to Le Bourget, from where she set off on the last lap of her long journey. Flying over the English Channel in stormy conditions, she was blown northwards as far as the coastal town of Deal in Kent. This left her so annoyed and cold that she landed for a cup of tea at Lympne Aerodrome near Folkestone before continuing on to Croydon. There she prepared herself for meeting the public and the media.

By now, her arrival was eagerly anticipated and two circling aeroplanes greeted her in mid-air. When she finally landed, she was surrounded by a crowd of cheering supporters. It was 17 May 1928 and her long adventure was finally over. She had become the first woman to fly solo from South Africa to London. It was also the first solo flight from any of Britain's overseas

Above: *A relaxed and refreshed Lady Heath prepared to depart Le Bourget on the last leg of her journey to Croydon on 17 May 1928. She wore her trademark leopardskin coat with lion-fur collar. 'I shot 'em both when I was in Africa, ma deah!' she frequently remarked.*
Courtesy Agence de Presse Meurisse, Paris via Bibliothèque Nationale de France

Above left: *The book* Woman and Flying *was co-authored by Lady Heath and Stella Wolfe Murray and published in 1929. It gives a detailed first-hand account of Lady Heath's journey from Cape Town to Croydon.*
Courtesy Trinity College Library, Dublin via Philip Bedford

Lady Heath relished the adulation of the throngs of supporters that greeted her at Croydon Aerodrome on 17 May 1928. She made a point of dressing impeccably when she anticipated meeting the media and the public.

COURTESY RONNY VOGT

*Lady Heath stepped from her Avro Avian, G-EBUG, on
17 May 1928 to a rousing reception at Croydon Aerodrome
after becoming the first woman to fly solo from Cape Town to
London, a distance of approximately 10,000 miles.*
COURTESY ASHFIELD PRESS, DUBLIN

colonies to London. Greeting her as she stepped from her aeroplane was her husband, Sir James Heath, along with a throng of journalists and the Bentleys, who had arrived at Croydon on 12 May.

If Lady Heath had been able to fly direct between each airfield on her route from Cape Town to Croydon in south London, the distance would have been approximately 9,150 statute miles. However, she had taken several off-track diversions and she probably flew in the region of 10,000 statute miles. She had told her husband that the journey would take three weeks, but as it turned out she did not get back to England for three months. When Lady Heath realised a record attempt was out of the question, she was all too ready to be distracted along the way by parties in her honour and chances to play tennis or even hunt. Her feat was to make headline news in newspapers all over the world. Few reports, however, did justice to her achievements and her mechanical ability, preferring to report on her glamorous appearance.

On 23 May at the Mayfair Hotel in London, a luncheon in her honour was hosted by the Air League of the British Empire, in cooperation with the Royal Aeronautical Society, the Royal Aero Club and the Society of British Aircraft Constructors. Among those attending were some of the most prominent names in British aviation, including the Duke of Sutherland, Sir Sefton Brancker, Sir Charles Wakefield, Sir Edwin Alliott Verdon Roe and Thomas Sopwith.

Soon after her return, the Ladies' Committee of the Air League of the British Empire was formed, with Lady Heath elected its first Chairperson. Top female pilots including Lady Bailey, Sicele O'Brien, Winifred Spooner and the Duchess of Bedford, as well as wealthy and influential wives and daughters (one of whom was Lady Cobham, wife of Sir Alan), were also involved.

Everything seemed to be going Lady Heath's way until 18 June 1928, when Amelia Earhart became the first woman to cross the Atlantic aboard an aircraft. Earhart may not have piloted the aeroplane but her fearlessness in flying over an expanse of water far vaster than the Mediterranean effectively eclipsed the achievements of every other woman pilot, including Lady Heath.

A week later, on 24 June, Lady Heath organised a secret rendezvous at Croydon Aerodrome for Earhart. Here Earhart took a de Havilland Gipsy Moth for a short flight to Northolt with Captain A.H. White. Earhart also flew a few circuits in Lady Heath's Avro Avian, G-EBUG. On landing, she declared that she was so impressed by the Avian that she wanted to buy one and take it home so that she could fly it on a planned 12,000-mile lecture tour of the USA. Lady Heath immediately offered to sell Amelia her aircraft. The little Avian was subsequently dismantled, put into a crate and shipped to the USA. On the fuselage was inscribed, 'To Amelia Earhart from Mary Heath. Always think with your stick forward.'

The Avro Avian, G-EBUG, was cancelled from the UK civil-aircraft register on 29 June 1928 and transferred to the US register as NC7083. It was shipped from Liverpool on 7 July 1928. Earhart had little subsequent luck with the aeroplane. Attempting to fly from Rye in New York to California, she smashed the undercarriage and the left wing on landing at Pittsburgh. Subsequently, she had forced landings in Utah and later at Utica, New York, when the engine failed. A year later, on 30 July 1929, Earhart sold it.

The DH.60X Moth G-EBZC was registered to Lady Heath on 3 July 1928 and she used it extensively at home and abroad until she sailed to the USA on 2 November 1928.
Courtesy Richard T. Riding

It had a variety of owners and incidents until it was finally cancelled from the US civil-aircraft register on 11 August 1936. A similar aircraft was restored to flying condition by Golden Wings Museum, Minnesota, and re-registered as G-EBUG on 14 June 2001 in Jackson, Wyoming.

The impulsive sale of her Avian caused problems for Lady Heath. At the Blackpool Air Pageant organised by the Lancashire Aero Club on the weekend of 6 July 1928, she was disqualified from competing because she had not produced an aeroplane in time. She lodged a protest, which was dismissed. She had purchased a new DH.60X Moth, registered to Lady Sophie C.T. Mary Heath as G-EBZC on 3 July 1928, but it was not available for Blackpool. This was the seventh aircraft registered to Lady Heath since she had obtained her Aviator's Certificate two and a half years previously.

Four days later, she was back in the headlines when she took an 84-horsepower, all-metal, British light seaplane to a height of 13,400 feet, or nearly 3 miles above the earth's surface, after taking off from the Medway at Rochester in Kent. The seaplane, a Mussell 1, G-ECMJ, was built by Short Brothers at Rochester. Fitted with water rudders, it gave Britain the first world record in a new class created by the Fédération Aéronautique Internationale. With Sicele O'Brien as passenger, she took 1 hour 32 minutes to reach the record height.

Lady Heath made a brief appearance at Brooklands on 20 July for the 1928 annual King's Cup Race. She then flew her new de Havilland Moth, G-EBZC, to the Netherlands to attend the Waalhaven Aviation Festival organised by the Rotterdam Aero Club between 20 and 23 July. Sicele O'Brien also participated. Lady Heath won one of the competitions and was presented with her trophy by Albert Plesman, founder and Managing Director of Royal Dutch Airlines (KLM). She took the opportunity at the award ceremony to ask Plesman for a job as co-pilot on a KLM multi-engined aircraft. He agreed. After the Dutch Air Ministry granted her a commercial licence, allowing her to act as a second pilot, he employed her. She was the first female co-pilot in the world on a scheduled air service.

Her short relationship with KLM began on 27 July 1928. Four days after Albert Plesman agreed to employ her, she flew as co-pilot on a Fokker F.VIII, H-NAEI, from Amsterdam to Croydon with Captain J.B. Scholte. (Scholte was later to pioneer the first Irish airmail service from Baldonnel to Berlin on 22 October 1932.) This luxury airliner could accommodate 15 passengers. She spent the next few weeks delivering airmail and carrying passengers all over Europe, eventually accumulating 30 hours' experience.

Meanwhile, Ireland had gone aviation mad, particularly after Commandant (later Colonel) James Fitzmaurice's pioneering flight across the Atlantic on

Lady Heath, on the left, posing with her secretary beside her de Havilland Moth, G-EBZC, at the Waalhaven Aviation Festival, Rotterdam, on 20 July 1928.
COURTESY LINDIE NAUGHTON

Lady Heath with Albert Plesman (left), founder and Managing Director of KLM, and Frederick Koolhoven, a Dutch aircraft designer and constructor. After the prizegiving ceremony on 23 July 1928 at the Waalhaven Festival, she asked Plesman for a job as co-pilot with KLM.
COURTESY JAN WILLEM DE WIJN VIA EUGENE LEEMAN

Lady Heath accompanied Captain J.B. Scholte from Amsterdam to Croydon in multi-engined Fokker F.VII H-NAEI on 27 July 1928. The occasion was Lady Heath's first flight as co-pilot with KLM on a passenger air service.

Lady Heath (second from right), in her KLM uniform, standing in front of Fokker F.VIIa trimotor, H-NADZ. Charles Kingsford-Smith's Southern Cross *was a similar Fokker trimotor, as was the* Friendship, *in which Amelia Earhart crossed the Atlantic as a passenger on 18 June 1928.*

12 April 1928, while Lady Heath was still in Africa. In the aftermath of this historic flight the Irish Aero Club was reborn. They purchased Ireland's first civil aircraft, an Avro Avian, registered EI-AAA, on 5 October 1928. Lady Heath's sales promotional work for A.V. Roe the previous year had not been in vain.

On 22 August 1928, Lady Heath returned to Ireland for a fortnight's visit at the invitation of Oliver St John Gogarty, an Irish surgeon, poet, senator, author and aviation supporter. Flying her newly acquired Moth, G-EBZC, she travelled north from London, preferring to cross the short channel of water from Scotland to Northern Ireland than risk the 56 miles of sea between Holyhead and Dublin. Because of low cloud, she realised it would be impossible to get to the aerodrome at Baldonnel as planned. Instead, she landed on Dollymount Strand, just north of Dublin's city centre, and the next day she flew on to Baldonnel. On Monday, 27 August she visited her Aunt Cis in Ballybunion, County Kerry. She stayed a few days before heading north along the County Clare coast and landing in a flat open space at South Park, just south of Galway City. With an increasing stream of curious onlookers, an Garda Síochána requested she position her aircraft to Oranmore, an aerodrome constructed by the RAF in 1918. The following morning, she set off to meet her husband at Gogarty's home in Renvyle in

Connemara, County Galway. Flying over Clifden, she saw the place where Alcock and Brown had landed after their historic transatlantic flight just nine years earlier. She landed on a beach near Renvyle. The next day she landed on Tullabawn Strand, where she caused damage to her propeller. A replacement was despatched by de Havilland from Stag Lane, London, and she returned to Baldonnel when it was fitted.

Lady Heath returned to England and soon afterwards she was at Orly Airport, Paris, to take part in the Light 'Plane Meeting, which commenced on 10 September 1928. She won the Dismantling and Erecting Competition in a time of 2 minutes 13 seconds. She beat 8 male competitors in the Quality Tests to achieve the best score of 80 points. In the Climb and Take-off Test she finished in a credible third position by taking off in a distance of 125.35 yards and reached a target altitude of 5,000 feet in 10 minutes 40 seconds. The Efficiency Tests involved competitors flying 250 miles without landing or refuelling and marks were awarded for speed and economy of fuel consumption. In this competition she finished in fourth position as she opted for speed rather than economy. The final competition was the Reliability Trial, which lasted from 14 until 21 September 1928. This involved flying eight stages in a tour of France between 8am and 4pm on each of the eight days, covering a total distance of 1,345 miles. Lady Heath had to make a forced landing in a field near Caen due to a cracked carburettor and another on the beach at Trouville. She lost valuable points but overall, over the 12 days of competitive flying, was placed in fourth position and was the only female participant. The overall winner was Herr Lusser, a director of the Klemm aircraft factory in Germany.

KLM was planning to expand its services to the colonies in the Dutch East Indies capital of Batavia (now Jakarta, Indonesia). Initially four Fokker aircraft were to fly the route but, when a fifth was added, Lady Heath was asked if she would like to join as second pilot. She jumped at the chance but was well aware that her flying had been restricted to smaller machines, so she asked to fly as second pilot on other KLM routes for experience. She was due to set off for Batavia on 11 October 1928 but it was not to be. Some of the publicity she had received was extraordinarily negative and underlined the deep prejudices facing the pioneering women pilots of the time. KLM realised that, if there was an incident involving a KLM aircraft while she was at the controls, they would never live it down – and thus it was easier not to employ her. As was so often the case, Lady Heath was ahead of her time and failed to anticipate the opposition she faced. She held on to her KLM uniform, which she would wear with pride when she returned to Dublin in the 1930s.

Lady Heath (left) holding Robin the dog while on a visit to her Aunt Cis Peirce (seated left). Seated on the right is Rosie D'Arcy and standing on the right is Richbel Curling. They are photographed outside Rosie D'Arcy's cottage in Ballybunion on 27 August 1928.

Courtesy Langford family

For the altitude-record flight on 4 October 1928 from Croydon, Lady Heath wore heavy, warm clothes, as it was very cold in an open-cockpit aircraft. A naggin hip flask was a welcome companion in the cold at altitude.

A stylish and glamorous Lady Heath and an unknown companion shortly after her arrival in the United States of America in November 1928.

Courtesy Ashfield Press, Dublin

Knowing her plans to fly with KLM were scuppered, she accepted an invitation to go to the USA. Before she left she would make an attempt to regain the world altitude record. She persuaded the Aircraft Disposal Company to take her Moth, G-EBZC, in hand, lend her a Cirrus Mark III engine which had ten extra horsepower, and make some other adjustments to streamline the aircraft. The morning of 4 October 1928 dawned brightly and Lady Heath remarked that 'the gods who have always been so good to me in flying were better to me than usual'. She and Harold Perrin, Secretary of the Royal Aero Club, who was to be the official observer, then drove to Croydon, 'armed with many barographs'. There Captain Neville Stack, Test Pilot at the Aircraft Disposal Company, was waiting with some last-minute advice while she donned her furry boots and a thick coat. At 11.55am, she took off 'with nose pointed to heaven' and took just 8 minutes to climb to 10,000 feet and another 7 minutes to reach 16,000 feet. In her tiny craft, the altimeter stopped working at 19,000 feet: 'Beyond that, I just had to guess; I estimated that I had got beyond 23,000 feet when the climbing became a little slow.' So high was she by then in her open-cockpit aircraft that frost formed on her goggles. Now, at least five miles above the earth's surface, the engine of her small plane cut out. Keeping calm, she pointed the plane downwards and let it pick up speed; the engine duly fired, although it was spluttering from the cold. She suffered no physical after-effects from her time at high altitude. Both barographs were sent to the National Physical Laboratory, which confirmed a new record height of 24,700 feet.

Her feat had made the front pages of several American newspapers and, a few days later, the public announcement that she planned to visit the United States in November 1928 was greeted with great excitement in New York. Lady Heath sailed from Southampton on board the SS *Leviathan* on 2 November 1928. She had invited her husband to come with her but he had refused, for reasons that would become clear later on. Before departing for the USA, she sold her Moth, G-EBZC, to the London Aeroplane Club. On 12 February 1929, while she was in America, the last of her aircraft, the SE.5a, G-EBPA, was transferred to F.G. Miles. Its Certificate of Airworthiness had expired on 11 April 1928.

On the afternoon of her arrival in New York, she made her first flight in the United States, a 15-minute flip at Hadley Field in New Jersey, which was widely reported. With her customary canniness, she made it quite clear to the Irish-loving Americans that she was Irish, not English. While the main reason for her visit was the International Air Conference in Washington, she also had an appointment with President and Mrs Coolidge at the White House.

While Lady Heath was enjoying the attention in the United States, trouble was brewing for her in London, where she had left an unhappy husband. On 17 November 1928, a notice from Sir James appeared in a number of British newspapers, announcing that he would be taking the drastic action of repudiating her considerable debts:

I hereby give notice that I expressly withdraw all and every authority which my wife Lady Sophia Catherine Mary Heath may have at any time, either expressly or by implication or otherwise acquired to contract for me or in my name or as my agent or in any way pledge my credit and that she has been since the 11th day of October 1927 (the day of our marriage) and still is in receipt of sufficient allowance from me for the purpose of providing herself with all sustainable necessaries and that I will not be responsible for her debts, whensoever or howsoever incurred, dated this 15th day of November 1928.

There is little doubt that Lady Heath had a weakness for high fashion and not much taste for the conventions of marriage. Her first husband of two years had also found her spending and her independent habits equally difficult to control. Eliott-Lynn had complained that his wife, then with the excuse of youth, had seen husbands as little more than 'cash-cows'. Sir James seems to have experienced the same problem.

But the publication of the notice was, at best, tactless and Lady Heath was deeply hurt. In a statement from New York, she emphasised that she was financially independent and that there was no question of a separation:

Lady Heath at Rochester, New York, early in 1929.

COURTESY JOE DURNHERR, *TIMES UNION* NEWSPAPER, NEW YORK, VIA LANGFORD FAMILY

Sir James has seen fit to commit a breach of etiquette by making public a matter which should be private. I am therefore reluctantly constrained to reply publicly. My husband's attitude is probably due to the fact that he is not aware of the courtesy and consideration which prevail in American business circles and of which I have had such happy experiences during the past week. Immediately upon receipt of my husband's action this morning, I deposited $1,000 (£200) with each house with which I am transacting business. This is a guarantee of good faith.

This was a carefully coded message to her new American friends concerning her solvency. Nowhere does she admit any responsibility for the problem: that she had left her husband to settle her financial affairs when already forbidden to pledge his credit. Although she had often consulted him about her flying plans before they married, all that had ceased once he became her husband.

For any ambitious aviator, the United States was the place to be during the 1920s. It was an exhilarating period for the air-minded. Anyone could attempt to fly at the start of the twentieth century, as Amelia Earhart pointed out in her 1932 book, *The Fun of It*: 'it wasn't really necessary to have any licence at this period. There were no regulations such as exist today. People just flew, when and if they could.' By the time Lady Heath arrived in the United States in November 1928, she was a vastly experienced pilot with more than 1,500 solo hours achieved in three years.

As a delegate of the British Empire Air League, she attended the International Air Conference on Civil Aviation in Washington on 9 December. As the only woman delegate at the conference, which she followed with a countrywide lecture tour, she hoped to interest American women in flying.

On 29 January 1929, she took an oath for American citizenship; after five years she would be able to apply for final papers. Her address was 112 Central Park South, New York. Under American aviation laws she was not licensed to fly in the United States. In early February 1929, she failed an examination because of her lack of local knowledge. She immediately applied for a re-examination, in which she was successful, at Curtiss Field, Long Island, New York. While she was at it, she passed a test qualifying as an aeroplane mechanic. She was the first woman to do so in the United States.

In September 1927, Elinor Smith, then aged 16, became the youngest US-government-licensed pilot on record. Her licence was signed by Orville Wright. She was the first pilot to fly under all four New York East River bridges and earned worldwide fame for endurance, altitude and speed records. In early 1929, a great friendship developed between the 17-year-old Elinor Smith and the 32-year-old Mary Heath.

The pair flew cross-country several times, always in separate aeroplanes. Lady Heath also supported her young friend in her battles with George Putnam, whose machinations promoting the career of Amelia Earhart were making it difficult for any other women pilots to earn a living in the United States. Smith, like many other Americans, considered Lady Heath to be a member of the British nobility, largely because of her accent: it never occurred to her that Lady Heath was not at least as well-born as her titled husband. The young Elinor noted with admiration Lady Heath's ability to court publicity; for much of 1929, no newsworthy aviation story in the United States was complete without either a quote from or a picture of the 'British Lady Lindy'.

Smith felt that Lady Heath tacitly accepted the risks every pilot took and suspected that this outwardly self-assured woman might have been superstitious: 'A large pair of wings was always in evidence, either on her attire or even in her handbag, but she would never tell me whose they were or why they were always with her.' These were possibly the wings she had received during her brief period with KLM, when she had come so

Lady Heath befriended Elinor Smith (pictured here)
after arriving in the USA.
Courtesy Cradle of Aviation Museum, New York

Lady Heath was employed by American Cirrus Engines Incorporated to demonstrate and sell Cirrus engines in early 1929, something she was very successful at.
COURTESY DE HAVILLAND MOTH CLUB ARCHIVE

Her role with Cirrus expanded after Bill Lancaster was involved in a disastrous accident in March 1929.

Lady Heath was not long in America before she began to submit articles to aviation publications. She was appointed Contributing Editor to the newly founded United States magazine *Flying Stories*. The May 1929 edition featured a ten-page article entitled 'Thrills I have Had in the Air' by Lady Heath. The article related her first attempt at obtaining her 'A' Certificate on her maiden flight test back in London, England, on 30 October 1925. After climbing to 6,000 feet the cloud below thickened and she lost sight of the ground. In a spinning descent she broke cloud cover a few hundred feet above the ground but lost the airfield. Suddenly her engine lost power and she was forced to land.

tantalisingly close to becoming permanently employed as the world's first female commercial pilot.

British record-breaking pilot Bill Lancaster was employed with American Cirrus Engines Incorporated as Chief Test and Demonstration Pilot, demonstrating their engines in various Avian aircraft. He persuaded the company to employ Lady Heath too as Demonstration Pilot. His salary began at $500 a month and was soon raised to $800; Lady Heath was paid about the same and did well financially from her first few months in the United States, using her title to good effect. Elinor Smith remarked on Lady Heath's ability to make money, a gift that had not struck many of her earlier acquaintances. According to Smith, she 'pyramided' her funds and dabbled in British and Canadian aircraft stocks. Wherever she stayed, she looked for a suite with a telephone in the bathroom: 'One must be in touch with one's broker at all times, m'deah!' By now she had begun a 3,000-mile tour of the continent, selling Cirrus engines and acting as her own mechanic. Her job as Aeronautical Advisor to American Cirrus Engines involved making test flights of American light aeroplanes, as well as selling engines to manufacturing companies. She was to claim that she flew 3,000 miles and sold 100 Cirrus Mark III engines, earning £10,000 in salary and sales commission during those six months.

Lady Heath continued to demonstrate and sell Cirrus aircraft engines for American Cirrus Engines Incorporated for several months in mid-1929.
COURTESY FLIGHTGLOBAL ARCHIVES VIA RBI LIMITED

She solved the problem with a crinkly hairpin, but the field was too small for a take-off run, so she revved up the engine and 'hopped' over a fence into a larger field to take off. This was her first unauthorised solo cross-country flight. As darkness was looming, she found another field to land in and stayed the night there. She was 18 miles from the flying field. She had to make another attempt for her 'A' Certificate and was successful on 4 November 1925 at Stag Lane Aerodrome.

This autobiographical article also related her attempts and frustrations at trying to earn a 'B' Commercial Pilot's Certificate, as she was the first woman in Britain to achieve such certification. She stated:

> I hoped to prove that a healthy woman properly trained is as reliable in the air as a man. I was determined to open the doors of civil aviation to women. It was a bumpy course I set for myself.

Another obstacle she encountered was the ability to obtain insurance as a female commercial pilot. She was eventually granted cover for a three-month probationary period. Lady Heath described an incident on the final day of the insurance trial period when she attempted a take-off on a wet grass field and the aircraft flipped over and left her suspended by her safety harness.

She also recalled the period when she instructed Lady Bailey, whose husband disapproved of her flying:

> Each morning I used to call for her dressed in white and carrying a tennis racket. Lady

Lady Heath (left) and Elizabeth McQueen, founder and President of the Women's International Association of Aeronautics.
COURTESY ASHFIELD PRESS, DUBLIN

Bailey decided not to tell them about her higher aims until she knew how to pilot a ship.

The article continued, recounting several mishaps she encountered during her first three and a half years' flying – incidents where she injured herself by hand-swinging the propeller and caused damage to aircraft.

In a subsequent article in *Flying Stories*, Lady Heath related details of her African flight along with other aerial adventures.

In late May of 1929 came news of the first ever Women's Air Derby, due to coincide with the annual National Air Races, the largest aviation event in the United States, in August. Starting from Clover Field, Santa Monica, California, on 18 August and touching down in 15 cities along the way, it would arrive in Cleveland in time for the opening of the National Air Races 8 days later. In April, Lady Heath wrote an enthusiastic letter to Elizabeth McQueen of the Women's International Association of Aeronautics from her New York address, signalling her intention to enter the Women's Air Derby. When McQueen wrote back, she invited Lady Heath to become President of the association. The hype surrounding the first Women's Air Derby continued. After her earlier doubts regarding the restrictions on the entrants, Lady Heath was now a committed supporter of the Women's Air Derby.

At the time, Lady Heath was working on the Redpath Chautauqua lecture circuit in the upper New York State area. Her Chautauqua work would take her to a different town every evening for 11 weeks. She was using a Great Lakes Trainer with a Cirrus Mark III engine to get herself and her 200 pounds of luggage around. She did her own mechanical work and used filling-station gasoline to keep herself airborne. Articles presenting her views continued to appear in numerous American newspapers and magazines. Lady Heath was described by one reporter like this:

> Lady Heath speaks in an unusually soft, well-modulated tone. Her appeal is distinctly feminine, pleasingly in contrast with the newspaper impression she may have created with many because of her amazing prowess in the sports arena. She is the ideal prototype

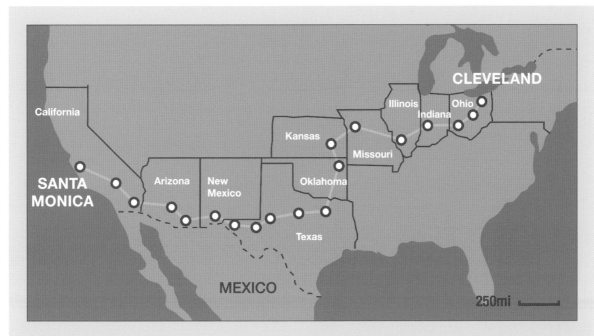

The planned course for the first 1929 Women's Air Derby from California to Cleveland. Lady Heath eventually withdrew her application as her aircraft was not suitable for the race.

MAP © MARTIN GAFFNEY

of the modern woman who plays outdoor games, who rides, flies, swims; who does a man's mental or physical labour, perhaps, but who outwardly at least, sacrifices nothing in the way of loveliness or personal charm.

But Lady Heath, charmer of journalists and brilliant manipulator of the media though she was, had met her equal in the publisher George Putnam, who was ruthlessly sweeping aside all threats to Amelia Earhart's position as the female face of American aviation. When Lady Heath had arrived in New York, Earhart had gathered as many women pilots as possible to honour the woman who had been so kind to her just a few months earlier in London. However,

Putnam increased his pressure and determination to see Amelia firmly established as the top woman pilot of the day. Lady Heath's friendship with Earhart quickly cooled. Although Lady Heath had filed an entry for the Women's Air Derby, in the end she opted out because her own aeroplane was too light and too slow and she failed to find anyone prepared to sponsor

Lady Heath posed beside her Great Lakes Trainer aircraft prior to taking off on her fateful flight at Cleveland on 29 August 1929.
COURTESY INTERNATIONAL WOMEN'S AIR AND SPACE MUSEUM,
CLEVELAND, OHIO

her in something faster: 'Her "superior" attitude didn't always sit well with many people which was really too bad,' said Elinor Smith, also left without an aeroplane. George Putnam's all-pervading influence could not be discounted, though he did not manage to prevent the country's top two female air-racing pilots, Louise Thaden and Phoebe Omlie, from entering a race he desperately wanted Amelia Earhart to win. In the event, Louise Thaden crossed the finish line first. Putnam later married Earhart, on 7 February 1931.

On 13 August 1929, just before she headed for Cleveland, Lady Heath damaged the strut of her de Havilland Moth while landing at Billings Field near the Canadian border at Ogdensburg, after flying in from Thousand Island Park nearby. She had escaped injury but, because the strut had cracked, the fabric was torn and she was forced to stay until the aeroplane was repaired.

In all, there were 35 closed-course races scheduled for the 1929 National Air Races at Cleveland, Ohio, including five for women only. Over 80,000 citizens watched, enthralled. Lady Heath entered the first Women's Race on Tuesday, 27 August 1929. Her skilled cornering won acclaim from newspaper commentators and it seemed she had won the race easily but, when the figures were added up, it turned out that Phoebe Omlie, in a Monocoupe, had put in an average speed of 111.63 miles per hour, compared to Lady Heath's 95.7 miles per hour in a Great Lakes Trainer. Lady Heath was still employed by American Cirrus Engines and was demonstrating a Cirrus engine in the aircraft she used for the air racing. In a 50-mile race on 27 August, Phoebe Omlie was disqualifed when a judge said she had failed to fly around one of the pylons. Lady Heath claimed she saw Phoebe Omlie correctly pass the pylon – and thus forfeited the race. Lady Heath was placed second with a time of 31 minutes 11 seconds. She later admitted that she had not seen Phoebe pass the pylon; in fact, she had given up victory in order to remain popular with the other (American) female pilots.

On Thursday, 29 August, the fifth day of the air races, Lady Heath, aged 32 years, dominated the headlines, but certainly not in the way she would have wished. At the worst possible moment, her luck finally ran out. According to the *Cleveland Plain Dealer* newspaper:

Lady Mary Heath, Ireland's premier woman flyer and one of the world's greatest woman pilots, was near death at the Emergency Clinic Hospital, 928E 152nd Street from injuries suffered when her plane crashed through the roof of the Mills Company's factory at 965 Wayside road this afternoon.

The plane, a Cirrus-engined Great Lakes Trainer, was manufactured by the Great Lakes Aircraft Corporation of Cleveland. Early that Thursday morning, Lady Heath went to the airfield of the Great Lakes aircraft factory and made two flights before bringing Erwin Kirk, a 28-year-old mechanic, with her on a third flight. After he climbed into the back seat, she took off from the short runway beside the Mills sheet-metal factory to fly to Cleveland Airport to take part in the 60-mile race for women pilots. She was also scheduled to take part in the Dead-Stick Landing Contest for Women that afternoon. She may have been practising an engine-off, dead-stick landing, since at about 100 feet she attempted one of her trademark vertical side-slips before the aeroplane went into a nosedive, accidently making contact with a chimney guy wire. Although she struggled frantically with the controls, the aeroplane failed to straighten and crashed

Point of impact with factory roof

Lady Heath's Great Lakes Trainer aircraft nosedived and crashed into the roof of the Mills factory near the Great Lakes factory airfield.
Courtesy *Cleveland Plain Dealer* Archive via
Bill Meixner

into the Mills factory roof. Its wings were completely sheared off when it burst through the heavy roof timbers.

Unconscious when taken from the aeroplane, Lady Heath was rushed to the Emergency Clinic Hospital in Cleveland. She was not expected to live. At the hospital, Dr A.R. Miller said that an X-ray examination disclosed two fractures of the skull, a broken nose, a fractured jaw and other injuries. Her passenger lost a finger and broke his ankle but sustained no more serious injuries.

Just a day after the crash, on 30 August, Lady Heath regained consciousness. For the first couple of days, chances of saving her life appeared slim. A three-hour operation was required to remove a portion of the jawbone that had been forced upwards against her brain. There was a risk of spinal meningitis and a fear that she would lose her eyesight. 'She withstood the operation well and is taking a liquid diet with apparent relish,' said the surgeon, Dr Elliott C. Cutler, in one bulletin. 'Sleeps most of the time, but responds when aroused and answers questions with yes or no,' he added. Her temperature was now 100 degrees, her pulse 108 and her respiration 36. Sir James Heath, when asked if he intended to travel to America, replied, 'There is nothing I can do!' She slipped in and out of consciousness for the next day or so, but was soon out

The crumpled wreckage of Lady Heath's aircraft was removed by trailer from the Mills factory, Cleveland.

COURTESY LAMMOT DU PONT JUNIOR VIA HAGLEY DIGITAL ARCHIVES

of danger, though still very ill. Doctors doubted that she would ever fly again.

Later in September 1929, a frantically worried Aunt Cis in Ballybunion received a letter from Dr Cutler reporting on Lady Heath's condition:

> She has made an excellent recovery. Everything is now healed and she gets out of bed today or tomorrow. Her damage is purely in the frontal lobe where she lost a considerable amount of brain. She sustained a compound, comminuted fracture of her skull and completely sheared off the face and both superior maxillae from the base of the skull. Everything is now healed back.

However, he baldly warned of possible side effects:

> The only disability which might remain would be some loss of her intellectual capacity such as disposition, will power or qualities of one's psyche.

On 10 October, Lady Heath was photographed outside the Lakeside Hospital in a fur coat, along with a pilot's cap and glasses, something she normally never wore when photographers were about. The outlandish garb only exaggerated her self-consciousness and distress at her scarred appearance. She had been told that it would be six months before she could take any active exercise. A muscle in one eye was permanently damaged and not even plastic surgery could correct it.

A few weeks later, on 29 October, her chances of ever again earning a good living in the United States took a further battering when Wall Street crashed, with devastating repercussions for the world economy.

Since her marriage of two years to Sir James Heath had now irretrievably broken down, money was again, as so often in her life, a primary concern for Lady Heath. At the end of October 1929, she was recognised by reporters in Reno, Nevada. She had taken out a three-month lease on an apartment, but she refused to respond to her name when approached and would not confirm that she was there to petition for divorce under Nevada state laws, which required a residential qualification of just three months.

Lady Heath (left) and her private nurse, Florence Madden, outside Lakeside Hospital, Cleveland, Ohio, on 10 October 1929.
COURTESY LANGFORD FAMILY

With terrible timing, the case of *Christobel Russell* v. *Sir James and Lady Heath* – in which a Curzon Street dressmaker was suing the couple over an unpaid debt – was heard in London's High Court, King's Division, before Mr Justice Talbot in late November 1929. When she had been contacted about the forthcoming case, Lady Heath had allegedly replied, 'Don't sue me. Sue my husband. He is liable.' She was not represented in court. Evidence was given in court and later published, giving detailed accounts of both the financial and personal relationships between Sir James and Lady Heath. The story made all the daily newspapers, and it was widely alleged that Lady Heath had resolved to spend as much of Sir James's money as she could before clearing off to the USA, declaring, 'I'll sting the old swine!' When telephoned in Reno about the sensational revelations made in court, she is reported to have fainted with shock.

Judgement was given against Lady Heath for £239 8s, plus costs. Mr Justice Talbot said that the case turned solely on questions of fact. On whether Sir James had authorised his wife to buy the goods claimed for on his credit, he was of the opinion that he had not. Already desperately trying to come to terms with the after-effects of her accident, Lady Heath was deeply affected by the case and was uncharacteristically muted in her response.

Following a gathering after the Women's Air Derby, invitations to a meeting on 2 November at Curtiss Field, Long Island, New York, were sent to 117 licensed women pilots and about 26 turned up. Eventually, 99 enrolled in the group of women aviators that was to use this number as its name. Among the original Ninety-Nines was Lady Heath, with Pilot's Licence number 5333.

In January 1930, Lady Heath filed for divorce in Reno's District Court, charging extreme cruelty. In her complaint, she cited the difference in age, her husband being 75 and she 30 when they married. Her husband, though extremely wealthy, was penurious and found fault with her expenditures. Lady Heath went to Boston for facial surgery in early 1930. She was visited by Elinor Smith, who later remarked, 'One of her eyes was not focusing and it was obvious that her cheekbone had been shattered.' Two months later, in March, it was announced that Lady Heath would receive her divorce a few days later. Sir James had accepted service of the divorce notice through the American consul in London, with the answer filed though a Reno attorney.

Lady Heath's life took several bizarre twists as she attempted to come to terms with her dreadful accident and its consequences. In March 1930, she received $3,000 from the Workmen's Compensation Bureau, Jersey City, in compensation for her accident. Since she had been working for the Cirrus Aircraft Company, based in New Jersey, at the time of the accident, she had been entitled to petition the bureau. Cirrus agreed to pay $350 in legal fees and $500 towards medical expenses. Later that year, in July, she was back in Cleveland and alleged to be mentally incompetent in an application by her nurse and companion, Florence Madden, to be appointed her guardian. The application revealed that Lady Heath had entered the Delhurst Sanatorium at Mentor, near Cleveland, a few days earlier for treatment. She was no longer able to look after herself and her only means consisted of a trust fund from which she received an annual income of $3,500.

In March 1931, she was back at Curtiss Field, New York, and took her first flight since her accident. By now, she had logged 2,447 hours and flown 67 different aircraft, including the Fokker and Ford trimotors. Her Commercial Pilot's Licence had lapsed but, rather than retake the rigorous exams, she opted to apply for a Private Pilot's Licence. She duly passed her written and flight exams. About a week later, also at Curtiss Field, Reginald 'Jack' Williams, secretary to Lady Heath, made his first solo flight after little more than an hour of dual instruction. Williams, in a Curtiss Fledgling, flew for eleven minutes and made three perfect landings, said Instructor John Trunk. He had taken only two lessons, one a week before and one earlier that same day.

George Anthony Reginald Williams had been born on 15 October 1900 to a wealthy family on the Caribbean island of St Lucia. A small, handsome man, he was usually called either Reggie or Jack. At the time of his first solo, he was already secretly engaged to Lady Heath and would become her third husband. He was four years her junior. They had met at a horse show, she would tell young admirers at Kildonan Aerodrome, north of Finglas, Dublin, a few years later. Williams was a keen horseman and, while competing in a showjumping competition, his horse had been startled by the movements of a woman in a red dress. After losing the top prize, he had made his way in a fury towards the woman who had spoiled his chances. It was Lady Heath.

In April 1931 Lady Heath was back in trouble again when she failed to appear in a magistrate's court in Windsor, Ontario, to face trial on a charge of drunkenness, which sadly was to become the first of many in the years to come. Two policemen had come across a traffic jam at a busy junction, caused by a car blocking the road. In the car, they had found Lady Heath, intoxicated and quarrelling loudly with her secretary, Jack Williams. Both were arrested.

After her Reno divorce, Lady Heath became Mrs G.A.R. Williams on 12 November 1931 in Lexington, Kentucky, but not without difficulty. Sir James Heath had vigorously contested her divorce through the London courts and refused to accept the Reno decision. Their honeymoon was in Mexico City, where Lady Heath became the second woman to be granted a Mexican Private Pilot's Licence. Whether she loved her new husband was open to question. Elinor Smith certainly thought not:

> I'm not sure at all she ever knew what real love was all about. I think her feelings for this man were based on his promises to take care of her. He had already been there for her when her drinking got out of hand.

Lady Heath was delighted to accept congratulations from the US Aeronautical Examiner on 6 April 1931 on having her Pilot's Licence revalidated. This flight test was 19 months after her near-fatal crash at Cleveland, Ohio.
COURTESY BRITISH PATHÉ

Certainly, she was never to take his name, remaining 'Lady Heath' to the end of her short life, despite many protestations that a title meant nothing to her.

With her reputation still intact in the United States, an article she had written entitled 'Why I Believe Women Pilots Can't Fly the Atlantic' appeared in *Liberty* magazine on 21 May 1932. She outlined her reasons and the dangers she perceived. She concluded her article: 'Of the seven women who had attempted an Atlantic crossing, only one had made it and she did no piloting.' Lady Heath was sadly unaware of that particular woman's plans and, with catastrophic timing, her article was printed on the very day Amelia Earhart set off on her historic flight across the Atlantic. Less than 15 hours later, Amelia landed in a County Derry field and, almost instantly, became a twentieth-century icon. Because of her almost pathological fear of flying over water, Lady Heath had got it badly wrong.

In July 1932 in London, Sir James Heath was granted a decree nisi to divorce his wife on the grounds of her adultery with Jack Williams. No defence was offered. By then in his eighties, Sir James took a fourth wife in 1935. She was Dorothy Mary Hodgson, a scientist from Hampshire, and when they married there

Amy Johnson (second from left) on Portmarnock Strand, Dublin, on Thursday, 18 August 1932 for the departure of Jim Mollison, Amy's husband of three weeks, on his solo transatlantic flight to New Brunswick, Canada. On the left is Lady Heath. With her arm around Amy's shoulder is her sister Molly.
Courtesy Independent Newspapers

was a congratulatory telegram 'from the first Mary to the second'. Sir James was to outlive the first Mary, dying on 24 December 1942, just over a month short of his ninety-first birthday.

After her dreadful accident, Lady Heath had decided to leave the United States, where, with aviation in a slump because of the Great Depression, she could no longer earn a living. Somewhat surprisingly, she opted to return, not to Britain, where she had made her name, but to the calmer backwaters of her native Ireland. By then Ireland had a well-founded reputation as a launching pad for some of the great aviation adventures of the early twentieth century and the country's citizens had made a notable contribution to flying. Lady Heath returned to Ireland in the summer of 1932 and, in mid-August, was at Portmarnock Strand, Dublin, when Jim Mollison set off for the United States in a de Havilland 80A Puss Moth, *The Heart's Content*. Though dressed smartly, she looked heavier than in the past and a hat was pulled down over her eyes. She accompanied Mollison's new wife, Amy Johnson.

On 21 September 1932, Lady Heath went through a second marriage ceremony with Jack Williams at the registry office in Tralee, County Kerry, with their address given as care of Miss Peirce, Ballybunion. On the wedding certificate he is described as a 32-year-old bachelor, a pilot by profession, and son of the Honourable George Williams, retired. She, Sophia Mary Heath (otherwise Peirce Evans), a 34-year-old *divorcée*, gave no profession. She had pared a year off her age – in September 1932 she was just over a month off 36. Aunt Cis was one of the witnesses to the wedding, as was Kate Flynn, her maid. The Registrar, William H. Giles, performed the brief ceremony. Afterwards, the pair settled in Dublin.

On 26 January 1933, a new DH.60G Gipsy Moth, G-ACBU, was registered in the name of Lady Heath's husband, G.A.R. Williams. She made several journeys to England, trying to renew her British Aviator's 'B' (Commercial) Certificate. She had also undergone a medical examination in Dublin the previous autumn. In her application, from a London address, she stated that she had flown about 70 hours over the past two years, approximately 50 of them since April 1931. In the previous 6 months, she had flown about 15 hours. She held Irish, American and Mexican Private Pilot's

Licences. She underwent a medical examination by the UK Civil Aviation Authority on 15 March 1933 and was found to be 'temporarily unfit'. At this time she stated:

> I am assistant manager to Iona National Airways Ltd and am their only 'B' licensed pilot. I have a great deal of instruction, joy-riding, and charter work to do and am kept pretty busy.

She was given an opportunity to resit the UK medical examination in July 1933 but she deferred this.

Lady Heath had returned to Ireland at a time when civil aviation was in its infancy. Before Iona National Airways was founded in September 1930,

only three private aircraft carried Irish registration marks, no commercial airline existed and the few aircraft operated by the Irish Army Air Corps were rarely seen by the local population. In Ireland, the only active aerodrome was at Baldonnel, an old RAF base to the west of Dublin, evacuated in February 1922 and left almost derelict for the fledgling Irish army that took over. Inadequate though it was and plagued with grazing sheep, Baldonnel continued to play a pivotal role in Irish aviation for the next decade, since all aircraft coming into the country had to land there to clear customs.

Learning to fly was not prohibitively expensive for Irish Aero Club members. Annual membership cost £5, with instruction 30 shillings an hour and a solo trip 5 shillings. With an average of 15 flying hours required, a club member could acquire a licence for little more than £20.

An enthusiastic member of the Irish Aero Club was Hugh Cahill, owner of the Iona Engineering garage

With her popularity in Ireland as great as ever, Lady Heath signed autographs for supporters and well-wishers in Rattery's Field, Ballybunion, County Kerry.

Kildonan Aerodrome, north Dublin, during the period when it was managed by Lady Heath.
COURTESY PEARSE CAHILL

Lady Heath, proudly wearing her KLM uniform, demonstrating the aircraft controls and instruments to enthusiastic boys at Kildonan in 1933. Note the sparsity of cockpit flight instruments.
COURTESY PEARSE CAHILL

at Cross Guns Bridge in Dublin. In June 1931, he based Ireland's first commercial airline, Iona National Airways, at an aerodrome at Kildonan, north of Finglas in County Dublin. By June 1932, the site was approved for use by civil and commercial aircraft and became Ireland's first commercial aerodrome. No longer would all aircraft coming into Ireland have to land at Baldonnel.

In the spring of 1933, Hugh Cahill approached Lady Heath to join Iona National Airways as Instructor. Lady Heath was already disenchanted with her treatment at Baldonnel, where she had hangared the de Havilland Moth G-ACBU. She had brought her aircraft over from England to Baldonnel and, despite her international reputation, she had been charged for routine maintenance of her aeroplane. There was plenty of interest in the National Irish Junior Aviation Club she founded, with hundreds of flying-mad local young adults attending lectures and practical demonstrations on the art of flying. Modelled on similar organisations in the USA, it was the first such club for youngsters in Europe and proved an enduring success, thanks to Lady Heath's immense organisational skills. Among the original Vice-Presidents were Sir Alan Cobham, Jim Mollison and Amy Johnson, even though

Johnson was always cool with Lady Heath, whom she felt had denigrated her friend Lady Bailey's African flight in her book *Woman and Flying*.

Chris Bruton was a prominent member and later Secretary of the National Irish Junior Aviation Club. In this role, he would meet Lady Heath perhaps once a week. He remembered her as a large but graceful woman with a prominent English accent. In her ability to organise and marshal those around her, she was exceptional, said Bruton:

> Her personal life was not at all organised. She was very mercurial and unreliable. I think a lot of her problems were due not so much to the drink as the unstable life she led – a bit like theatrical people. They're in bed during the day and working when other people want entertainment, so they don't mix with normal people. Even when she was here, you didn't know if you had her. It was a life with no normal keel to it.

In May 1933, Lady Heath was one of a number of people elected as Vice-Presidents of the inaugural committee of the National Aero Club, set up for pupils of the Iona Flying School. The prominent aviator and socialite Lady Nelson was elected Chair and President. A few weeks later, on Whit Monday, 5 June 1933, Lady Heath took part in an air race as part of the Air Pageant organised by Iona at Kildonan, which included Irish Air Corps personnel for the first time. Four other pilots lined up with her for the Irish Cup race, which was won by C.F. French, Assistant Instructor of the Irish Aero Club, who finished just ahead of his boss, William Elliott. Lady Heath was fifth and last, underlining the loss of her considerable skills as a racing pilot.

While she settled into Dublin life, taking a basement flat at Fitzwilliam Street and later at Pembroke Road, Lady Heath attempted to revive her social life in the city she had so enjoyed as a schoolgirl and student. In 1934, she and her husband were admitted as members to the Arts Club, where her old neighbour from Newcastle West, the artist Dermod O'Brien, still played a pivotal role.

The Irish Free State had a begrudging attitude towards civil aviation and refused to subsidise flying clubs like the British government had done. The Irish government believed that flying clubs could become a security risk and felt flying should be confined to the defence forces. These were the reasons behind Hugh Cahill's decision to close Iona down in November 1933. Not even the establishment-friendly Irish Aero Club could persuade it otherwise, although key members of the Irish Air Corps, particularly Charles Russell, were arguing strenuously for the formation of a national aviation company. They would eventually get their way but, in the meantime, private enterprises struggled on.

In February 1934, Lady Heath was declared unfit to fly by the British Air Ministry because of her 'below standard' sight and her history of 'morbid mental trouble' since the American accident. She was told emphatically never again to apply for a UK 'B' Certificate. She wrote another pleading letter to Colonel Shelmerdine, Director of Civil Aviation in the UK:

A signed portrait of Lady Heath given to Chris Bruton.

Courtesy Chris Bruton via Ashfield Press, Dublin

Lady Heath and her third husband, Jack Williams, relaxing at Kildonan beside her de Havilland Moth, G-ACBU, named The Silver Lining.
COURTESY CHRIS BRUTON
VIA BRENDAN BRUTON

As I have been failed twice, and never having passed the examination better than the last time I took it last year, I am reluctantly obliged to consider that there must be some personal animosity in the matter.

Colonel Shelmerdine's reply must have come as a crushing blow:

The result of my enquiries indicate without doubt that as you are well below the ICAO [International Civil Aviation Organisation] standards of eyesight, you are permanently unfit for the grant of either an 'A' or a 'B' licence.

It was clear that, at 37 years of age, Lady Heath's flying career was over. Her alcoholism and other personal problems had made her something of an embarrassment. Even the National Irish Junior Aviation Club she had founded neglected to keep her informed of meetings and developments. The Irish Air Corps, which still had considerable influence over local aviation matters, wished to have nothing to do with the maverick Lady Heath. An alternative view is that Lady Heath was by now incapable of taking on any position of responsibility.

With Iona gone, Everson Flying Services, a short-lived company formed by Lady Nelson and George Everett, had taken over Kildonan in December 1933. (Lady Nelson's period of operation at Kildonan is detailed in another chapter of this publication.) In February 1935, Everson was reorganised, first as Free State Air Ferries and shortly after, as Dublin Air Ferries, a company formed by Lady Heath with her husband in an attempt to save the airfield. Around the same time, the Dublin Aero Club was founded for pupils of the flying school at Kildonan. With Lady Heath and Jack Williams co-opted as members, some 140 quickly joined. Two de Havilland Moths were registered in Lady Heath's name − *The Silver Lining* was the plane she had brought with her from England and initially kept at Baldonnel while still registered G-ACBU. She re-registered it as EI-AAW on 29 May 1934. The Gipsy Moth EI-ABE was registered to her on 1 March 1935.

On Saturday, 2 March 1935, the new company was inaugurated with an air display at Kildonan. Public interest in aviation was clearly still high. The company owned four aircraft − three de Havilland Gipsy Moths and the ex-Iona de Havilland Fox Moth, EI-AAP. Three pilots were employed, mostly on charter work, and photographs of the day show Lady Heath wearing her trademark leopardskin coat over a smart navy uniform.

A highlight of the week came on Sundays, when members would fly over Dublin City in formation. Weekends were also the time for joy-riding at five shillings a time, mostly to Glasnevin Cemetery, a few miles south of the airfield. The company got plenty of good publicity in the first months of its existence. In

A ticket typical of those issued by Lady Heath's Dublin Air Ferries. This one was for a 30-minute instruction flight in their DH.60G Moth, EI-AAK. Its issue date was 11 July 1935 and it scheduled a flight at 1930h.

COURTESY RONNY VOGT

May 1935, the new company held an aviation camp at Kildonan that went on for a fortnight, with lectures, practical demonstrations and social events, either in the clubhouse or in a number of tents pitched nearby. Williams continued to do most of the charter work from the airfield.

By now, Lady Heath's drinking was out of control. She would drink anything, so long as it was strong and alcoholic. 'She was always drunk,' remembered the late Sister Katherine Bayley-Butler in an interview: 'Young people would come out from Dublin to meet the famous Lady Heath and she would be slumped in a corner with her bottle. We would be so ashamed.'

Every now and then, her husband would book her into the local clinic at Farnham House, Finglas, described on contemporary maps as a 'mental hospital', to dry out. 'She was what we called a dipsomaniac in those days − a hopeless alcoholic,' said Sister Katherine. She had lost her looks:

> We always thought of her as a lot older than she was. She had been very attractive in her young days, but by the time she came to us, her face was all dragged and haggard. But she could still be charming.

Pearse Cahill, whose father, Hugh, founded Iona National Airways at Baldonnel in September 1930, remembered knowing her in his youth, and recalled in an interview: 'She was a sad case by the time we knew her. Her face was distorted, as she had a lot of plastic surgery after the accident, though she was still a fine big woman.'

Although Lady Heath had stopped flying by this time, she occasionally got the notion to take a machine up. The young aviators like Pearse Cahill came to dread these occasions:

> You would try and put her off or avoid her, but

The de Havilland Moth EI-ABE was operated by Dublin Air Ferries at Kildonan from 2 March 1935.
The company logo is visible on the tail section.
Courtesy Meath Aero Museum

sometimes nothing would work. I remember having to go up with her once and when it came to landing the plane, she started shouting and swearing. I was terrified – I learned a few new words that day I'm telling you!

Jack Williams did his best for his wife. Sister Katherine recalled:

He was terribly good to her. She really would get herself into an awful state and he would clean up after her with no fuss. He was a nice man, though not always a good man. He looked after Lady Heath, but always had a bit extra going on the side, and while we were very innocent at the time, we would have known enough to guess what he was up to.

In May 1935, the National Aviation Day took place in the Phoenix Park, after a similar event, planned by the Irish Aero Club from Baldonnel the previous August, was cancelled because of a newspaper strike. This was the largest air display ever seen in the country, with the Irish Air Corps, the Irish Aero Club and Sir Alan Cobham's Air Circus all in action. Some 60,000 spectators packed the flat, open spaces of the Fifteen Acres, paying admittance fees of ten shillings for a car or one shilling per person. The Irish Aero Club made £2,966 from the day. As in 1933, not a single aeroplane from Kildonan was invited.

On 22 September 1935, an American of Lithuanian descent crash-landed in bad weather near Ballinrobe, County Mayo. Felix Waitkus had left Floyd Bennett Field, New York, 23 hours earlier and, after battling atrocious weather across the Atlantic and running low on fuel, had been forced to land his Lockheed Vega *Lituanica II* in a field. Lady Heath flew from Dublin with the intention of bringing Waitkus onward to Dublin. However, she also damaged her aircraft on landing in the same field. This was her last known public appearance.

By now Lady Heath was living in England and just before Christmas 1935 came her first arrest for drunkenness since the episode in Canada four years earlier. When charged at Paddington Police Station with being drunk in a public place, she gave her name not as 'Mrs Williams' but as 'Lady Mary Heath'. A day later, when she failed to appear in Marylebone Police Court, enquiries made at the address she had given revealed that she was no longer living there and so a warrant

was issued for her arrest. Two days later, she was picked up again and charged with another offence of being found drunk in a public place. This time she gave her name as 'Sophie Mary Williams', of no fixed abode. In court, the magistrate dismissed the case, imposing costs. A Harley Street doctor, Elizabeth Sloan Chesser, spoke on her behalf and said that Mrs Williams wished to return to her native Ireland. She agreed to pay the costs and said she would look after Mrs Williams until her return to Ireland.

In September 1936, probably because of Lady Heath's increasing health problems, Dublin Air Ferries shut down for a 'change of direction and re-

Lady Heath jovially greeted Felix Waitkus after both of them damaged their aircraft landing in a field at Ballinrobe, County Mayo, on 22 September 1935. Waitkus had just flown the Atlantic solo. On the left is Jack Williams.

*Carreras Cigarette Company, London, produced a series of
cigarette cards in 1936 under the title 'Famous Airmen
and Airwomen'. One of the cards commemorated the
aeronautical achievements of Lady Heath and her Avro
Avian, G-EBUG.*

Courtesy London Cigarette Card Company

organisation'. It was not quite the end, however, and in March 1937 the
company, now with three aircraft, re-emerged with an entirely new board
led by Managing Director J.M. Clarke. Neither Lady Heath nor Jack
Williams had any involvement with the company, which was plagued with
bad luck from the start: one plane was sold and the other two grounded
after minor accidents soon after it reopened. It was not altogether surprising
that Dublin Air Ferries ceased operations in August 1938, when the last of
its three planes, the venerable *Alpha Papa* (EI-AAP), was put up for sale. By
now Irish aviation was moving on, and it was left to Percy William 'Darby'
Kennedy to continue the fight for the advancement of private aviation. He
set up Weston Aerodrome and Flying School at Leixlip, County Kildare, in
1938, with members of Dublin Air Ferries transferring to this venue.

Now estranged from her husband, Lady Heath headed for England.
With no one to look after her, she was regularly drunk. In December 1937,
she was found drunk in London's Gerrard Street and remanded in custody
at Bow Street. A policeman said he had found Mrs Williams sitting at the
foot of a flight of stairs. He helped her into the street but she was incapable
of taking care of herself. He brought her to Vine Street Police Station,
Piccadilly, where a doctor reported that she had a black eye, a bruised knee
and a sprained wrist. In her possession she had one penny, a handbag and
half a bottle of rum. Mrs Williams said that she had gone to a café in
Kingston to meet a close friend after receiving a letter from him. She told
the court:

> After that I remember absolutely nothing until I found myself
> unconscious in an outhouse in Kingston. I picked up the bottle
> not knowing what it was. My eye was shut up and I was in great
> pain. My knee was badly cut. I thought of getting back to where
> I was staying. I could not get any help. I went into town by
> getting a lift on a lorry.

The magistrate pointed out with some exasperation that she had lost one entire day in her fragmented account and requested a further report on her mental state.

As she made more frequent appearances in front of the judges, their patience finally wore out and she was sentenced to 28 days in Holloway Women's Prison for drunkenness.

Work by now had begun on a new airport at Collinstown, an old RAF base in north County Dublin, which finally opened in January 1940. Baldonnel would survive, but there was little hope for nearby Kildonan and it duly closed down. Jack Williams left Ireland when Kildonan folded. He returned to the Caribbean where, as Flight Lieutenant George Williams, he became Second in Command at the Empire Training School at Piarco Aerodrome in Trinidad. After the war, he returned to England and, with his second wife, Muriel Marjorie, lived at 14 Cherimoya Gardens, West Molesey, Surrey, until his death from pneumonia aged 87 on 13 December 1987.

In a newspaper article written shortly before her death, Lady Heath spoke of her drink problem:

> People wonder why I took to drink after I had been fearless and rose from a poor Irish girl to become a titled lady. It was the failure of my struggles for happiness. My frequent romances have ruined my life. Now I have given up drink forever. I went to church last Sunday and now I am studying my medicine and surgery books again. I shall start life all over again and be what I wanted to be when I was a girl — a doctor.

Lady Heath founded the National Irish Junior Aviation Club in 1933. The photograph below shows club members on a visit to Baldonnel in 1938. The Club Secretary, Chris Bruton, is in the centre of the front row.
COURTESY CHRIS BRUTON VIA BRENDAN BRUTON

But it was not to be. On Monday, 7 May 1939, Lady Heath, a shabbily dressed woman, boarded a tramcar at Highgate Hill, some way from her then-residence in Princes Square, Paddington, and ascended the stairs to the upper deck. When the conductor, Alfred Stokes, came to collect her fare, she failed to respond to him and seemed 'very vacant'. Later he found her dozing in her seat and, when he woke her up, she burst out laughing. He asked her where she was going and she claimed to have a date in the East End. In that case, he told her, she should get off at Old Street. He then went back to the platform and gave the signal to start moving. The tram set off again with no noticeable jerking or bumping.

He then heard a noise. 'I was still on the platform when I heard a commotion on the stairs and a thud I shall never forget,' he told the inquest a few days later. The shabbily dressed woman had fallen down the steps. 'Her head was lying on the controller, her body was on the stairs and her feet on the staircase.' The woman, still not identified, was rushed to St Leonard's Hospital, Shoreditch. She died within a day. Her identity was not established until she was recognised by a police officer as a woman he had seen many times before the court. She was only 42 years of age.

The inquest heard that she had not been 'quite right' since the accident of 1929, although she was able to walk quite normally afterwards. Dr Cedric Keith Simpson gave his medical opinion:

> I found nothing which would indicate that the dead woman was under the influence of alcohol. I found an old depressed fracture on the left side of the head consistent with an old injury. Underneath it was an old blood clot pressing on the brain. This clot could have caused epilepsy, black-out and unconsciousness for a short time or led to her fall.

After evidence from the car driver that the tram had started normally and without a jerk and had travelled only about 30 yards when the accident occurred, the jury returned a verdict of accidental death, exonerating the driver and conductor from blame.

One of those present at the inquest was an old friend and legal advisor of Lady Heath, Colonel S.H. White. He added that, in accordance with what relatives and friends felt would be her wish, her body was cremated at Golder's Green Crematorium on 15 May. The cremation was under the name Sophie Mary Catherine Theresa Williams and the arrangements were made by Francis Carnegie Peirce. Her ashes were collected by relatives.

She was remembered kindly. Most newspapers carried glowing references to her athletic and aeronautical achievements in Ireland, England and the United States of America, and reported that she once was a commanding figure among the world's women. There was passing mention of her final unpleasant years battling with alcohol addiction: the London magistrates nearly always treated her with leniency and probation officers strove hard to recapture the strong personality that had once been hers. They were attempting the impossible. *Flight* magazine also opted to remember her at her best: 'as a woman who took on men on their own terms and often beat them'.

There is a codicil to Lady Heath's story, although it is possibly apocryphal. The ashes of Mrs Williams were duly brought back to Ireland, according to the wishes of her family, most notably of her beloved Aunt Cis, still alive at the time, to whom she had left all her worldly goods – a total of £204 7s 10d. (Cis died aged 77 years on 27 May 1942, seven months before the death of Sir James Heath.) Lady Heath had apparently requested that her ashes be scattered over the houses adjoining the south-west side of the Square at noon precisely. At the time, the houses there consisted of the

A London tramcar similar to the type on which Lady Heath accidentally fell down the stairs on 7 May 1939. She died as a result of her injuries.
COURTESY LONDON TRANSPORT MUSEUM

former Peirce home, by then a Munster and Leinster Bank, and the home of Captain Richbel Curling, a former agent of the Earl of Devon's Limerick lands and a man Lady Heath had disliked intensely as a child. At an angle was a Church of Ireland chapel, enclosed by a stone wall facing the Square. Every day at noon, Curling would emerge from his house, stroll over to the church wall and lean against it to survey the passing scene.

At midday precisely, a small aeroplane passed overhead and all that remained of the town's most famous daughter drifted slowly earthwards. The Captain, in his usual position, could not escape inhaling the scattered ashes, which caused a prolonged coughing fit. He soon learned why the aircraft had caused such a commotion and, in later years, when the wind picked up and raised the dust around the Square, the Captain would salute passers-by, saying, 'There's that Peirce lady at it again. Will I ever be clear of her?'

A replica of Lady Heath's 1927 Avro 594 Avian III, photographed at Oshkosh, Wisconsin, on 27 August 2001.
COURTESY DARREN PITCHER

The plaque commemorating Sophie Peirce in her home town of Newcastle West, County Limerick. Note: the birth date should read 1896.

COURTESY JOHN CUSSEN

EPILOGUE

A plaque commemorating Sophie Peirce in her home town of Newcastle West, County Limerick, was unveiled on 20 July 1990 outside the AIB in the Square. The property was once the location of the Peirce family home.

The showhouse for a new development of 72 townhouses and apartments near Finglas village, Dublin, opened on 5 October 2000. The development was called Heath Square and was named in honour of Lady Heath, who had flown from the nearby aerodrome at Kildonan, located 1.5 miles north-west of the development.

Lady Heath's Avro 594 Avian III was replicated when another Avian was restored to flying condition by Golden Wings Museum, Minnesota, USA.

British pilot Tracey Curtis-Taylor undertook a flight from Cape Town, South Africa, to Goodwood, south of London, in an effort to replicate Lady Heath's 1928 flight. Curtis-Taylor landed her 1942 Boeing Stearman on 31 December 2013 after an eight-week flight. The flight was the subject of a documentary entitled *The Aviatrix: The Lady Who Flew Africa*, broadcast on BBC Four on 17 March 2015. It was followed by the launch of a film by Nylon Films and a DVD of the same name on 22 April 2015.

An Post, the Irish Post Office, issued four stamps on 24 February 1998 commemorating pioneers of aviation in Ireland. One of the four commemorated was Lady Heath.

COURTESY JOHN CUSSEN

The locations of Heath Square, Finglas, and the former Kildonan Aerodrome in north Dublin.

COURTESY ORDNANCE SURVEY IRELAND

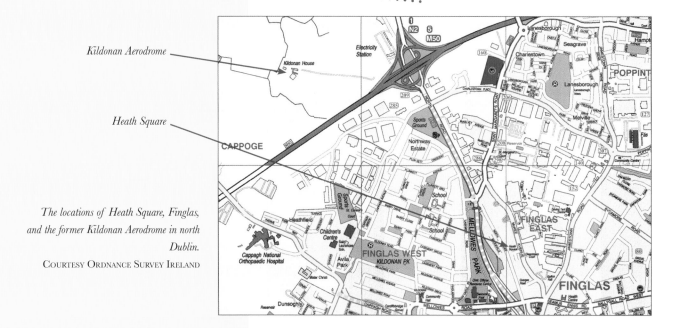

BIBLIOGRAPHY

Lady Heath and Stella Wolfe Murray, *Woman and Flying* (London: John Long, 1929).

Lindie Naughton, *Lady Icarus: The Life of Irish Aviator Lady Mary Heath* (Dublin: Ashfield Press, 2004). This publication also contains an extensive bibliography.

ACKNOWLEDGEMENTS

John Cussen, historian, Newcastle West, County Limerick.

Richard Langford, Shanagolden, County Limerick.

Lindie Naughton, who very kindly supplied the substance of this chapter, abridged from her book, *Lady Icarus: The Life of Irish Aviator Lady Mary Heath*.

Above: *On 9 November 2004 a book,* Lady Icarus: The Life of Irish Aviator Lady Mary Heath, *written by Lindie Naughton and published by Ashfield Press, was launched in Dublin.*
COURTESY ASHFIELD PRESS, DUBLIN

Left: *Lady Heath's flight was the subject of a 2015 documentary.*
COURTESY WWW.THEAVIATRIXFILM.COM

Below: *An authentic 1927 Avro Avian restored to flying condition and registered G-EBUG as a tribute to Lady Heath's aeronautical achievements.*
COURTESY GREGG HERRICK, GOLDEN WINGS MUSEUM, MINNESOTA, USA

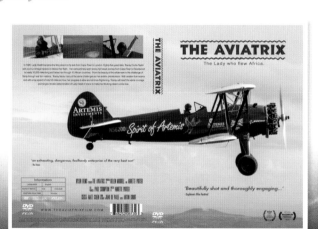

SICELE O'BRIEN
ONE OF THE STAG LANE TRIO

Sir Timothy O'Brien was a wealthy aristocrat who lived in a castle in County Cork, where his ten children were reared. His eldest daughter, Sicele, was educated at boarding school in England and, in November 1925, she commenced flying lessons at Stag Lane Aerodrome, London. Undergoing pilot training at the same time were fellow Irishwomen Sophie Eliott-Lynn and Lady Bailey. Sicele O'Brien became the second Irish female to earn her Aviator's 'A' Certificate and the second female in Britain to earn her 'B' (Commercial) Certificate. She entered several air races, in which she was successful, and attempted many aviation records. Following a serious air crash, she had part of her leg amputated. After her Aviator's Certificate was restored, she was possibly the first disabled female pilot in Britain. She purchased her own aircraft to take part in aeronautical events. She was taking delivery of her latest acquisition in June 1931 when she crashed. Tragically, 44-year-old Sicele O'Brien is recorded as the first Irishwoman to be killed in an aeroplane crash.

Sicele O'Brien in 1926.
COURTESY ROYAL AERO CLUB TRUST

I N THE WAKE of the Great Famine, Queen Victoria paid her first visit to Ireland between 2 and 12 August 1849. Timothy O'Brien (1787–1862) was Lord Mayor of Dublin and welcomed the Queen. In return she conferred the first Baronetcy of Merrion Square and Borris-in-Ossory on him on 24 September of the same year.

The O'Brien family pedigree is among the oldest in Europe, with lineage back to Brian Boru (who died in 1014) and beyond. The particular family line in question here is the O'Briens of Ara Castle on the shores of Lough Derg, near Portroe, County Tipperary, and can be traced back to 1272. The lineage continues to Turlogh O'Brien, who died in 1399. Colonel Mortagh O'Brien of Annagh, near Puckane, north County Tipperary, was in command of the Irish Brigade from 1641 to 1652. Along with 4,000 of his men, he surrendered to the Commonwealth forces near Ennis, County Clare. The O'Briens of Dromoland Castle are part of this family, going back to the sixteenth century, from which Sir Lucius O'Brien (1731–95) and the Earls of Inchiquin descended.

The family remained in Counties Clare and Tipperary. Timothy O'Brien married a daughter of Timothy Madden from County Galway. One of his sons was Timothy (1787–1862), who married Catherine Murphy of Flemingstown, County Dublin, in August 1821. He moved to Dublin, where he became a successful merchant. As a member of the Repeal Movement, he was one of Daniel O'Connell's foremost lieutenants. During his lifetime, Sir Timothy (first Baronet) held several offices, including Justice of the Peace, Deputy Lieutenant for Dublin City, Member of Parliament for Cashel (1846–9) and Lord Mayor of Dublin for 1844 and 1849. He had a townhouse at 14 Merrion Square East, Dublin, and two country houses, Tudor Lodge in County Dublin and another in Borris-in-Ossory, Queen's County (later County Laois). He was also a barrister and a prominent businessman and owned several public houses in the city. However, he was known for his miserliness as a publican in the Liberties of Dublin, where he owned an inn on Patrick Street. The suspicion was, according to one issue of the *James Joyce Quarterly*, that 'his battered cups enabled him to serve his customers less than full measure'. For this he was immortalised by James Joyce in *Ulysses* as 'Timothy of the Battered Naggin'.

Catherine bore Sir Timothy six children, three sons (Patrick, John and Timothy) and three daughters (Kate, Mary and Ellen). Catherine died in 1836, before her husband. Following Sir Timothy's death on 3 December 1862, his son Patrick (1823–95) became second Baronet. Patrick married Ida Sophia Perry on 29 August 1866, widow of the late Lieutenant General James Perry and daughter of Commander Parlby, Royal Navy. Sir Patrick was elected Member of Parliament for King's County (later County Offaly) in 1852 and held the seat until the general election in 1885. They had no children and Sir Patrick died on 23 April 1895.

Sir Patrick's brother, John, was Captain in the 30th Foot and Fusiliers. The youngest of the three brothers was Timothy, who married Mary O'Dwyer, only daughter of Andrew Carew O'Dwyer, on 3 September 1860. They had three sons: Timothy Carew, born on 5 November 1861; John George, born on 10 January 1866; and Edmond Lyons, born on 27 November 1868. The title of third Baronet fell to Timothy Carew O'Brien on 25 April 1895. Like his predecessors, he was a Justice of the Peace and Deputy Lieutenant for Cork.

Timothy Carew O'Brien was born in Baggot Street, Dublin. His father died on 25 April 1869 when Tim was seven years of age. He was educated at Downside, a leading Catholic monastic public boarding school in Bath, Somerset, for boys aged between 11 and 18. His sixth-form education was at St Charles College, Notting Hill, London. At school he excelled and impressed at cricket. In 1881, aged 19, he joined the Middlesex Cricket Club after his talents were spotted when he was playing with his local Kensington Park Cricket Club.

As a result of Tim's brilliance at cricket, he went to New Inn Hall, Oxford, with the intention of winning a Blue. (A Blue is an award earned in competition by men and women in university sport who have excelled in that sport to the highest university level.) At the time Tim was rated the second-best batsman in England. He was classed as a right-hand batsman and a left-hand bowler. He did receive a Blue in 1884, and his international test debut was England *versus* Australia

Sir Tim O'Brien when he represented England in test cricket.
Courtesy Michael Healy

in Manchester on 10–12 July of that year. One of his notable achievements was an innings of 92 against Australia on that occasion.

Described as red haired, tall and strong, 23-year-old Tim married Gundrede Annette Teresa de Trafford on 22 September 1885. She was the daughter of Sir Humphrey de Trafford, second Baronet, and Lady Annette Mary Talbot, who were married on 17 January 1855. Sir Humphrey (1 May 1808–4 May 1886) was a prominent English Catholic and resided at the family home of Trafford Hall, Trafford Park, Manchester. Trafford Park, in close proximity to Manchester city centre, was the seat of the de Trafford family for many centuries. Sir Humphrey had five daughters and three sons. The de Trafford boys also attended Downside School. One of the sons was Charles Edmund, who played cricket for Lancashire and Middlesex Cricket Club and captained Leicestershire for 17 seasons. It may well have been through these cricket associations that Tim became acquainted with Charles's sister Gundrede, who was born on 9 October 1860. Sir Humphrey was a wealthy businessman who owned vast tracts of land in Cheshire and was High Sheriff of Lancashire in 1861. Construction began on the Manchester Ship Canal, of which he had been a staunch opponent because it cut through his lands, in 1887, the year after he died, aged 78. Lady Annette died on 1 July 1922.

Another son was Sir Humphrey Francis de Trafford (1862–1929). Sir Humphrey was the largest landowner in that area of Lancashire, with Trafford Park then occupying 1,183 acres. He sold the park in 1896 and it became the first planned industrial estate in Europe. Indeed, it remains the largest in Europe to the present time. One of the park's involvements with aviation was the location of the Rolls Royce factory, where from 1936 Merlin engines were manufactured. At its peak the factory was producing 200 engines per week for many aircraft types, including the Supermarine Spitfires, Hawker Hurricanes and Avro Lancasters used during the Second World War.

Meanwhile, Tim O'Brien continued his cricket career and represented England for a second time in Australia in 1887–8 and South Africa in 1895–6. By the time of the third tour he had inherited the Baronetcy of Merrion Square and Borris-in-Ossory and was called Sir Timothy O'Brien, third Baronet. Around the same time as the team arrived in South Africa, the tensions that would lead to the Second Boer War were simmering. O'Brien was awarded the captaincy of the England team in Port Elizabeth in February 1896, with his team winning over the two days.

On 1 December 1890, Sir Tim purchased Lohort Castle, Cecilstown, County Cork, between Mallow and Kanturk, from Charles George Perceval, seventh Earl of Egmont. Sir Humphrey de Trafford was named as a party to the transfer of ownership, joining Sir Tim and Gundrede. The Norman castle was built during the reign of King John in 1184. Following the end of the Williamite War in 1691, Sir Phillip Perceval, Baronet, succeeded to the lands at Lohort. The tower house was restored by the Perceval family in 1750, converting this historic castle into a place of residence. The building is a seven-storey fortified tower with rounded corners, standing over 80 feet tall, with walls 10 feet thick at the base. Originally it had an eight-foot-wide moat and drawbridge. It was further modernised in 1879 by Charles, Earl of Egmont.

Sir Patrick O'Brien purchased Lohort Castle in 1888; in 1890 it was acquired by his nephew, Sir Timothy Carew O'Brien. The view from the battlements of the surrounding countryside was quite spectacular. According to the *Irish News*, 'Mr O'Brien can well sustain the style of the place, as his wife inherited largely at her father's death.' Sir Humphrey had died four years previously.

Trafford Hall in Trafford Park, Manchester. This was home to Sicele O'Brien's mother, Gundrede de Trafford.
COURTESY TRAFFORD LOCAL STUDIES

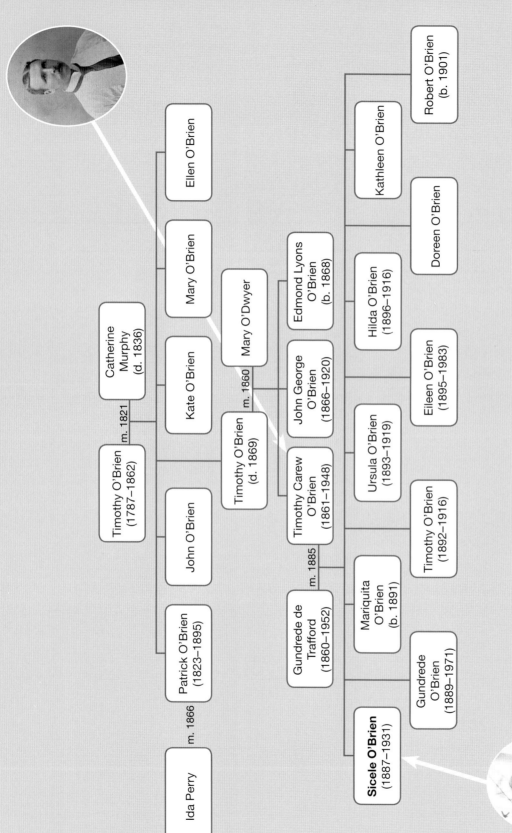

Sicele O'Brien's family tree.
COURTESY ALICIA MCAULEY

Lohort gatehouse and castle.
COURTESY MICHAEL HEALY

Map showing locations associated with Sicele O'Brien.
MAP © MARTIN GAFFNEY

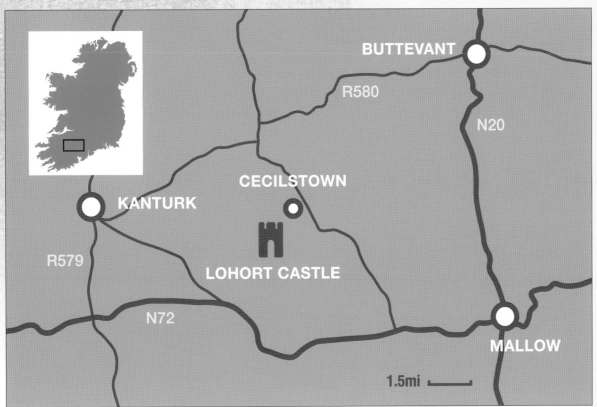

Lohort Castle, Mallow.

Lohort Castle, Mallow, County Cork, where Sicele O'Brien and her siblings lived between 1898 and 1912.
COURTESY MICHAEL HEALY

Sir Tim enjoyed hunting and travelled around Munster to partake in equine events. He was a familiar figure at Punchestown Racecourse, County Kildare. He was a noted follower of the local Duhallow Hunt Club and a director of Cork City Racecourse Limited. He is reputed to have owned some of the best horses in Ireland at that time and was a regular prizewinner at Dublin and Cork horse shows. The entry in *Thom's Directory* for 1896 gave Lohort Castle as his address.

After his cricket tours were concluded, Sir Tim settled in County Cork and his family relocated there from London in 1898. Between 1881 and 1898 he scored a remarkable 7,377 runs for Middlesex Cricket Club. The O'Brien children grew up enjoying the trappings of a rural lifestyle as the sons and daughters of a wealthy country squire.

The census of Sunday, 31 March 1901 records the O'Brien family residing at Lohort Castle. In addition to

Sir Tim, Lady Gundrede and six of their children, the census includes twelve staff (three servants, a governess, a cook, two housemaids, a launderer, a gardener, a butler, a coachman and an agricultural labourer). By this time nine of their ten children were born. The eldest was Sicele, born on 1 April 1887 at 69 Oxford Terrace, Paddington, London, and christened Cecilia Julia Mary Annette O'Brien. The following were born in succession: Gundrede Mary Gwendoline, Mariquita Winefrede Aloysius, Timothy John Aloysius, Ursula Mary Annette, Eileen Mary Frances, Hilda Moira Clare, Doreen Moira and Kathleen Moyra. The youngest, Robert Rollo Gillespie, was born on 9 June 1901. On the night of the census three sisters were absent from the house. The census for England, taken the same night, listed Sicele, Gundrede and Mariquita as boarding at Princethorpe School, Rugby, Warwickshire. At that time the school had 71 nuns and 31 female boarders, three of them being the O'Brien sisters.

When Cecilia was ten years old her family moved to Lohort Castle. By the time she attended Princethorpe she was using the name Sicele, which was adapted from her mother's sister's name. Another of her mother's sisters was Hilda (1875–1965), who became a Benedictine nun in the French enclosed order and entered the convent at Princethorpe Priory. Lady Annette de Trafford was a generous benefactor to Princethorpe and, in addition to providing the school with a handsome dowry for her daughter Hilda, she assisted financially with the construction of a school church, which was built between 1897 and 1901. Sicele's mother and the remaining four de Trafford sisters were all boarders at Princethorpe. The school catered for female boarders aged 10 to 18. At one time the convent was the largest in England, with over 200 nuns.

The three O'Brien sisters seemed to enjoy their stay at Princethorpe and, as well as being academically talented, they were active in many sports and performed roles in school plays. On the sports field, during the Tournament of Games in 1902, Sicele

Below: *The junior classroom at Princethorpe School, circa 1900.*
COURTESY PRINCETHORPE FOUNDATION

Bottom: *The dormitory at Princethorpe School that accommodated boarders including the O'Brien sisters.*
COURTESY PRINCETHORPE FOUNDATION

gained the croquet prize, while Gundrede carried off the tennis prize. In the same year, five students in the school were successful in the Examination in Music, among them Sicele, Gundrede and Quita (Mariquita) O'Brien. On 22 July 1902, the distribution of the year's prizes was held and included Quita (aged 11) taking the prize for English in Form II. In Form III, the prizes for English and Mathematics were taken by Gundrede (aged 12) and in Form IV, Sicele (aged 15) took the first prizes for English, Mathematics and Languages. Sicele contributed articles for the annual school magazine, *Peeps of Princethorpe*. The Irish students were allowed to celebrate St Patrick's Day, which was a school holiday. One St Patrick's Day a fancy-dress ball was held and Gundrede gave a performance entitled 'Shamrock'. She also took part in several other plays. By 1904, the fourth O'Brien daughter, Ursula (aged 11), had entered the school. Gundrede excelled on the hockey pitch and was singled out for praise as someone 'whose strong and well-directed strokes do her great credit' in her right-back position.

The girls also played cricket and the experience and influence of Sir Tim carried through to Gundrede, who performed well for the school team and in 1905 was credited 'with a splendid stand, keeping up her wicket until she had completed a very well-played innings of about 45 minutes'. In 1906, Sicele had left the school and returned to Lohort Castle. The remaining O'Brien girls were joined by their first cousin Clare de Trafford (aged 11).

St Mary's Priory, Princethorpe, circa 1900.

COURTESY PRINCETHORPE FOUNDATION

During the years when Sicele and her sisters attended Princethorpe, their aunt Mère Mary Hilda (de Trafford) was a nun at the college. In 1930 she celebrated her Clothing Ceremony. By 1951, at the age of 76 years, she is recorded as having become the Sacristan to the Priory and Second Chantress. In 1955 she celebrated her Silver Jubilee. She died in 1965, the year before the Benedictine nuns vacated Princethorpe and relocated to Fernham in Oxfordshire.

Meanwhile, in County Cork, Sir Tim became involved in local cricket and went on to become Captain of the Irish team on its inaugural tour in 1902 against his *alma mater*, Oxford University. He scored 169 runs in 4 hours, which remained an Irish record for 71 years until 1973.

Shortly after Sicele returned to Lohort Castle, her father became embroiled in the ruinous litigation that was ultimately to destroy him financially and result in the family having to leave their beloved County Cork.

Sir Tim's life in County Cork was not devoid of controversy. Along with cricket, his other love was hunting. He purchased a horse at Cahirmee Fair, Buttevant, County Cork, on 13 July 1891, from the Honourable Alexis Burke-Roche, son of Lord Fermoy. According to Sir Tim, the horse was later determined to be lame and proved to be a 'broken winded nag'. Burke-Roche refused to accept the return of the horse or refund O'Brien the £140 purchase price. The incident was not forgotten, and 17 years later, while attending the Duhallow Hunt at Cecilstown on 7 March 1908, Sir Tim rode up to Burke-Roche and characterised him as 'a liar, a thief and a swindler'. He declared, 'You live by swindling and to my knowledge you have lived by swindling for over 20 years.' Burke-Roche immediately sued for slander, seeking £3,000 in damages. The case was heard before Cork Assizes, commencing on 21 July 1908. Witnesses were subpoenaed in England and America. The *New York Times*, reporting on the case on 23 July 1908, stated:

> An audience of fashionable Irish people has filled one of the local courts since the beginning of the week to hear the trial of the suit for libel brought by Alexis Burke-Roche against Sir Timothy O'Brien. Mr Burke-Roche is a son of Baron Fermoy, whose family is well known in America. The trial collapsed today after the hearing of statements that Sir Timothy had tried to tamper with a juror. The Judge then dismissed the jury. The plaintiff applied for an attachment against Sir Timothy for contempt and the application was referred by the Judge to the higher court.

On the third day, the case came to a sudden halt and the jury was dismissed. The presiding judge, the Right Honourable Charles Pallas, Lord Chief Baron of the Exchequer in Ireland, subsequently granted a conditional order 'attaching' Sir Timothy for contempt of court. Sir Timothy was heavily fined for contempt of court in attempting to influence a juror. Australia's *Adelaide Register* reported on the contempt hearing in Dublin on 6 November 1908. It advised readers:

> The defendant was fined £300 and ordered to pay the costs of the present hearing and also those of the abortive slander trial.

Grangewilliam House, Maynooth, County Kildare, as it appeared when it became home to Sicele O'Brien in 1912.

A retrial of the slander case took place, commencing on 2 June 1909 in the High Court in Dublin. After nine days of hearing evidence and considering a verdict, the jury found in favour of Burke-Roche, although it awarded him only derisory damages of £5. Many of the witnesses at the Duhallow Hunt, who had heard the utterances at the confrontation between Sir Tim and Burke-Roche, attended the case in Dublin. O'Brien also had to cover their expenses. Sir Tim was also ordered to pay costs for both the plaintiff's and his own legal teams. The amounts involved left him almost financially ruined and this had serious consequences for the family. The ruination of his name, reputation and fortune caused him to move away from County Cork. In the census of 2 April 1911, Sicele, Gundrede and Mariquita were the only children residing at Lohort Castle with their parents. The staff in the past decade had reduced to eight (a cook, two housemaids, a coachman, a butler, a footman, a gardener and a chauffeur). Sir Tim was still supporting 22 people, including his staff and their families. He became interested in Grangewilliam House in Donaghmore, near Maynooth, County Kildare, and he began paying rates on the property from 1909.

The first ever aviation meeting to be held in Ireland was at Leopardstown Racecourse, Dublin, on Monday and Tuesday, 29 and 30 August 1910. It included an air display featuring four aircraft that were crated and brought by sea from the United Kingdom and assembled in specially constructed hangars on the racecourse. The three pilots were Cecil Grace, in a Farman biplane, Captain Bartram Dickson, also in a Farman biplane, and J. Armstrong Drexel, who brought two Blériot monoplanes to Ireland. Among the thousands that flocked to Leopardstown to get their first glimpse of a flying machine was Sir Tim O'Brien. Sicele was back from college by then and there is every possibility she attended the event with her father. If so, then that would have been the first time she witnessed aviation at first hand. Even if she did not attend, she would no doubt have heard stories of the day's events from her father.

Sir Tim appeared in Oldtown, Kildare, for the County Cork cricket team against a County Kildare selection on 14 June 1911, at the age of 49. The *Kildare Observer* of Saturday, 23 March 1912, visited Grangewilliam House and reported to its readers:

> Grangewilliam House, Maynooth, the residence of H.F.H. Hardy, Esq has been improved so much by its present owner since we formerly had the pleasure of looking over this property that

some of the departments have been changed beyond recognition. The residence has been greatly enlarged and renovated while some fine boxes and buildings have been arranged in a very convenient yard. The gardens and avenues have been nicely planted and laid out, while neat and attractive cottages for those employed on the property have been erected. The land has been enriched and made much more productive.

The article goes on to describe the type of animals and agricultural production taking place on the estate. This was shortly to become the residence of the O'Brien family. On 8 July 1912, Sir Tim's father-in-law, Sir Humphrey Francis de Trafford of Hill Crest, Market Harborough, Leicestershire, along with John

Cecil Grace's Farman biplane is prepared for flight outside one of the specially constructed hangars during the 1910 Aviation Meeting at Leopardstown. This was possibly Sicele's first experience of aircraft.
COURTESY ROYAL IRISH AUTOMOBILE CLUB ARCHIVE

George O'Brien of Lakefield, Fethard, County Tipperary, and Humphrey Walmesley of Hungerford, Berkshire, completed the purchase of a total of 237 acres at Barrogstown and Donaghmore, Maynooth, from Harry F.H. Hardy. Situated on these lands were Grangewilliam House and buildings, containing one and a half acres that had been leased from the Duke of Leinster by Cornelius Kehely of Carrig House, Douglas, County Cork, since 13 March 1911.

In late summer 1912, Grangewilliam House became Sicele O'Brien's second family home after she left London in 1898. Her cousins, children of her father's brother Edmond, were living in Celbridge Abbey, about five miles away. Edmond had purchased the property from the Dease family, who moved about a mile and a half away. One of the Dease children was Ernest, born on 7 January 1899 and raised at Celbridge Abbey. He was educated at Sandhurst Military College, Camberley, Berkshire. Ernest's father, William, served with the Army Remount Service during the First World War and, in a letter dated 14 July 1917, William wrote that Ernest wanted to learn to fly. Ernest did take flying lessons and went on to serve with the Royal Flying Corps. Maurice Dease from Coole, County Westmeath, was a cousin of Ernest's. Maurice was also educated at Sandhurst and joined the Royal Fusiliers. On 23 August 1914, aged 24, Lieutenant Maurice was killed during an intense battle at Mons, Belgium. For his actions and bravery while in command of a machine-gun section defending Nimy Railway Bridge, he earned the distinction of being the first person to be awarded the Victoria Cross in the First World War. Ernest returned to Ireland in 1920 and subsequently he became involved in the Irish aviation scene.

Ernest Dease was the first instructor with the newly formed Cork Aero Club, which commenced flight training on 21 May 1934 at Fermoy. Within a week, one of his first students was Ruth Hallinan from Fermoy, followed a few weeks later by Lily Dillon from Listowel. In October 1935, he was appointed Chief Flying Instructor with the Irish Aero Club. He did not hold this post for long and, in January 1936, resigned to take up an instructional posting with the Royal Air Force (RAF). There was an urgent requirement for military pilots to be trained to service the additional squadrons and thereby boost RAF strength. On 20 September

1938, Ernest was promoted to Flight Lieutenant. He served in the Second World War. On 11 July 1940, he was invested as Member of the Most Excellent Order of the British Empire (MBE). He gained the rank of Acting Squadron Leader and retired to Cannes, France, where he died in 1982. Sicele would have been acquainted with Ernest Dease and it is possible this is where her interest in learning to fly was kindled.

Meanwhile, back in County Kildare, the O'Brien sisters became involved in local activities. The *Kildare Observer* of 18 January 1913 reported:

> On 28 December 1912 a high class concert was given to inmates of Celbridge hospital. The Misses O'Brien, Grangewilliam were much appreciated in a humorous sketch and in several excellently rendered recitations.

The *Kildare Observer* regularly published articles relating to the social activities of the local gentry and titled families in the area. An example was their 'House Parties' section, which detailed visitors to each estate in the county. The edition of 25 January 1913 detailed the Kildare Hunt Ball and listed Sir Timothy and Lady O'Brien along with Misses Quita and Gundrede O'Brien in attendance. The O'Briens settled into the local culture and social scene within a short space of time. In summer months the O'Briens featured in floral, fruit, vegetable and horticultural shows, winning prizes for their displays. Hunting was an activity that Sir Tim relished and regular reports appeared in local media of his involvement in that sport during his tenure at Grangewilliam. In 1914 Sir Tim was selected for a fixture in England which was to prove his farewell to cricket. He was 53 years old and scored 90 and 111 in his final first-class match. He received 266 caps and was the first, and so far only, Irishman to captain both England and Ireland at cricket.

By summer 1914, war was looming and Sir Tim joined the Remount Service as part of the Royal Army Service Corps. The Remounts were responsible for the provisioning of horses and mules to all other army units. Remount squadrons consisted of approximately 200 soldiers who obtained and trained 500 horses. These squadrons were critical to the war effort in all theatres of the First World War. By December 1917, these facilities had trained 93,847 horses and 36,613 mules. Sir Tim served as Lieutenant with the Derbyshire Yeomanry Cavalry. He also served with the 5th Battalion, Royal Irish Fusiliers. For his service he was mentioned in Despatches and his promotion to Major was posted in the *London Gazette* on 29 March 1915.

Sicele's sister Mariquita married Sergeant James Thirkell Price on 20 October 1915. He enlisted with the 1st Battalion, Royal Dublin Fusiliers and was posted to France, but was killed on Good Friday, 21 April 1916 (a few days before the start of the Easter Rising in Ireland) and buried in Vermelles British Cemetery, France. He was posthumously awarded the Military Cross. His address was given as Ballylinan, Athy, County Kildare. His marriage to Mariquita had taken place six months previously. Their only child was born after his death, on 24 October 1916.

Sicele's brother Timothy John Aloysius O'Brien was born on 21 June 1892. He was educated at St Anthony's, Eastbourne, and at Beaumont College. He joined the Royal Field Artillery and went to the front with the original British Expeditionary Force. He took part in the Battles of Mons, the Aisne and Ypres and in numerous other military engagements, escaping without injury until 7 August 1916, when he was fatally hit by shell fire in Delville Wood, aged 24. The Battle of Delville Wood was one of the fiercest battles and bloodiest confrontations of the Somme, with German shells raining down at a rate of up to 400 per minute. Like his father, the late officer was an accomplished horseman, cricketer and all-round sportsman and a prominent member of the Kildare Hunt.

Sicele's youngest brother, Robert Rollo Gillespie O'Brien, aged 15 at the time of his brother's death, as the only other male in a family of ten children, then became fourth Baronet.

The Tablet of 9 September 1916 reported in its 'Social and Personal' column:

> The first Mass, in perpetuity, for the late Lieutenant Timothy John

Aloysius O'Brien, RFA, son of Sir Timothy O'Brien, Bart., was said in the Soldiers' and Sailors' chapel, Westminster Cathedral, on 7 September, at 11.30. A Solemn Requiem Mass was sung on the same day at Maynooth, Co. Kildare.

Sadly, the day before this ceremony, tragedy again struck the family. Following the fatal wounding of her brother Timothy, Sicele's sister Hilda died on 6 September 1916, aged 20. Her tombstone in Grangewilliam Cemetery bears the inscription:

> In loving memory of our darling child Hilda Moira Clare O'Brien who died on September 6 1916 aged 20. Daughter of Sir Timothy O'Brien, Bart., DL and Lady O'Brien of Lohort Castle, Co. Cork and Grangewilliam, Maynooth.

The *Kildare Observer* of 4 November 1916 summed up the family's tragic losses:

> The first grandchild of the famous baronet, Sir Timothy O'Brien has been born under pathetic circumstances. The mother married Capt. Price just a year ago and he was killed on Good Friday. Recently, Sir Timothy lost his elder son in action and a 20-year-old daughter died in a nursing home last month.

Settlement of the libel case had forced Sir Tim to dispose of some of his assets. On 12 July 1918,

Delville Wood, Somme, France where Timothy O'Brien was killed by shell fire, 7 August 1916.
COURTESY IMPERIAL WAR MUSEUM, LONDON

ownership of the 223 acres at Lohort Demesne was transferred to Eustace and Company Limited, Leitrim Street, Cork, who were suppliers to the building trade. Sir Tim retained the castle and continued to pay rates on it until 1921. He was credited with many improvements to the Lohort Demesne and to the castle, including the installation of an electricity-generating plant.

An auction took place at Grangewilliam on Tuesday, 10 February 1920 of horses, cattle and implements belonging to Sir T.C. O'Brien. The O'Briens vacated the house and ownership of the lands surrounding Grangewilliam House was transferred to Cornelius Kehely on 18 February 1920. Sir Tim owned other properties jointly with Sir Humphrey de Trafford on the Main Street in Borris-in-Ossory, Queen's County. These were also sold, with the deals completed by 31 December 1920.

Their seven years of residency at Grangewilliam constituted a deeply tragic period for the O'Brien family. Lieutenant Timothy and his sister Hilda both died in 1916, and Sicele also suffered the loss of another sibling. Ursula was a nun with the Society of the Holy Child Jesus at Mayfield Convent in East Sussex. In religion she took the name Sister Maria Mercedes. She developed influenza and died on 12 March 1919, aged 26.

On 15 August 1920, the death occurred at Dr Steevens' Hospital, Dublin, of Captain John George O'Brien (1866–1920), Royal Field Artillery, brother of Sir Tim. He was involved in a motor accident with his niece in the Phoenix Park, when the car skidded and overturned, pinning John O'Brien underneath. Miss O'Brien was thrown clear and suffered shock and injuries to her shoulder and arm. She was able to leave hospital a week later. John, however, was killed. According to the *Irish Times* of Monday, 16 August 1920:

Grangewilliam House and stables at the time of purchase by the Rogers family in 1965. Considerable renovations and extensions have taken place over the past 50 years.
COURTESY SONIA ROGERS

Captain O'Brien was educated at St Charles College. He married Marion Dora who predeceased him leaving no issue. Captain O'Brien was formerly a Captain in the Monmouth Engineers (Militia) and also held a commission with rank of Captain in the Shropshire Light Infantry. On the outbreak of war he joined the 16th Divisional Field Artillery as a Lieutenant being then in his 49th year. He was invalided home but rejoined and served in France until the end of the war when he was invalided home from Cologne.

He had been living at Lakefield, Fethard, County Tipperary, and was buried in Fethard on Wednesday, 18 August 1920.

Grangewilliam was the location for a large-scale incident of the Irish Civil War (1922–3). On 1 December 1922, around 40 National Army soldiers surrounded a local Irish Republican Army (IRA) unit that had taken over Grangewilliam House. The ensuing gun battle lasted four hours and resulted in the capture of 22 IRA volunteers, five of whom were tried for army desertion and executed.

In 1965, Grangewilliam House and the adjoining lands were acquired by Captain Anthony (Tim) Rogers and his wife, Sonia. Considerable refurbishment of the buildings and gardens and development of the lands turned the estate into a prime stud farm and Airlie Stud evolved to become one of Ireland's premier thoroughbred-horse-breeding farms.

Lohort Castle near Mallow remained unoccupied during the War of Independence (1919–21) and became a strategic location for Crown forces, who used its 80-feet-high battlements as an observation post. Its extensive outbuildings in the courtyard were used as stables by cavalry patrols, thus making it a target for the IRA. The *Cork Examiner* reported on Thursday, 7 July 1921, under the heading 'Lohort Castle Burned. Sir T.C. O'Brien's Residence':

> On Tuesday night Lohort Castle, situated near Cecilstown, for many years the residence of Sir Timothy O'Brien, Bart., was destroyed by fire. The building had the appearance of an old mediaeval castle. Only the walls at present are standing. The outbuildings have also been burned. The castle and demesne attached had for some years past been the property of Messrs Eustace and Co. Ltd of Cork that firm having purchased from Sir Timothy O'Brien.

The redoubt (gatehouse) at Lohort Castle, photographed during the 1970s, bearing the scars of the 5 July 1921 IRA arson attack and the ravages of the Irish weather in the subsequent decades.

COURTESY *SEANCHAS DÚTHALLA* MAGAZINE (1978) VIA SEÁN RADLEY, MILLSTREET MUSEUM, COUNTY CORK

The roof of the castle tower had been broken up by the insurgents to improve airflow to the incendiary material – hay soaked with petrol. The tower was totally gutted from

the third to the seventh floor and never restored following the fire. Also destroyed was the gatehouse or 'redoubt'. In historical military terms, the redoubt was the part of a fortress that acted as a place of retreat for soldiers. It formed the entrance to the tower, with the eight-foot-wide moat lying between the redoubt and the tower. Evidence remains almost a century later of the burnt wall joists and rafters in the redoubt.

The newspapers of the time were reporting on atrocities including kidnappings, shootings, sabotage, and executions, resulting variously in the deaths of soldiers, Royal Irish Constabulary officers and civilians. The truce to end the War of Independence was declared six days after the burning of Lohort Castle. The top half of the structure was destroyed. Eustace and Company claimed compensation amounting to £101,500 but the judge, on 9 October 1921, aware of the impending sale of the castle, awarded nominal damages of £14,000. The McCabe family took ownership of the property in the mid-1920s and it remained in that family until 2007. They resided in the lower two floors of the tower, which were not destroyed in the fire. In March 2012

it was acquired by Lohort Management Limited with plans to restore the castle and associated buildings. The restoration began with the courtyard outbuildings.

In late 1919, the O'Briens were residing at Rockford Manor on the Stradbrook Road, Blackrock, south County Dublin. The registration to complete the purchase of this property was finalised on 11 April 1919. The Tudor-style mansion was erected by Sir William Betham. It had a splendid view of the Dublin and Wicklow Mountains. It was described thus:

> The house is approached from the high road by a handsome carriage drive, with an excellent two-storey gate lodge at the entrance. The dwelling house contains three reception rooms, four large and four small bedrooms, w.c., with five servants' bedrooms, kitchen, larder, pantry, dairy, wine cellar, two store and harness rooms. The granite built mansion is distinguished by its many gables, stone buttresses, diagonal chimney stacks and mullioned windows.

During the summers of 1921, 1922 and 1923, the O'Brien sisters, while residing at Blackrock, returned to County Kildare and took part in local tennis tournaments. On Thursday, 7 September 1922, Sicele, aged 35, along with Reverend Canon Craig, won the mixed open tennis doubles. The competition included her sisters Gundrede and Eileen as entrants. Again on Monday, 30 July 1923, Sicele was a competitor at the open lawn tennis tournament at Oldtown, Naas.

The O'Briens were still a very proud family and they recovered from the financial destruction they had endured in Cork. They were able to provide a lavish wedding for Sicele's younger sister Eileen, born on 1 February 1895, when she married Brigadier Edward Thomas A.G. Boylan on 3 January 1923 in the Church of St John the Baptist, Blackrock, County Dublin. Britain's Pathé News covered the ceremony and film footage shows police containing the crowd of well-wishers outside the church. Eileen's sisters, Gundrede and Doreen, were two of the four bridesmaids. Rockford Manor was the location for the elaborate and well-attended reception, where gifts were displayed in two rooms. This marriage bore four children: Edward Anthony, born on 24 February 1925; Anne Cecilia, born on 6 April 1928; Doreen Gundrede, born on 30 December 1931; and Desmond Francis, born on 26 November 1934.

Brigadier Boylan served in the First World War with the Royal Horse Artillery and was decorated with the Distinguished Service Order and the Military Cross. After service in the Second World War he was given the title of Commander of the Most Excellent Order of the British Empire (CBE). Along with Eileen, he retired to Hilltown, County Meath, and died there on 24 September 1959, aged 65. Eileen entered the Medical Missionaries of Mary, Drogheda, County Louth, on 8 March 1968, aged 73. The Boylan family were well known to this order and, in view of Mrs Boylan's age, she was only required to do one year's novitiate before making her first profession on 3 October 1969 and her final profession on 24 August 1975. She died on 1 August 1983 and is buried in St Peter's Cemetery, Drogheda, in the Medical Missionaries of Mary plot.

At Bonhams auction rooms, Montpelier Street, Knightsbridge, London, Brigadier Edward Boylan's war medals were sold for £3,240 on 26 September 2012. Brigadier and Eileen Boylan's eldest son, Major Edward Anthony Boylan, was a racehorse owner and served in the Royal Horse Artillery. He obtained his Aviator's Certificate and, having accumulated over 1,000 flying hours, entered the Rothmans International Air Rally at Ballyfree, Glenealy, County Wicklow, on Sunday, 4 June 1967. His entry was in Auster J.1 EI-AMK, and he won the Handicap Race from a field of 60 entrants. He entered the following year in the same aircraft and finished in nineteenth position in a field of 72 entrants. Major Boylan was a nephew of Sicele O'Brien.

Rockford Manor was sold on 9 May 1924 to Charles T.J.G. Walmesley. In recent years the manor became part of a

Brigadier Edward Boylan and Eileen O'Brien leaving the church in Blackrock following their marriage service, 3 January 1923.
COURTESY BRITISH PATHÉ

development of modern residential properties. The O'Briens returned to London and lived at 40 Hans Mansions near Brompton Road, Kensington, in the south-west of the city. In 1928, Sir Tim and the family moved to 282 Earl's Court Road, near Kensington Gardens, close to the centre of London. Following the outbreak of the Second World War, they made their final move, to Myndon Ville, Ramsey, in the Isle of Man, and Sir Tim died there on 9 December 1948 at 87 years of age. At the time of his death he was the oldest England cricketer to have played in a home test against Australia. His widow, Gundrede, died on 17 December 1952, aged 92. Their daughter Gundrede relocated to the Isle of Man to care for her parents. While there she met a widower, Richard Forbes, whom she married on 1 September 1947. Richard Forbes died on 30 May 1960 and Gundrede died on 14 March 1971. There were no children from their marriage.

Mariquita also moved to the Isle of Man. Her only child, James Timothy Noel Price, married Anne Margaret Younger on 13 March 1943. They had five children: Jenifer Mary, born on 6 January 1944; Timothy James, born on 15 September 1945; Jacqueline Anne, born on 15 January 1948; Simon Anthony, born on 15 January 1951; and Mary Elizabeth, born on 26 April 1953.

In 1925, Sir Tim's youngest son, Robert, married Ester Ethel Coghill and they had three daughters: Patricia Mary, Sheelagh Tessa and Shaunagh Gundrede. At the time of his father's death, Robert, fourth Baronet, was residing at Red House Farm, Monk Sherborne, Basingstoke, Hampshire.

Meanwhile, Sicele had developed an interest in aviation. She joined the London Aeroplane Club at Stag Lane Aerodrome, Edgware Road, west London, a distance of nine miles from her home. Stag Lane had been the home of the de Havilland Aircraft Company ever since Geoffrey de Havilland established it there in September 1920. In 1925 the Air Ministry introduced a scheme for encouraging the formation of light-

Stag Lane Aerodrome in 1926. Sicele O'Brien underwent pilot training here with the London Aeroplane Club.
Courtesy de Havilland Moth Club Archive

aeroplane clubs throughout Britain. It was conducted under the auspices of the Royal Aero Club and they formed the London Aeroplane Club at Stag Lane, which was officially opened 19 August 1925. At Stag Lane, two separate organisations coexisted. The more commercial of the two was the de Havilland School of Flying, run by Geoffrey de Havilland and catering largely for RAF reservists, with lessons costing £5 an hour. Thanks to its annual government grant of £2,000, the London Aeroplane Club, which leased its land from the canny de Havilland, was able to give lessons for about half that rate. Having passed the various tests, a new pilot could use the club's machines for a fee of £1 per hour and take part in races, displays and stunts.

In a later article, 'When You Learn to Fly', Sicele O'Brien gave some indication of the cost and requirements for an Aviator's Certificate at the time:

> The flying costs varied from £2 to £2.10s with an instructor or £1 or 30s solo due to the generous subsidy provided by the Government. An average person will fly solo after about 10 to 12 hours instruction. After three hours solo you will be eligible to pass the tests for a Private Pilot's Certificate, commonly called the 'A' ticket. So that for £25 to £35 you could qualify as a private pilot. You will need a medical certificate. For clothing you will need a good fitting leather flying helmet complete with speaking tube, googles and a fur or leather coat. The flight instruments are basic – altimeter, oil gauge and an air-speed indicator.

Sicele's training commenced during the week ending Saturday, 7 November 1925 with Captain F.G.M. Sparkes as her instructor. Also undergoing flight instruction at Stag Lane at that time was Limerick woman Sophie Eliott-Lynn, who had recently taken her first solo flight. Sophie Eliott-Lynn successfully completed tests for her Aviator's 'A' Certificate on Wednesday, 4 November 1925, the same week that Sicele began her training. Sicele received further instruction during the weeks ending 14 November 1925, 5 December 1925, 19 December 1925 and 23 January 1926. This training was irregular and erratic in its scheduling.

In April 1926, Sophie Eliott-Lynn purchased her own de Havilland Moth, G-EBKT, and used it to continue instruction for her 'B' (Commercial) Certificate, which she earned in June 1926. The 1926 fifth King's Cup Race commenced and finished at nearby Hendon Aerodrome on the weekend of 9 and 10 July. Sicele O'Brien, along with other members of the London Aeroplane Club, were granted free admission to the event as flying was suspended at Stag Lane on the Saturday afternoon. Her presence at this event would have whetted her appetite for the sport of air racing. From March 1926 the weekly aviation magazine *Flight* indicated that Sicele was now showing more enthusiasm and receiving instruction at Stag Lane more frequently, with training flights almost every week and through the summer. She achieved her first solo flight during the week of 26 August 1926.

The club was represented at the Bournemouth Race Meeting on Saturday, 21 August 1926. Successful entrants were Sicele's instructor, Captain Sparkes, and her close friend Sophie Eliott-Lynn. Another Irishwoman that showed an interest in flying was Lady Bailey from Rossmore Castle, County Monaghan. Lady Bailey received her introductory flight with Sophie, on 7 June 1926 at Stag Lane and commenced formal flight instruction during the first week in September. While flying solo during September, Sicele crashed the club's Moth, G-EBLI. There were no injuries and the aircraft was repaired.

By the beginning of October, the trio of Irish female aviators were a regular sight at Stag Lane. Lady Bailey was undergoing *ab-initio* instruction, while Sicele was preparing for her examination for her Aviator's 'A' Certificate and Sophie was giving flying instruction to student pilots and clocking up hours flying her own machine. On Monday, 18 October 1926, both Sicele, aged 39, and Lady Bailey, aged 35, successfully completed the tests for their Aviator's Certificates. Sicele wasted no time in lodging her application with the Royal Aero Club and was issued with Aviator's Certificate number 8045 on 20 October 1926. Before 1925, only eight women in Britain had been issued an Aviator's 'A' Certificate. Sophie was the ninth and Sicele was the tenth. Had Lady Bailey been as prompt as Sicele in submitting her application to the Royal Aero Club, the Irish trio would have received their certificates

O'BRIEN, Miss Sicele   8045

        41, Hans Mansions, S.W.l.

Born 1st April 1887   *at* London, England
Nationality   British
Rank, Regiment, Profession
Certificate taken on D.H."Moth", 27/60 h.p. Cirrus
At London Aeroplane Club, Stag Lane Aerodrome
Date 20th October 1926.

        Competition Licence No 2   12 July 1928

The Royal Aero Club Aviator's Certificate issued to Sicele O'Brien on 20 October 1926 along with the photograph that accompanied the certificate. An amendment made by hand on the certificate states: 'Commercial Licence No 2, 12 July 1928'.

COURTESY ROYAL AERO CLUB TRUST

in succession. Instead, Lady Bailey became the twelfth when hers was issued on 26 January 1927.

Within six months of obtaining her Aviator's Certificate, Sicele was entering aerial competitions and races. Her first was the Bournemouth Easter Meeting, held over three days on Good Friday, Easter Saturday and Easter Monday, 15, 16 and 18 April 1927, at Ensbury Park Racecourse. The meeting was the largest such event of its type to date in Britain, with a record 28 machines accumulating 153 entries into a variety of events and races. The de Havilland Moth was the aircraft type best represented. Sicele used the de Havilland 60 Moth with a Cirrus Mark I engine, G-EBKT. This particular aircraft was a prototype, first flown by Geoffrey de Havilland on 22 February 1925. Alan Cobham had used it successfully in his record-breaking flight from Croydon to Zurich and again when he entered the 1925 King's Cup Race. It had been purchased by Sophie Eliott-Lynn on 17 April 1926 and she had entered it in the Paris Concours d'Avions Économiques in August 1926. The London Aeroplane Club had acquired it from Sophie on 4 February 1927. The club then permitted Sicele to enter it in Bournemouth. Thus, the aircraft had a proven track record by the time of the air meet.

Saturday, 16 April 1927 started off with better weather than the previous day. The third event of the day was the Bournemouth Aerial Oaks Handicap Race over two laps of the five-mile course. This race was for female pilots only. Lady Bailey was absent owing to a recent mishap she had had at Stag Lane and Sophie Eliott-Lynn was in Africa. J.R. Bell started scratch in the Moth, G-EBNO, and handicapping allowed Sicele a 50-second headstart in G-EBKT. *Flight* summarised the race thus:

> Miss O'Brien handled her machine splendidly, her cornering being particularly good. Mrs Bell, although flying very well indeed, did not appear quite so certain of herself and Miss O'Brien deserved her win. She got 75 mph out of 'KT around the course, which was by no means bad.

In July the London Aeroplane Club made a presentation to Sicele of a gold wristlet watch to commemorate her victory in the first Aerial Oaks.

Lady Bailey and Sophie Eliott-Lynn entered their names in the aviation record books when, on 18 May 1927, they ascended from Hamble Aerodrome,

Southampton. With Sophie as pilot and Lady Bailey as passenger in an Avro Avian, they reached an altitude of 15,748 feet, establishing a new height record. On 5 July Lady Bailey, piloting a de Havilland Moth with Geoffrey de Havilland's wife, Louie, as passenger, attained a new height record for a two-seat light aeroplane of 17,283 feet.

The summer of 1927 saw Sicele enter more aviation races and events. The Bournemouth Whitsun Meeting, organised by the Royal Aero Club, took place on Saturday, 4 June 1927. The trio of Irish ladies all entered. A dark shadow was cast over the aerodrome before the events commenced, however. During the morning a crash occurred that proved fatal for the passenger and caused serious injury to the pilot. The day was dampened by the event but the meeting continued. A report in *Flight* magazine 9 June 1927 stated:

> The second race of the day was open to lady pilots only and two of the five machines entered for this race were non-starters. The three starters were Miss S. O'Brien in the de Havilland Moth (G-EBMF) with Cirrus Mark I engine; Lady Bailey in her Moth (G-EBPU), Cirrus Mark II engine and Mrs Eliott-Lynn in G-EBPW the Westland Widgeon III monoplane, Cirrus Mark II engine. The machines started on the order indicated, Miss O'Brien being 'limit man' and Mrs Eliott-Lynn being scratch. All three handled their machines excellently, making very good turns at the aerodrome turning point, those of Mrs Eliott-Lynn being particularly good and practically vertical. The race was won by Mrs Eliott-Lynn, with Miss O'Brien second and Lady Bailey third.

Hucknall near Nottingham was the venue for the sixth King's Cup Race, which took place on Saturday, 30 July 1927. Sophie Eliott-Lynn and Lady Bailey were the only two female entrants. Prior to the race, Sophie withdrew in protest at the new handicap formula. Lady Bailey was the only woman to begin the prestigious race but she was forced to retire because her aircraft suffered a broken valve spring. On the following Monday the

trio featured again at the Nottingham Flying Meeting at Hucknall Aerodrome. They were the only entrants in the Ladies' Purse Race. The course was a triangular one of 8.5 miles in which rounded corners, about 200 yards apart, were used instead of the usual sharp-angled turning points. This made for much greater safety, especially when several competitors rounded a corner together. Also for safety's sake, the number of competitors flying at the same time in any event was limited to six. *Flight* reported to its readers on 4 August 1927:

> The race for the Ladies Purse was a good race. The three competitors were: Miss O'Brien on Moth Cirrus I, G-EBLI; Mrs Eliott-Lynn on Moth Cirrus I, G-EBMV and Lady Bailey on Moth Cirrus II, G-EBPU. The ladies got away in fine style, Lady Bailey gaining on Mrs Eliott-Lynn who had already passed Miss O'Brien. The finish was most exciting, for flying down the final leg it seemed that Lady Bailey was leading but when crossing the line Mrs Eliott-Lynn dived and got across first – but only by about two yards!

The trio of Irish female pilots from the London Aeroplane Club who took part in various air races during 1927. Left to right: Sophie Eliott-Lynn, Lady Bailey and Sicele O'Brien.
COURTESY DAVID RUSHWORTH VIA MARK ASHFORD

The de Havilland 60 Moth G-EBOS at Stag Lane in 1927, before it was owned by Sicele O'Brien. This aircraft was involved in the crash on 20 October 1928 in which Sicele lost part of her leg.

COURTESY DE HAVILLAND MOTH CLUB ARCHIVE

That weekend, Sicele took ownership of a de Havilland 60 Moth that had been operated from new by the de Havilland School of Flying at Stag Lane since 5 July 1926 and was registered G-EBOS. It was placed on the UK civil-aircraft register in Sicele's name on 2 August 1927. She had it painted blue and silver and, in order to match the colour scheme, she purchased a blue leather coat and beaver-lined flying helmet. The average price of a new Moth in those times was £675 and such a machine could be hangared at Stag Lane for £3 5s per month.

The body of Sophie Eliott-Lynn's estranged husband was discovered in the River Thames on 1 May 1927. On 11 October 1927, 30-year-old Sophie married 75-year-old mine owner Sir James Heath. This marriage entitled Sophie to be addressed as Lady Heath. On 18 November 1927, along with her new husband, they sailed to Cape Town, South Africa, and on 5 January 1928 she commenced her epic and historic solo flight back to London, where she arrived on 17 May 1928. (Further detail about Lady Heath is contained in another chapter.) As Lady Heath was on the final stages of this journey, Sicele was in California, where she entered for an air race. Under the headline 'Aviatrix Places in Race after Hand Is Caught in Propeller', the front page of *The Sun* newspaper for San Bernardino County of 6 May 1928 reported to its readers:

> Miss Cecily [*sic*] O'Brien, daughter of Sir Timothy O'Brien of Dublin and one of England's well known airwomen, won second place today in a 70 mile race with a bottle of smelling salts beside her to prevent fainting from the pain of an injured hand. Before the race Miss O'Brien had caught her hand in the propeller of her plane, tearing the palm. She declined to quit the race, but had a surgeon bandage it and used it on the controls throughout the race.

The Air Pageant at Squires Gate, Blackpool, Lancashire, was held in stormy and blustery conditions on Friday, 6 July 1928. Several races were cancelled and some aircraft were blown over. The races proved a challenge even to experienced aviators and landing safely required great skill and luck. Sicele entered for the Open Handicap Race in her Moth, G-EBOS. She received a handicap allowance of 11 minutes and 27 seconds and finished in second position in the first heat with an average speed of 83.5 miles per hour. The heat winner was Flight Lieutenant Tommy Rose, with an average speed of 84.5 miles per hour. Two laps of the course were flown, totalling 29 miles. Unfortunately, in the finals the following day, Sicele was not among the top three finishers. She did enter the *Daily Sketch* Nomination Handicap Race on

Saturday, 7 July 1928. There she fared better, winning the final of this event with Miss Mawdsley as passenger, again entering her own aircraft, G-EBOS. She had a handicap allowance of 2 minutes and 33 seconds and completed the race in a time of 10 minutes and 42 seconds, at an average speed of 84 miles per hour. Second position went to Captain Valentine Baker, Chief Flying Instructor at the London Aeroplane Club, Stag Lane. (In 1934, he joined with James Martin to form the Martin-Baker Aircraft Company Limited). Sicele beat Captain Baker by one second. Her prize was the *Daily Sketch* Challenge Cup and £60.

Lady Heath and Sicele joined forces a few days later to make an attempt at another altitude record. *Flight* magazine 12 July 1928 reported:

> On 10 July 1928 Lady Heath accompanied by Miss S. O'Brien ascended from Rochester in the Short 'Mussel' G-EBMJ, an all-metal light seaplane (Cirrus engine) in an attempt to create a world's altitude record for the light seaplane class. The flight lasted 1 hour 50 minutes during which, according to the sealed barograph, an altitude of 13,400 feet was attained.

Sicele (left) and her passenger, the Honourable Miss Mildred K. Leith, in front of Sicele's Moth, G-EBOS, on arrival at Rotterdam, 20 July 1928.

COURTESY MICHAEL HEALY

Sicele was so thrilled with her experience of flying in a Short Mussel seaplane that she remained at Rochester to learn to fly this type of aircraft. By now Sicele was a member of the Royal Engineering Society, which she joined while studying aircraft engineering.

In the early months of 1928, Sicele began taking instruction at Stag Lane for her 'B' (Commercial) Certificate. This was issued to her on 12 July 1928 and she became only the second female in the United Kingdom to earn such a certificate, the first being Sophie Eliott-Lynn in June 1926.

The King's Cup Race was the most important race in British aviation and was scheduled for 20 July 1928. Lady Heath had designs on promoting her intention of flying commercially with an airline. The Dutch airline KLM was recruiting air crew and she decided to forgo entry in the King's Cup Race. Instead Lady Heath travelled to Holland to partake in the Rotterdam Meeting on 20, 21 and 22 July 1928 in Waalhaven and to show KLM her flying skills. She arrived just before the appointed time of 4pm, along with her secretary, in the de Havilland Moth G-EBZC purchased two weeks earlier on 3 July 1928. About an hour later, Sicele and her passenger, the Honourable Miss Mildred K. Leith, touched down in Sicele's Moth, G-EBOS. Sicele had understood the nominated arrival time to be 4pm Greenwich Mean Time; instead, it was local time. This error cost her a

Photographed on 20 July 1928 in front of Lady Heath's Moth, G-EBZC, in Rotterdam are (from left to right): Sicele O'Brien, the Honourable Miss M.K. Leith, Captain Cordes and his passenger, Mr Cooke, Lady Heath and her private secretary. In the background are Moths G-EBXG and G-EBOS, the latter of which belonged to Sicele.
COURTESY ROYAL AERO CLUB TRUST

considerable number of points. That evening a dinner was hosted at the De Maas Yacht Club.

Sunday was reserved for the more serious sections of the weekend's programme. Both Irish ladies entered for the take-off and landing competitions. In the section to determine the shortest take-off distance, Lady Heath was placed third, with a take-off run of 63.7 metres. Sicele took ninth and final place, with a run of 109 metres. In the Landing Competition, Lady Heath was second, having come to a halt with a landing distance of 108 metres, and Sicele was fourth, with a recorded distance of 116.5 metres. In the afternoon the first event was the Speed Test, which was flown over a triangular course of 20 kilometres' length, which had to be covered twice. The winner was Lady Heath, with an average speed of 98.8 miles per hour. Sicele recorded an average speed of 79.2 miles per hour to finish fifth in the event.

The Relay Race followed and Sicele was a member of the winning team. In the Rally she finished in third position. In the final classification Lady Heath took overall first place with 176.5 points; Sicele was seventh with 104.3 points. That evening the participants were guests at a banquet hosted jointly by the Rotterdam Aero Club and KLM. The weekend had an added bonus for Lady Heath, as she was recruited by KLM to fly as co-pilot on their large Fokker aircraft.

Saturday, 20 October 1928 was the second anniversary of the date Sicele was issued her Aviator's 'A' Certificate. Tragedy struck when she was giving instruction to Miss Leith in her de Havilland Moth, G-EBOS. The accident occurred at Mill Hill Golf Club, Barnet, north London, about five miles north of Stag Lane. The student accidentally caused the aircraft to enter a spin, whereupon Sicele discovered, to her horror, that she had gone up with her dual-control rudder bar disconnected – otherwise she would have been able to initiate the normal spin-recovery procedure. With

the joystick alone she managed to induce a wide spiral turn before impact – a course of action that saved their lives. The crash caused Sicele serious injury, however, resulting in the amputation of one leg below the knee. Her passenger suffered only concussion.

At the time of the crash, Sicele was living with her parents at 282 Earl's Court Road, London. The aircraft was written off and unfortunately, as the insurance had lapsed a few days before the crash, her loss was total. The aircraft was cancelled from the UK civil-aircraft register on 2 November 1928. By Christmas, Sicele was making a good recovery and was contemplating resuming her flying career.

Miss Leith was involved in another incident on 8 June 1929, when flying the London Aeroplane Club's de Havilland Moth, G-AABL. She collided with Captain Guest's de Havilland Airco, G-EBVS. According to *Flight* magazine of 13 June 1929:

> The two aircraft were about to alight and were a few feet off the ground when the collision took place. The damage to both aircraft was somewhat considerable but both pilots were unhurt.

While unable to fly, Sicele did not forsake the occupation to which she was so attached. She began to write aviation articles for *Air*, the monthly magazine of the Air League. In the December 1928 issue, she colourfully portrayed for readers a two-hour journey in her Moth from Stag Lane to the south coast near Bournemouth, where she stayed overnight and returned to London the next day. She concluded the

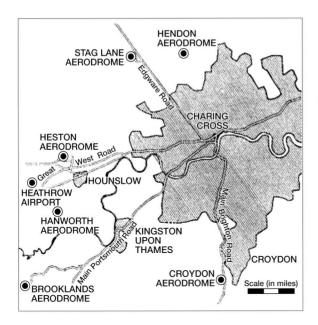

The articles compiled and submitted by Sicele O'Brien for *Air* magazine in 1929 and 1930 were:

'Is Aviation a Profitable Career for Women?'
'Suitable Flying Kit for Women'
'Flying as an Education for Women'
'Private Flying in Britain'
'When You Learn to Fly'
'The First Lessons in the Air'
'About Flying Licences'
'The £.s.d. of Flying'
'Cross-Country Flying'
'Keeping an Aeroplane of One's Own'
'Some of the Light Aeroplanes for the Private Owner'
'What is the Use of Airships?'
'The Latest Types of Light Aeroplanes'
'When you Attempt Aerobatics'

article with, 'Aeroplanes do bring the unbeaten tracks and quiet places within easy reach of London.' The following year, her articles gave advice and tips to fellow pilots, based on her experiences. November 1929's article was entitled 'Cross-Country Flying for Beginners'. The following month it was 'The Choice of Light Aeroplanes', offering advice on what to look for when buying an aeroplane. She contributed articles to *Air* throughout 1930.

The Girl's Own Paper was a monthly magazine aimed at young women in Britain, which had been in circulation for 50 years. The monthly editions were combined and published annually as *The Girl's Own Annual*. While continuing her recuperation and recovery, Sicele also subscribed to this popular monthly magazine. Her articles first appeared in 1929 and continued through 1930 (Volumes 50 and 51).

Little more than six months had elapsed from the time the accident that almost cost Sicele her life, when she was the main organiser of the first successful air rally to be held in Scotland. The location was the grounds of the Gleneagles Hotel, Perthshire. (The hotel was opened in 1924 and is now established as one of the premier locations in the world for golfing tournaments, including the 2014 Ryder Cup.) An improvised aerodrome was staged on a suitable piece of ground, selected by Sicele, just a few

The Gleneagles Hotel, Perthshire, was the location for the first Scottish Air Rally, held on 11 May 1929. The event organiser was Sicele O'Brien.

COURTESY ROYAL COMMISSION ON THE ANCIENT AND HISTORICAL MONUMENTS OF SCOTLAND VIA GLENEAGLES HOTEL

Suitable Flying Kit for Women

By SICELE O'BRIEN

One of Sicele's several articles published in The Girl's Own Paper *during 1929 and 1930.*

COURTESY THE GIRL'S OWN PAPER

I FEEL so thankful that our lady pioneers in aviation had not the modern craze for dressing up as men, discarding skirts—such as there is of them—for breeches and leggings. For skirts are no handicap in the air, but if our first lady aeroplane owners had been another type, they would have started the fashion of breeches or "plus fours"!

If you set forth to break height records, it is certainly extremely cold above 10,000 feet, and a Sidcot suit, consisting of coat and trousers in one piece, fleece-lined, is a comfort up there. But the usual cross-country flying is done between 15,000 and 2 or 3,000 feet, and you are far more sheltered in a light plane than in the back of an open car. You sit low, the sides of the cockpit coming about up to your neck, and have a little talc windscreen in front of your face.

If piloting the machine, you certainly need goggles, as you look outside the talc when you want to see specially clearly, and even for a passenger in an open machine they are far pleasanter. Triplex glass are advisable in case of a possible crash. Though in civil aviation fatalities are happily rare, machines are crashed more frequently, and the occupants usually scramble out smiling.

A leather flying helmet is the most comfy head-gear, and if pilot and passenger have them fitted with speaking-tubes attached to the ear-pieces they can carry on conversation, which adds to the interest of the flight, especially if one of them knows and can describe the country over which they are flying.

Hard Fur is Better than Soft Fur.

In winter a leather coat with woollies underneath, or a hard fur coat, is good. I suggest a hard fur,

Miss O'Brien about to Start.
Photo by Photopress.

as soft, pretty ones, like moleskin, not only wear badly, but are none too warm. And if you are doing a cross-country flight of several hours in winter your feet and legs get cold unless you wear thick shoes and gaiters, or woollen stockings over your silk ones. Waterproof Cording's boots are good, especially as many of the aerodromes are quagmires in winter.

There is a locker behind in which you can take thin shoes, hats, and even suit-cases. Going solo, I have filled the front cockpit with enough clothes, including hats, evening frocks and riding habits, for a visit and a month's hunting!

Some of the women aviators favour coats to match their machines. Miss Winifred Brown, of the Lancashire Flying Club, has a red and silver Avian, and used to wear a smart red suède coat and flying cap at the air race meetings last summer. When I bought my Moth and had it painted blue and silver, I got a blue leather coat and beaver-lined flying helmet to match.

A Warm Coat is Essential.

Even in a shut air liner you want a good warm coat in winter, and would be safe in having one by you in the vagaries of our English summer—though on the Paris trip you are only

in the air one and a half to two hours, and not much longer to Cologne or Rotterdam. I think keeping warm is the great secret of warding off both sea and air sickness, which some people suffer from in these big three-engined machines. But in our light aeroplanes, with one engine and comparatively little vibration, breathing the purest air, one has no excuse for not feeling one's best.

When Travelling to India.

The air service we are just starting to India is scheduled to take six days—a great difference from the three weeks it takes by boat. And some day, doubtless, parts of the route will be lit for night flying, as is already the case on the United States air routes, and we could then get to Karachi in three days.

The present scheme is to fly to Basle the first day and then go by train under the Alps to Genoa during the night. The other nights will be spent in hotels. From Genoa all down the Italian coast to Sicily sounds a most lovely flight, and this and the stage across the Mediterranean to the African coast will be done in big flying boats. At Cairo you change to the air liners that are already on the Far East route to Bazra for the last couple of years, and they will now continue the trip along the Persian Gulf to Karachi.

I have never flown over the regions of the Equator, but am told that it is not unpleasantly warm up at a couple of thousand feet; however, I expect you will want your solar topees when you land.

Isn't it wonderful to think how these air routes will draw the Empire together, and tighten the bonds between the Mother Country and her Dominions, let us hope, to the advancement of our mutual esteem.

minutes' walk from the hotel. The rally took place on Saturday, 11 May 1929. The Arrivals Competition was won by a Mr Jackson, who had flown from Slough, Berkshire. He had covered the 350 miles in a time of 4 hours and 10 minutes. This first Scottish Air Rally included 20 aircraft from throughout the United Kingdom and attracted over 2,000 spectators. The events passed off without a hitch and that evening a ball was held at the hotel, attended by the Captain and members of the recently defeated American Ryder Cup team. Sicele did not participate in any events, as her Aviator's 'A' and 'B' Certificates had been revoked by the Air Ministry after her crash.

With a persistence that showed her remarkable determination as well as her love of aviation, Sicele took and passed a medical examination to attest that she had recovered from such post-crash effects as would incapacitate her for flying. Her artificial foot would not necessarily be a serious handicap in controlling an aeroplane. On receipt of the medical certificate in March 1930, 16 months after the crash, the Air Ministry renewed her 'A' Certificate. However, her 'B' Certificate, permitting her to fly for hire or reward, remained revoked. Sicele may have been one of the first disabled women in the world to fly. It was announced in *Flight* magazine of 21 March 1930 that she would embark on a 'Buy British Goods' campaign, whereby she would fly around the country and give a series of flying lectures. After each lecture she would give joy-rides to members of the audience.

A new aviation group of the Forum Club was formed in April 1930. The President was Lady Bailey and the Honorary Secretary was Sicele O'Brien. Their first outing, by means of a group flight, was to Hedon Aerodrome, Hull, to attend the official opening of the clubhouse on Saturday, 12 April 1930. The Forum Club was the first British women's club to form an aviation group.

Parnham Country Club near Beaminster in Dorset was the location for another flying display organised by Sicele, on Saturday, 10 May 1930. Weather prevented some of the events from proceeding. The opening event was the Arrivals Competition. The field selected by Sicele was on top of a hill and close to the country club, where a lunch was held. This was followed by an aerobatic display by Flight Lieutenant Rose. Despite the rain that afternoon, a large crowd gathered to witness the aerial activities.

Sicele was flying with some of the most famous female aviators in Britain at that time, including some world-famous pioneers. Lady Heath departed solo from Cape Town, South Africa, on 5 January 1928 and arrived in Croydon, London, on 17 May 1928. Lady Bailey departed solo from London on 9 March 1928 and arrived in Cape Town on 30 April 1928. She departed Cape Town on 21 September 1928 and arrived back in London on 16 January 1929. Amy Johnson, the first woman to fly solo to Australia, departed London on 5 May 1930 and arrived in Darwin on 24 May 1930. In July 1931 Amy Johnson flew from London to Tokyo via Moscow in record-breaking time and in November 1932 she broke the solo record for the London to Cape Town flight. Winifred Spooner was placed second in the 1928 King's Cup Race and fifth in the 1929 race. In 1929 Winifred Spooner was awarded the Harmon Trophy as the world's most outstanding female aviator. Jean Batten was a New Zealand-born aviator who also received instruction at Stag Lane, qualifying in December 1930, and embarked on flights from England to Australia, New Zealand and Brazil. Throughout the world these women were presented with medals, trophies and diplomas of honour for their achievements and contributions to aviation. They were all contemporaries of Sicele's at the London Aeroplane Club.

On 8 August 1930, a Westland Woodpigeon, G-EBIY, was registered to Sicele. This aircraft was the result of a competition by the Air Ministry in September 1924 to 'Produce a two-seat light aeroplane with folding wings and an engine capacity not exceeding 1,000 c.c. Its minimum control speed below 45 mph should be accompanied by a maximum speed of more than 60 mph.'

Westland's entry in the competition was G-EBIY, with seating for the pilot aft of the passenger. It bore constructors' serial number one. On 8 September 1930, a month after acquiring the aircraft, Sicele had it withdrawn from use and, less than six months later, on 27 February 1931, it was officially removed from the UK civil-aircraft register.

Aston Clinton, between Tring and Aylesbury in Buckinghamshire, was the location for a flying display organised by Sicele on Saturday, 18 April 1931. As there was no proper aerodrome at Aston Clinton, the 20 competitors for the treasure hunt commenced at nearby Hanworth Aerodrome and sought clues in the vicinity of the country club. The event went ahead, despite much rain and snow, during which an aerobatics display thrilled the spectators.

Sicele, along with Enid Merlin Gordon Gallien, purchased a Blackburn Bluebird III biplane from H.R. Law. H.R. Law had bought the wood-and-fabric machine in May 1930 from the original owners, the Suffolk and Eastern Aeroplane Club, who had purchased it new in March 1929. G-AABF changed registration to both women on 10 June 1931. Enid Gallien's explorations in Tanganyika (now Tanzania) earned recognition from the Royal Geographical Society, before whom she lectured. She also took an expedition, of which she was the only European member, along the Sudanese border of Abyssinia. One of her journeys was from Damascus to Baghdad and she also travelled

Sicele's Westland Woodpigeon, G-EBIY, prior to registration, when it was a prototype model, in September 1924.
Courtesy Ray Watkins

The Blackburn Bluebird III biplane registered to Sicele O'Brien and Enid Gallien on 10 June 1931.
COURTESY JOHN CLIFFORD

through central Australia. Enid Gallien had learned to fly at Hanworth Club, and received her Aviator's 'A' Certificate (number 9222) from the Royal Aero Club on 27 June 1930. She would have been more celebrated by the public if she had not, for obscure reasons, been at great pains to prevent her achievements from being known. Her husband, Ronald, was also a private pilot and an engineer with the Anglo-Persian Oil Company Limited. He earned his Aviator's Certificate (number 8938) on 31 January 1930.

After purchasing the machine, the new owners had it sent to the Blackburn Aeroplane Company at Brough, west of Hull, Yorkshire, to be reconditioned. The aeroplane was delivered to Hedon Aerodrome, east of Hull, after overhaul and Enid and Sicele called there to collect it on 18 June 1931. H.A. Love, Pilot in Charge at Hedon Aerodrome, tested the aeroplane and went up with Sicele while she became familiar with its handling characteristics. The owners then set off south towards Hatfield, a journey of approximately 120 miles. Their intended final destination was Hanworth Aerodrome

at Hounslow in west London, where the aircraft was to be based. The stop at Hatfield was a fuel stop, with a further 25 miles to Hanworth. It was close to the longest day of the year.

Hatfield Aerodrome, 1931, viewed from the north.
COURTESY JANIC GEELEN VIA JOHN CLIFFORD

Flight magazine of 26 June 1931 announced to its worldwide readers:

> It is with extreme regret that we have to announce the death, as the result of a flying accident on June 18 of Miss Sicele O'Brien and Mrs Gordon Gallien. They had arrived at Hatfield Aerodrome from Brough, in a Blackburn Bluebird en route for Hanworth and had just taken-off to resume the journey when the machine was seen to nose-dive in a spin. It crashed into a hayfield outside the aerodrome and immediately burst into flames. The machine was completely destroyed within a few minutes and it was impossible to rescue the unfortunate occupants. The bodies were charred beyond recognition.

Hatfield Aerodrome from the south-east, showing the departure route from the hangars. Sicele's flight proceeded clockwise (instead of anti-clockwise) around the white directional circle, then veered right before crashing and bursting into flames in a hayfield.
Courtesy Philip Birtles via John Clifford

Several eye-witnesses to the tragedy ran to the scene. Mr Grovenstock of Harpsfield Hall Farm, who arrived at the location a few minutes afterwards, said that 'it was quite impossible to get anywhere near the aeroplane to help the occupants whom he could see through the flames. There was however no sign of life from either of them.' In his opinion the pilot made a poor take-off but managed to clear some trees and then side-slipped and spun into the ground.

Hatfield Aerodrome had been opened in June 1930 specifically as a new home for the de Havilland School of Flying, which had been operating at Stag Lane since 1923. (The London Aeroplane Club followed to Hatfield in 1933.) The aerodrome site is presently the location for the University of Hertfordshire. Sicele O'Brien's crash was the first fatal incident at the aerodrome. A white circle on the aerodrome indicated the direction of arrival and departure – anti-clockwise, to avoid collision with other landing or departing aircraft. Sicele's take-off run broke this rule: she took off to the left of the white circle in a clockwise direction.

The Requiem Mass for Sicele O'Brien was held at the London Oratory, Brompton Road, south Kensington, London. Father John Talbot officiated. There was a large attendance at the Mass and accompanying Sicele's family was a wide circle of friends, dignitaries and aristocrats. The burial took place afterwards at the cemetery attached to the church of St Thomas of Canterbury, Rylston Road, Fulham. Sicele was 44 years of age.

The fatal departure route viewed from the north.
Courtesy BAE Systems via Reg Willoughby and John Clifford

The inquest into the deaths of both pilots was held four days later on 22 June 1931 at St Albans, seven miles west of Hatfield.

Sir Tim O'Brien said he recognised a ring that belonged to his daughter. Inspector Goodship said that 'other articles found on Miss O'Brien were too charred to be recognisable'. Donald Alsop, an accountant, of Shepard's House, Shepard-Market, Mayfair, added that he had 'known Mrs Gallien all his life'. A latch-key found in the wreckage corresponded with a key of Enid Gallien's London home, which was in the possession of Mrs Alsop.

Dr Percy M. Brittain of Hatfield told the inquest that, when he arrived at the scene of the accident, the aeroplane was on fire with two bodies inside. In his opinion, death in each case was due to shock from burns. Arthur Potter of Hatfield, timekeeper and night-watchman at the de Havilland School of Flying, said that 'at 8pm on Thursday a two-seater biplane made a good landing on the aerodrome. The machine was refilled and later the pilot and her passenger had tea in the club room.' When he was pushing the machine towards the petrol tank the pilot said, 'Don't lift too high, because I am rather heavy on the nose.' After he got the machine started, Sicele went a few yards and called to him, 'You will have to come and help me, I can't turn this thing across there.' He pointed out:

The Honourable Mrs Enid Merlin Gordon Gallien.
Courtesy Royal Aero Club Trust

> The spot which Miss O'Brien indicated was not the one from which pilots usually took off but Miss O'Brien appeared to be in a hurry. She began to taxi and went a considerable distance in comparison with what other pilots usually did before her machine left the ground.
>
> She left the ground about 18 inches or 2 feet then dropped again, took on a little more speed and eventually got off the ground and climbed against the wind. I thought that the trees were sheltering the wind but when I saw she was above the trees I was satisfied that she had got off all right.

The witness continued:

> When she rose she turned right, which is against the rules of the aerodrome. A gamekeeper who saw her take-off suddenly cried to me 'Look, Arthur, she's down.' I saw the machine spinning to the ground. The aeroplane struck the ground with her nose and burst into flames immediately. The machine crashed just outside the aerodrome in a hayfield.

Herbert Catlin, a Hatfield labourer, told the inquest that he saw the machine spin once or twice before crashing to the ground and bursting into flames. Harry Albert Love, Pilot in Charge of the Hull Aero Club, said:

> On Thursday morning Miss O'Brien and Mrs Gallien arrived by car at the club to call for the machine. Miss O'Brien said she was going to a gymkhana or something.

He added:

> She asked me to give her a few landings and racing turns as she intended to go in for a race there. Weather conditions were unfavourable, so she hung about a bit. Later conditions improved, so I took the machine up to test it. I found everything quite satisfactory.

After the test he went up with Sicele, who piloted the machine. He also told the inquest:

> Miss O'Brien before leaving asked to have the rudder-bar in Mrs Gallien's seat adjusted so that Mrs Gallien could work it. Miss O'Brien would perhaps find difficulty in getting the machine out of a spin because of her artificial leg and I thought she wanted the rudder bar adjusted so that Mrs Gallien could help her out of a spin.

Major James Cooper, Inspector of Accidents, Air Ministry, gave his opinion:

> The machine had hit the ground after a spin. The conditions were consistent with a stall. No part of the structure of the machine had failed in the air and none of the controls were defective. It was quite impossible to say if engine trouble had developed. It appeared Miss O'Brien took the shortest run into wind and one was forced to the conclusion that probably she pulled the machine off the ground a little early.

The Deputy Coroner, F. Turner, said he did not think there could be any blame attached to the pilot or the passenger. A verdict of 'accidental death' was returned. It was also stated during the course of the inquest that there was no reason to suppose that any purely physical defect was responsible for the accident. At the time of Sicele's death, the O'Briens were residing at 282 Earl's Court Road, London.

After Sicele's death, the *Peeps of Princethorpe* annual school magazine for 1931 recorded:

> Whilst tendering our heartfelt sympathy to Lady O'Brien on the sad death of her daughter, Sicele, whose early school days are a happy memory for us, we wish at the same time to offer our thanks for the beautiful gift of her own and Sicele's Court trains to be made up into vestments and we can assure her this shall be done and trust it will afford her some little consolation in her bereavement.

Thus ended the life of the second Irishwoman to be issued an Aviator's 'A' Certificate and the second woman in Britain to earn an Aviator's 'B' (Commercial) Certificate. Sicele O'Brien may also have earned the distinction of being the first disabled female pilot in Britain, and perhaps the world. Tragically, she is also recorded as the first Irishwoman to be killed in an aeroplane crash.

BIBLIOGRAPHY

Jane Falloon, *Throttle Full Open: A Life of Lady Bailey, Irish Aviatrix* (Dublin: Lilliput Press, 1999).

Lindie Naughton, *Lady Icarus: The Life of Irish Aviator Lady Mary Heath* (Dublin: Ashfield Press, 2004).

Flight magazine (1925–31).

ACKNOWLEDGEMENTS

John Clifford, aviation historian, Hatfield Aerodrome.

Alex Darkes and Celia Scott, Princethorpe College, Rugby.

Michael Healy, Lohort Castle, County Cork.

Liam Kenny and colleagues, historians, County Kildare.

Clare Walker, former Chairman of the British Women Pilots' Association.

Per Ardua ad Astra.

Of your Charity
Pray for the Repose of the Soul of
SICELE J. MARY ANNETTE O'BRIEN
Killed while flying on
JUNE 18th, 1931
On whose Soul sweet Jesus have Mercy.

———o———

ABSOLVE, we beseech Thee, O Lord, the soul of Thy servant SICELE that being dead to this world, she may live to Thee; and whatever sins she may have committed in this life, through human frailty, do Thou, of Thy most merciful goodness forgive, through Jesus Christ our Lord.   AMEN.

May she Rest in Peace.—Amen.

My Jesus Mercy.—(*100 days Ind.*)

Our Lady of Lourdes pray for her.

Sicele O'Brien is sadly immortalised as the first Irish female pilot to be killed in an aviation accident. She died on 18 June 1931 in her own aircraft.
COURTESY CLARE WALKER

LADY BAILEY
THE LONE LONG-DISTANCE AVIATRIX

Mary Westenra was born into an aristocratic family in County Monaghan and, at the age of 20, married one of South Africa's wealthiest entrepreneurs, who had made his fortune in the rich gold mines. After giving birth to five children, she decided to take up flying and set about creating altitude records and taking part in air races. She was the first woman to enter the King's Cup Race in 1927. In March 1928, aged 37, she embarked on a solo flight from London to Cape Town and back, which established world records as the longest solo flight by a woman and, indeed, the longest ever flight by a woman. Lady Bailey, as she was by then known, was lauded as a heroine and was one of the most famous women in the world at that moment. The International League of Aviators awarded her the Harmon Trophy as the most outstanding woman aviator in the world for 1927 and 1928. She was honoured with the title Dame Commander of the Most Excellent Order of the British Empire (DBE) for her services to aviation.

Lady Bailey at Léopoldville, Belgian Congo, in 1928.
COURTESY PROSPERO BAILEY

FOR CENTURIES THERE have been strong links between Ireland and Scotland. Through generations, families have transited in both directions. The largest movement was during the years of the Plantations, in particular the Plantation of Ulster, which began in 1609. Military leaders of the Crown were frequently rewarded with large areas of land in Ireland. One such Scottish officer was Major General Sir Alexander Cairnes, who settled in County Monaghan. In 1680 he bought a large estate from the fifth Lord Blayney. In future years this was to become the Rossmore Estate, adjacent to Monaghan town. In 1704 Cairnes fought at the Battle of Blenheim, Bavaria, and for this he was created a baronet in Monaghan. General Cairnes had only one daughter, Mary, born in 1705. On 3 August 1724, at the tender age of 19, Mary was married, against her will, to 31-year-old Cadwallader Blayney, the seventh Baron Blayney, whose family seat was at Blayney Castle near Castleblayney, County Monaghan. Mary became Lady Blayney, a title she retained for the rest of her life. Their marriage was childless.

Mary's husband died on 19 March 1732 and she inherited a portion of his large estates. When her father died on 30 October of the same year, Lady Blayney inherited all of his estates. Her fortune was further increased following the death of her uncle, Sir Henry Cairnes, who died childless in June 1743. This left Mary, the dowager Lady Blayney, a woman of considerable wealth and influence. She found happiness in her second marriage to Colonel John Murray, a wealthy landowner in County Monaghan. This marriage produced five daughters.

Mary was determined that her four surviving daughters would marry well. Her eldest daughter, Frances Murray, married William Fortescue in 1752.

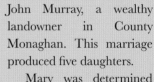

Blayney Castle, Castleblayney, County Monaghan, on the shores of Lough Muckno.
COURTESY LAWRENCE COLLECTION, NATIONAL LIBRARY OF IRELAND

He became the first Lord Clermont in 1770 and was reputed to be one of the richest men in Ireland at the time. Lord and Lady Clermont were close friends of royalty, including the future King George IV and Queen Marie Antoinette. They had no children. Lady Blayney moved to Corke Abbey, Bray, County Wicklow, and spent the last years of her life there. She died on 24 July 1790, aged 85. Frances inherited the entirety of her mother's vast fortune. The four daughters took precedence over entitlement to her estate over any males that might be born to them.

Another soldier of the Crown forces was General Robert Cunningham, who fought at the Battle of Culloden, Inverness, on 16 April 1746 and came to Ireland a few years later. General Cunningham married Lady Blayney's second daughter, Elizabeth Murray, on 29 May 1754. They had no children either. Robert became Member of Parliament at both Dublin and Westminster. In 1769 Elizabeth and Robert bought the magnificent Mount Kennedy House, Newtownmountkennedy, County Wicklow, along with 10,000 acres, for £19,691. In 1793 Major General Robert Cunningham was promoted to Commander in Chief of His Majesty's forces in Ireland and on 19 October 1796 was granted the title Baron (Lord) Rossmore of Monaghan. He died suddenly on 6 August 1801.

Lady Blayney's third daughter was Anne, who married a wealthy man, Theophilus Jones. Theophilus was the grandson of Sir Theophilus Jones, a Welsh-born Irish soldier, whom Oliver Cromwell sent to Dublin to prepare for his visit on 15 August 1649. Subsequently Cromwell made Jones the Governor of Dublin. During the Cromwellian era Jones acquired Lucan Manor, the confiscated property of Patrick Sarsfield's family in County Dublin. According to the Act of Settlement of 1661, Jones was granted a large tract of land in County Meath by King Charles II. Anne lived near her mother in County Wicklow and had one son, Alexander, who tragically died young while travelling abroad. Had he survived, the future Rossmores would have had the surname Jones instead of Westenra.

Lady Blayney's youngest daughter, Harriet Murray, did not enjoy the same wealthy lifestyle as her sisters. Harriet was born in 1742 and, on 29 November 1764, aged 22, she married Henry, son of Warner and Hester Westenra. The name Westenra is an adaptation of the Dutch name Wassenaar, which can be traced to Philip van Wassenaar, who died around 1225. Three Westenra brothers fought for King Charles II and were granted lands, so that by 1662 they were naturalised citizens of Ireland. Warner Westenra married Lady Hester Lambart, daughter of the fourth earl of Cavan, on 13 December 1738. They had one son, Henry, and one daughter, Castiliana.

The Westenras held a position of wealth and rank in Ireland. That changed, however, and by the time of Harriet Murray's marriage to Henry Westenra they were considered by other family members to be almost in poverty. This was in part due to the fact that Henry and Castiliana's widowed mother, Lady Hester, had retained the proceeds from the family estates in King's County (later Offaly) and Queen's County (later Laois). Fortunately, Lady Blayney came to their financial assistance.

Castiliana married Captain Henry Dod. Following his death, she married Sir Edward Crosbie, fifth Baronet, on 14 December 1790, and they lived in Carlow. Sir Edward was accused of partaking in an attack on Carlow town by United Irishmen on 24 May 1798. He was summarily tried by courts martial and hanged on 5 June 1798. Sir Edward was an older brother of the balloonist Richard Crosbie, who is celebrated as Ireland's first aeronaut, having ascended in a balloon from Ranelagh Gardens, Dublin, on 19 January 1785.

Harriet and Henry's first son, Warner William Westenra, was born on 14 October 1765. Warner married twice. His first wife, whom he wed on 3 October 1791, was Marianne, a Roman Catholic and the daughter of Charles Walsh of Walsh Park, County Tipperary. Their first son, Henry Robert, was born at Walsh Park on 24 August 1792. They also had a daughter, Frances Maria.

When Warner's uncle, General Robert Cunningham, the first Lord Rossmore, died on 6 August 1801, Warner, aged 35, became the second Lord Rossmore, as he was the only surviving male of the next generation. Alas, the title brought no wealth, since General Cunningham left his house and money to his Cunningham relations, some residing at Mount Kennedy. That property would remain in the Cunningham family for another century, until the Land Acts divided the estate among the tenants.

Marianne died on 12 August 1807 and Warner married Lady Augusta Charteris in 1819. No children were born of this marriage. Under the terms of his grandmother's will, Warner's aunts would each, in succession, have to inherit the estate and die before he would inherit anything. Unfortunately for him, they all lived to a ripe old age. Frances Fortescue (Lady Clermont) died aged 86 in 1820; Elizabeth Cunningham (Lady Rossmore) died aged 92 in 1827; Anne Jones also died in 1827, aged 87. His own mother, Harriet, died in 1822, aged 80. On 25 January 1820, Warner and Marianne's son, Henry Robert, then aged 28, married Anne Douglas-Hamilton, the illegitimate daughter of the Scottish Duke of Hamilton. She became Lady Anne Douglas-Hamilton and inherited the Scottish island of Arran. During the elections of 1826, Henry won a seat representing County Monaghan. During the 1820s, Warner championed the cause of Catholic Emancipation and was by then a close friend of 'the Liberator', Daniel O'Connell.

In 1827, when Warner William Westenra was 62 years old, Lady Blayney's inheritance finally became his. He set about the mammoth task of restoring Rossmore Park. He oversaw the building of a Tudor Gothic castle, dominated by a square tower and turret, with crow-step battlements. Just after Queen Victoria's Coronation on 28 June 1838, she granted Warner Westenra an English peerage with a seat

Sir Richard Crosbie, Ireland's first aeronaut, was a great-great-granduncle of Mary Westenra (Lady Bailey).
COURTESY NATIONAL LIBRARY OF IRELAND

RICHARD CROSBIE *Esq.*
The Celebrated Irish Aeronaut

in the House of Lords. He now became the second Lord Rossmore in Ireland and the first Lord Rossmore in England. It was at Rossmore Castle that Warner resided until his death on 10 August 1842, aged 77. Lady Augusta had predeceased him two years earlier. Their son Henry Robert, now aged 50, inherited the (Irish) title third Lord Rossmore. Henry represented Monaghan as Member of Parliament for the majority of the period 1818–42. Henry Robert Westenra's finances were helped considerably by his marriage to Lady Anne. However, she died on 20 August 1844 and bore Henry no children. Two years later, on 19 May 1846, Henry Robert Westenra married his much younger first cousin once removed, Josephine, daughter of Henry and Harriet Amelia Lloyd of Farrinrory, County Tipperary. Harriet Amelia was the daughter of Frances Maria Westenra, a sister of Warner William Westenra. Thus a double bond of Westenra blood was formed for future generations.

Frances Maria Westenra married Sir John Craven Carden, first Baronet of Templemore, County

Tipperary. Their daughter Harriet Amelia Carden married Henry Jesse Lloyd and they had one daughter, Josephine Julia Helen Lloyd. (Josephine was the paternal grandmother of Mary, Lady Bailey). Josephine's marriage to Henry Robert Westenra in 1846 produced six children. The eldest son and heir was Henry Cairnes Westenra, born on 14 November 1851, who acquired the nickname Rosie.

In 1858 the conversion of Rossmore Castle from a Tudor Gothic building to a Renaissance-style creation of immense size and grandeur was completed. It was set high on a hill and included a massive tower with polygonal turret. It boasted 117 windows. The drawing room was extended five times until it became the largest room in County Monaghan. Henry Robert did not live long in the luxurious castle whose elaborate development he had overseen, as he died on 1 December 1860, aged 68. His eldest son, Henry Cairnes, as male heir, inherited the title fourth Lord Rossmore at the age of nine.

Henry's death in 1860 left Josephine a young widow with six children, the eldest being 13 years of age. On 18 June 1863 Josephine married Lieutenant Colonel George William Stacpoole

Rossmore Castle, Monaghan, following extensive restoration and extension by Henry Robert Westenra in 1858.
Courtesy Eason Collection, National Library of Ireland

of the Royal Irish Regiment, a native of Edenvale, County Clare. Josephine died on 12 September 1912 in Retford, Nottinghamshire.

Tragically, Henry Cairnes Westenra died aged 22, as a result of a fall from his horse, Harlequin, at Windsor on 28 March 1874. Queen Victoria was in attendance at those races and was said to be deeply affected by the tragedy. Henry was buried in the family mausoleum at Rossmore. The title fifth Lord Rossmore then passed to his younger brother, Derrick Warner William Westenra, who was born on 7 February 1853. He had been seven when his father died.

Following Henry Robert Westenra's death, his widow and six children had relocated, along with their tutors and governesses, to Pau, at the foot of the Pyrenees in southern France. After Pau, Derrick, who was nicknamed Derry, was educated at Boulogne, Brighton, Monaghan and then Rugby. At 16 he was sent to Hanover, Germany. When he was 18 years of age, Derry was accepted as a member of the prestigious gentlemen's United Service Club and the Kildare Street Club in Dublin. In 1871, at 18, he joined the 9th Lancers. Following the death of his brother Henry (Rosie), Derry was transferred to replace him as Lieutenant with the 1st Life Guards on 10 June 1874. Derry resigned his commission on 23 October 1875.

The following year, Derry and his brother Richard (Dick) went to South Africa with the intention of spending a leisurely couple of years big-game hunting. On his return to Ireland in 1878, Derry took an interest in horse racing. He was known to take foolish risks, to gamble, to philander and to spend recklessly. He also engaged in duelling. Thus commenced the slow demise of the Rossmore dynasty.

Racing became a passion for Derry and also the means of losing an enormous amount of money. He did have some racing successes, however, and achieved his greatest win as the owner of Passaic, the winner of the City and Suburban at Epsom on 26 April 1882. The race coincided with an interview with Sir Richard Christopher Naylor at the latter's fashionable Downshire House, 24 Belgrave Square, London, to ask for the hand of his eldest daughter, Mittie, in marriage. (In recent years, the property at 24 Belgrave Square has been the Embassy of Spain in London.) Several years later, in July 1907, during dinner at this residence, Bruce Ismay, Chairman and Managing Director of the White Star Line, and Lord William Pirrie, Chairman of the shipbuilders Harland and Wolff, conceived plans for a new class of transatlantic liner, operating a two-liner express service to New York. The new liners were to be far larger and more luxurious than any vessel in service in the world at the time. They were to be one-third as large again as the Cunard Line's competitor ships, RMS *Lusitania* and RMS *Mauretania*, and would exceed 800 feet in length. The vessels would bear the names *Olympic, Titanic* and *Britannic*.

Sketched portraits of Lord Derrick and Lady Mittie Rossmore (née *Naylor*) *on the occasion of their marriage on 14 June 1882.*
Courtesy National Library of Ireland

Twenty-nine-year-old Derry Westenra duly married twenty-two-year-old Mittie Naylor on 14 June 1882 at All Saints' Church, Ennismore Gardens, London. Sir Richard Naylor was a wealthy banker of Leyland and Bullins Bank, Liverpool, who resided at another of his properties, the magnificent Hooton Hall, near Ellesmere Port, Cheshire.

Naylor had purchased Hooton Hall for 80,000 guineas in 1854 and proceeded to spend a further 50,000 guineas to extend the property greatly, adding a racecourse, a polo ground and a heronry, to establish it as one of the grandest estates in north-west England. Naylor also owned Kelmarsh Hall in Northamptonshire and, of course, Downshire House in Belgrave Square, London. He had two daughters, Mittie and Doods. Mittie moved in the smartest circles of English society. During the First World War, Hooton Hall was commandeered as a military hospital. Hooton Park, the grounds of Hooton Hall, was converted in 1917 for use as an airfield for pilot-training American and Canadian cadets in aircraft shipped across the Atlantic and offloaded at Birkenhead and Liverpool. Naylor moved to his other extensive property, at Kelmarsh Hall, in 1875. Following years of neglect and unoccupancy, Hooton Hall was finally demolished in 1925.

The fact was that Derry needed to marry a wealthy lady to support his lavish lifestyle. In 1891 he decided to sail to Australia to indulge his appetite for adventure and pleasure. Three children were born from Derry and

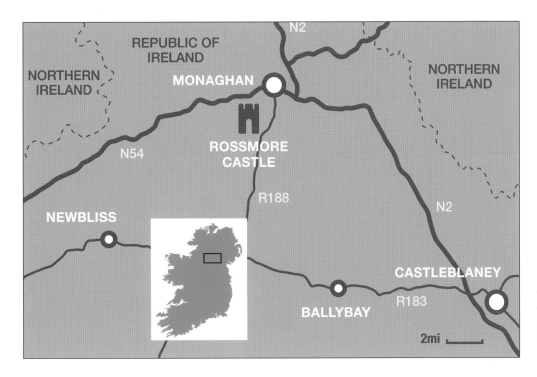

Locations associated with Lady Bailey.
Map © Martin Gaffney

Mittie's marriage: Mary on 1 December 1890; William on 12 July 1892 and Richard on 15 October 1893.

The pattern of their year was clearly defined. From August until March they were at Rossmore in Monaghan. From April to July they were in London, where they enjoyed race meetings, house parties and yachting events with the Prince of Wales's set and where their engagements filled spaces in social columns. Mittie's life could not have been easy, complicated as it was by her father's contempt for her husband and her position as a go-between, continually having to provide her father's money for Derry's profligate ways. Alcohol and infidelity would have made things worse. Lord Rossmore's autobiographical book, *Things I Can Tell*, published several years later in 1912, gives an account of his careless, lavish and almost foolhardy lifestyle. In it he acknowledged, 'I lost far more than I won at the sport of kings, and racing and gambling and I were at last obliged to part company.'

Although born in London, the children spent most of their childhood at Rossmore Castle, Monaghan.

Hooton Hall, Ellesmere Port, near Liverpool, was extended and renovated by Richard C. Naylor in 1854. This was the home of Mary Westenra's mother, Mittie Naylor.
Courtesy Cheshire Archives and Local Studies (ref. c09973)

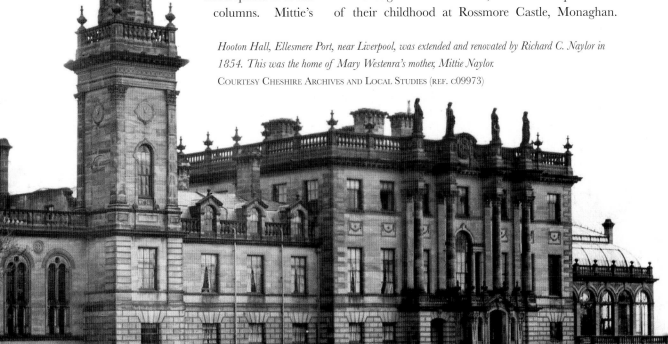

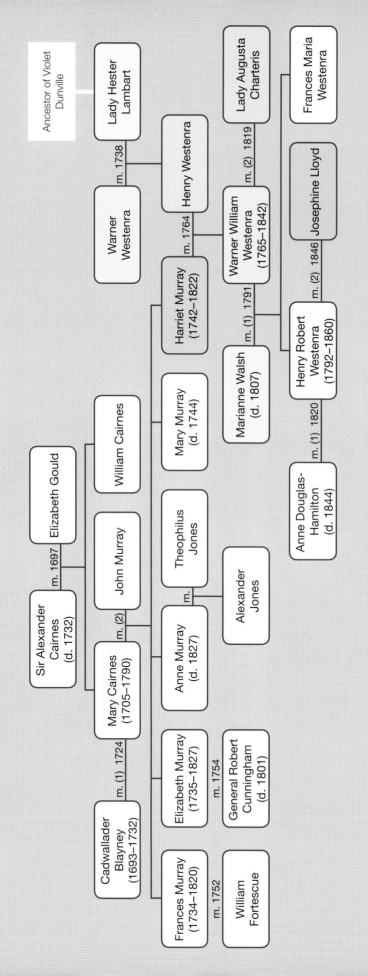

The Cairnes family tree.
COURTESY ALICIA MCAULEY

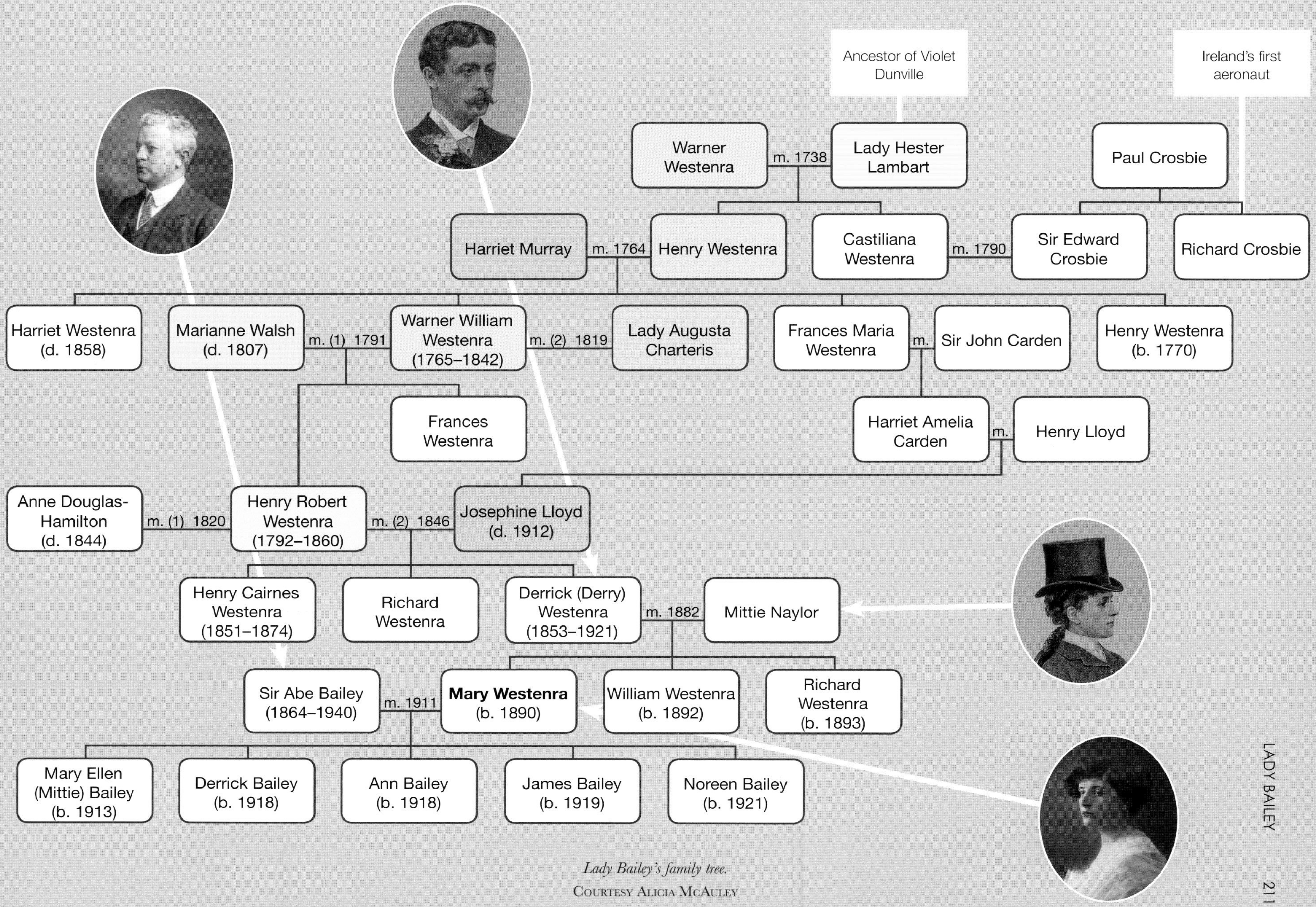

Lady Bailey's family tree.
COURTESY ALICIA MCAULEY

Ireland's first aeronaut

Paul Crosbie

Richard Crosbie

Sir Edward Crosbie

Henry Westenra (b. 1770)

Ancestor of Violet Dunville

Lady Hester Lambart

m. 1790

Castiliana Westenra

Sir John Carden

Henry Lloyd

Warner Westenra

m. 1738

Henry Westenra

Frances Maria Westenra

m.

Harriet Amelia Carden

Harriet Murray

m. 1764

Lady Augusta Charteris

Mittie Naylor

Richard Westenra (b. 1893)

Warner William Westenra (1765–1842)

m. (2) 1819

Frances Westenra

Josephine Lloyd (d. 1912)

m. 1882

Derrick (Derry) Westenra (1853–1921)

William Westenra (b. 1892)

Noreen Bailey (b. 1921)

Marianne Walsh (d. 1807)

m. (1) 1791

Henry Robert Westenra (1792–1860)

m. (2) 1846

Richard Westenra

Mary Westenra (b. 1890)

James Bailey (b. 1919)

Harriet Westenra (d. 1858)

Anne Douglas-Hamilton (d. 1844)

m. (1) 1820

Henry Cairnes Westenra (1851–1874)

Sir Abe Bailey (1864–1940)

m. 1911

Ann Bailey (b. 1918)

Derrick Bailey (b. 1918)

Mary Ellen (Mittie) Bailey (b. 1913)

They each had a nanny and each function of the great house was performed by its own band of servants. Twenty cottages on the enormous estate housed the large workforce required to maintain Rossmore Park.

On 29 July 1896, Derry was appointed Honorary Colonel of the 5th Battalion, Royal Irish Fusiliers. On 18 June 1897 he was appointed Lord Lieutenant of Monaghan, a position he held until his death, representing the third generation of Westenras to hold that office. Despite Derry's grandfather's support for Catholic Emancipation and loyalty to Daniel O'Connell, Derry did not think it odd that he was the County Grand Master of the Orange Order. He had considerable influence over several thousand Orangemen in the county. He resigned this position in 1904.

Mary Westenra was the eldest child and was treated as a princess. In nearby Monaghan town she would have been well known and the inhabitants would have taken an interest in her as she was growing up. She developed a strong affection for her roots – for her Irish home and her Irish background, despite her ancestry being part-Scottish, part-Dutch and part-English. The Westenra/Rossmore family were typically Anglo-Irish and enjoyed sport. Their upbringing produced a courageous attitude to life and Mary's family had a remarkable degree of daring in their makeup. Her relationship with her father was fostered by a mutual love of horses and hunting. In 1904, aged 13, she hunted with the Monaghan Harriers and continued to do so during the winter of 1904–5, which suggests that she was not away at boarding school but was being educated at home. In 1906 she attended Heathfield School, Ascot, Berkshire, a few miles from the principal royal residence of Windsor Castle. Mary disliked the college and ran away after one term. She never returned. Her education was continued back at Rossmore by two Franco-Russian sisters. In 1907 Mary won third prize in the horse-jumping competition at the Monaghan County Show.

Eighteen-year-old Mary Westenra (second from right at rear) attended many social engagements as a débutante. This photograph was taken in December 1908 at Elveden, Thetford, Suffolk, the stately home of Edward Cecil Guinness, Earl of Iveagh. The future King George V is standing second from left.

Courtesy Jane Falloon
via Julieanne McMahon

In 1908, Derry Westenra purchased the first automobile in County Monaghan. Shortly afterwards, Mary purchased a motorbike. A passion for speed and danger was part of her psyche. In 1909, Mary was presented at court in London as a débutante. After this watershed, young girls were considered to be grown-up enough to join their parents' social events and were also expected to find eligible and wealthy husbands. Because of her mother's friendship with the King, they attended the evening party at Buckingham Palace on 9 July 1909 along with 1,700 other guests. Mary's life was then full of the things she enjoyed most – hunting, shooting, house parties, race meetings, balls and formal receptions at Dublin Castle and Buckingham Palace. However, during these years, her father's drinking was a source of unhappiness to Mary and her mother. It fed his appalling temper, something which Mary inherited from him and which she always found difficult to control.

Shortly after her nineteenth birthday, in December 1909, Mary was elected Master of the Monaghan Harriers, something unusual for such a young woman. She encouraged young ladies to become more involved in horse-riding events. Her aunt Doods was reported to be one of the finest horsewomen in the hunting field of her day. On 20 August 1911, 20-year-old Mary was staying at Cowes on the Isle of Wight when she wrote to her brother Richard:

> I have news to tell you but at present it is an absolute secret to be told to no-one – I am engaged to be married to Sir Abe Bailey, a man of 46, a widower with two children, a boy of 11 and a girl of – I don't know a bit older I imagine!! I suppose you will laugh, we are going out to South Africa on the second of September and going to stay at his two places out there and then at Cape Town and then go to Durban. I don't know if he will come back here again or not. I am trying to get a maid who will travel. This morning I went for a swim at 5.30. Yesterday we went sailing in Lord Iveagh's yacht and after breakfast I am going again to sail with Mrs Ernest Guinness. Best love. Your loving Mary. Love to Daddy.

A portrait of 20-year-old Mary Westenra on 1 September 1911, four days prior to her marriage to Sir Abe Bailey.
COURTESY NATIONAL PORTRAIT GALLERY, LONDON

Two weeks later, on 5 September 1911, Mary married Sir Abe and acquired the title Lady Bailey. While the engagement may have been hurried, the marriage survived until Abe died, 29 years later.

Abraham Bailey was the son of an immigrant to South Africa. His father, Thomas, emigrated from the Manor House, Keighley, Yorkshire, in the late 1850s with his Scottish-born wife, Ann Drummond McEwan. Abe was born on 6 November 1864 and, of the three children born to Thomas and Ann, he was the only son. He was also a bit of a rebel. His mother died when Abe was seven and he ran away from home for about a year. After this he was sent to be educated at a no-nonsense grammar school in Keighley. From there he was sent to Clewer House School in Windsor for 3 years, until he was 15. This school had such a profound effect on Abe that in later life he called his business, his farm, his houses and even his yachts by the name Clewer. At 15 Abe was employed in a textile firm in London. Two years later he returned to South

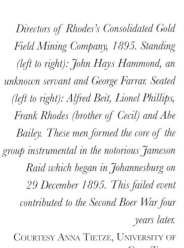

Africa to find that his father's business as a general dealer had prospered. In 1885, when Abe was aged 21, there were reports of gold finds in Kimberley and he decided to move to Barberton. He dabbled in stockbrokering but eventually he headed to the gold mines. He undertook menial jobs to survive but persisted with the mining business. In 1887 Abe returned to the Witwatersrand, which was the largest gold field ever discovered and where fortunes were being made. He bought the Kleinfontein mine and then the Transvaal Gold Mining Estates. Another name associated with gold mining in South Africa at the time was Alfred Beit, who made his fortune in the diamond mines in Kimberley and whose nephew, of the same name, eventually settled in Russborough House, Blessington, County Wicklow. By 1894 Abe Bailey had £100,000 in his bank account and was Chairman of the Johannesburg Stock Exchange. At 29 he was described as 'the most daring speculator of the Golden City'.

That year he married Caroline Paddon, daughter of a wealthy Kimberley merchant who owned a large house in south London. They lived at Clewer House in Johannesburg. In December 1895 he was a supporter and financial backer of the failed Jameson Raid on Johannesburg and this support incurred a three-year prison sentence, although it was reduced on payment of a fine of £2,000. This event was one of the sources of antagonism between the British and the Boers that resulted in the Second Boer War in 1899. Abe took part in this also, and it led to his friendship with Winston Churchill. His close

Abe Bailey became a successful and wealthy entrepreneur after the discovery of gold in South Africa towards the end of the nineteenth century.

Directors of Rhodes's Consolidated Gold Field Mining Company, 1895. Standing (left to right): John Hays Hammond, an unknown servant and George Farrar. Seated (left to right): Alfred Beit, Lionel Phillips, Frank Rhodes (brother of Cecil) and Abe Bailey. These men formed the core of the group instrumental in the notorious Jameson Raid which began in Johannesburg on 29 December 1895. This failed event contributed to the Second Boer War four years later.

business companion Cecil Rhodes died in 1902, which was also the year his young wife, Caroline, died suddenly, leaving him the lone parent of a six-year-old daughter, Cecil, and a two-year-old son, John.

The years between 1902 and 1911, during which he married Mary Westenra, were a period of extraordinary activity for Abe. In 1905 he completed his dream house looking out across Muizenberg Bay, about 20 miles outside of Cape Town, called Rust-en-Vrede, meaning 'Rest and Peace' in Afrikaans. Abe had a business relationship with Cecil Rhodes (who controlled 90 per cent of the world's diamond production) and the culmination of this relationship was that Abe acquired a 1.25-million-acre ranch in Rhodesia (now Zimbabwe), which made him the largest landowner there. He also acquired several large landholdings near Colesberg in the Karoo, purchased in the name of the Wernher Beit Bailey Consortium. His own farm, called Grootfontein, was near Colesberg. Also acquired was a 300-square-mile farm in Karoo National Park, about 300 miles north-east of Cape Town, called Clewer.

Abe entered politics and was made whip in the Pretorian Government in 1908; he also became a newspaper magnate. In March 1911 Abe was created Knight Commander of St Michael and St George and was one of the invited guests at the Coronation of King George V at Westminster Abbey, London, on 22 June 1911. It was possibly at this royal occasion that the 46-year-old Abe Bailey met the 20-year-old Mary Westenra. They were married ten weeks later, on 5 September 1911, at Holy Trinity Church, Sloane Street, London. Abe was three years younger than Mary's mother, Mittie.

The home that Abe Bailey completed in 1905, which he called Rust-en-Vrede, was 20 miles west of Cape Town and overlooked Muizenberg Bay.
COURTESY ANNA TIETZE, UNIVERSITY OF CAPE TOWN

To a young girl like Mary, Abe must have seemed something of a colossus and she must have been amazed and flattered that he wanted to marry her. The wedding was a typical lavish occasion and Mary had six bridesmaids, including Abe's 16-year-old daughter, Cecil. Numerous titled ladies and gentlemen attended. A special reception had been held the day before, where the presents were laid out, diamonds featuring prominently. Three days after the wedding, Abe and his new bride travelled by steamer to Belfast and onward to Monaghan by train. It was Abe's first visit to Ireland. A large crowd greeted the newlyweds at Monaghan Railway Station – the Westenras were the nearest thing to royalty the inhabitants had. Banners and bunting adorned the town as they made their way in cars to Rossmore Castle. After three days in Monaghan, the bride and groom returned to England. They sailed first class for South Africa on 23 September 1911 on board the Harland and Wolff-constructed RMS *Saxon*.

The three-week sea journey was an opportunity for Mary to start getting to know the most interesting but strange man she had just married, who had a life behind him full of experiences totally unknown to her. Shortly after their arrival, Abe took Mary around his estates and properties in his beloved country. On 27 October they visited the Victoria Falls and a few days later paid their respects at Cecil Rhodes's grave. They travelled for two months as their honeymoon. In mid-December 1911, Mary's parents, Derry and Mittie, along with Mary's two brothers, William and Richard, arrived to spend three months in South Africa. Prior to their departure from England, Derry and Mittie had been granted a grace-and-favour residence at Hampton Court, London, by the newly crowned King George V.

Over the next few years Mary and Abe made numerous sea journeys between South Africa and England, but Mary realised that her heart still lay in Monaghan. In 1912 her father, Derry, published his memoirs, *Things I Can Tell*. Due to the titillating content of the autobiography, it became a best seller and made Derry notorious.

Mary and Abe's first child was a daughter, born on 1 August 1913 and christened Mittie Mary Starr (to be known as Mary Ellen). Mary and Abe decided that their children would be reared in England and Abe rented a five-storey house, 38 Bryanston Square, near

The house at 38 Bryanston Square was the fashionable London residence that Abe rented for Mary and their children while he was in South Africa.

COURTESY ANNA TIETZE, UNIVERSITY OF CAPE TOWN

fashionable Mayfair in London. Mary and Abe hosted lavish parties in Bryanston Square, and many relished an invitation to dine at this exquisite residence. Abe's compassion was evident, in that he tended to employ war-wounded men as staff in his Bryanston Square house.

When the First World War broke out in the summer of 1914, Abe returned to South Africa, leaving Mary and baby Mary Ellen behind in Yewhurst, near East Grinstead, Sussex. Mary and her two stepchildren were kept busy there making splints for hospitals. In October 1914, Mary and her stepdaughter, Cecil, sailed for South Africa. Fifteen-month-old Mary Ellen was left in England with a nanny and her Westenra grandparents. Abe formed a unit of 20 top-grade marksmen as sharpshooters to join the British Expeditionary Force in France. He received the Croix de Guerre and was made a baronet by the British government at the end of the war in recognition of his contribution.

One very important political meeting that Abe facilitated in his home on 3 December 1916 was a private meeting between Prime Minister Herbert H. Asquith and David Lloyd George. During this meeting Asquith was persuaded to resign to enable Lloyd George to become British Prime Minister, with effect from 6 December 1916. The incoming Prime Minister was also persuaded at this meeting to have Winston Churchill included in his new cabinet, a decision that was to have a profound effect on British and world affairs for many years to come.

When Lady Bailey came back to England in 1916, she joined the Women's Legion, which had been formed in July 1915 by the Marchioness of Londonderry. In February 1917 it became the Women's Army Auxiliary Corps. She then joined the Royal Flying Corps. Whilst she was not permitted to learn to fly, she was a driver and mechanic and was exposed to flying. She was trained to deal with the mechanical problems of motor engines, something that would help her in years to come. She got close to the fighting in France as a driver but had to return home when she became pregnant with twins, Derrick Thomas Louis and Ann Hester Zia, who were born on 15 August 1918 in Marylebone, London.

Lady Bailey had a terrible temper and her children later recalled how it got worse as she grew older. They remember her beating the older children and having rages with servants. However, they also recalled happier times spent with her outdoors. After the war Abe spent more time in South Africa than England, where he enjoyed successes with his racehorses, which were trained on the Clewer Estate in the Karoo.

Lady Bailey and Abe's fourth child was James Richard Abe, born on 23 October 1919. Two years after the birth of James, her father, Derry Westenra, died. He had been the person who, until she married Abe, had shown her the most love and affection. Her family was completed with the birth of Noreen Helen Rosemary on 27 July 1921.

Lady Bailey and Abe continued to sail between England and South Africa during the early 1920s,

Lady Bailey in 1924 with her five children. Standing are Mary Ellen (11) and Ann (6). Kneeling is Derrick (6) and seated is Jim (4), with Noreen (3) on her mother's lap.

COURTESY JANE FALLOON
VIA JULIEANNE MCMAHON

Abe Bailey (right) with HRH the Prince of Wales at Abe's farm, Grootfontein, in the Karoo during the Prince's tour of South Africa in 1925.
COURTESY JANE FALLOON VIA JULIEANNE MCMAHON

despite such sea journeys taking up to 24 days. Abe had befriended Edward, Prince of Wales (later King Edward VIII) and invited him to visit his ranch in South Africa during a three-month royal visit between 30 April and 29 July 1925. The Prince was a keen aviator at that time and was owner of several aircraft, one of which was de Havilland 80A Puss Moth, G-ABFV, an aircraft he sold to Adelaide Cleaver in September 1931. On Abe's visits to London, the Prince frequently invited him and Lady Bailey to St James's Palace and often dined in 38 Bryanston Square. It was on these visits to England that Abe entered his horses for races. He had victories at Epsom, Goodwood and Newmarket and his horse Foxlaw won the 1927 Gold Cup at Ascot.

A general strike in Britain took place on 3 May 1926. Abe was a friend of Winston Churchill, Chancellor of the Exchequer, Ramsay MacDonald, the Leader of the Opposition, and Jimmy Thomas, a trade-union leader. Behind the scenes Abe arranged meetings in his Bryanston Square home between Thomas and Churchill and then between Churchill and MacDonald. As a result they found a means of calling off the general strike after nine days. Abe's reputation as a negotiator grew. The miners' strike, unfortunately, continued.

In September 1925 Mary Ellen started at Malvern St James Girls' School, Malvern, Worcestershire. She was aged 12. Her younger sister, Ann, followed her during spring term 1928, when she was just nine years and eight months old. This was the girls' preparatory boarding school where Jean 'Shamrock' Trench also spent

The Junior House, where Mary Ellen, Ann and Noreen Bailey would have attended on first entry at Malvern School as boarders.
COURTESY KATIE POWELL, MALVERN ST JAMES GIRLS' SCHOOL, WORCESTERSHIRE

Above: *A tennis match in progress on the top terrace around the time the three Bailey sisters attended Malvern St James Girls' School in Worcestershire.*
COURTESY KATIE POWELL, MALVERN ST JAMES GIRLS' SCHOOL, WORCESTERSHIRE

The outdoor swimming pool, tennis courts and other areas of recreation for the all-female boarders at Malvern St James Girls' School.
COURTESY KATIE POWELL, MALVERN ST JAMES GIRLS' SCHOOL, WORCESTERSHIRE

one term in 1924. Shamrock would become the first woman to earn an Aviator's Certificate in the Irish Free State in 1931. (She is the subject of a separate chapter in this publication.) Ann Bailey was the youngest in the college until Noreen was sent to join her.

Derrick and Jim Bailey went to a preparatory school in Wixenford, Wokingham, Berkshire, about 40 miles west of London. Wixenford claimed to be a school for 'the sons of gentlemen and minor princes'. The *Wixenford School Notes* for December 1928 recorded that both Bailey boys took part in school football matches. They reported that Derrick, aged ten, was the best player and that Jim was one of the most promising players. Another passion that the boys had was horse riding, which they had inherited from their mother. During the Senior-Division Riding Competition, Derrick took the Junior Prize. Derrick finished at Wixenford in 1931. In the academic year 1931–2, Jim continued to excel at sports, particularly at rugby and shooting. Derrick and Jim Bailey were both sent to Christ Church College, Oxford, having attended Winchester College in the interim.

With her five children now at boarding school, it was time for Lady Bailey to indulge in a new passion. The London Aeroplane Club at Stag Lane was nine miles from Bryanston Square. There a club-qualified pilot member could hire an aircraft for 20 shillings an hour; instructional lessons were 30 shillings an hour.

In order to gain an Aviator's Certificate a total of 20 lessons, covering 10 hours' flying time, was required. Lady Bailey started taking flying lessons secretly, not wanting to tell Abe until she discovered whether she could do it or not. Since Hilda Hewlett had become the first woman in England to earn an Aviator's Certificate on 18 August 1911, only eight other women had achieved such an entitlement by 1922. In 1925 only one woman qualified, Sophie Eliott-Lynn.

Lady Bailey's first flight was on 1 June 1926. She was flown nine miles from Stag Lane Aerodrome by Mr Dudley Watt in his 1919-constructed Sopwith Grasshopper aircraft, G-EAIN, to see her horse, which was running at Epsom that afternoon. Her instructors were Sophie Eliott-Lynn and Captain F.G.M. Sparkes.

By 19 September 1926, Lady Bailey was flying solo. On Monday, 18 October 1926 she successfully passed her tests for her 'A' Certificate. On the same day another Irishwoman, Sicele O'Brien, also passed the tests for her 'A' Certificate at Stag Lane. Lady Bailey then felt able to tell Abe what she was doing and that she wanted her own aeroplane. A DH.60 Moth was the most popular light aircraft of that period and Abe duly bought her one for her thirty-sixth birthday, at a cost of approximately £600. The new aircraft was all silver. It was registered as G-EBPU to the Honourable Lady Bailey on 1 December 1926 and kept hangared at Stag Lane.

Wixenford Boys' Preparatory School, Wokingham, Berkshire, which Derrick and Jim Bailey attended.
Courtesy Sally Whittaker, Ludgrove School, Wokingham

The 88 acres available to the London Aeroplane Club at Stag Lane in 1927. This was the home base for three Irish female pilots: Sophie Eliott-Lynn, Lady Bailey and Sicele O'Brien. Take-off and landing runs were multidirectional, depending on weather conditions.
Courtesy Richard T. Riding

Below: *Lady Bailey's brother Richard Westenra, who commenced flying lessons in January 1927 (from a portrait taken on 22 April 1921).*
Courtesy Royal Aero Club Trust

Lady Bailey did not complete the application for her 'A' Certificate until 26 January 1927 and she was issued Aviator's Certificate number 8067. Her first flight in her new aircraft was on 21 February 1927. By now Lady Bailey had become friends with aircraft manufacturer Geoffrey de Havilland and his wife, Louie, and been elected to the committee of the London Aeroplane Club. In the week that Lady Bailey obtained her certificate, her brother Richard Westenra enjoyed his first joy-ride at the London Aeroplane Club.

The first press coverage of Lady Bailey's flying was on 25 February 1927 – a report on her visit to a rally in Norwich. Geoffrey de Havilland described an incident he witnessed involving Lady Bailey in April 1927:

BAILEY, The Hon. Lady ~~Bailey~~ (may)   8067

38, Bryanston Square, W.1.

Born 1st December 1890   *at*   London
Nationality   British
Rank, Regiment, Profession
Certificate taken on D.H."Moth", 60 h.p. Cirrus
At London Aeroplane Club, Stag Lane, Edgware
Date   26th January 1927

The Royal Aero Club Aviator's Certificate issued to the Honourable Lady Bailey on 26 January 1927, along with the photograph that accompanied the certificate.
Courtesy Royal Aero Club Trust

She started her engine at Stag Lane by hand-swinging the propeller in the usual way and slipped forward on the wet grass. The result of this sort of miscalculation was often fatal but Lady Bailey was only scalped. I happened to be there at the time and retrieved a large patch of skin and hair from the ground; and I believe it was later cleaned and bound into place. When I next saw her she was wearing a sort of turban; but this did not prevent her from flying.

Her children later believed the head injury might have contributed to the deterioration of her temper and her inability to control her outbursts. In spite of that gruesome injury, she appeared later that month, on Easter Saturday, 16 April 1927, at Bournemouth, wearing the head dressing which she wore for the rest of that year. Because of her recent injury she was unable to partake in any race and the winner of the Aerial Oaks Race for female pilots was Sicele O'Brien, flying the London Aeroplane Club Moth, G-EBKT.

Lady Bailey had found her vocation. Flying was a combination of so many different elements: challenge, escape, skill and sheer exhilaration. She was once quoted as saying, 'I do it to get away from prams.' By the time of her first instructional lesson, Mary Ellen, her eldest child, was 12 years old and her youngest, Noreen,

Lady Bailey enjoying a flight in Herr Lusser's Klemm-Daimler L20 at Stag Lane on 3 July 1927.
Courtesy John Illsley

was 5. Flying was now Lady Bailey's drug of choice and her fascination with it lasted the rest of her life.

By Saturday, 14 May 1927, she had recovered sufficiently from her head injury to partake in both the Wakefield Light Aeroplane Handicap Race and the President's Challenge Cup Race at the Hampshire Air Pageant. She was not a placed finisher in either race in her Moth, G-EBPU, however. On 18 May, Lady Bailey was a front-seat passenger at Hamble Aerodrome when Sophie Eliott-Lynn set a world altitude record for a light aircraft of 15,748 feet. The Bournemouth Whitsun Meeting took place on 4 and 5 June 1927. It was sadly preceded by a fatal crash but continued nonetheless. Lady Bailey entered for five events over the weekend, including the race open to women pilots only. There were just three entrants to that race: Sophie Eliott-Lynn was the winner, Sicele O'Brien came second and Lady Bailey placed third. She was third also in the semi-final of the Sweepstake Race. *Flight* magazine on 9 June 1927 further reported on another escapade of Lady Bailey's:

> Lady Bailey, who flies nearly every day in her Moth, was flying over Leicestershire when engine trouble developed and a forced landing became imperative. This she accomplished very skilfully in a field near Peatling Hall, the home of Colonel Gemmell, where she remained for the night.

Cramlington Aerodrome was the venue for the Newcastle Aero Club's meeting, attended by 20,000 spectators, on 11 June 1927. Lady Bailey won the Private Owners' Handicap Race when she beat Squadron Leader Rea in the final. Eleven days later she finished in third position in the first event at the Bristol Air Pageant and fourth in the utility event. On 3 July 1927 two Klemm-Daimler L20 aircraft arrived at Stag Lane, flown by German pilots on a short visit. Lady Bailey went for a flight in one of them, piloted by Herr Lusser, and took control.

On 5 July 1927 Lady Bailey, accompanied by Louie de Havilland, broke the altitude record in the DH.60X Moth G-EBQH over Stag Lane Aerodrome, reaching 17,283 feet. This aircraft was available for sale at £650. That year she became the first woman in

Louie de Havilland disembarked after extending the world altitude record to 17,283 feet in the de Havilland Moth G-EBQH on 5 July 1927. Lady Bailey piloted from the rear seat.

<small>COURTESY DE HAVILLAND MOTH CLUB ARCHIVE</small>

England to obtain her blind-flying certificate. A couple of weeks later, on Saturday, 16 July, Lady Bailey won the Low Power Handicap Race at the Birmingham Air Pageant in her Moth, G-EBPU, with an average speed of 92 miles per hour, while Sophie Eliott-Lynn was second, with an average speed of 82.75 miles per hour. Over 100,000 spectators witnessed her victory. In the afternoon she was one of eight entrants in the Air League Challenge Cup Race and finished 49 seconds behind the second-place aircraft in a race of 116 miles, at an average speed of 97.25 miles per hour. The following weekend she flew to attend Marchioness Townsend's Aerial Fete at Raynham Park, Norfolk, to raise funds for a local hospital.

On 30 July 1927, Hucknall Aerodrome, Nottinghamshire, hosted the 1927 King's Cup Race.

Within three months of her serious head injury, Lady Bailey became the first woman to enter the King's Cup Race. She is photographed at Hucknall on 30 July 1927, examining her charts for the 540-mile air race and wearing a turban to conceal her head injury.

<small>COURTESY RONNY VOGT</small>

Lady Bailey beside her DH Moth, G-EBPU, at Hucknall, Nottinghamshire, on 30 July 1927, prior to the King's Cup Race.

<small>COURTESY PROSPERO BAILEY</small>

Lady Bailey became the first woman to enter the round-Britain race in her Moth, G-EBPU. She broke a valve cotter and was compelled to land in the vicinity of Doncaster. The following day she finished second in the final of the Pelham Stakes and second in the Ladies' Race that Sophie Eliott-Lynn won at the Nottingham Flying Meeting.

Following this meeting, Lady Bailey flew her Moth to Dublin via Holyhead for the Horse Show. As a safety precaution she carried a larger fuel tank and an inflated motorcycle inner tube for buoyancy in case she ditched. Her record-making flight commenced from Hooton Park Aerodrome, the former home of her mother's ancestors, the Naylor family, at Hooton Park, near Ellesmere Port, Cheshire. This flight earned her the distinction of becoming the first woman to fly solo across the Irish Sea.

Lady Bailey was back at Stag Lane on 16 August 1927, where she christened Lieutenant Richard Bentley's Moth, G-EBSO, *Dorys*, in honour of his soon-to-be bride in Johannesburg, South Africa. After the ceremony he departed on a solo flight to Cape Town; he was a member of the South African Air Force (SAAF). He completed the flight on 28 September 1927.

Christening Lieutenant Bentley's Moth, G-EBSO, Dorys at Stag Lane, London, on 16 August 1927 in advance of his solo flight to Cape Town, was Lady Bailey.

On Saturday, 24 September, the Hooton Air Pageant took place. Over 100,000 spectators were expected but in wretched weather many stayed away. Although most events went ahead, Lady Bailey was unsuccessful in the three races she entered.

At the end of the summer of 1927 Lady Bailey became President of the Suffolk Aeroplane Club at its new base at Hadleigh Aerodrome, Ipswich. The Sherburn Air Pageant in Yorkshire on 1 October was affected by adverse weather and reduced to one day of racing. In the Ladies' Race, Lady Bailey, flying the London Aeroplane Club's DH.60 Moth, G-EBMF, finished ten seconds behind the second-placed Sicele O'Brien. She entered the Wattle Handicap Race in another DH.60 Moth, G-EBUA, and finished fourth.

Saturday, 8 October 1927 was the official opening of the Bristol and Wessex Aeroplane Club. Despite poor weather in the morning, many managed to arrive by air, including women pilots Lady Bailey, Maia Carberry and Sicele O'Brien, all in Moths. Sophie Eliott-Lynn did not attend as she was at Woodford, Manchester, where she surpassed Lady Bailey's altitude record of 17,283 feet to establish a new record height of 19,200 feet. As President of the Suffolk Aeroplane Club, Lady Bailey attended their first air meeting at the Hadleigh Aerodrome on Sunday, 30 October. It was successful and many pilots and dignitaries were in attendance, with over 400 people given flips at 5 shillings a ticket. Where possible, Lady Bailey attended at the club and gave joy-rides to as many members as possible. She was one of the first members to donate £100 towards the cost of a second club aeroplane.

On 29 November 1927, Lady Bailey was nominated to represent the London Aeroplane Club as its delegate at the Royal Aero Club. On 8 November 1927, her brother William married Dolores Cecil Lee. He was heir to the family title of Baron Rossmore along with the estate and castle. Thereafter Lady Bailey was less inclined to return to Monaghan.

While Lady Bailey triumphed in the air, Sir Abe was winning on the racecourses and trophies from both sporting activities adorned the dining room at 38 Bryanston Square. On 14 January 1928 the International League of Aviators awarded Lady Bailey the title Champion Airwoman of the World for 1927. Colonel Charles A. Lindbergh was proclaimed the Champion Airman for 1927 for his solo transatlantic flight to Paris. This was all before Lady Bailey's epoch-making solo return flight from London to Cape Town.

On 26 January 1928, she attended the inaugural meeting of the Liverpool and District Aero Club, of which she was elected Vice-President. Flying commenced at Hooton Park two days later, with Lady Bailey giving exhibitions and free flights to new members. The Chief Flying Instructor was Lieutenant Richard Bentley.

A posed photograph of Lady Bailey from late in 1927.
COURTESY RONNY VOGT

A family photo taken beside the Moth G-EBPU in January 1928. In the rear cockpit is her daughter Noreen and Ann is in the front cockpit. Standing is Derrick with Jim on the wing. Mary Ellen was at boarding school at this time. Lady Bailey stood nearby.
COURTESY JANE FALLOON
VIA JULIEANNE McMAHON

Courtesy Lilliput Press, Dublin,
via Jane Falloon

On 17 February 1926, Alan Cobham arrived in Cape Town, having flown from Stag Lane Aerodrome, London, on 16 November 1925. Reports of such long-distance flights excited and thrilled Lady Bailey. With so many servants to attend to her every need, she was becoming bored and frustrated at home and she began to contemplate a solo flight to South Africa. She discussed her future flying plans with her confidant Geoffrey de Havilland, who agreed to sell Lady Bailey his latest aircraft, an 80-horsepower DH.60X Moth, G-EBSF. Adaptations were made to the aircraft in secret. Abe funded the adventure and Sir Charles Wakefield, the distributor of Castrol Oil, assisted with fuel provision. She decided to follow the route Alan Cobham had plied between 16 November 1925 and 17 February 1926. Fuel would be available for her at the same locations.

Jane Falloon's publication, *Throttle Full Open: A Life of Lady Bailey, Irish Aviatrix*, published in 1999 by Lilliput Press, Dublin, gives extensive coverage of Lady Bailey's journey from Croydon to Cape Town and back. What follows is a summary of that journey in extract form.

On 6 March 1928, Lady Bailey's DH.60 Moth, G-EBPU, was registered to Geoffrey de Havilland; his DH.60X Moth, G-EBSF, was registered on the same day to the Honourable Lady Bailey. Both aircraft had been subjected to rigorous fuel-consumption tests during the first week of March 1928. It was established that G-EBSF, with 44 gallons on board, would cruise at 79 miles per hour, burning 4.3 gallons per hour. The front cockpit occupied the extra

Aircraft manufacturer Geoffrey de Havilland stood to the starboard rear as Lady Bailey warmed her engine prior to take-off in her converted single-seat open cockpit de Havilland Moth, G-EBSF, from a wet and muddy Stag Lane Aerodrome on 9 March 1928.
Courtesy de Havilland Moth Club Archive

fuel tank, giving the Moth a range of ten hours. Two small suitcases contained Lady Bailey's luggage for the journey. She departed Stag Lane Aerodrome at 12.30pm on Friday, 9 March 1928. By the time she left Croydon it was snowing. She wore heavy winter clothes to protect herself in the small open-cockpit aircraft.

Next stop was Lympne, Kent at 3pm, then across the English Channel to Berck-sur-Mer at 4.30pm. The French press were intrigued by this intrepid 37-year-old woman. Her first night was spent at Sacy-le-Petit, north of Paris. Thick fog prevented her from getting beyond Le Bourget Airport, Paris, the next day. On Sunday, 11 March, she reached Lyon in appalling weather conditions. Despite warnings of further deteriorating weather, she continued to Marseille, where she landed at 5.30pm. Overnight the weather improved and, with an escort of numerous French light aircraft, she departed and flew across the Gulf of Genoa and landed at Pisa at 3.35pm. The next morning she explored the city before taking off for Rome. She was not trying to break any records, just to prove the flight could be done by a woman flying alone. After Rome she continued down the western-Italian coast to Naples and arrived at 5.30pm that Monday evening. She was flying without radio communication. A lot depended on good eyesight and chance. On Tuesday, 13 March she reached Catania in Sicily, where she dined alone that evening.

At 9.45am the next day she departed for the island of Malta, arriving at 1.30pm at Halir Aerodrome. Royal Air Force (RAF) officers advised her not to fly over the 200 miles of open sea to Libya until the next day, when they would escort her halfway on her sea crossing with three of their seaplanes. She landed at Tripoli at 11.40am on Friday, 16 March 1928. Her next stops were the Libyan cities of Khoms, Sirte and Benghazi. By now her total flying time was 33.5 hours. The night of Sunday, 18 March was spent at Aboukir (now Abu Qir), Egypt, after a flight time of eight and a half hours that day.

On Monday, 19 March she flew into Heliopolis Aerodrome in Cairo, where she met the first serious obstacle on her journey. The British authorities in Egypt refused

The Moth G-EBSF taxiing in the sand at Heliopolis Aerodrome, Cairo, on 19 March 1928.
Courtesy Prospero Bailey

Above: *RAF officers looked on as Lady Bailey checked the cockpit of G-EBSF, while temporarily grounded by the military authorities at Heliopolis Aerodrome, Cairo, on 19 March 1928.*
COURTESY DE HAVILLAND MOTH CLUB ARCHIVE

Above: *Lady Bailey preparing to hand-swing the propeller of G-EBSF at Wadi Halfa in the north-Sudanese desert on 29 March 1928.*
COURTESY PROSPERO BAILEY

Left: *Engine checks were performed by Lady Bailey on her Moth, G-EBSF, during a four-day stopover at Khartoum between 1 and 5 April 1928. RAF officials refused her permission to continue south across the Sudanese desert.*
COURTESY PROSPERO BAILEY

to give her permission to fly south over the barren desert of southern Sudan by herself. They insisted she should be escorted by a man. High-ranking RAF officers were determined in their efforts to prevent Lady Bailey from crossing these dangerous, swampy areas alone. Despite Lady Bailey's desire to continue on her own, a compromise was reached after seven days of negotiations. Abe Bailey contacted the *Johannesburg Star*, which was sponsoring the South Africa to London flight, via Khartoum and Cairo, of Dick Bentley and his wife, who were about to set out. Dick Bentley had flown from London to the Cape in 28 days in September 1927. He had already been contacted by another damsel in distress, Lady Heath, to escort her across the Sudan on her flight north from Cape Town. He agreed to do the same for Lady Bailey, who continued through the desert heat until she arrived in Khartoum on Sunday, 1 April, joining the Bentleys and Lady Heath, who were already there.

Lieutenant Richard Bentley discussing plans to accompany Lady Bailey south over the southern Sudanese desert on 5 April 1928 at Khartoum.
COURTESY PROSPERO BAILEY

The world's press were following the flights of both Lady Heath and Lady Bailey with keen interest. The aviators rested for four days in Khartoum.

On Thursday, 5 April the three small aircraft departed Khartoum. Lady Heath flew north to continue her journey towards London and the Bentleys accompanied Lady Bailey for 420 miles from Khartoum south to Malakal. Here the barren desert turned to green areas of forest and the Bentleys turned around to continue their journey northward. Lady Bailey was again solo when she continued past Kisumu, Kenya, and headed to Tabora, Tanganyika Territory, after a stop at Shinyanga. Tabora Airport is almost 4,000 feet

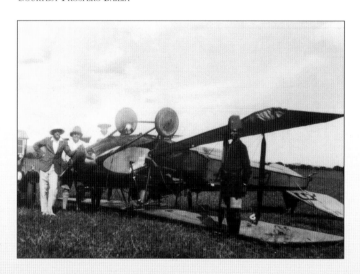

above sea level and it was the hottest part of the day when, after a flight time of six and a half hours, she made a disastrous mistake in judging her approach on 9 April 1928. She landed heavily and crashed G-EBSF, coming to a halt inverted. She escaped unhurt.

Lady Bailey contacted her husband to ask him to secure another aircraft to continue her journey. Several solutions were considered until he purchased another Moth for her. The replacement aircraft was rapidly sourced and registration was completed within three days. The de Havilland 60X Moth, G-UAAL, was placed on the South African civil-aircraft register on 13 April 1928 under the name Sir Abe Bailey. This aircraft had been registered on 8 March 1928 to Mr J.H. Veasey, the de Havilland agent in Johannesburg. On 16 April 1928 Major Mentjes of the SAAF flew it from Pretoria to Tabora and he reached Lady Bailey on 19 April. The engine, the larger fuel tanks and other enhancements were

The inverted Moth G-EBSF at Tabora, Tanganyika, on 9 April 1928, when Lady Bailey made a disastrous landing but fortunately escaped unhurt.
COURTESY PROSPERO BAILEY (TOP)
COURTESY JOHN ILLSLEY (ABOVE)

A humorous sketch by Lady Bailey of her crash at Tabora on 9 April 1928.
COURTESY PROSPERO BAILEY

transferred from her crashed machine, G-EBSF, to G-UAAL. On Saturday, 21 April, she was finally able to continue her journey south after a delay of 11 days. The remainder of the wreckage of G-EBSF was transported to Pretoria by railway and, when it was eventually repaired in May 1928, Lady Bailey presented it to the newly formed Johannesburg Flying Club.

It was now six weeks since she left London and she was heartily sick of Tabora. Four hours after taking off, she landed at Abercorn, 5,400 feet up in the mountains. The next morning she was in Broken Hill, where she was delayed by one day because she was suffering from a short-term fever. On Tuesday, 24 April she arrived at Livingstone in Rhodesia. While circling the majestic Victoria Falls, she reminisced about the first time she had seen them – on her and Abe's honeymoon, 16 years previously.

She had a very bumpy flight as she followed the railway line to Bulawayo, where she was greeted by the Mayor. Here the fever finally left her and the next day she was tracking towards Pretoria, the starting point of Lady Heath's journey proper two months earlier on 25 February. However, she was following the wrong rail tracks and had to land to find directions. She was forced down a second time when she ran out of petrol. Villagers used buckets, jugs and other utensils to gather fuel to get her going again. These delays caused her to spend a night at Warmbaths (now Bela-Bela) in the Transvaal, where she landed in an area surrounded by anthills.

On 27 April 1928, Lady Bailey departed Warmbaths and, as she approached Pretoria, she was welcomed by several aircraft of the SAAF and Miss Douglas, the first woman pilot of the Johannesburg Flying Club. At Zwartkop Military Base, Pretoria, there was great rejoicing from the huge crowd assembled to meet her.

That evening she flew the short hop to Johannesburg, from where she departed at 1pm the following day to fly to Bloemfontein for an overnight stay. Another night was spent at Beaufort West.

This spectacular photograph of the Victoria Falls was taken by Lady Bailey on 24 April 1928. She had spent her honeymoon in that area in October 1911.
COURTESY PROSPERO BAILEY

Lady Bailey taxiing her Moth, G-UAAL, to a halt at Zwartkop Aerodrome, Roberts Heights, Pretoria, on 27 April 1928.
COURTESY PROSPERO BAILEY

The last day of her flight to Cape Town was dramatic and she described it in a long, barely punctuated scrawl:

I had heard about difficulties in the Hex River Mountains which had to be crossed. So I thought I'd get up very high and go over like that and have no bother. I took a lot of trouble climbing all the way to get a good height but it was all wasted as the machine sank as I got over the mountains. Then I at last got to one big range where when I went high enough to go over the wind came so strong against me that I could not make any headway and when I went lower I could advance but was too low to fly so I went off to the south over a lower bit and came back low down up to the next valley and when I climbed up again to look over the next range I saw it was the last one and I could see the top of Table Mountain sticking up out of a sea of cloud in the distance.

Assistance with her leather flying jacket was offered to Lady Bailey as she prepared to depart Johannesburg for Bloemfontein on 28 April 1928.
COURTESY PROSPERO BAILEY

Sir Abe (right) gazing skywards, anxiously awaiting the appearance of his wife's aircraft from the east of Cape Town, 30 April 1928.
COURTESY PROSPERO BAILEY

Table Mountain was Cape Town. Table Mountain was home and Abe. At Young's Field Military Base, Wynberg, east of Table Mountain, a great assembly had been waiting since early in the day, anxiously looking into the north-eastern sky for the first sight of Lady Bailey.

When she became overdue, aircraft from the local flying club went up to look for her. Eventually, a very small shape in the sky developed a faint distant sound and shortly the Moth could be seen. The landing was perfect. Lady Bailey climbed out of the cockpit and Abe was the first person to greet her. She remarked to him, 'Hello Abe! I'm a bit late – I got muddled in the mountains.' After many interviews and photographs with the press, the tiny aircraft was locked away to prevent souvenir hunters from tearing pieces off it. Lady Bailey and Abe retired to Rust-en-Vrede.

The flight of 8,000 miles to Cape Town ended at 12.15pm on 30 April 1928 and took 52 days. Lady Bailey calculated the flying time at 121 hours and 35 minutes. No records had been broken but the world's press were

G-UAAL on arrival at Cape Town, 30 April 1928.
COURTESY PROSPERO BAILEY

Above: *Well-wishers greeted Lady Bailey at Cape Town on 30 April 1928, following her flight from Croydon, London, which had begun on 9 March 1928. Looking on was her husband, Sir Abe.*
COURTESY ANNA TIETZE, UNIVERSITY OF CAPE TOWN

Right: *Lady Bailey disembarking from G-UAAL at Cape Town, 30 April 1928.*
COURTESY PROSPERO BAILEY

The wings of G-UAAL were folded before the aircraft was placed in a hangar to protect it from souvenir hunters at Young's Field, Cape Town, on 30 April 1928.
COURTESY PROSPERO BAILEY

Rodd Douglas, Director of the
de Havilland Aircraft Company,
South Africa, stood behind the cockpit
of Moth G-UAAL as Lady Bailey
prepared to depart from Cape Town on
14 May 1928.
COURTESY JANE FALLOON
VIA JULIEANNE MCMAHON

rapturous nonetheless. Three days later, a luncheon in Cape Town, hosted by both parties of government, honoured Abe's retirement from parliament. Senior politicians and dignitaries were present and toasted Lady Bailey's success, acknowledging her Irish heritage. In Abe's reply to the toast, he spoke in praise of his wife's achievement. Abe had planned to sail back to England on 5 May 1928 but Lady Bailey wanted to complete a return trip by air. Abe did not succeed in persuading her not to fly back; neither did any of the others who tried to publicly dissuade her from undertaking the return journey. Lady Bailey made her own plans.

Her departure in the Moth G-UAAL from Young's Field, Cape Town, was on Monday, 14 May 1928. Weather immediately caught her out and, during a forced landing beside Humansdorp, the undercarriage collapsed, damaging the nose and shattering the propeller. The damaged plane was taken by road to Port Elizabeth and Lady Bailey spent ten days at Colesberg, Abe's farm in the Karoo, while it was repaired. While waiting there she did some local flying in a Westland Widgeon III, G-UAAH (later ZS-AAH), belonging to the Port Elizabeth Light Aeroplane Club.

While the Moth G-UAAL was repairable, Lady Bailey was not happy with it and she telegraphed Geoffrey de Havilland in London, who advised her of one

Unknown onlookers inspecting the crash at Humansdorp, south-west
of Port Elizabeth, South Africa, on 14 May 1928. This accident
caused Lady Bailey to delay her departure from South Africa until
September 1928.
COURTESY PROSPERO BAILEY

Unknown onlookers inspecting the crash of G-UAAL at Humansdorp, South Africa.
Courtesy Prospero Bailey

similar to the crashed Moth G-EBSF that would be available in Nairobi, Kenya. This aircraft was a de Havilland demonstration machine and was registered as G-EBTG to Commander Lionel Robinson, the de Havilland agent in Nairobi. G-UAAL was repaired by volunteer members of the SAAF and became the first aircraft operated by the Defence Flying Club based at Zwartkop Military Base, Pretoria. When the South African civil-aircraft register started using the prefix ZS on 1 January 1929, G-UAAL became ZS-AAL. It was written off at Muldersdrift, north of Johannesburg, on 6 December 1937.

Major Mentjes flew G-EBTG from Nairobi to Pretoria and then to Lady Bailey at Colesberg, arriving there on 25 May 1928. Despite having lost two weeks already, Lady Bailey deferred the recommencement of her journey and spent the next four months with Sir Pierre van Ryneveld, Director of Air Services in the Union Air Force and a long-distance solo flier of renown. He had the distinction of having piloted the first flight from London to Cape Town, which had commenced on 4 February 1920 and concluded 45 days later on 20 March 1920. The flying time had been just 109 hours but in the process he had wrecked two aircraft.

During that stay, Lady Bailey enjoyed her first experience of a big-game hunt in the Transvaal. One reason for the delay was the determination of the British authorities to refuse her permission to return alone over the Sudanese desert. She eventually planned a route along the west coast of the continent – virtually unknown territory for aviators. This involved flying over the Belgian Congo, French Equatorial Africa and the Sahara Desert.

On 14 September 1928, while Lady Bailey was still staying with the van Rynevelds, a new DH.60G Gipsy Moth was registered to her as G-AABN. She had ordered this aircraft with the intention that she would be back in the UK by the time of its delivery. It was instead operated by the London Aeroplane Club and registered to them on 5 March 1929.

During her stay she endeavoured to obtain information about her planned route home. However, she admitted, 'I found that maps were unobtainable and that definite information about petrol and oil was not to be had. It was a question of just seeing how far one could go.' By mid-September, her latest Moth, G-EBTG, was ready at Pretoria for the return journey to London. On 16 and 17 September 1928 she tested the aircraft in an eight-hour round trip to Lourenço Marques (later Maputo), the capital city of Mozambique. At 7am on Friday, 21 September 1928, Lady Bailey arrived at Zwartkop Aerodrome, two miles east of Roberts Heights, Pretoria. Zwartkop is located 4,780 feet above mean sea level.

The heavy Moth lifted off at 10am for Bulawayo, where it landed over 6 hours later at 4.10pm, having endured a headwind of 30 miles per hour. Lady Bailey spent the night at Government House and departed

The converted single-seat de Havilland Moth G-EBTG arrived at Salisbury, Rhodesia, on 22 September 1928. The front cockpit was modified to contain the extra fuel tank.
COURTESY JOHN ILLSLEY

the next morning, 22 September 1928, at 7.10am for Salisbury (now Harare), Rhodesia. She had no maps for this area but based her route on the railway line. She took it leisurely, enjoyed sightseeing and arrived at 10.30am. Next day saw her departure at 8am for Broken Hill. The route was mountainous, with considerable haze to hinder her view and lots of barren land with no landmarks to guide her. She was greeted at Broken Hill at 12.30pm by some friends and, after replenishing her petrol and oil stocks, she continued

The aircraft selected for the return journey to London was a DH.60X Moth, G-EBTG. It is pictured here ready for departure from Zwartkop Aerodrome, Roberts Heights, Pretoria, on 21 September 1928.
COURTESY PROSPERO BAILEY

A smiling Lady Bailey was greeted at Elisabethville, in the south-east section of the Belgian Congo, by Pat Murdoch. She arrived there on 23 September 1928 and stayed for three days.
COURTESY PROSPERO BAILEY

at 2.05pm for Elisabethville (now Lubumbashi). High trees made her take-off challenging, forcing her to bob her head from side to side rapidly to navigate the plane clear of the trees. With no maps, the railway line should have been her reference. However, haze and poor visibility prevented her from locating it and she landed at Elisabethville at 5.15pm on 23 September, more by luck than anything else. She stayed there for three days.

On Wednesday, 26 September 1928, Lady Bailey departed Elisabethville at 7.30am and, flying over grassland and bush, she landed at Kamina for petrol and oil at 11.15am. Low oil pressure forced her to land at Tchumba for the night. On Friday, 28 September she arrived, after an adventure with low clouds and flying over dense forests, at Bandundu at 4pm. The next day she was in Léopoldville (now Kinshasa), where her concern was whether or not she could obtain petrol and oil further north. Availability of these products was unknown through the Belgian Congo and French territory to Fort-Lamy (now N'Djamena) in Chad. While awaiting replies from telegrams to London she decided to fly to the Portuguese west-coast town of Luanda, Angola, where she arrived 10.55am on 1 October, chasing herds of rhinoceros on the way. She was greeted by crowds of excited locals after she touched down. Problems with a front magneto caused Lady Bailey an unanticipated delay of over two weeks at Luanda, during which time she enjoyed some more big-game hunting.

Finally, on 19 October 1928, with the magneto repaired, she departed Luanda and arrived back at Léopoldville the next afternoon. As a result of

scratching some mosquito bites, however, she had developed abscesses on her legs and feet. It was almost a month before she could continue her journey. Finally, on 16 November, she left her friends in Léopoldville and arrived back at Bandundu at 11.15 that morning. The Belgian and French governments had been working tirelessly in previous years to develop air routes and aerodromes in that part of lower-central Africa. She was advised to depart without delay because there

A relaxed Lady Bailey at Léopoldville, Belgian Congo, on 29 September 1928.

were tornados and lightning storms on the way north to Coquilhatville (now Mbandaka) on the River Congo. The area below was a combination of lakes, marshes and forests, providing few places for landing if necessary. The town hall in Coquilhatville was two miles north of the geographic equator line and was the closest town in the world to the equator. She left Coquilhatville the next day and arrived at Bangui where, because of the presence of tornados, she could not leave for two days. At Fort Archambault (now Sarh) she was greeted by the native population with a marching-band reception and escorted to the Administrator's House.

Petrol and oil were supplied at Fort Archambault and Lady Bailey departed for Fort-Lamy at 10.30am on 21 November 1928, where she arrived four hours later and commenced a clean-up of the Moth's engine. From Fort-Lamy her journey turned westward to the Nigerian town of Kano. However, she lost her way because of fog and strong winds. To determine where she was, she landed on the sandy main street of Potiskum village. A Ford car carrying the King of the village arrived with speed and, scattering dust in all directions, stopped beside the Moth. The King gave her onward directions and she took off again for Kano, where she touched down on the sandy aerodrome at 1.30pm on 23 November, having experienced further difficulty locating it. She departed Kano the next morning at 8.30am, accompanied by G.R. Boyd-Carpenter in his de Havilland Moth, G-EBZL. They followed the railway line through Zaria to Sokoto in north-west Nigeria, where locals had the aerodrome marked out most elaborately for her. Greeting her were horsemen wearing colourful clothes and ornamental saddles and harnesses. These riders belonged to the retinue of the Sultan of Sokoto, the 'fifth most important Mohammedan in the world'. According to his religion, the Sultan himself was not supposed to see a woman without a veil, so as soon as Lady Bailey arrived he drove off.

After Sokoto she stopped at Niamey and followed the River Niger to Gao in French West Africa, where she arrived on Wednesday, 28 November. She found little cooperation in finding fuel supplies to continue her journey to Tesalit. She was very unimpressed with the lack of assistance from the French towards her. This was explained by the fact that they assumed she was

Lady Bailey at Kano, Nigeria, with her Box Brownie camera, on 24 November 1928.
COURTESY PROSPERO BAILEY

English. She was 'detained' for 14 days at Gao due to the non-cooperation of the French in supplying petrol and oil for her journey north across the Sahara Desert. She had to forgo an opportunity to transit the Sahara and consider an alternative route. On Wednesday, 12 December at 8am, she left Gao and headed towards the west-African coast. Her intended destination was Mopti. However, she got lost and landed at Goulambo, where she made a heavy landing and broke an axle. She was given a horse to ride the 11 miles to the nearest town for assistance and accommodation. After three days, the axle was repaired and she took off for Mopti, where she stayed for two nights. It was Sunday, 16 December 1928 before she departed Mopti for the aerodrome at Bamako. Here she fell foul of mosquitoes again and found it difficult to sleep. From Bamako she flew to Kayes and arrived on 19 December 1928 at Dakar, the capital of Senegal, and terminus of the French Air Service from Paris.

The next day, 20 December 1928, Lady Bailey continued north to Saint-Louis. Then onward through

Lady Bailey was welcomed at Dakar, French West Africa, by Commandant Bouska on 19 December 1928. Her annotation regarding this photograph read: 'The lady pilot is neither tidy, pretty nor clean.'

COURTESY PROSPERO BAILEY

Port-Étienne (now Nouadhibou), Mauritania and the Spanish aerodrome at Villa Cisneros (Dakhla) in southern Morocco. The journey from Villa Cisneros to Cape Juby was 400 miles and she arrived there on 23 December. At Cape Juby a Spanish Air Force officer insisted she needed clearance from Madrid to proceed to Agadir. While waiting there, the NCOs and their wives gave a tea party in Lady Bailey's honour. She remarked:

> To anyone muddling along on a trip like this, to meet with such kindness and friendliness

was a wonderful experience, because it necessarily helped me along so very much and I deeply appreciate this, not only here, but in every stopping place that I went to.

The coastal Moroccan aerodrome of Cape Juby, where Lady Bailey landed on 23 December 1928. The Airfield Manager was the famous French aviator Antoine de Saint-Exupéry.

COURTESY PROSPERO BAILEY

While at Casablanca, Morocco, on 29 December 1928, Lady Bailey studied charts for her flight north towards mainland Europe.
COURTESY PROSPERO BAILEY

The permit arrived after a 14-hour delay and, on 24 December, she journeyed to Agadir and spent the night there. The next morning was Christmas Day, though Lady Bailey made no reference in her diary to any celebrations. That day she planned to fly to Casablanca. As the engine was not firing well, she replaced the plugs and flew onwards. However, over the mountains north of Agadir, the machine cut out. She found what she thought was a dried-out lake but, to her surprise, it turned out to be the landing ground at Tamanar. She landed and secured her aircraft, then followed a native, who brought her to the local Administrator's House and there put her in touch with the British Consul in Mogador (now Essaouira), who arranged for a mechanic to meet her the next morning.

It was Friday, 28 December before she got airborne from Tamanar and flew the short distance to Mogador, where she spent the night. Although the engine problems confounded her, she was able to proceed and a flight of two and a half hours the next day brought her to Casablanca. Here she stayed until 1 January 1929 and then made the four-hour flight across the Straits of Gibraltar to Malaga in the south of Spain. Further engine problems were to dog her journey back to London.

The following day, she travelled along the eastern coast of Spain to Alicante; the next day brought her to Barcelona, where she spent two nights. On Saturday, 5 January, she crossed into France and landed at Bordeaux, after a flight of 4 hours and 55 minutes. Her trip to Paris was fraught with difficulties. She had to choose the western route through France because of very strong winds in the Rhône Valley and Massif Central:

> At Paris I was unable to find Le Bourget due to heavy fog and was lucky to find the airfield at Villacoublay. There wasn't a soul about and it was too dark to go on so I got a taxi into the Ritz in central Paris.

The fog remained too thick to fly for several more days and she waited there until Tuesday, 8 January, when she made the 25-minute short hop north to Le

Bourget. Here she spent a week, before embarking on the final French leg to Berck-sur-Mer near Le Touquet on the north-west coast. By the time she got to Berck, snow had become a problem.

On Thursday, 16 January 1929, she completed the round trip in G-EBTG with a two-hour flight to Croydon, London, as that was the official landing place for all long-distance flights. The weather over the English Channel was poor. There was a huge crowd of people waiting in the snow at Croydon to greet her, including her mother, two of her daughters and her brother Willie.

The flying time from Pretoria to London was 124 hours, not including the excursion from Bandundu to Luanda in Angola. She expressed her surprise at finding an excellently run and organised air service flying regularly across the Belgian Congo and a similar air service running along the west coast of

Lady Bailey taxied her Moth, G-EBTG, in the snow at Croydon Aerodrome on 16 January 1929, followed by a large crowd of well-wishers.

COURTESY RONNY VOGT

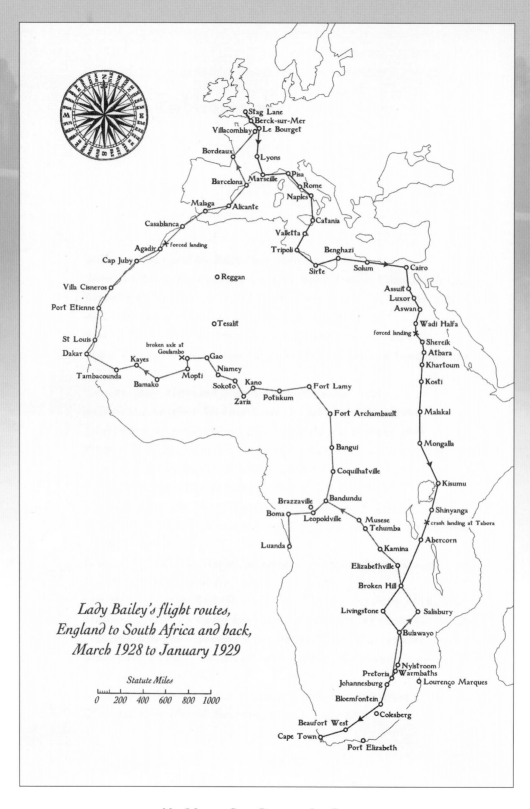

Lady Bailey's flight routes,
England to South Africa and back,
March 1928 to January 1929

The above four pages are from Lady Bailey's diary recording her historic flight from London to Cape Town and back to London between
9 March 1928 and 16 January 1929.

COURTESY PROSPERO BAILEY

Africa between Dakar and Paris. The sad fact was that the same did not exist in the British colonies in Africa. She remarked, 'My trip was too slow to count as anything wonderful but as a tour I think it was the most marvellous means of travelling   for seeing interesting places that anyone could wish for.'

Lady Bailey's total distance during her ten-month absence was about 18,000 miles and her Moths, G-EBSF, G-UAAL and G-EBTG, performed as well as could be expected over such a journey. She had achieved an all-time distance-flying record. No one had flown so far by themselves before. The flight was the longest ever accomplished by a woman and the longest solo achievement by any woman aviator at that time. She was a heroine, probably the most famous woman in the world at that moment. On 19 January 1929 she made the 25-minute final hop to her base at Stag Lane, where she was welcomed by Geoffrey de Havilland and his wife, Louie. Then it was home to 38 Bryanston Square, where three of her children were recovering from influenza. She remarked on how much they had grown in the ten months. Her husband was in Cape Town, recovering from a minor operation, but wrote her a warm, glowing letter praising her achievement. Lady Bailey's riveting journals of this return flight have survived and are reproduced in Jane Falloon's book, *Throttle Full Open*.

Newspapers of the world had followed her journey and, whenever she had not been able to send a telegraph giving updates, they reported her lost. This had occurred frequently. Adulation, praise and honours were heaped upon her from the moment she landed at Croydon that snowy morning on 16 January 1929. The following evening the Royal Aeronautical Society and the Royal Aero Club hosted a hastily organised luncheon at the Savoy Hotel, London. Despite the short notice, it was attended by over 100 guests and presided over by Lord

Thompson, Minister for Air. Lady Bailey's mother, Mittie, and her aunt Doods were there, as well as Sir Alan and Lady Cobham, the de Havillands, Winifred Spooner and Bert Hinkler. Speeches were delivered by Marshal of the RAF Sir Hugh Trenchard, and he acknowledged the lack of assistance she had received from that service.

The London *Daily Telegraph* commented: 'This is the most remarkable flight made by any woman of any country.' The *Times* went further: 'This long, lone African journey will rank as one of the finest and most daring in the world's story of light aeroplane flying.' The Moth G-EBTG was formally placed on the UK civil-aircraft register in Lady Bailey's name in March 1929.

The Harmon Trophy is a set of three international trophies awarded annually to the world's outstanding male aviator, female aviator and aeronaut (balloon or dirigible). They are awarded by the International League of Aviators. The first year an award was made for a woman aviator was 1927. Lady Bailey was the inaugural winner and Charles A. Lindbergh won the award for male aviator. For the most outstanding female aviator for the year 1928, Lady Bailey was again the recipient. The male aviator trophy went to the Italian pilot Colonel Arturo Ferrarin.

The honours and awards kept piling up. In March 1929, Lady Bailey was elected Chairperson of the Ladies' Committee of the Air League, replacing Lady Heath. Lady Bailey acquired another new DH.60G Gipsy Moth Coupé, registered G-AAEE to the Honourable Lady Bailey on 20 February 1929, and based it at Stag Lane Aerodrome. By now Lady Bailey was Vice-President of the Hampshire Aeroplane Club, which had been formed on 2 March 1926 with Lord Louis Mountbatten as President. She was honoured at many events in the months following her return to England and received many accolades.

Meanwhile, her daughters Mary Ellen and Ann were

The Harmon International Trophy was awarded annually to the world's outstanding woman aviator. Lady Bailey was the inaugural recipient in 1927 and won the trophy again in 1928.

COURTESY MUSEUM OF TRANSPORT AND TECHNOLOGY (MOTAT), AUCKLAND, NEW ZEALAND (REF. 2003.551)

enjoying their time at Malvern St James Girls' School. On 2 February 1929, Lady Bailey was at Paddington Railway Station to meet her two daughters off the steam train from Malvern. The girls were in London to attend the Hors Concours prizegiving ceremony by the Lord Mayor at the Mansion House. A few weeks later, on 8 March 1929, Lady Bailey went to the school to attend Mary Ellen's confirmation. While there, she gave the students a first-hand account of her recent African flight, which interested them immensely.

Lady Bailey soon got back to her favourite activity – partaking in aeronautical events. The Cinque Ports Easter Meeting at Lympne, Kent, on 30 and 31 March 1929 saw Lady Bailey enter the Handicap Race of 36 miles in her new Moth, G-AAEE. She finished in a very creditable second place with a speed of 93 miles per hour. On 19 April 1929, she was at Croydon Aerodrome to christen Frank Mase's Simmonds Spartan *The All Black* prior to his attempt to fly solo to New Zealand. During the ceremony, Captain Neville Stack performed some exhibition flights. On 13 June she attended the Cambridge Aero Club Air Display, where she did some display flying and led the fly-past. The following day, she flew from London to Belfast in G-AAEE. She departed Stag Lane at 1.30pm and arrived at Liverpool at 4.30pm, then crossed to Belfast, landing at Aldergrove shortly after 8pm.

On 22 and 23 June 1929, the Ostend Air Rally took place. Twenty-six machines arrived from England, with Lady Bailey one of the first to get there. They were met by the Belgian Air Minister. Lady Bailey was awarded first prize in the Airwoman's Division, a special class for single-seat light aeroplanes. She remained on the Continent and on 27 June she was at Waalhaven Aerodrome, Rotterdam, Holland, to partake in the International Light Plane Meeting organised by the

Lady Bailey enjoyed the luxury of the enclosed cockpit in her DH.60G Coupé, G-AAEE, which she purchased on 20 February 1929.

COURTESY PROSPERO BAILEY

Rotterdam Aero Club. Here she was part of the English team that won the Relay Race, with the Dutch team second and the Belgian team third.

In June 1929, Abe was well enough to travel back to England and Lady Bailey and the children sailed to Madeira to meet him. They attended a dinner organised by the Royal Institute of International Affairs on 8 July 1929 at the Mansion House. (Abe had made a generous and substantial donation of £100,000 to the RIIA.) The Prince of Wales (later King Edward VIII) proposed toasts to both Lady Bailey and Abe. Jimmy Thomas, a former trade-union leader and now Privy Seal, spoke, as did Winston Churchill. Sir Abe also spoke and paid warm tributes to his wife's achievements.

On Friday, 5 July 1929, the annual King's Cup Race took place from Heston Aerodrome. The weather conditions were poor but the three ladies that entered succeeded in finishing. Flying her de Havilland Gipsy Moth Coupé, G-AAEE, Lady Bailey finished in twenty-sixth place. On 27 July, she attended the seventh International Aero Exhibition at the Savoy Hotel,

London, where Louis Blériot was a distinguished guest and Sir Arthur Whitten Brown was a speaker.

Mary Ellen (16) and Ann (11) finished the 1929 school term on a high. In cricket, Mary Ellen was described as 'a promising wicket-keeper' who has 'improved generally' and Ann was a 'good bat and a keen player with time for improvement'. They were both members of the Girl Guides and one of their leaders was Heather Baden-Powell, the 14-year-old daughter of Robert Baden-Powell, the founder of the Scout Movement. The sisters were also in the Dramatic Society. Mary Ellen was a member of the Speaker's Society and the Literary Society, while Ann was awarded a prize in the Gardener's Society and the highest mark in the Grand Concours.

The International Light Plane Tour of Europe began on 3 August 1929, with 82 aircraft entered. The following map indicates the extensive course of the race, which started at Orly Airport, Paris. Great Britain was represented by three pilots: Lady Bailey, Winifred Spooner and Captain Hubert Stanford Broad; they

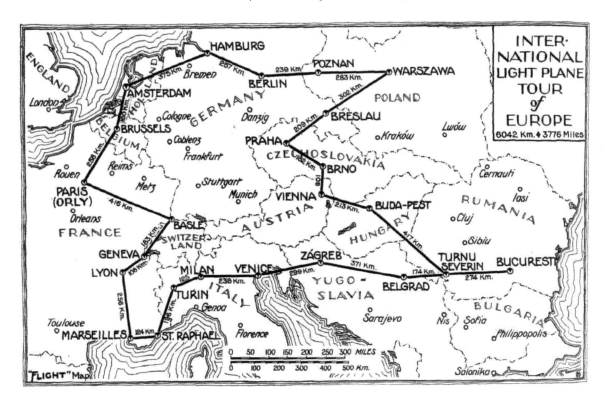

The route of the 3,776-mile International Light Plane Tour of Europe, which commenced in Paris on 3 August 1929.

COURTESY FLIGHTGLOBAL ARCHIVES VIA RBI LIMITED

were all flying Gipsy Moths. Lady Bailey and Winifred Spooner were the only women among 55 entrants. Lady Bailey damaged the undercarriage of her aircraft at Croydon and was deemed a non-starter. She did, nonetheless, fly the course as was laid out, to prove she was equal to such a challenge.

On 23 September 1929, over 20,000 spectators enjoyed the aviation display hosted by the Lancashire Aero Club at Morecambe. Despite the bad weather, Lady Bailey was one of several that gave a good display for those in attendance. She departed Croydon in G-AAEE on 12 October and reached Amsterdam that afternoon. On 14 October she was prevented from progressing beyond Gothenburg by bad weather and continued to Oslo by train.

So successful had been the creation of an aviation group in the Forum Club that it was decided to hold an inaugural dinner on Monday, 22 October 1929. Lady Bailey, the first President of the group, officiated. Three days later she was guest of honour at the Yeovil branch of the Royal Aeronautical Society and delivered a talk on her flight to Cape Town and back.

Lady Bailey's younger brother Richard earned his Aviator's 'A' Certificate (number 8678) on 11 July 1929 with the Bristol and Wessex Aeroplane Club. His wife, Alice

Winifred Spooner was the only female pilot other than Lady Bailey to represent Great Britain during the International Light Plane Tour of Europe in August 1929.
COURTESY PROSPERO BAILEY

WESTENRA, Hon. Richard,   8678

Bullyhaven, Bishopsteignton, S. Devon.

Born   15th October 1893 *at* London.
Nationality British
Rank, Regiment, Profession   Gent.
Certificate taken on D.H. Moth 30h.p. Cirrus
At   Bristol & Wessex Aeroplane Club, Filton
Date   11th July 1929.

The Royal Aero Club Aviator's Certificate issued to Richard Westenra, a brother of Lady Bailey, on 11 July 1929, along with the photograph that accompanied the certificate.
COURTESY ROYAL AERO CLUB TRUST

WESTENRA, Hon. Mrs. Alice Florence   9067

Ballyhaven, Bishopsteignton, Devon

Born 20th January 1895   at   Dublin

Nationality   British

Rank, Regiment, Profession

Certificate taken on   D.H. "Moth" 90 h.p. Gipsy

At   Brooklands School of Flying.

Date   29th April, 1930.

The Royal Aero Club Aviator's Certificate issued to Alice Florence Westenra, wife of Richard Westenra,
on 29 April 1930, along with the photograph that accompanied the certificate.

COURTESY ROYAL AERO CLUB TRUST

Florence, was successful in earning her Aviator's 'A' Certificate (number 9067) on 29 April 1930 with Brooklands School of Flying.

On 6 December 1929, *Flight* magazine published a list of private aircraft owners. Lady Bailey and her relatives were well represented, along with several other owners of Irish extraction, as follows:

Registration	Owner	Type
G-EBTG	Lady Bailey	Moth
G-AABO	Messrs T. and Q. Naylor	Moth
G-AAEA	Mrs A. Cleaver	Moth
G-AAEE	Lady Bailey	Moth
G-AAFC	Hon. Richard Westenra	Moth
G-AAFM	Hon. Arthur Guinness	Moth
G-AAJO	Hon. Loel Guinness	Moth
G-AAJZ	Hon. Mrs A. Westenra	Moth
G-AARL	John Carberry	Moth

By this time Lady Heath, who had owned several aircraft prior to December 1929, had disposed of them as she travelled to the United States of America in November 1928. Out of 174 privately owned machines in Britain on the register on 30 November 1929, 9 had Irish owners.

During the winter of 1929–30, Lady Bailey studied for her 'B' (Commercial) Certificate at the de Havilland Technical School at Stag Lane. In her class was Amy Johnson and they frequently practised their Morse code in 38 Bryanston Square. Amy Johnson was 13 years younger than Lady Bailey.

On 1 January 1930 Lady Bailey was awarded the title Dame Commander of the Most Excellent Order of the British Empire (DBE) for her services to aviation. She was the first woman aviator to be so honoured. She now had an hereditary title, a title by marriage and one that she had earned herself. A month later she was informed that she had been awarded the 1929 Royal Aero Club's Britannia Trophy for:

> The most meritorious performance of the year. Her lone flight from England to the Cape and return by the west coast of Africa has set a new standard and blazed a new trail for the private owner.

On Saturday, 5 April 1930, Lady Bailey performed the opening ceremony of the new clubhouse at Park Aerodrome as Vice-President of the Liverpool and District Aero Club. While she had been away in Africa, the Liverpool and District Aero Club had prospered. Among its early members were husband and wife Thomas Humphrey and Quenelda Naylor, who had been undergoing flying instruction at the Hooton Park Aerodrome during the summer of 1928. Lady Bailey's maternal grandfather was Richard Christopher Naylor (1814–99), who once owned Hooton Park. Richard had an older brother, John Naylor (1813–89), who had a son, also called John (1856–1906). Thomas Humphrey Naylor, who was born five months before Lady Bailey on 1 July 1890, was this John's son.

Quenelda Naylor made her first solo flight on 26 August 1928 and became the first female member of the Liverpool club to earn her 'A' Certificate (number 8454) when she passed her tests on 25 October 1928. Thomas, meanwhile, earned his 'A' Certificate (number 8475) on 15 December 1928. They became the first members of the Liverpool Aero Club to own an aircraft when they acquired de Havilland Gipsy Moth G-AABO and flew it from London to Hooton Park on Sunday, 10 February 1929.

Lady Bailey and her cousin Thomas H. Naylor flew to Gleneagles, Scotland, in their machines to attend the first air rally held in Scotland. It was organised by Sicele O'Brien. On 10 August 1929, Thomas Naylor won a race from Wythenshawe Aerodrome, Manchester, to Hooton Park, Liverpool, comprising a return journey of 70 miles, in G-AABO, at an average speed of 98.53 miles per hour. The previous record for the Manchester to Liverpool

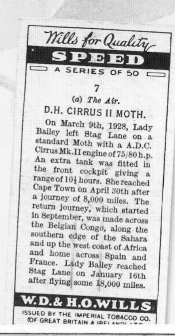

In 1930, Wills's Cigarette Company, UK, issued a series of 50 cigarette cards under the series title 'Speed'. Lady Bailey's DH Cirrus II Moth, G-EBTG, was among the aircraft commemorated.

Courtesy London Cigarette Card Company Ltd

Stag Lane Aerodrome in May 1930, when the London Aeroplane Club was at the peak of its success. Lady Bailey was active in the club and partook in several aviation events.
COURTESY DE HAVILLAND MOTH CLUB ARCHIVE

Air Race had been set on 7 July 1911 by Henry G. Melly, in a time of 1 hour 55 minutes.

In June 1930, she sold the Moth G-EBTG, which had brought her from South Africa, and a new de Havilland Puss Moth with a Gipsy III engine was registered to the Honourable Lady Bailey as G-AAYA. Whit Monday, 9 June 1930, was the date of the Reading Air Fête, hosted by the Berks, Bucks and Oxon Aero Club at Woodley Aerodrome. The first item on the programme was the Handicap Race, in which Lady Bailey finished third in G-AAEE, at an average speed of 99 miles per hour. She was the only female entrant.

The following Saturday, she was among 800 guests at RAF Manston for a garden party. Lady Bailey made her third entry into the annual King's Cup Race on 5 July 1930, flying her Moth, G-AAEE. There was an entry list of 101 aircraft but only 88 started, and of these only 61 completed the course. The total distance was 750 miles, starting and finishing at Hanworth Air Park, south-west

London. *Flight* magazine reported on 11 July 1930: 'Lady Bailey, when it was her turn to go away, made the best take-off up to then, leaving the ground after a very short run and turning smartly on to her course.' She was placed in fifty-third position at the end, with an average speed of 101 miles per hour. The weather on the day was very favourable and the winner was Winifred Brown. Female pilots occupied three of the first four finishing positions. Thomas Naylor also entered in his Gipsy Moth, G-AABO, and finished in twenty-seventh place. The following weekend he entered the Yorkshire Air Race and finished a fraction of a second behind the third-place finisher. He entered the annual Manchester to Liverpool Air Race again on 31 August 1930 and finished in third position. There is no evidence, however, that the Naylors took part in racing to the extent of their famous cousin. In April 1931, Thomas Naylor purchased a de Havilland Gipsy Moth, G-ABLN, and sold G-AABO the following month.

By July 1930 Lady Bailey's eldest daughter, Mary Ellen, finished her education at Malvern St James School, aged 16 years 11 months. When the next term commenced, on 24 September 1930, Lady Bailey's youngest daughter, Noreen, started at the same school aged nine years and two months. Ann (aged 12) was elected representative for Form IV in the school parliament.

Almost 100 entries were received for the 1930 International Touring Competition (as the Tour of Europe was then called), which increased in length from 3,776 miles the previous year to approximately 4,700 miles. The starting point, on 20 July, was Berlin, and Britain entered eight machines. Two of the pilots had Irish heritage – Lady Bailey and John Evans Carberry (formerly tenth Lord Carberry). In addition to the gruelling flight throughout Europe, lasting about ten days, there were also technical tests in Berlin up until 7 August 1930. Of the 60 starters, Lady Bailey finished in thirty-first position in her Moth, G-AAEE, despite tough flying conditions. John Carberry finished in a creditable sixth position.

Sir Abe Bailey with his youngest daughter, Noreen, around the time she started boarding school at Malvern St James in September 1930, aged nine. On the left is Sir Abe's son Derrick, who was boarding at Wixenford, Wokingham.
COURTESY PROSPERO BAILEY

Below: *Lady Bailey carrying her journey log book for her Moth, G-AAEE, at Vienna during the International Touring Competition in August 1930.*
COURTESY PROSPERO BAILEY

Below: *Standing beside her Moth, G-AAEE, while a steward confirmed her arrival time at Lausanne, Switzerland, during the International Touring Competition in August 1930. Her race number was K6.*

On 8 February 1931 Lady Bailey left Croydon for a flight to north Africa. On 12 February she covered the distance from Marseille to Tunis in five hours. She was carrying out survey flights over the Libyan and Egyptian deserts in connection with an archaeological and geological survey of the Kharga Oasis. Important information regarding sand-buried sites was obtained by aerial photography. Lady Bailey's contribution to the Kharga Oasis expedition was both innovative and impressive. She arrived back in Croydon on 12 March 1931. Before she departed Croydon, she completed her training with the London Gliding Club for her Glider's Certificate (number 109), which was issued on 11 February 1931.

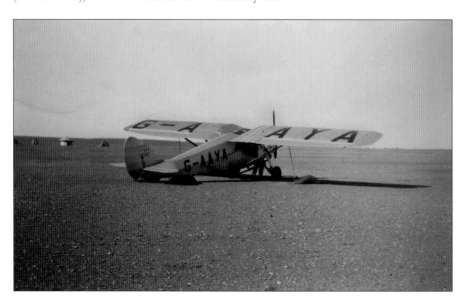

Puss Moth G-AAYA at Kharga
in the Egyptian desert, where
Lady Bailey took part in an
archaeological and geological
survey in
February 1931.
COURTESY PROSPERO BAILEY

*Prime Minister Ramsay
MacDonald's election-campaign
posters at Heston Aerodrome,
London, on 19 October 1931.
Lady Bailey flew the posters to the
north of England.*
COURTESY RONNY VOGT

In March 1931 Richard Westenra purchased two new aircraft. One was a DH.60G
Gipsy Moth, registered as G-ABJL to himself; the other was DH.80A Puss Moth,
registered to his wife, the Honourable Mrs Alice Florence Westenra, as G-ABJO.
In May 1931 Lady Bailey sold her Moth G-AAEE to Alfred Lovesay, a Rolls-Royce
development engineer at Derby.

Flight magazine reported on 29 May 1931: 'Lady Bailey and Miss Amy Johnson
were presented, in Paris on 23 May, with medals and diplomas of honour of the
International League of Aviators.'

Lady Bailey's fourth entry for the King's Cup Race was in her Puss Moth, G-AAYA.
The entrants departed Heston Air Park in rainy conditions at 6am on 25 July 1931,
which was particularly unpleasant for the 40 starters, as most of the aircraft were
open-cockpit machines. This compared to 88 starters in 1930. The course had been
extended to 982 miles and finished back at Heston. Unfortunately, heavy rain and bad
visibility meant that Lady Bailey failed to get beyond Stag Lane and retired.

The inaugural Ladies' Flying Meeting at Sywell Aerodrome, Northampton, took
place on 19 September 1931. This was attended by a large proportion of the female
pilots in England at the time. The first pageant at the new Cardiff City Aerodrome
took place on Saturday, 3 October 1931, and its first event was a race from Heston
Aerodrome, London, to Cardiff. Lady Bailey, in her Puss Moth, G-AAYA, arrived in
fifth position, in a time of 1 hour 29 minutes, with an average speed of 114 miles per
hour.

Lady Bailey supported Prime Minister Ramsay MacDonald during his campaign
for the general election on 27 October 1931. She assisted by flying his campaign
posters around the United Kingdom.

By the end of 1931 Lady Bailey was undertaking qualifying flights for her 'B' Certificate at Croydon Aerodrome. She had previously obtained her certificate for blind flying after a course of instruction with Air Service Training Limited at Hamble, for which she earned the third-highest marks of 1931. On Saturday night, 7 February 1932, Lady Bailey completed her night-flying course at Croydon for her 'B' Certificate and thus became a fully qualified commercial pilot. She then commenced studying for the second-class Navigator's Certificate.

Not to be outdone by her sister-in-law, Quenelda Naylor undertook a flight from London to South Africa and back. She departed from Stag Lane Aerodrome, London, on 6 November 1931, along with Captain Robert Henry McIntosh, as pilot in her de Havilland Puss Moth, G-ABJO. The Puss Moth had an enclosed cabin, which was a luxury Lady Bailey had not enjoyed. They were greeted on arrival in Cape Town on 2 December 1931 by Sir Abe Bailey and his daughter Mary Ellen. Their departure from Cape Town was on 15 December and they followed the central-African route across the Sahara Desert. This was the first flight by a light aeroplane across the vast Sahara. They arrived back at Stag Lane on Saturday, 16 January 1932. They had flown 23,000 miles over 249 flying hours. A detailed account of the two-way flight is recounted in McIntosh's autobiography, *All-Weather Mac* (1963). On 16 September 1927, Captain McIntosh and Colonel James Fitzmaurice made an unsuccessful attempt to fly the Atlantic Ocean westbound from Baldonnel, County Dublin. Both Richard and Alice Westenra commenced a blind-flying course at Brooklands School of Flying in April 1932.

Following Lady Bailey's return flight to Cape Town, her mission was to persuade the British authorities to develop an air service through the African colonies to Cape Town. This aspiration was realised when Imperial Airways inaugurated a route between London

and Cape Town on 20 January 1932. This represented the realisation of Lady Bailey's dream, for which she had worked so hard.

One of the world aviation highlights of 1932 was the landing in Culmore, County Derry, of Amelia Earhart, following her successful solo crossing of the Atlantic Ocean on 21 May. Lady Bailey flew to Derry to greet the transatlantic flier, but Amelia had already left for England. Lady Bailey immediately returned to England but had to land *en route* due to bad weather and was officially missing until the following day. Along with Amy Johnson and Winifred Spooner, she was a guest

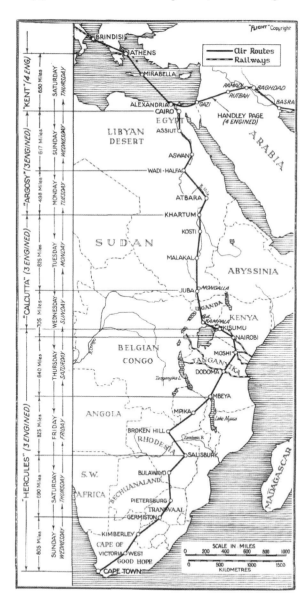

The route taken by the Imperial Airways inaugural mail-only flight from London to Cape Town on 20 January 1932. The route was similar to that taken by Lady Bailey in January 1928.
Courtesy FlightGlobal Archives via RBI Limited

Throngs of onlookers and supporters gathered at Croydon Aerodrome, London, to witness the departure of Imperial Airways's Handley Page 42, G-AAXF, named Helena, *on 20 January 1932, on its maiden flight to Cape Town, South Africa. This was the culmination of Lady Bailey's aspiration to develop an air route between London and Cape Town.*

COURTESY PROSPERO BAILEY

at a reception at the Royal Aero Club on 26 May in honour of Amelia Earhart. Amelia's Lockheed aircraft was placed on view to the public at Selfridge's, Oxford Street, London.

The 1932 King's Cup Race took place at Brooklands Aerodrome on Friday, 8 July. The Westenra aviation racing bug was not confined to Lady Bailey. While she did not enter the race, her brother Richard made his first participation in his de Havilland Gipsy Moth, G-ABJL. He finished in twenty-third position. The following month he entered the same aircraft for the London to Newcastle Air Race, which commenced from Brooklands Aerodrome on 6 August 1932 and ended 264 miles later. Richard was successful and won the race in a time of 2 hours 13 minutes at an average speed of 118.75 miles per hour. His Gipsy II engine was fitted with KLG spark plugs, which were the most successful of the time. The designer of these plugs was Kenelm Lee Guinness, a member of the Irish brewing

Following Amelia Earhart's solo transatlantic flight she met three other prominent women aviators at the Royal Aero Club on 26 May 1932. Left to right: Lady Bailey, Amelia Earhart, Amy Johnson and Winifred Spooner. Standing on the right is Lord Wakefield. Within eight years Lady Bailey would be the only survivor of these four women.

COURTESY JANE FALLOON VIA JULIEANNE MCMAHON

family, and they were used by successful motor-racing drivers as well as air-racing pilots.

Lady Bailey's air racing continued throughout 1932, but on a considerably smaller scale than previous years. On Sunday, 25 September 1932, the second Ladies' Flying Meeting took place at Sywell Aerodrome, Northampton. A competition based on pilots' navigational skill was the main event. Lady Bailey, in her Puss Moth, G-AAYA, was judged the winner.

Lady Bailey took the exam for her 'B' Certificate in December 1932. By the end of that year she was contemplating a second solo journey to the Cape to beat Amy Johnson's record of five and a half days. Though her friend and mentor, Geoffrey de Havilland, was among those who tried to dissuade her, she nonetheless departed Croydon on a bitterly cold 15 January 1933 at 2.35am. She was flying her Puss Moth, G-AAYA, which was fitted with extra fuel tanks, giving her an endurance of 20 hours. Because of the weight of the batteries, she dispensed with a radio, navigation lights and instrument lights. This was deemed by some to be foolhardy in the extreme.

The first leg of her journey was south through France and Spain and across the Mediterranean Sea to Oran in Algeria. This she negotiated without incident. However, the second leg of the 1,500-mile trip ended with her fuel tank almost dry near the southern edge of the Sahara Desert. She was stranded there for four days until a French reconnaissance aircraft searching for her located her aircraft. A Caterpillar tractor was sent for to bring her fuel.

Lady Bailey, had had enough and the next day she decided to return to London. C.G. Grey, the outspoken, misogynistic editor of *The Aeroplane* magazine, was highly scathing about her attempt and stated, 'In the best interests of British aviation she should not have undertaken this journey.' On 28 January 1933 she commenced her journey home from the Algerian oasis town of Ain Salah. Her return journey was a horrific time for her, beset by the worst possible weather; she was stranded again at Alicante in eastern Spain. It was 14 February 1933 when she arrived back in London. Soon after she got home she became seriously ill with typhoid fever. There were no further attempts at long-distance flights.

On 13 February 1933 Richard Westenra purchased a new DH.60G Gipsy Moth III, registered G-ACCW.

For the fifth time in seven years, forty-two-year-old Lady Bailey entered the King's Cup Race at Hatfield Aerodrome on Saturday, 8 July 1933. This time she flew her Puss Moth,

Below: *The Moth G-AAYA was stranded for four days at Ain Salah in the southern Algerian desert at the end of January 1933 while awaiting fuel supplies.*
COURTESY PROSPERO BAILEY

Bottom: *Lady Bailey hand-swinging the propeller of G-AAYA at Ain Salah in the southern Algerian desert on 28 January 1933. She abandoned her attempt to reach Cape Town again and returned to London.*
COURTESY PROSPERO BAILEY

G-AAYA, which by then had been fitted with a more powerful Gipsy Major engine. Her entry registration was number one and she was joined by her brother Richard flying his Gipsy Moth, G-ACCW. Richard was eliminated in heat seven; Lady Bailey was eliminated in heat eight. Cardiff Aeroplane Club held their annual air display on 22 July 1933, attended by approximately 25,000 spectators. The event included a race from Heston Aerodrome, London, to Cardiff of approximately one hour's duration. Lady Bailey finished fifth in her Puss Moth, G-AAYA. Handicapping was so effective that the fourth-, fifth- and sixth-place aircraft landed within 58 seconds of the third-place finisher. This was the last time Lady Bailey would enter a competitive air race. It was seven years since she had taken flying lessons during the summer of 1926.

The third annual London to Newcastle Air Race took place from Brooklands Aerodrome on Saturday, 12 August 1933. Richard Westenra again entered, but this year he flew his Moth, G-ACCW, fitted with a Gipsy Major engine. After the 264-mile race, he was first across the finish line, with a lead of 1 minute 22 seconds over the second finisher. His time was 2 hours, 6 minutes and 27 seconds, at an average speed of 125.27 miles per hour. The change of engine reflected his improved performance from the previous year. His prize was a trophy and a cheque for £75.

Throughout the years 1933 to 1936, Lady Bailey spent more time enjoying the company of her five children and less time in the air. On 7 July 1933 she visited the girls at school. Ann completed her education at Malvern St James in April

With residential properties encroaching, Stag Lane Aerodrome was sold in March 1933 for housing development and the London Aeroplane Club relocated further north to Hatfield Aerodrome.

COURTESY DE HAVILLAND MOTH CLUB ARCHIVE

1935. She was aged 16. Ann played an active role in numerous activities including the Dramatic Society, the Country Dance Society, the Royal Life Saving Society, the Photographic Society and the Girl Guides and she obtained honours in the Royal Drawing Society examinations. Her critics at lacrosse in December 1932 commented: 'A promising player who should improve with experience in match play.' She also played tennis and hockey.

Noreen remained at Malvern for a further year, until 28 July 1936, when she was one day past her fifteenth birthday. Like her older sisters, she was an active participant in many of the school's extracurricular societies and sporting activities. At the end of the 1936 academic year Noreen's tennis critics reported: 'A promising player with an excellent serve.'

The fact that Lady Bailey was now available to spend more time with her children may have been, in part, due to the relocation of the London Aeroplane Club from Stag Lane to Hatfield. This created a longer distance for her to travel to enjoy flying. On 26 April 1935, she sold her sixth and final aircraft, the Puss Moth G-AAYA, to the RAF Flying Club at Hatfield.

By the early 1930s she no longer enjoyed living in the city and she and the children moved to the Earl of Jersey's mansion at Middleton Park, Middleton Stoney, near Bicester, Oxfordshire.

It was a large Georgian house that was well equipped with servants. The children looked forward to the comforts of the country and learned the aspects of country life their mother had enjoyed as a young woman in Monaghan: shooting, hunting and looking after their own dogs and ponies. The children remembered these years as the happiest of their childhood. They stayed in Middleton Park from 1930 until the house was demolished in 1934 to make way for a new building. They then lived at Lord Valencia's place at Bletchington, Oxfordshire, until 1940. In 1932, Mary Ellen, aged 19, went to South Africa. On 12 December 1932, Abe's 32-year-old son John married 23-year-old Diana, daughter of Winston Churchill. Abe's daughter Cecil had been married since 16 March 1919 to Major

During the early 1930s Lady Bailey spent more quality time with her children. At the Bicester Show, 6 September 1932, were (left to right) Ann, Lady Bailey and Noreen.
COURTESY PROSPERO BAILEY

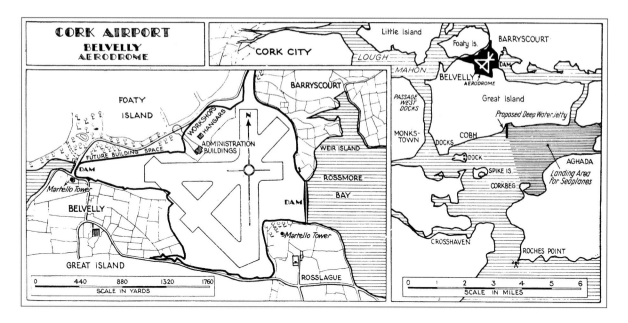

The layout and location drawings for the proposed airport at Belvelly, County Cork, as drawn up in March 1934.
Lady Bailey was a supporter of the project.
COURTESY BERNARD SHARE, THE FLIGHT OF THE IOLAR: THE AER LINGUS EXPERIENCE 1936–1986 (1986)

William Christie. Mary Ellen Bailey married Robin Grant Lawson on 23 May 1934. This marriage ended in divorce the following year. Ann married Pierce Synnott on 6 September 1939.

While Lady Bailey was spending more time with her family, she remained actively involved with the development of civil aviation. Throughout 1934, she became associated with proposals to establish an Irish airline, which were being led by Richard O'Connor, Cork County Surveyor, who was also advocating an airport at Cork. John King examined Irish government files relating to this attempted aviation venture. On 15 March 1934, O'Connor wrote to Lady Bailey at her home at Middleton Park, inviting her to his home at Clydeville, Mallow, County Cork, to discuss the plans for a transatlantic airport at Belvelly, near Little Island, County Cork. Lady Bailey's success in persuading Imperial Airways to establish an air route between London and Cape Town in January 1932 probably inspired the Cork men to contact her. On 19 March, she met with two of O'Connor's supporters in London, who were *en route* home from meeting KLM representatives in Amsterdam. They confirmed her support for such a venture. KLM would become involved in establishing

a new Irish airline catering for transatlantic services. An unlicensed airfield existed at Ballincollig and this location was also considered as an option.

Correspondence between the parties continued in an optimistic vein and, on 24 April 1934, O'Connor wrote to Lady Bailey, asserting that the formation of Irish Airways was going ahead rapidly. The discussions also involved Imperial Airways, the Air Ministry in London and the Department of Industry and Commerce in Dublin. On 27 April 1934, Lady Bailey attended a meeting in the Shelbourne Hotel, Dublin, with the Cork group. On 12 May, O'Connor updated her on positive meetings he had had with Éamon de Valera, President of the Executive Council, and his Minister for Defence, Frank Aiken. By 7 June Seán Lemass, Minister for Industry and Commerce, also supported a scheme for an airport at Cork and a Cork-based airline to undertake transatlantic flights. By now O'Connor's venture was referred to as the 'Aer Lingus Éireann' scheme. Lady Bailey again flew to Dublin to attend a meeting on 12 June 1934. Two days later she and Richard O'Connor were both hospitalised following a car crash at Portlaoise.

Surprisingly, by 20 June, hopes were fading of success for the Cork delegation and they approached members of the Board of Directors of the Munster and Leinster Bank in Cork to attempt to garner support. Only one showed interest. Thirty-nine-year-old Major Thomas Hallinan from the influential and successful Hallinan milling family, which owned three large flour mills and had just merged their business with the British millers Joseph Rank Limited. Thomas Hallinan joined the Munster Fusiliers and was wounded at the Dardanelles in 1915. By the end of the First World War he was aged 23 and held the rank of Major. He oversaw the sale of his family business to Joseph Rank Limited in 1932 and became Deputy Chairman of Joseph Rank Limited (Ireland). He became a very successful businessman and was appointed Senior Director of the Munster and Leinster Bank. (Major Thomas Hallinan was a first cousin of Ruth Hallinan, whose aviation exploits are discussed in a separate chapter of this publication.)

On 16 July 1934, Richard O'Connor presented the transatlantic scheme to Seán Lemass. Lady Bailey was kept briefed on progress. Despite the efforts of all involved throughout 1934, however, the Fianna Fáil government declined to support the Cork airport and airline scheme. An airport was not constructed at Farmers Cross, Cork, until 1961. The government instead decided to set up an interdepartmental committee to investigate a state-aided air service between the Irish Free State and Britain. The state airline, adapting O'Connor's suggested name, Aer Lingus, was established and its inaugural flight to Bristol was on 27 May 1936. A new airport at Collinstown in north County Dublin was opened on 19 January 1940.

While plans for an international airport at Cork were being developed, members of the Fermoy-based Cork Aero Club obtained a licence to operate from a field at Rathmacullig, Farmers Cross, from 4 September 1934. Seán Lemass granted the licence; one of the club's foremost members was Ruth Hallinan from Fermoy.

Sir Abe Bailey was equally supportive of the development of civil aviation. He demonstrated this by offering £10,000 for the encouragement of civil aviation in South Africa, as confirmed by *Flight* on 17 September 1936. Two months later, he offered the Prime Minister of Southern Rhodesia a gift of £3,500 to promote civil aviation in that country. This was followed in May 1937 by an offer to the Rand Flying Club of £5 to each member towards the cost of renewing their 'A' Certificate.

Meanwhile, having completed their preparatory-school education at Wixenford, Wokingham, both Bailey sons went to Winchester

The chapel at Wixenford School, Wokingham, around 1937. Derrick and Jim Bailey finished preparatory education there in 1936 and 1938 respectively. In 1937 the school became Ludgrove School.
COURTESY SALLY WHITTAKER, LUDGROVE SCHOOL, WOKINGHAM

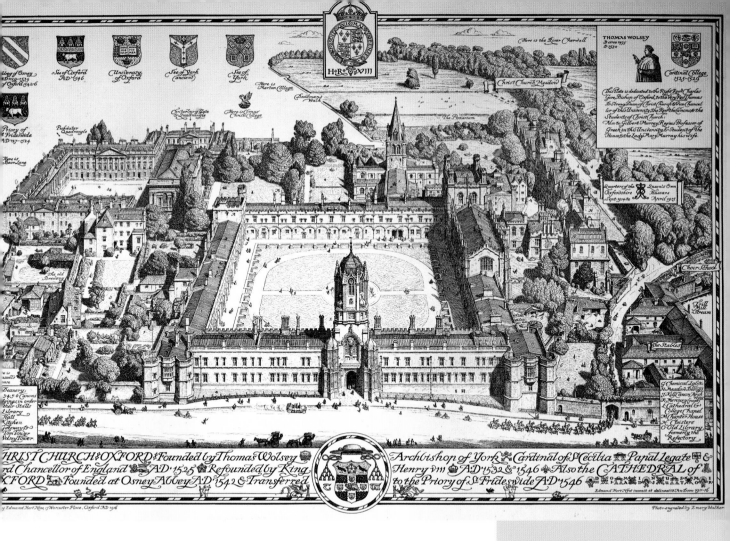

CHRIST CHURCH OXFORD Founded by Thomas Wolsey Archbishop of York Cardinal of St Cecilia Papal Legate &
Lord Chancellor of England AD 1525 Refounded by King Henry VIII AD 1532 & 1546 Also the CATHEDRAL of
OXFORD Founded at Osney Abbey AD 1542 & Transferred to the Priory of St Frideswide AD 1546

College and then to Christ Church College, Oxford. Derrick entered the latter in October 1936, aged 18, and Jim in October 1938, aged 19.

By 1936 Abe's health had deteriorated and he returned to London for treatment for arthritis, which caused him to be lame. While there he was also diagnosed with peripheral vascular disease, which ultimately led to a left-leg amputation above the knee in August 1937. The disease continued to develop and, in 1938, it was necessary to amputate the other leg. Lady Bailey travelled to Cape Town to be with him during his recovery period. Abe recovered from the amputation to return to Bryanston Square for the coming-out ball for his 17-year-old daughter Noreen in 1938. On 11 November 1938 Abe left

Sir Abe Bailey was carried off-ship after his final journey from England to Cape Town, following the diagnosis that confirmed his terminal illness in 1940.
COURTESY ANNA TIETZE,
UNIVERSITY OF CAPE TOWN

Above: *An engraving of Christ Church College, Oxford, founded in 1525, where Derrick and Jim Bailey studied.*
COURTESY EDWARD NEW VIA THE
GOVERNING BODY OF CHRIST CHURCH,
OXFORD

his London home and returned to Cape Town. Abe's disease, which caused him great pain, was not halted by two amputations. In 1940 he was told that he would also have to have his two arms amputated. He firmly said he would rather die. In the last months of his life, in Muizenberg, Cape Town, his chief pleasure was going out in his yacht *Clewer* and taking neighbouring children out with him. Abe died on 10 August 1940.

That was the bleakest and most perilous period of the Second World War. The Battle of Britain was at its height and Lady Bailey could not return to South Africa. Abe was buried high on a cliff above his house, Rust-en-Vrede, on a level platform of ground he had specially chosen for its wide views on all sides of surrounding bays and far-off mountains. To reach this remote burial site his coffin had to be carried down 100 precipitous steps.

Abe's will had been written in November 1937 with several codicils added in 1938 and 1939. He left the bulk of his fortune of over £2 million to be administered as a trust, 80 per cent of which was to be spent in Africa. His valuable fine-art collection in Bryanston Square went to the National Art Gallery in Cape Town. From his trust fund and business interests his wife was to receive a handsome £10,000 *per annum* for her lifetime. His children were to be provided for from the trust but, owing to the outbreak of war and the uncertainty of the outcome, he requested that his estate remain intact for ten years after his death. However, lack of clarity in his will and codicils resulted in his assets being disposed of prematurely at bargain prices. Lady Bailey's inheritance was not affected but she was worried about her children's.

Aged 50, Lady Bailey applied to the Air Transport Auxiliary (ATA) for a position as a ferry pilot. Even though she was above the age limit of 45, she was accepted, probably because of her flying experience and her influential contacts. However, she was ridiculed and humiliated by C.G. Grey of *The Aeroplane* and she left the ATA after one week. She then took up a non-flying role with the Women's Auxiliary Air Force (WAAF) and remained with them for the duration of the war. Her home at Bryanston Square took a direct hit from a German V 1 'doodlebug' bomb in 1944 and was considered so unsafe thereafter that it had to be demolished. Lady Bailey moved to a house in Oakham, Rutland, in the east midlands, for the remainder of the war. Her youngest daughter, Noreen, married Wing Commander Peter Simmons on 27 January 1941.

Both of Abe and Lady Bailey's sons were involved in the war. Derrick served as Second Lieutenant in the South African Irish Regiment. He later became Captain in the SAAF and later again in the RAF. Jim joined the RAF and became a fighter pilot in the Battle of Britain.

Lady Bailey (left) as an officer with the WAAF in 1941.
COURTESY JANE FALLOON
VIA JULIEANNE MCMAHON

The Martin Baltimore medium-range bomber of the type flown by Derrick Bailey during missions with the Desert Air Force in Italy in 1943.
COURTESY IMPERIAL WAR MUSEUM, LONDON

Both were awarded the Distinguished Flying Cross for bravery.

Derrick's two godfathers were General Louis Botha (first Prime Minister of the Union of South Africa) and Field Marshal Sir Douglas Haig (the most controversial British military figure of the First World War). Derrick attended Christ Church College, Oxford, and played cricket with success for Oxfordshire in 1937. He then returned to South Africa to help his 70-year-old father. Derrick was 21 years of age when the Second World War broke out in September 1939. He joined the South African Irish Regiment and, in 1940, transferred to the SAAF. Derrick joined No 223 Squadron of the RAF, which was part of the Desert Air Force. In January 1942 the squadron was based at Shandur, Egypt, and operated the first batch of 150 American-built Martin Baltimore medium bombers to be flown by the RAF. These aircraft had a maximum speed of 302 miles per hour and could climb to 12,000 feet in 12 minutes. Their armament included: 4 wing-mounted machine guns; two 7.7-millimetre Browning machine guns in dorsal turret; 2 more in ventral position; plus a bomb load of 2,000 pounds. Derrick's squadron took part in the bombing offensive against Luftwaffe airfields in Sicily and flew many sorties during an intensive period of operations. These missions were in support of the Allied attack on Salerno, south of Naples, which led to the surrender of the Italians to the Allied forces in September 1943. He flew over 50 operational bombing sorties throughout the Italian campaign.

In June 1944, he was posted to the Middle East and then to South Africa for the remainder of the war. No 223 Squadron was later renamed No 30 Squadron SAAF. The *London Gazette* of 25 August 1944 recorded that Captain Derrick Thomas Louis Bailey (88789) was awarded the Distinguished Flying Cross by the SAAF. The annotation included: 'awarded in recognition of gallantry and devotion to duty in the execution of air operations'. He left the RAF in 1946 with the rank of Captain. When his stepbrother John died on 13 February 1946, Derrick inherited his father's baronetcy, becoming the third Baronet of Cradock in the Province of the Cape of Good Hope. For the remainder of his life he became known as Sir Derrick Bailey. Lady Bailey's brother Richard Westenra died on 26 July 1944, aged 50.

Derrick returned to England in 1948 and farmed in Herefordshire, where he purchased Brinsop Court Estate. The property remained in the Bailey family for 60 years. He resumed his successful cricket career with Gloucestershire County Cricket Club, of which he was Captain for 1951 and 1952. He was a middle-order batsman and occasional medium-pace bowler. Between 1949 and 1952 he played 60 first-class matches for Gloucestershire, scoring 2,029 runs.

He retained his strong interest in aviation and established Glos-Air, an aircraft-maintenance business based at Staverton (now Gloucestershire) Airport, and became involved with the Isle of Wight Britten-Norman Company in the development of their Islander eight-seater passenger plane. He was head-hunted by the States of Alderney, Channel Islands, to establish Aurigny Air Services, to maintain a regular air service between the Channel Islands, the English mainland and France. This he inaugurated on 1 March 1968. The airline's colours, gold and black, were chosen to echo Sir Abe Bailey's horse-racing silks. In its first year of operation the fledgling airline carried 45,000 islanders.

Derrick died at his home on Alderney aged 90 on 19 June 2009. He was succeeded in the baronetcy by his son, Sir John Bailey, fourth Baronet. By the time of its fiftieth anniversary of operations, in March 2018, Aurigny operated eight aircraft to ten destinations from the Channel Islands and employed three hundred staff.

Derrick's younger brother, Jim, also graduated from Christ Church College, Oxford, and in 1939, aged 19, he joined the University Air Squadron. With war looming, he joined the RAF and was commissioned as Pilot Officer on 26 September 1939. In January 1940 he was sent to the RAF College at Cranwell in Lincolnshire. At the conclusion of his training, on 19 June 1940, three weeks before the Battle of Britain

The first aircraft operated by Aurigny Air Services on 1 March 1968 was the Britten-Norman Islander G-AVCN. It is shown here in the gold and black horse-racing colours of Sir Abe Bailey.
COURTESY BARRY FRIEND VIA BRITTEN-NORMAN HISTORIANS

commenced, he was posted to No 264 Squadron, flying Boulton Paul Defiants with rear-facing gun turrets. His squadron was then based at RAF Manston in Kent, tasked with protecting part of the English Channel. On 28 August 1940, at the height of the Battle of Britain, his squadron encountered numerous Heinkel He 111 bombers over Folkestone, Kent. Jim's rear gunner succeeded in downing one of them. His Defiant, N1569, was attacked and shot down by a Messerschmitt Bf 109 and he force-landed it near Petham, Canterbury. He escaped injury but his aircraft was destroyed.

On 26 September 1940, Jim Bailey was promoted to Flying Officer and posted to No 85 Squadron at Castle Camps, Cambridgeshire, where he was trained in night-fighting. Here he flew Hurricanes and Havocs. The Douglas A-20 Havoc was an American aircraft and was chiefly called the Boston in RAF service. The first Bostons for the RAF were part of a French order taken up for delivery from the USA after the fall of France. They entered RAF service with No 85 Squadron on 7 April 1941. No 85 Squadron lost 25 of its 37 pilots during Jim Bailey's period with them. On 26 September 1941 he was promoted to Flight Lieutenant and returned to No 264 Squadron. On 1 January 1942 he joined No 125 Squadron flying Bristol Beaufighters and hunting Luftwaffe reconnaissance aircraft over the Irish Sea and up to the Orkney and Shetland Islands. On 20 September 1942 he damaged a Junkers Ju 88, 65 miles south-west of Waterford. A few weeks later, on 10 November 1942, on patrol between Scotland and Norway, he destroyed another Ju 88. On 1 April 1943 he was temporarily assigned to the United States Army Air Forces 615th Night Fighter Squadron to train American crews in night-fighting. On 3 December 1943 he was assigned to duties in Italy.

A formation of Boulton Paul Defiant fighters of the type flown by Jim Bailey when he was attached to No 264 Squadron during the Battle of Britain in August 1940.

COURTESY IMPERIAL WAR MUSEUM, LONDON

He had five enemy 'kills' in four months in 1944, while operating from bases in Italy in Beaufighters attached to No 600 (City of London) Squadron, RAF, and operating night-time missions. He destroyed two aircraft on the night of 2–3 June 1944.

The *London Gazette* of 8 September 1944 recorded that Acting Squadron Leader James Richard Abe Bailey (74325), RAF Volunteer Reserve No 600 Squadron, was awarded the Distinguished Flying Cross by the SAAF. This was two weeks after his brother was awarded the same honour. Lady Bailey would have undoubtedly been proud of her two sons. On 1 July 1945 Jim Bailey was promoted to Squadron Leader and commanded a ferry unit, bringing aircraft back to England from Europe. His wartime victories totalled six enemy aircraft destroyed and two damaged. He is commemorated as one of the nine South African aces of the Second World War.

When war was over he returned to Christ Church College, Oxford, for Hilary Term 1946. He obtained a Bachelor of Arts degree in 1948 and a Master of Arts in 1949, after rejoining the University Air Squadron. In 1950, 30-year-old Jim returned to Cape Town and took control of his father's affairs. In 1951 he established the monthly African publication *The African Drum*, the title of which was later changed to *Drum*. It became a successful forum for black people to express themselves and define and describe their world. By the late 1950s its monthly circulation was 450,000 copies throughout 15 African countries. It was arguably one of the most successful magazines in Africa. Jim inherited Grootfontein in the Karoo from his father's estate. Jim, married Gillian Parker in 1958. They were divorced in 1963 and he married Barbara Epstein on 16 April 1964.

Lady Bailey subsequently followed Jim to South Africa to resolve outstanding matters concerning Abe's will. She purchased a house in Kenilworth, a suburb of Cape Town.

In 1946, Lady Bailey's brother Willie and his wife, Dot, decided they must move out of Rossmore Castle, as it was suffering from dry rot. In May 1946, Battersby and Company conducted an auction of the furniture and Lady Bailey purchased some items to bring to South Africa. On 5 December 1946 an auction by Samuel Brown, Rockcorry, involved 400 lots of sections of the castle that could be disposed of. This marked the end of this Westenra family home. It was finally demolished in 1974. Lady Bailey rarely returned to Europe after that. Her first son, Derrick, married Katharine Nancy Darling (known as Nancy) on 18 July 1946. Mittie Westenra died on 8 February 1953, aged 93.

Lady Bailey occasionally visited the airfield at Young's Field, Wynberg, Cape Town, where Abe had greeted her on 30 April 1928. In her later years she travelled a few times by commercial airline back to England, following the route she had fought to develop during the early 1930s.

Her brother William Westenra died on 17 October 1958, aged 66. That same year Lady Bailey was diagnosed with lung cancer and, in typically courageous fashion, fought the disease for two years. She succumbed to the cancer and died on 29 July 1960 – four months before her seventieth birthday. Even though the house at Rust-en-Vrede had been sold, the burial ground attached to it was where Lady Bailey was laid to rest, alongside her husband. She did not want to be buried in her native County Monaghan. The headstone erected to her had engraved on it an image of one of her international flying trophies. Two of her children have joined her there – Mary Ellen, who died eight months after her mother, on 10 April 1961, and Ann, who died in December 1979. Noreen died in Johannesburg on 26 July 1999, aged 78. The first marriages of all of Lady Bailey's five children ended in divorce.

It was 1984 when Jim Bailey finally sold the highly successful *Drum* magazine and his other local publishing interests to Nasionale Pers, an Afrikaans publishing house. On 14 September 1990, Jim Bailey and his wife, Barbara, were at Buckingham Palace as part of the fiftieth-anniversary commemorations of the Battle of Britain.

Jim and Barbara's last visit to Ireland together was the first week of June 1992, when they were guests of Thomas Pakenham and Desmond Guinness. They

The first issue of The African Drum *magazine, published in March 1951 by Jim Bailey.*
COURTESY AFRICA MEDIA ONLINE

The image below shows Rossmore Castle in all its splendour during the early twentieth century. Dry rot was identified in Rossmore Castle in 1946. Thereafter it was abandoned and left to the ravages of the Irish weather. Its demolition was completed in 1974.

COURTESY JANE FALLOON VIA
JULIEANNE MCMAHON (BELOW)
COURTESY JULIEANNE
MCMAHON (ABOVE)
COURTESY EUGENE
CLERKIN (TOP)

also spent time with Paddy and Jane Falloon in County Kildare. In the New Year's Honours list for 1996, Jim Bailey was awarded the honour of Commander of the Most Excellent Order of the British Empire (CBE). One of his nominees was Bishop Desmond Tutu, Anglican Archbishop of Cape Town, who stated:

> James Richard Abe Bailey must be the single most important individual British contribution to magazine and newspaper publishing for Africans throughout the continent. For years *Drum* magazine was unique in the spread of its circulation across Africa. In recent years we have seen the richness of Mr Bailey's photographic archives reflected in a number of books tracing Africa's history during the years of its decolonisation.

Jim Bailey died 29 February 2000, aged 80, in his home, Monaghan Farm, between Johannesburg and Pretoria. In the previous months, cancer had spread to several organs and he had been bedbound in considerable pain.

Little remains around Monaghan of the once-extensive Westenra dynasty. The current holder of the title seventh Baron Rossmore of Monaghan is William Warner Westenra, born on 14 February 1931. He is known locally as Paddy Rossmore. The Bailey legacy continues several thousand miles away in Johannesburg, where the 20-year-old Mary Westenra first travelled on her honeymoon in October 1911.

BIBLIOGRAPHY

Barbara Bailey, *An Eccentric Marriage: Living with Jim* (Cape Town: Tafelberg Publishers, 2005).

Jim Bailey, *The Sky Suspended: A Fighter Pilot's Story* (London: Bloomsbury Publishing, 1990).

Benjamin Bennett, *Down Africa's Skyways* (London: Hutchinson, 1932).

Jane Falloon, *Throttle Full Open: A Life of Lady Bailey, Irish Aviatrix* (Dublin: Lilliput Press, 1999).

Robert Henry McIntosh, *All-Weather Mac: The Autobiography of Wing Commander R.H. McIntosh, DFC, AFC* (London: MacDonald, 1963).

Julieanne McMahon, *Lady Mary Bailey: A Life in the Sky* (unpublished, n.d.).

Peter Richardson, *Hooton Park: A Thousand Years of History* (South Wirral: Hooton Airword, 1993).

Derrick Warner William Westenra Rossmore, *Things I Can Tell* (London: Eveleigh Nash, 1912).

Bernard Share, *The Flight of the Iolar: The Aer Lingus Experience 1936–1986* (Dublin: Gill and Macmillan, 1986).

Flight magazine (1926–34).

ACKNOWLEDGEMENTS

Prospero Bailey, grandson of Lady Bailey.

Jane Falloon, from whose book *Throttle Full Open* a considerable amount of the text of this chapter was extracted.

Julieanne McMahon, researcher.

So many people have played their part in Aurigny success over the past 50 years, but without the effort of one man – the late Sir Derrick Bailey – none of it would have been possible.

AURIGNY FOUNDER
SIR DERRICK BAILEY

In March 2018 Aurigny Air Services in the Channel Islands celebrated their fiftieth anniversary. In an article in their in-flight magazine they acknowledged the contribution made by the airline's founder, Sir Derrick Bailey.
COURTESY AURIGNY AIR SERVICES

The additional fuel tank was located in the converted front cockpit of Lady Bailey's Moth, here being examined at Wadi Halfa on 29 March 1928.
COURTESY PROSPERO BAILEY

NOTE ON VOLUME TWO

The second volume of *Petticoat Pilots* contains the following chapters:

7 ADELAIDE CLEAVER
DESCENDED FROM THE LINEN TRADE

The prominent Pollock and Cleaver families of Belfast were united when Adelaide Pollock married Arthur Cleaver in 1905. The couple relocated to England and, when her two sons were at boarding school in February 1929, Adelaide began to take flying lessons. The following month she embarked on a three-month flight to India as a passenger in her de Havilland Moth. She earned her Aviator's Certificate in June 1930 and shipped her aircraft to the United States to embark on a transcontinental flight from New York to San Diego, California. Back in Europe she entered several long-distance flying competitions and organised an air show at Aldergrove, near Belfast. Her eldest son was tragically killed in 1934. Adelaide herself was diagnosed with cancer and died in the south of England in 1939. Her younger son, Gordon, a Royal Air Force (RAF) Hawker Hurricane pilot, had a near-death experience when he was shot down during the Battle of Britain. The resultant damage to his eyes led to the discovery of a cure for cataracts.

8 SHAMROCK TRENCH
IRELAND'S FIRST

The Trench family had been resident in County Galway for three centuries when Wilbraham FitzJohn Trench obtained a position as Professor of English Literature at Trinity College, Dublin in 1912 and moved to County Wicklow. Jean, who acquired the pet name 'Shamrock', was his second daughter. While receiving education in Germany in April 1928, she met the crew of the aircraft *Bremen* following their successful crossing of the Atlantic. On her return to Ireland, she took flying lessons at Baldonnel near Dublin. In August 1931, 22-year-old Shamrock Trench earned the distinction of being the first female in the Free State to earn her Aviator's Certificate. However, promises of an opportunity to achieve a 'B' (Commercial) Certificate never materialised and a disappointed Shamrock gave up flying. She moved to England and her second marriage produced her only child, who was tragically killed at the age of 20. Shamrock Trench died in London in 1974, aged 65.

9 LADY NELSON
AVIATION ENTREPRENEUR AND EQUESTRIAN ENTHUSIAST

Cathleen Bryan was born into one of the leading gentry families in County Wexford. Her brother Anthony became a pilot with the Royal Flying Corps in 1912. In 1923 she married Sir James Hope Nelson of the successful Nelson Shipping Line and they developed a stud and horse-racing farm in County Meath. She acquired the title Lady Nelson and, with ample free time and financial resources, she obtained her Aviator's Certificate in 1932. One of the equestrian farm's jockeys had a brother who was a pilot, George Everett, and Lady Nelson joined forces with him to take over the running of the aerodrome at Kildonan in north County Dublin. She had enthusiastic plans to develop commercial and private aviation but these failed to materialise, despite considerable investment in the enterprise. Thus, she retired from aviation and returned to her love of horses.

10 Margaret, Helen and Mairi Stewart
THE LONDONDERRY LADIES

Many Anglo-Irish families rose to prominent political and military positions while they occupied grand mansions in Ireland. One was the Stewart family, who resided at Mount Stewart in Newtownards, County Down. The seventh Marquess of Londonderry held senior positions at the Air Ministry and eventually obtained his Aviator's Certificate. Three of his daughters also learned to fly, at Heston near London, and witnessed the development of an aerodrome on their lands at Newtownards. A private airstrip was developed on the family estate. They had their own single-engine aircraft and commuted by air between the family's mansions in Great Britain and their home in Northern Ireland. Their enthusiasm for aviation continued for many years and the family were involved in various aspects of aviation for a number of decades.

11 Mabel and Sheila Glass
THE INTREPID FLYING SISTERS

The linen industry was one of the greatest employers in the north-east of Ireland during the nineteenth century. One family heavily involved was the Glass family from Lurgan, County Armagh. When Henry Glass was orphaned at the age of 11, he began his career as a ship's draughtsman with Workman, Clark and then Harland and Wolff. He later moved to London, where his two daughters took flying lessons and earned their Aviator's Certificates in 1934. Their mother bought them a de Havilland Moth and, with guidance from their friend Amy Johnson, they embarked on several long-distance flights. In 1937 they flew to Egypt and took part in the Oases Race. Back home, the sisters entered several air races in the UK and were commended by several of their (male) peers. Mabel Glass ferried over 900 aircraft for the Royal Air Force (RAF) while serving with the Air Transport Auxiliary (ATA) during the Second World War. Following the death of Henry Glass in 1947, his widow and two daughters established new lives in South Africa, where Mabel continued her involvement in aviation.

12 Ruth Hallinan
MUNSTER'S FIRST WOMAN AVIATOR

The Hallinans of County Cork were a successful milling family that owned several flour mills. Ruth Hallinan from Fermoy contracted polio as a young girl. This did not deter her from achieving her ambition to become the first female in Munster to earn her Aviator's Certificate. She purchased her own aircraft and was instrumental in the formation of the Cork Aero Club during the summer of 1934. Despite several mishaps, she continued to enjoy the pleasures of flying throughout the island of Ireland. The 'Emergency' brought an end to her flying activities, but she enjoyed an interest in motoring and in later years her charitable interests came to the fore.

13 Nancy Corrigan
ACHILL'S AVIATRIX: FROM ÉIRE TO ERIE

Nancy Corrigan lost her father at the age of three. When she was 16, her mother brought her to Cleveland, Ohio, to escape a life of poverty and hardship in her native Achill. Within three years she hit the local headlines when she made her first solo flight with less than five hours' training. She became a model with a top agency in New York and continued her pilot's training in Tulsa, Oklahoma. She taught military cadets to fly in Columbia, Missouri, where she was the Chief Flying Instructor, and in 1948 she competed with the best female pilots in America when she entered the National Air Races in Cleveland, flying her own AT-6A. She later became a full-time Lecturer in Aeronautics at the University of Kansas. She retired to Florida and died there in 1983. Hers was quite an amazing journey for a lady with a primary-school education in poverty-stricken Achill.

INDEX

Note: Page numbers in italics refer to illustration captions.